THE REAL
LIFE STORY
OF ONE
MAN'S WAR
AGAINST
TERRORISM

THE
INFORMER
SEAN O'CALLAGHAN

'A cracking story... O'Callaghan is one of the
greatest friends of peace in Ireland'
Observer

Acclaim for *The Informer*

'A compelling account of the psychology and the personalities behind a movement which until a year ago waged brutal war on the British state'
Philip Stephens, *Financial Times*

'One of the most extraordinary stories to have emerged from the Troubles . . . a milestone in writing about the last thirty years of violence on this island . . . As a read, the book rips along'
Jim Cusack, *Irish Times*

'An extraordinary memoir of life within the murky republican world . . . *The Informer* is filled with astonishing insights into the personalities and politics of the Provisionals . . . a huge leap forward in our under-standing of the internal machinations of the Provisional movement'
Kevin Toolis, *Guardian*

'Stands out in the emerging genre of critical auto-biographies of contemporary Irish republicanism for its astute humanism . . . the best work yet on the lethally sick, sad world of republicanism . . . *The Informer* will be an indispensable almanac of where they [the IRA] are coming from'
Austen Morgan, *Observer*

'The IRA has long been and remains by far the most important terrorist organisation in Western Europe. His book gives a uniquely valuable account of how it works, how it thinks and how it feels'
Daily Telegraph

'*The Informer* will prove to be an invaluable guide to the mind of the IRA'
Lord Tebbit

'O'Callaghan's devastating story about his life in the IRA
... the information he has to impart is political dynamite
... a book of major significance ... told with the
suspense of a thriller'
Mary Kenny, *Daily Express*

'A fascinating, and in some ways disturbing, account of
his transformation from an IRA killer and senior
commander to a highly prized informer for the Garda'
Country Life

'An enthralling, disturbing story of our times, told with
honesty and clarity, needing little embellishment. In a
dirty war, it takes men of exceptional bravery and moral
strength to stay in an organisation they hate, in order to
destroy it'
Belfast Telegraph

'The extraordinary story of an extraordinary man ...
His well-written unpretentious book sheds an unprecedented amount of light on the inner working of the
"Republican Movement" (Sinn Fein–IRA). It is
especially illuminating on the motivation of Sinn Fein's
commitment to the "peace process" and the political
dividends it has earned from that processed commitment, in the service of the IRA, while the IRA retains all
its weapons. Warmly recommended'
Conor Cruise O'Brien, *Sunday Telegraph*

'A valuable memoir. It details many aspects of the IRA's
modern campaign, and casts a wider light on the broad
culture of Irish republicanism ... a chilling and
fascinating tale'
The Times Literary Supplement

'IRA secrecy is being increasingly breached by memoirs
from former members. This readable bestseller is easily
the most important'
Tribune

THE INFORMER

Sean O'Callaghan

with a foreword by
Dr Liam Kennedy

CORGI BOOKS

THE INFORMER
A CORGI BOOK : 0 552 14607 2

Originally published in Great Britain by Bantam Press,
a division of Transworld Publishers Ltd

PRINTING HISTORY
Bantam Press edition published 1998
Corgi edition published 1999

Some of the names in this book have been changed or
omitted where this has been necessary for reasons of
the individual's security.

Set in 10/12pt Sabon by Falcon Oast Graphic Art

Corgi Books are published by Transworld Publishers Ltd,
61–63 Uxbridge Road, London W5 5SA,
in Australia by Transworld Publishers , c/o Random House Australia
Pty Ltd, 20 Alfred Street, Milsons Point, NSW 2061
and in New Zealand by Transworld Publishers, c/o Random House
New Zealand, 18 Poland Road, Glenfield, Auckland.

Reproduced, printed and bound in Great Britain by
Cox & Wyman Ltd, Reading, Berks.

This book is dedicated primarily to organizations working for lasting peace in Northern Ireland; to New Dialogue, a London-based cross-party peace group, which has been unyielding in its opposition to political violence in Northern Ireland; to Families Against Intimidation and Terror, a Belfast-based human rights group that has fought a long and sometimes lonely battle against the abuse of human rights by terrorist groups; to the Peace Train Organisation, which mobilized public opinion against the terrorists. And to all of the other organizations and individuals who, each in their own way, have stood up to the terrorists. Northern Ireland owes all of you a huge debt of gratitude.

THE INFORMER

Over a pint of Guinness
In Quane's pub in the village
I got to thinking about the value
Of being an informer.

On our television screens
I know that friends and neighbours
See the ghost of Roger Casement
March on Banna Strand.

I see seven tons of American
Guns and bullets,
Towed into Queenstown, or Cobh
As we call it now.

My Guinness and my secrets satisfy.
Seventy-six thousand bullets
Will not shatter one limb,
Or spatter brain on a pub floor.

I finish my pint and walk
The forty yards home.

It's been a long, hard week.

Autumn 1985

FOREWORD

There are few darker figures in the folk history of Ireland than the informer. In Liam O'Flaherty's novel of murder and betrayal, *The Informer*, written soon after the Irish War of Independence, the very notion of giving information is presented as a breach of human nature: 'a monstrous idea had prowled into his head, like an uncouth beast straying from a wilderness into a civilized place where little children are alone'. Thus Gypo Nolan, the central character in the novel, entertained his first thoughts of selling a former comrade, a murderer-on-the-run, for the reward money of twenty pounds. It is a tale as old as the Bible, and yet retains the power to shock, and invite retribution. On the red-bricked walls of Belfast the graffiti proclaim: Touts Beware.

This is the real-life story of Sean O'Callaghan. Starting as a 'boy-soldier' with the IRA in County Kerry, by the age of twenty he had become an accomplished terrorist, operating along the border with Northern Ireland. Later, disgusted by the sectarianism of the northern IRA, he took on a more dangerous role: informer for the Garda, the Irish police force. As a high-ranking member of the IRA, attending meetings of the General Headquarters Staff of that organization, and as a member of the

National Executive of Sinn Fein, he was well placed to report on the hidden world of conspiratorial Irish nationalism. Today O'Callaghan is a tireless campaigner for peace in Ireland, albeit still working from the shadows. An IRA death threat hangs over his every moment, waking or sleeping. It's been a long, long way from a Kerry childhood to a life in exile.

The personal may be political but, in the end, it is experienced personally. Inevitably, the burdens of a double-life took their toll. Some of the most poignant moments in this book relate to Sean's mother, his ex-wife, and his former partner who fled with him to England. How much they suffered can only be surmised. His father, with whom he had a relationship largely characterized by the unspoken, died soon after he was released from jail in 1996. His mother had died earlier. Yet hers is the quiet voice that whispered down the years of his IRA involvement: 'no good will come of it'. At the end of the day, her son had to bear responsibility for his own actions. Sean, the romantic revolutionary, the warrior against British imperialism, could not still this voice – the *agenbite of inwit*, as Joyce put it – within his own head. Eventually he listened to another Mother Ireland.

O'Callaghan's memoirs challenge stereotypes and comfortable assumptions – shared both by terrorist organizations and the wider society – that informers are necessarily depraved, cowardly and, above all, avaricious. To take on voluntarily, and without recompense, the role of informer for the Irish police was an act of extraordinary courage. Some time ago, at a presentation to John Hume MP, the historian Joseph Lee remarked that Irish history was brimful of acts of physical bravery but instances of moral courage were in shorter supply. John Hume, in his life's work, has epitomized the latter. O'Callaghan may be said to embody both qualities, in plenty. He knew only too well the fate which awaited him, should he have been suspected of informing on his comrades. Interviews at the RUC's Castlereagh interrogation station have come in for strong criticism in the past, and rightly so. Loyalist and republican interrogation methods, however, routinely involve torture: hooding, repeated half-drownings, burns to the body, mutilation and sometimes sexual assault. In the face of such physical danger, O'Callaghan undertook his work for seven years on behalf of the gardai, acting for the Irish people. In the process, he ensured that many, many lives, both Irish and British, were saved. To borrow from Othello: he has done the state some service. And we need to know it.

One of the least understood corners of Irish society is that of the 'republican family'. Participation in this introverted, twilight world has its attractions: the experience of a shared sense of ideals, comradeship and commitment to a transcendent goal. The downside, which is explored sensitively and self-critically by O'Callaghan, includes acquiescence in sectariarism towards Ulster Protestants, racism towards the English and the Scots, and an almost unforgivable cruelty to all who stand in the way of the forcible incorporation of the different peoples of the island into a unitary state. Revealing this 'hidden Ireland' to a mass audience may be O'Callaghan's enduring contribution to the cause of democracy and freedom in Ireland, Britain and Irish America.

O'Callaghan is far from being the only prisoner of conscience in western Europe, nor the only one subject to a *fatwa* or death threat. In his own self-deprecating and humorous way he would probably say: 'To hell with that; it's more important that Kerry win the Sam Maguire Cup.' But like Salman Rushdie, another writer in internal exile, he continues to speak out on behalf of principles of justice and fairness, and of the democratic route to political change. No doubt he is sometimes wrong in his analysis and in his prognostications. It would be surprising if his memory were not faulty in places. His past holds sordid as well as good deeds. But the integrity of his current project – to advance the cause of democratic politics in these islands by weakening the forces of terrorism – shines through. He may be a priority target for the IRA; he should be a priority case for the Irish government. His personal dream, the day he abandoned his home in Kerry with his girlfriend and daughter, just before Christmas 1985, awaits fulfilment. 'Driving out of our house, past the familiar windmill and the canal at Blennerville, I felt sadness mixed with relief. I really loved this place and I determined then that one day I would come back.'

Dr Liam Kennedy
Reader in Economic and Social History
The Queen's University of Belfast
April, 1998

PROLOGUE

On 4 December 1996 came the news I had been waiting for. I had been in jail since 1988, when I had walked into a police station in Tunbridge Wells and admitted my involvement in IRA murders and bombings in County Tyrone in Northern Ireland in the mid-1970s. From that time I had been held in a variety of prisons in Northern Ireland and England: Crumlin Road in Belfast, Full Sutton in Yorkshire, Parkhurst on the Isle of Wight and Maghaberry outside Lisburn, where I was presently held. The prison official who had pursued my case for some time came to see me. He told me my release had been sanctioned and it would take place on Thursday 6 December. I must talk to no one about it, with the exception of the person who would collect me. I had always made it clear that I did not want any assistance from the State in the form of protection or financial assistance. I would be on my own.

In two days' time I would be released. I felt surprisingly calm about it. During that time my mind wandered back over the years. I thought of Peter Flanagan and Eva Martin, who were dead and could never be released. I thought of the years as an informer when I had had to operate entirely inside my own head. I thought of Sean

Corcoran, himself a Garda informer, who was murdered by the IRA. I thought of my two very serious hunger and thirst strikes when I could quite easily have died, of my almost fatal poisoning and of my mother's death. I had had no contact with my family for many years and had not seen my children since I handed myself up. I knew that I had done the right thing by turning myself in, but over the years I had sometimes questioned whether it had been worth it, whether it had changed anything. It certainly had not brought back people I had murdered, but at this stage what else could I have done? I had walked freely into jail and admitted my crimes. It had been a long road from young republican idealist to murderer and eventually informer. Former comrades had gone to jail as a result of my information. I felt no blame on that score; their own involvement in the IRA had decided their fate. They took their own decisions and paid the price for it. It would have been preferable had there been no one killed or injured, had no one gone to jail, but I bore the responsibility only for my own actions. The sheer stupidity and fanaticism of republican leaders had helped to condemn a generation of young nationalists to prison, death or years on the run in pursuit of a cause for which the price was always too high in terms of human suffering.

On Wednesday, the day before my release, I had a visit from the RUC officer in charge of the protection programme run on the British mainland for informers or supergrasses whose lives are deemed to be at risk from terrorist organizations. He tried, halfheartedly, to persuade me to enter into the programme. We had engaged in similar conversations in the past and he was well aware of my attitude: I didn't want anything to do with it, not because of distrust but simply because I had much to do and wanted to get on with it. I didn't want to be encumbered by continuing to be in the system. He told me that the offer of protection remained open indefinitely and that he would help in any way he could.

I really had no idea of what I was going to. I wanted to continue in some way to work against violence. I was certain that there would be another ceasefire but any pressure that could be put on the IRA was helpful. In the meantime, however, I had no money, no place to live, no job, no passport, no bank account and I would be under very serious threat from republicans for as long as I lived. I felt confident that these obstacles could be overcome, but perhaps I did not understand the real difficulties I would have in trying to get to grips with so many things at once. I did not know what to expect. I knew that there would be a degree of media interest but after eight years in jail it is difficult to focus. Concentration becomes impaired and what should provoke clear thoughts often remains fuzzy.

On 6 December I was up early as usual. There was an air of unreality about the events around me and I had a curious lack of excitement. By now the other prisoners in the unit knew that I was being released and inevitably while everyone wishes you well they are wondering when their day will come. From the minute other prisoners know you are being released you become a different person. A chasm opens up between you and them that can't be bridged. Although you're the focus of attention and conversation, your departure is discussed amongst the other prisoners almost as if you had already gone.

At 11 a.m. the security governor and the principal uniformed security officer came to see me. I had known the uniformed man for eight years; we got on particularly well and had enjoyed some real laughs, as well as the occasional spat. I'd known the security governor for a couple of years, and we too had a friendly relationship.

There were papers to sign and the governor had to read out the conditions of my release. I was shown a copy of the royal prerogative signed by the Queen, but I wasn't allowed to take a copy with me.

As 12.30 approached I could feel myself becoming very nervous and wanting to be away. I had packed my few possessions the night before and they were sitting by the grille beyond which would park the van that was to take me out of the prison. Everyone, prisoners and staff, were standing there waiting for the van to appear. I walked back to my cell for one last look and I felt the emotion hit me. My head was telling me, 'Get your act together and stay calm,' but my heart wanted to scream out loud with sheer delight. I said goodbye to everyone, had a final round of handshakes and jokes along the lines of 'We'll keep your cell ready for you,' and then I was out through the grille and into the back of the van.

We drove out of the prison, through two gates that opened as we approached without being instructed to do so. We were obviously expected. Within minutes we were driving through the open countryside surrounding Maghaberry. We drove for about two miles until we came to a petrol station off the main road. I could see Liam Clarke, the *Sunday Times* Ireland correspondent, getting out of his car and walking towards us. We shook hands warmly – Liam was obviously delighted to see me. I collected my possessions from the prison van and shook hands with the prison officers as we wished each other all the best for the future. It was the end of an important, challenging and emotional period of my life. Twenty-six years after I had joined the IRA, seventeen years after I had become an informer, I was finally free.

1

I was born in 1954 in Tralee, a small, unpretentious market town in the remote south-west corner of the Irish Republic, famed more for its annual International Rose of Tralee beauty contest than for anything else. County Kerry – of which Tralee is the major urban centre – has long been Ireland's best-known tourist centre.

At that time Tralee and its surrounding hinterland were only just beginning to emerge slowly from the suffocating stranglehold of a narrow Irish Catholic nationalist ethos that had stifled economic, intellectual and social development ever since the foundation of the Irish Free State, after the War of Independence, the subsequent Treaty and the bloody Civil War that followed. Thirty years on, memories of the Civil War in which the recalcitrant IRA was quickly and brutally crushed by the new Irish Free State government were alive and festering, particularly in Kerry, where the war had been fought with awful savagery. On three occasions, within days, the government forces had taken republican prisoners from jails and army barracks and tied them together before blowing them to pieces with landmines.

My father's family had taken the IRA's side in the Civil War and was steeped in hatred of the British presence in Ireland and of subsequent native governments, who, they believed, had sold out the ideal of an Irish Republic. Kerry had long been fertile ground for the IRA. Bitter memories of the Civil War remained, but it was the execution of two Kerry IRA men by de Valera's government in the 1940s that had really proved to be the catalyst for a rebirth of the IRA. In 1942 Dan Spring, a local Labour member of parliament (and the father of Dick Spring, until recently deputy prime minister in the Irish Republic), was elected to parliament following an emotional wave of protest at the execution of Maurice O'Neill, a Kerry republican. Shortly afterwards, Charley Kerins, also from Tralee and a boyhood friend of Dan Spring, was executed in Dublin for the murder of a Garda officer. Spring staged a noisy protest in the Irish parliament. Later, he erected a large monument to the memory of Charley Kerins, close to the Spring family home, and also named a nearby local authority housing development after him. The local Gaelic Athletic Association club, the Kerins O'Rahilly GAA Club, to which all the Spring family have belonged, is partly named in Kerins' honour. For reasons such as these and because of Kerry's isolated geographical position, republican feeling there remained bitter towards the Irish State.

Our family home was a small, terraced council house in Marian Park on the outskirts of Tralee. To the east, west and north rose the Sliabh Mish and Stacks Mountains. Even the memory of watching the mist quickly envelop Sliabh Mish and claw its way across the surrounding fields can still evoke awe in me. Our housing estate was built in 1954, mostly to rehouse families who had lived in slums in the 'lanes' familiar to anyone who has read *Angela's Ashes*, Frank McCourt's heart-rending description of poverty in Limerick City.

Throughout my childhood and youth older people would speak of the 'lanes' with a mixture of sentimentality and horror: no running water or toilets, bad damp and cramped housing conditions. Despite that, with the glow of nostalgia, no doubt, many of them maintained that they were happy. But my father had no such illusions and often got angry, asking aloud how anyone could ever see anything positive about such poverty.

Thinking or writing about my father – indeed, any of my family – is not easy. Childhood memories are not without their difficulties and their objective veracity is hard to establish. But I do have memories of a happy childhood with an absence of fear, either from the present or about the future. Memories of my father in particular are many, varied and complex. He was a stockily built, argumentative man, one minute full of laughter and fun, the next raging over some little thing that most found difficult to understand. He left school at twelve but he read widely and was in many ways an intelligent and sensitive man. Locally he was well known and regarded as a bit of a character. Small-town life ground him down in the end: the meanness and spite, lost ambition and the anguish of wasted years. I think I understood him almost from my very early childhood.

We were an ordinary working-class family, no different in most respects from our neighbours and friends. But throughout my early years the IRA was once again active – albeit in an ineffectual way – in Northern Ireland, and my father was still a member of that army which dreamed romantic but deadly dreams of driving the British out and establishing their Irish Republic by any methods.

Surrounded by such natural beauty and coming from – in memory at least – a happy home, I was surprised many years later to read a Christmas card received while I was in prison from a nun who had taught me in my first school. She described how many years before, I, aged five, and my older brother Donie had decided to run away from home. My father found us at the local railway station and had us back at school for the eleven o'clock break. In her description, it seemed to be regarded as no more than a boy's adventure – a hilarious and harmless occurrence. I suspect that my brother was railing against some decision of my father's and I adored my brother and was more than happy to go along for the ride.

I started school at Moyderwell Convent – which was run with brisk efficiency by the Sisters of Mercy and was just yards from my paternal grandmother's house – when I was two. It was unusual to begin so young and this was possibly a result of my mother being seriously ill with tuberculosis: TB was still the scourge of Ireland, particularly among the poor, and was prevalent in our area.

My childhood memories of my mother's illness are vague and fractured. She was ill for some years and spent a long period in a sanatorium at Edenburn, a few miles outside Tralee. I remember little of that period except that I recall my father getting us ready to visit her some Sundays with much excitement on our part and frustration on his. But of actually going to see my mother in the sanatorium I have no memory. I suspect that I have blotted it out. She never really recovered, and remained rather frail physically, but extremely tough mentally, for the rest of her life. Photographs of her when she was young show a very beautiful woman with lustrous black hair and deep brown eyes. She was very quiet – almost detached – and would listen to my father's endless and often loud dissertations on politics and history with an air of amused impatience. Did they love each other? There was certainly little or nothing in the way of any demonstrative affection, but that would not have been so unusual for their generation in rural Ireland. They were easy in each other's company and tolerant towards each other, and I have only vague memories of occasional arguments, which never lasted very long. Perhaps they did love each other in their way, but there seemed to be no great passion there – or at least not by the time I would have been old enough to observe it.

Born in 1920, when the War of Independence was being fought, my father came from a strong republican background. His mother in particular was fiercely anti-British – indeed, anti-authority. She once told me when I was about nine: 'Never trust a policeman, even a dead one. They should always be dug up and shot again just to be sure.' She was a very large woman, with a strong, domineering personality, but she was full of fun and mischief. She and I always got on very well and she was the adult I spoke to more than any other. It was from her, in particular, that I inherited my lack of fear of authority, something that has remained with me all of my life.

My father's leaving school coincided with his joining the Fianna – an IRA-controlled boy-scout-type movement that prepared young men for the IRA. His early teenage years saw ugly confrontations in Tralee between republicans and the Blueshirts, a quasi-fascist movement styled on Hitler's Brownshirts. The Blueshirts were allied to those who had taken the government side during the Civil War and were ferociously anti-IRA. Some of them went on to fight on Franco's side in the Spanish Civil War, opposite IRA men who had enlisted in the International Brigade. By 1936, at the age of sixteen, my father was a fully fledged member of the IRA.

In 1939, at the start of the Second World War, the

IRA began a bombing campaign in England. An old republican saying had it that 'England's difficulty was Ireland's opportunity'. Some went even further and tried to enter into an alliance with Nazi Germany. Many of the big names that had remained loyal to the IRA since the Civil War resigned in protest at what they saw as a futile and politically dangerous course of action. The IRA, or what remained of it, fell under the control of ultra-militarists dominated by a veteran of the War of Independence, Sean Russell, who later died on a German U-Boat returning to Ireland after trying to enlist aid from Hitler.

Shortly after the outbreak of the war Eamonn de Valera, the Irish taoiseach (prime minister), worried about the possible effect of the IRA's activity in Britain and Northern Ireland on Ireland's neutral status in the war, interned hundreds of IRA suspects. The great republican icon wanted nothing to do with people who had failed to grasp the new political realities arising from the war. My father and his brother Gerry were among over forty IRA suspects from the Tralee area who found themselves behind barbed wire at the Curragh military camp outside Kildare.

He spoke very little about that period. Sometimes he would see a death notice in a local or national newspaper and I might hear him saying to Mother: 'He was interned with us in the Curragh.' In fact, because the Curragh was the headquarters of the Irish Army I thought that he must have been in the army. It wasn't until much later that I realized that he was in the IRA and had been interned by an Irish government.

My first clear memory of my father and the IRA was early in 1963, shortly after the IRA campaign that had lasted from 1956 until 1962 had ended in complete failure. I was going to Mass with him early one Sunday

24

when I saw slogans painted on walls and the roadway: 'JOIN THE IRA – FREE THE PRISONERS'. It was the first time I had seen slogans like this, but I think that I knew that my father was somehow connected with them. Something in his expression told me that he knew about it. I remember feeling a little buzz of excitement without knowing why. He never said anything but I didn't expect him to. The silent knowledge of a secret shared made me feel very close to him.

I was the middle child of three, with an older brother Donie, four years and two months my senior, and a sister Mary, almost two years younger. I worshipped Donie, but he inevitably resented having to look after me. I would be sent along with him to the local picture-house matinée on Saturday – a boring chore when you are nearly twelve and your young brother is seven. He never let me forget who was in charge, either. Out of earshot of my parents I would frequently be told, 'One gug out of you and you're dead!'

The age difference between us made it certain, I suppose, that we would grow apart once he entered his teens. He never had any interest in politics and from about thirteen his world was dominated by judo and the martial arts in general. He went to work in Dublin when he was seventeen, which meant I saw him sporadically every other weekend. By then he was going out with the woman he was later to marry, so we saw little of each other in any meaningful sense from when I was twelve or thirteen.

My sister was different. We were closer in age and inevitably much closer over a longer period of time. We fought almost every day. I would often reduce her to tears by chanting, 'Who's the baby? Who's the baby?' She fought back either verbally or physically, but it would all be quickly forgotten. Mary had all of my father's characteristics: dogmatic, never slow to speak her mind and never, never wrong, but generous to a fault and always ready to stand up to a bully. We knew from early on that Mary could extract almost anything from my father and many a subtle hand we played between us.

My mother was ill for much of my childhood. While she was in hospital I often had my meals with a family in the neighbourhood called Rusk, who were related to her. My sister stayed with our next-door neighbours Flor and Cis Conway and their daughter, also called Mary. Flor Conway is still alive and I will always remember him as one of the most gentle and decent of men. Flor and I were always very close and when I was in jail – even after it became public knowledge that I was an informer – he sent me the local papers without fail each week.

There was one respect in which our house differed from those of most of our neighbours. It was awash with books – boxes of them, all gathered by my father, an inveterate collector of junk. Everything from encyclo-paedias and collections of Irish history to American detective stories. From a very early age I read everything I could get my hands on.

I was always getting into trouble when I was a kid. Once my sister Mary and I were sent to some kind of convalescent home in Foynes, County Limerick, after a local nurse examined us. I suppose the idea was to check that we hadn't contracted TB from our mother. We stayed there in the home, an austere, authoritarian establishment, for some weeks. There were only a few children among a variety of sickly and elderly patients, and Mary, who was a very pretty, endearing child, was popular with them.

To me it was the most tedious way to spend the summer holidays that I could imagine and I remember deciding that if I did something really bad they would have to send me home. The worst thing I could think of, short of burning the place down, was to flood it. There seemed to be hundreds of sinks and baths, but eventually I had them all blocked and the taps turned on at full strength. By the time the first baths were pumping water out onto the floorboards – and the ancient plastered ceilings underneath were leaking water – I was only just running down the back stairs after turning on the last ones. Three or four nurses were running down the corridors, draining baths and pulling out plugs. They were soaking by the time they caught up with me and while there was no lasting harm done to the home, I was punished by being confined to my bedroom for a couple of days.

The summers of my childhood seem now to have been one long warm dreamtime; no doubt the reality was rather different. Along with a gang of friends from the estate I spent my days playing football, raiding local orchards for apples and simply playing in the fields and foothills of Sliabh Mish.

Our favourite place for a while was the local grave-yard just yards from our home. It was divided into two sections: new and old. The new part held no interest for us, but the old part, with a tenth-century ruined abbey, old derelict tombs, alder trees and masses of under-growth, was a wonderland. Sometimes we spent whole days there, and in the winter we would issue dares to go into the old graveyard at night. I never had any fear of the old graveyard because we had played there so often as kids; even the sight of remnants of skeletons or coffins meant little to us. For a number of years I had a small terrier and I would often walk him in the graveyard at night. I was devastated when he was stolen one evening and a neighbour reported seeing him being put into a strange car near the graveyard as we played on oblivious. But in spite of this that graveyard was as much a part of our youth as football. It was, you could say, our amusement arcade.

A short distance from where we lived was a farm: 'McCarthy's farm', we called it. The owner, Tom McCarthy, was an old friend of my father's. I remember going there on summer evenings with my father and often on Sunday afternoons our whole family would join us. Tom's land sloped down to a river, on the other side of which lay Ballyseedy Wood, one of Ireland's oldest surviving woodlands with trees dating back to before the Treaty of Limerick in 1612. I can still remember the warm, sweet, almost suffocating smell of damp grass and the ground mist rising in the early morning soft sun.

Tom still ploughed with horses in those days, as did most small farmers; but he also kept the odd steeple-chaser. I was scared of them. I thought they would bite me if they could and I would stroke the gleaming necks of the Clydesdales only if Tom or one of his sons held me up to them. One day, however, Tom took it upon himself to amend what he saw as this flaw in my character. He had just acquired a beautiful stallion, which the previous owner had told him had a gentle and forgiving nature. Certainly he did appear to be very placid. Tom eventually persuaded me that no harm could come to me and showed me how the horse would nuzzle into his neck, as if he were kissing him. This beguiled me and I decided to give riding a go.

As soon as I was sitting astride the horse I knew it was a mistake. My heart pounded and I thought I was going to vomit. The horse must have sensed my fear, because he immediately bolted down the steep hill leading to the river. Tom and his son John were doubled up laughing at me. I can still remember my father shouting at me to

28

'get a grip'. The horse eventually came to a stop just before the river, miraculously without unseating me. I was white and shaking and it was a long time before I ever sat on a horse again. Several years later in my early teens I became much more comfortable with them and sometimes rode one of Tom's horses at the farm just for fun.

Ballyseedy Castle, on the edge of the wood, which has now been turned into a hotel, was very close to Tom's farm. Right beside it was a huge monument to the IRA prisoners who were blown up during the Civil War at this spot. When I was a child, although there was a caretaker for the castle, it was derelict and tumbledown. The grounds were overgrown, with wonderful bamboo gardens the like of which we had never seen before. We would play there for hours before returning home for our tea. When I was a little older we would walk out along the disused canal to the White Wall and Cockleshell and would paddle in the water at the edge of Tralee Bay. That part of the world has been my favourite place for as long as I can remember. Perhaps there are more beautiful or scenic places but I always felt at home and comfortable there. Many years later, as an adult, I would walk out to the bay early in the morning or late at night and let the silence and the sea take over. Near by is the little village of Blennerville, where many thousands set sail for America during the Famine Years in the mid-nineteenth century. Little more than a hamlet centred on a couple of pubs, Blennerville marks the gateway to the Dingle peninsula. For some reason in my youth it always had a particular haunted quality. You could stand where the sea met the canal by the then derelict windmill and imagine the thousands of people queueing to get on a boat to begin new lives in America.

It was common for our gang to be out all day without

our parents worrying about us. Certainly we had no sense of fear. We were aware that most people in the area knew our parents and that was usually enough to keep us in check. We were a pretty normal bunch of kids. We fell out, alliances changed from day to day. I know that I often wanted to be the one in charge, which led to many rows. Some of the kids were older than me and I got thumped now and again if they thought I was getting a bit above myself. We hunted for rabbits with a motley collection of dogs – with more enthusiasm than success, it must be said. We fished in any one of the two or three rivers within walking distance. We played games, we teased and tormented certain neighbours, knocking on their doors and then running off before they answered. We concentrated on those who took it worst and chased us as we ran off in the dark, our hearts pounding with fear. When Kerry won the All Ireland Gaelic football final, which they often did, we would scavenge the area for material for a big bonfire on a piece of wasteground where the triumphant team passed by in cavalcade, bearing the cup as we shouted and cheered.

During the winter we were more often confined to home by the weather. I joined the local library when I was about seven and would spend winter evenings sitting by the fire reading. My mother was happiest when I was immersed in a book, for her education was all about reading and she would often sit calmly with me by the fire while I read. Our family and everyone who knew us seemed to believe that I was my mother's favourite. There might well have been some truth in that but she was scrupulously fair and treated us all equally. Of course football and other sports went on through the winter, so like many other kids I often came home covered in mud and soaked to the skin.

My father was the kind of man who could decide on

a Monday that the earth was flat and hold to that opinion tenaciously despite all evidence to the contrary. Mary and I would argue with him ceaselessly. Donie – more like my mother in temperament – would usually keep out of it. My mother would just shake her head before eventually saying, 'I don't know which of you is worse.' At that stage things would almost inevitably quieten down.

At one point my father was working for an agricultural supplier. Some days he would collect me when the truck was passing by our house and we would spend the day in the country delivering animal feed. It was unusual if those visits weren't punctuated by my father arguing with one or more of the farmers. Sometimes I think he did it just because it was expected of him. Most times it seemed to end amicably enough.

He was a powerful, strong man, full of energy. As well as his daytime job he was also a part-time fireman in the local fire brigade. The fire station was equipped with a siren that sounded like it was announcing an air raid, and part-time firemen had a bell installed at home. When ours went off at night it woke everybody in the house. One of the benefits of this job for us was the 'fire-damaged goods'. Everything from fishing rods and tennis rackets to yet more books made their way through our door.

Like most Irish children I was taught by nuns and Christian Brothers. I enjoyed Moyderwell Convent, where the nuns were kind in their rough way, even though they forced me to write with my right hand, against my natural left-handed inclination, tying my left hand behind my back. Truth is, they weren't being cruel: they just didn't know any better. Forty years ago left-handedness was regarded as a handicap that should be cured. I remember getting into trouble at the convent only once. Fighting with another kid, I pushed him and he fell against a window, breaking it. Unfortunately this was witnessed by one of the nuns who dragged us off to the Mother Superior's office. Thankfully she didn't seem to regard this as a terribly serious incident. They knew we hadn't meant to break the window and they didn't make much of it. Many of the nuns were excellent teachers with an infectious enthusiasm about them. They liked teaching; for many of them it was a vocation rather than just a job.

I left the convent when I was seven and went to the Christian Brothers Primary at Clounalour in Tralee. Here teaching was conducted by a mixture of Christian Brothers and lay teachers. For the first time in my life I was at school with kids drawn from a wide area and I began to make many new friends. Some of the Christian Brothers were friendly, decent men who went out of their way to help; others were sour, frustrated individuals who seemed to enjoy verbally or physically abusing kids. I still had difficulty in making up my mind which hand I should be writing with, but the brothers had none. I was right-handed and that was that. Until I was twelve or thirteen I could write badly with either hand, but I was losing the ability to write with my left. I ended up with a right-handed, often illegible scrawl. In later years I wrote in block capitals so that my writing could be understood.

One of the lay teachers at the school was the son of a well-known local republican who had once been elected as a TD (Irish MP). I remember being sent into his class by our teacher to borrow some chalk. He asked me my name and when I told him he made much of who my father was. I felt both embarrassed and proud. I knew that the teacher was an important man in the republican movement. Every Easter he helped the republicans organize an Easter Sunday concert in the Ashe Memorial Hall to commemorate the Rising of 1916. It was a matter of some local pride and the whole town seemed to be there, even some local priests and gardai.

The concerts followed a set pattern: Irish dancers and traditional ceilidh groups would be followed by melo-dramatic and sentimental re-enactments of the Rising. Mournful and evocative republican ballads like 'Kevin Barry' – about a young medical student hanged by the British in the War of Independence – or 'The Ballad of James Connolly' would be followed by rousing tunes like 'A Nation Once Again'. Melodramatic tableaux from the Rising, which were designed to pluck a tear from your eye, would be acknowledged by rapturous applause and a standing ovation. I found them really moving until I entered my teens, when I cringed at their sentimentality. They seemed mawkish and old-fashioned.

Primary school was essentially about passing your Primary Certificate, the equivalent of the British 11-plus. After four years at the school I sat the exam. I cannot remember my exact results but I know that I did reason-ably well and that my parents and teachers seemed very happy with them. I don't think I cared much about it. I was much more interested in running and playing soccer; I had won a few medals at local athletic competitions in under-age events and I knew that at soccer I was as good as or better than anyone else around.

During the last summer holiday before I entered secondary school, I was playing around at home one day when I found two revolvers hidden in a water tank in the attic. One was an old Webley .45 and the other was a newer Smith & Wesson .32. I rushed off to show the guns to my friends and we had a lot of fun with them for a few days. Then for some reason I hid them under a

33

bush beside a lane not far from home. A few days later I heard my father say to my brother: 'They'd better be back when I come in this evening. If they are there'll be no more about it.' My brother protested his innocence but my father said, 'It had to be you. Your brother's too small to climb up there.' I knew exactly what he was talking about. I tried to leave the house before my father went and I was left alone with my brother, but there was no way out. After my father left my brother grabbed me and forced me to admit that I had taken the guns. He made me take him to where I'd hidden them and he brought them back home. Because I'd simply dumped them in the hedge without any covering they had already begun to rust and he had to clean them before he returned them to the attic. My father never mentioned the subject again. Years later I told him that it had been me who had taken them. He just laughed and said, 'I should have known.'

Entering St Mary's Secondary School, known locally as 'The Green' because it was situated by the town park, was a big leap – the first real step into the adult world. For the first time I became strongly conscious of the structured way in which the narrow Catholic nationalist attitudes dominated rural Ireland.

The Irish Catholic Church was the single most influential institution in daily life. Even as a youngster I recognized this fact in some vague way. Its influence was everywhere – from no meat on a Friday to the banishment of unmarried mothers. To be forced to go to England with an unborn child was bad enough; to have the child taken from you and handed over to anonymous foster parents chosen by the Church was perhaps even worse. At primary school we were marched to confession on the first Friday of every month; ranks of schoolchildren drilled in obedience to Holy Mother Church.

Rule by fear was the order of the day. I still remember the strut and swagger of the young priests, who knew only too well how powerful they were. We 'learned' that God and Irish nationalism marched hand in hand to a tune shrouded in mystery but which was always clear to the faithful. We were taught, over and over again, as part of our daily school routine, that Irish Catholics were special to God. The Virgin Mary was an Irish colleen. Padraig Pearse and the other rebel leaders executed by the British after the Easter Rising of 1916 were painstakingly interwoven with images of Christ and Catholic martyrs into a seamless mix of blood sacrifice for faith and fatherland. I felt that I was drowning in a sea of ignorance and superstition. For me most of it was mumbo-jumbo and superstition and I never really took it seriously, partly because, of course, at thirteen I was already beginning to rebel against the beliefs of my parents' generation.

On our first day in secondary school, under the scrutiny of the Christian Brothers, we sat an exam which purported to grade us according to ability. Those who performed best were placed in the A class, where every subject, where possible, would be taught through the medium of the Irish language. I was lucky enough to be one of the chosen few. I objected, saying that I did not want to be forced to submit to such dictatorial teaching methods. The assistant headmaster, a Christian Brother, was sent for. The Brother forced me to stand in front of the class while the other pupils were told to kneel and pray that I might repent and see the error of my ways. It seems comical today, but when you are thirteen years old and a giant of a Christian Brother is booming out prayers and abuse in equal measure, fear is the only emotion you feel.

The master capped it all by ordering me to leave the

room: 'You are a disgrace to Ireland's noble dead.' This was followed by a rendition of a song about Thomas McCurtain, a former Lord Mayor of Cork, 'murdered' by the British. The Brothers lived in a world of Gaelic games, the Irish language and endless songs and stories about noble Irish patriots, and the treachery of the English, which was at the root of all Ireland's ills. To be fair, most of them had left home as early as thirteen or fourteen and had been held in an authoritarian, vice-like grip by the diocesan colleges and, later, the residential training schools. Free-thinking had not been encouraged.

For years growing up in Marian Park I had played mostly soccer rather than Gaelic football. Though this did not meet with the approval of my father, it was not a source of friction until I was at secondary school. Football – Gaelic football, that is – was about the only sport taught at school, and games between classes and teams picked at random were fiercely contested. I liked sport but wasn't much good at Gaelic football. I was enthusiastic but by no means one of the better players. The standard was very high; many kids nurtured an ambition to go on to win the All Ireland Championship with the Kerry team. I was much more interested in soccer and long-distance or cross-country running. By then I was a member of the local St John's Athletic Club and spent a lot of time training. I wasn't the fastest runner in the world, but I could keep going for much longer than almost anyone my age.

My father didn't understand why a son of his wanted to play a 'foreign game'. This was one area of serious disagreement between us. At that stage my father and I had little in the way of a relationship and I avoided his company whenever possible. Any period alone almost inevitably ended in argument and I considered him stupid, thought that he knew nothing and couldn't be bothered to listen to him. Along with some friends I started a local soccer club in the area, which finally made it clear to my father that I would plough on and do what I was interested in, without feeling that it was necessary to have a major debate about the issue. He didn't like it but eventually seemed to accept that I was entitled to play whichever sport I was interested in. It was a pattern that was to repeat itself in the years to come.

2

Every Easter Sunday the annual commemorations were held at the republican plot in the cemetery where I had played as a child. The parades passed by our house, so after I had watched the bands and the colour party of IRA men pass I would tag on to the tail-end like all the neighbouring kids. One year, some of us made a rough crown of thorns and put it on top of the monument in the cemetery and tied a homemade Union Jack to it. Then we went on out to the cemetery to watch the fun. When they reached the monument one of the stewards removed our adornments, and we knew from their faces that they weren't pleased. There was quite a bit of muttering between them. I was sure they would catch us, and we laughed so hard we nearly wet ourselves.

At first I thought that the dwindling band of IRA veterans were a touch silly and old-fashioned, like 'Dad's Army', but it gradually dawned on me that most people seemed to have a fair deal of respect for them. They were very much a part of the town and its history and I suppose a lot of people said, 'Good luck to them.'

In June 1966 I went to Bodenstown for the first time. The annual pilgrimage to Bodenstown, in County Kildare, where Theobald Wolfe Tone, the father of Irish republicanism, is buried is, together with the Easter Commemoration, one of the key events in the IRA calendar. A Protestant, Tone was born in 1763 and became one of the founding members of a group called the Society of United Irishmen, which, heavily influenced by the French Revolution, sought aid from France to free Ireland from British rule. He and the United Irishmen proclaimed that they would substitute the common name of Irishman for Protestant, Catholic and dissenter, but in reality set off a squalid round of sectarian slaughter in 1798. Tone slit his throat in jail rather than be hanged by the British. As kids we were taught that he had not committed suicide – to do so would have been both cowardly and a sin – but had been murdered by the British. It was indicative of much of the rubbish we learned as 'history', particularly that concerning the relationship between Britain and Ireland. Most political parties in the Irish Republic still hold a parade to his grave on a Sunday in June. For the majority of them it is a matter of lip service, but for republicans it is a duty taken very seriously. The annual oration is an almost holy event; it gives meaning to the events of the previous year, explains and justifies the actions of the IRA/Sinn Fein and, most crucially, sets the scene for the forthcoming year.

There was a carnival atmosphere, starting with the bus journey organized by the local Sinn Fein, which took several hours and left early in the morning. Almost everyone on the bus was much older than me so I was a little inhibited. There were no women present and many of the men were farmers. In fact, there was only one other boy around my age on the bus. From the odd scrap of conversation or angry remark about 'selling out' or 'going communist', I became aware that my father and his friends and associates in the republican movement in

39

North Kerry were worried, even angry, at the direction the leadership was taking – away from physical force and traditional republicanism and towards constitutional politics and Marxism. Armed struggle was no longer the priority. The parade itself was quite an exciting affair for a twelve-year-old: men in paramilitary uniforms, bands and lots of friendly joking and laughter as people renewed old friendships. The speeches went completely over my head, I'm afraid, but I remember being impressed by the solemnity and sense of history as people listened attentively to every word. On the way back to Tralee some folk sang the occasional rebel song, usually laments about dead heroes. Others played cards, slept or talked quietly among themselves.

Soon afterwards, most of the North Kerry members of Sinn Fein/IRA were expelled by Cathal Goulding, then Chief of Staff of the IRA, and his assistant, Seamus Costello, after an article was published in the IRA newspaper, *United Irishman*, condemning as sectarian the practice of reciting the rosary at republican commemorations. Sean MacStiofain, the Sinn Fein organizer in the area at the time, stopped the distribution of the paper, and was suspended by Goulding for six months. Most of the North Kerry organization walked out in sympathy, playing right into Goulding's hands. Up until Goulding's speech, there were always bundles of Sinn Fein circulars lying about the house. I used to sneak off to the toilet to read the *United Irishman*, which always – at least for me – had a certain air of mystery and excitement.

That summer Donie bought our mother a transistor radio in Dublin. I had heard of the pirate radio stations such as Radio Caroline from older friends and was keen to listen to them. My mother and father still preferred the old radio which sat on a table in the living room for years. My sister was still a little young to be much interested in pop music, so the transistor as good as became my property. I remember weeks, perhaps months, when I seemed to do little else except listen to music on the transistor in my bedroom.

Around this time in my early teens I started to become wild and a little reckless. I and my friends were certainly hard to control, but looking back on it our activities were fairly harmless small-town stuff. In fact there was an air of innocence about it all. There was endless talk about drugs and yet I don't believe any of us ever even saw a joint. Drinking Coke with aspirin in it and smoking dried banana skins was about as close as we got. We were just growing up, struggling against the claustrophobia of provincial life, wanting to be sophisticates when in reality we knew little of the world beyond what we saw on Irish television and read in newspapers like the *Irish Press*. It would, however, be true to say that coming from a home where my father ensured that politics were discussed I perhaps had a better grasp than most of my friends that change was coming in Ireland.

The combination of the romantic myth of Che Guevara, the student riots in Paris, the anti-Vietnam War protest sweeping Europe, and the emergence of the Civil Rights movement in Northern Ireland began to capture my imagination. On 5 October 1968 I was sitting watching television along with childhood friends, brothers Martin and Billy, when the news clearly showed Royal Ulster Constabulary (RUC) officers brutally attacking Civil Rights marchers in Derry. We saw RUC officers kick, punch and baton completely defenceless and peaceful marchers. We were totally shocked by the naked hatred and violence of some of the police.

The march had been banned by William Craig, Northern Ireland's Home Affairs Minister, but nothing could excuse the brutality with which the police enforced

41

the banning order. That event had a huge effect on me. All of my sympathy was with the marchers and I formed the opinion there and then that the RUC were a totally bigoted police force on a par with the Nazis; this conviction was to remain with me powerfully for many years. Most nationalists were angered by the scenes in Derry, and the Northern Ireland Civil Rights movement went from strength to strength in the coming weeks and months. My two friends and I, who sat and watched the events of that day, were all to join the Provisional IRA.

On most Saturdays during this period a small group of Marxist students from University College, Cork, came to Tralee to sell their newsletter and to recruit. From them I bought my first copy of Mao's *Red Book*, and it was around this time that I formed an organization called the Young Socialists. We booked the local Irish Transport and General Workers' Union hall for our first meeting and a few people showed up, mainly older students who were home from university for the weekend. I don't think they were too impressed with the half-dozen fourteen- and fifteen-year-olds sitting around talking about the revolution. Later we produced a leaflet condemning the American involvement in Vietnam.

All of this has to be seen in the context of young, rather naïve, perhaps even idealistic youngsters looking for a cause. At our second meeting in the trade union hall one of my friends was chased from the meeting by his umbrella-wielding, very red-faced father, who screamed abuse at us, particularly me, the ringleader of this 'communist' conspiracy.

My own parents were fairly relaxed about our activities. As ever, my mother passed little if any comment, regarding it all as part of growing up. My father would have disagreed with me politically but we were disagreeing on everything by that stage. In many respects our ignorance of the situation in Northern Ireland was quite incredible. I had never, to my knowledge, met or spoken with a unionist. My image of unionism was formed almost entirely by the rabid bigotry of the Reverend Ian Paisley. Paisley had first risen to prominence in 1964, during a British general election, when he objected to the flying of an Irish Tricolour from the window of a Sinn Fein election office in Divis Street in the nationalist Falls Road area of Belfast. The subsequent removal of the flag by the RUC resulted in the worst rioting seen in Belfast for many years. A powerful and charismatic orator, Paisley held a Messianic quality for his followers. He was a rabid opponent of republicanism, homosexuality and 'popery', seeing 'papish' conspiracies around every corner. For Paisley the Civil Rights Movement was nothing more than a republican plot to force Northern Ireland into an All-Ireland Republic. Many Protestants agreed with him and it was during this period that he became a serious political force. For me he was the personification of Northern Ireland's unionists, and I doubt I was much different from most people of my age in the Irish Republic. The first time I saw Paisley on television was in 1968. When he referred to 'Roman Catholics' my friends and I looked at each other in bewilderment: 'We're not Italians,' one of them said. We really had no sense of ourselves as 'Roman'. We were Irish Catholics and felt insulted by his use of the prefix 'Roman'.

The only thing I knew of Protestants and unionists was that they were what is known as the 'Ascendancy': they stole the land from the Catholics and persecuted them. The Protestant working class in Northern Ireland were simply dupes of the British government. The Catholics would throw the British out by force, of course, and then the poor stupid Prods would see the error of their ways. There was little, if any, consideration given to the question of what would be done with the Protestants.

At the start of 1969 another event took place that was to harden my heart even more. The People's Democracy, a far-left group that had been formed in Queen's University just days after 5 October, when the RUC had attacked the Civil Rights march in Derry, planned a 'long march' from Belfast to Derry: it would take four days.

By this stage Terence O'Neill, the moderate, pragmatic prime minister of Northern Ireland, had already legislated to outlaw the discrimination that was rife against Catholics in housing allocations. Plans had also been announced to review the by now notorious Special Powers Act. In fact, O'Neill had already moved considerably closer to granting the initial demands of the Civil Rights movement – equalizing the allocation of housing points, for example, and passing a one-man, one-vote rule by removing the property qualifications. All of this came too late for some nationalists and provoked fury among hardline loyalists like Ian Paisley and William Craig, who saw O'Neill as 'selling out' to republicans.

Loyalists perceived the students' march as highly provocative and harassed the protesters at several points along the route. The loyalists were assisted by the worst elements in the RUC, who diverted the marchers into areas where they would be attacked. On 4 January at Burntollet Bridge near the village of Claudy, County Derry, a heavily armed loyalist mob who had been lying in wait for the remnants of the exhausted marchers pelted them with a hail of bottles and stones from either side of the road. After the initial assault they closed in on the students with cudgels and iron bars. The police –

some of whom actually attacked the marchers themselves – made no attempt to arrest the loyalists. It appeared obvious, at least to me, that the source of the bigotry was inherent in Northern Ireland's very existence and that reform was impossible. If justice was to prevail Northern Ireland and unionism would have to be destroyed.

The violence was to escalate throughout 1969. That summer, Protestant mobs raided the Catholic Falls and Ardoyne areas of Belfast, burning out many houses that bordered Protestant streets. A steady stream of Catholic refugees began to appear in Kerry and I began to learn from first-hand reports what was really going on. I got to know one of those families particularly well – the McKennas, a widow and her three young sons and young daughter – who had been burned out of their Falls Road home and forced to flee with only the clothes they wore. Somehow, they turned up in Tralee and were eventually housed in a particularly squalid two-room flat. I lost track of them after a year or two but heard that they later returned to Belfast. That family and others like them had never had much and what little they did have had now been destroyed by the sectarian brutality of Northern Irish Protestants. Because I had no knowledge of living conditions or the general standard of living in Northern Ireland I didn't know that people there, including Catholics, enjoyed a better standard of living than most people in the Irish Republic.

In Belfast the IRA was weak and badly armed. Many of the older members had left in protest at Goulding's new Marxist theories; it was even claimed that he had sold off most of the IRA's arsenal to the Free Wales Army in order to raise money to print pamphlets. A slogan appeared on gable walls: 'IRA – I Ran Away'. It was left to a group of the old-timers, most of whom had been inactive in the IRA for a number of years, to defend Catholic districts using whatever guns they could find. These men were to become the driving force behind the Provisional IRA.

On Friday, 15 August 1969, British home secretary Jim Callaghan acceded to the unionist request for troops to relieve the RUC, who were exhausted after nights of unsuccessfully trying to contain the sectarian riots in Belfast and Derry. The sorrow and the rage that swept nationalist Ireland after the events of August '69 proved to be the funeral pyre for the old leadership of the IRA. In the weeks to come, local defence committees sprang up in West Belfast, makeshift barricades were erected and a new generation of republicans took up the struggle. By the end of the year a new image had replaced the old: a regal phoenix, its wings poised vengefully, appeared from a mound of dead ashes. Painted beside it were the ominous words: 'Out of the ashes of '69 arose the Provisionals'.

3

At the end of 1969, after months of bitter wrangling and factionalism, the IRA finally split into the Marxist Official IRA, led by Cathal Goulding, and the right-wing Provisional faction, led by Sean MacStiofain.

Now, I see the birth of the Provisional IRA as the greatest tragedy in modern Irish history, but that was not how I felt at the time. I was fifteen years old and in a hurry to enlist. My own political views were to the left of the leadership of the Provisional movement and, left to my own devices, I would naturally have been closer to the socialism of the Goulding tendency. The Provisionals' romanticizing of violence and death worried me, but I saw them as a popular front that would sweep away partition and the British presence. We would then be able to have a realignment of the left in Irish politics, and after that it would be full-steam down the road to the socialist republic. There in a nutshell you have the political wisdom of a fifteen-year-old would-be Irish Revolutionary. For men like my father the formation of the Provisional IRA proved that the original dissenters had been right all along: only physical force would drive the British out of Ireland. They were happy now: the movement was back on track.

Many of the boys my age boasted that they were going to join the IRA. Most of them moved on to something else after a few days of enthusiasm, but the difference between me and them was that I knew exactly *how* to join up. Early in 1970 a friend and I approached a local shop-owner in Rock Street called Dennis Fitzgerald, who I knew was well connected to the new Provisional IRA. 'We want to join the IRA,' I told him. 'Well now,' he said, 'you'll have to join Sinn Fein first.' This would not have happened a few short years later. Then, we would have been taken quietly aside and told not to talk politics with anyone, or, if we did, to express opposition to the IRA. But these were early days and the shopkeeper was a republican from a different era. Shortly after this I attended my first Sinn Fein meeting in the same trade union hall I had booked for Young Socialist meetings. My father wasn't at that meeting but I had told him I was going and though he didn't say much I had no doubt that he was pleased.

The meeting was chaired by a successful local businessman, who was probably the best-known republican in Kerry at the time, and was also in charge of the IRA in Kerry. Attending the meeting were people who had been expelled from the republican movement by the Goulding leadership in 1966. As far as they were concerned it was they who had been proved right. Along with a handful of others, they had taken a stand against the direction in which Goulding and his colleagues had tried to go, leaving nationalists in Belfast defenceless. They held 'politics' in deep contempt, regarding them as a corrupting influence. They were also, in the main, very right-wing Catholic nationalists.

In his introduction to the meeting the IRA man said, 'The best way to explain the difference between us and the Official IRA is to describe the Provisionals as the green IRA and the Officials as the red IRA.' I wondered for a while if I was in the wrong meeting, but the Provisionals seemed determined to fight the British and that interested me above any consideration of political ideology.

Within a few weeks of signing up to Sinn Fein I made it clear that it was the IRA I wanted to join. Word was sent to me one day via a man very active in Sinn Fein, and whom I had assumed was also in the IRA, that I was to be at the local IRA leader's house at a certain time one evening. Several people whom I knew were already there. We drove together to a large farm on the outskirts of Tralee, where there were about twenty IRA men gathered. The farm had several outbuildings, including a large grain store.

Dried barley was piled high in one corner of the store. We cleared it away with large wooden shovels, and underneath was a substantial collection of guns and ammunition wrapped in plastic bags and boxes: Lee Enfield .303 rifles, Thompson and Sten sub-machine-guns, and a large selection of pistols and revolvers. These were the guns the local IRA had held on to after being expelled in 1966. Our job was to clean them and sort the ammunition into the correct calibre to suit the guns before the bulk of them was moved to Northern Ireland a few days later. Everybody was quite friendly, if serious. I knew most of those present even though they were all over ten years older than me. No one was surprised to see me. They knew my family and relatives; many of them had known me since I was a child.

I have never really been fascinated by guns. There were always a couple of shotguns and .22 rifles at home because my father often went shooting on a Sunday with a group of friends. I was used to having guns around from an early age and had no romantic illusions about them. I was, however, full of excitement because now I was in the IRA. This was the real business and I was part of it. When I got home that night my father spotted some pieces of grain that had fallen from my trousers or had got dislodged from my shoes. He remarked, 'I know where you were tonight. Be careful.' He said nothing else and I wouldn't have expected him to – such was our relationship. No one would have told him that I had joined the IRA and I knew that I wasn't allowed to talk to anyone, even my father, about it.

After this I became part of the local IRA unit in Tralee, attending meetings once or twice a week in farmhouses near the town. One of the more experienced members would take us through basic weapons training – stripping the guns down, cleaning and loading them – and explain the safety precautions that were always to be followed: never point a gun at anyone, always check to make sure it isn't loaded and that the safety catch works. Sometimes there was a lecture on the IRA's constitution or its General Standing Orders or maybe a little republican history. Ostensibly I was a member only of Sinn Fein but the police and most local people assumed I was in the IRA. After a couple of months I told the local IRA leader of some young people who were interested in joining the IRA, and after a few weeks I was given the go-ahead to recruit them. Among the new members were my childhood friends Billy and Martin. They did not remain long in the IRA, both later going on to join the Irish police force. Another recruit, who stayed only a couple of weeks, was Christy, who had been chased out of the local trade union hall by his umbrella-wielding father.

Our new unit was allocated three guns by the local IRA leader. He asked me sternly, as I recall, if I had a safe place for them. I assured him that I had; in fact I did not, but I was desperate to get the guns for the unit. He arranged to meet me at night near the old graveyard. I waited inside the wall until he drove up in his car. The guns, wrapped in sacking and plastic, were on the back seat of the car. He handed them to me, saying, 'Mind those,' as I disappeared into the darkness of the grave-yard. I went to the old abbey and with the aid of a torch examined the guns: a mark 4 .303 Lee Enfield rifle, a Thompson sub-machine-gun and a .45 Webley revolver, all old but in good condition. I was responsible for their safekeeping. As I wondered what to do with them the answer came to me: Tom McCarthy, whose farm I had played on as a child. I had no reason to suppose that Tom was an IRA supporter but some memory from childhood must have stayed with me. I called to his house after dark, the guns with me. I knocked on the door and when he answered I told him my problem. 'I wondered how long it would take you,' was all he said. He told me to leave the guns inside an open window. 'I'll look after them for you. Whenever you want them just let me know.' I realized that Tom was not about to tell me where he would hide the guns – a sure sign that he had done this kind of work before. In fact, Tom's farm-house was to become the regular meeting place for the unit.

One Sunday morning in the early autumn of 1970 I was collected from my home by the local IRA leader. We drove out of Tralee towards Killarney. I knew I was going to an IRA training camp but had no idea where it was to be. I was the only one from our unit who had been told about this and I knew that that meant I was the most highly regarded and the best trusted. About halfway between Tralee and Killarney, near the village of Farranfore, we turned right on to a small, winding road. The road narrowed into a track covered in potholes and bordered by high, heavily overgrown hawthorn hedges and wild fuchsia. When we halted we faced a long, low, whitewashed farmhouse. There was an inscription above the front door: 'Officially burned by Crown Forces, May 9th 1921'. I realized where I was.

I had heard many stories about Mai Dalaigh. My father had worked for her election campaign when she had stood for Sinn Fein in the Irish general election of 1957, and she had been a member of Cumann Na Mban, the women's IRA. Her brother had been executed at Drumbo in County Donegal by the Free State government during the Irish Civil War. Her house had been burned down by the Black and Tans during the War of Independence as a reprisal for IRA activity in the area. She now lived at the foot of the mountains in an old house with stone flags and a large open fireplace. It was crammed full of IRA propaganda tracts, training manuals – even British Army training manuals. At the back was a beautiful garden where Mai spent much of her time.

Mai was a woman of startling contrasts. Then in her late sixties, she was tall, gentle and deeply religious, yet steeped in a violent, almost anarchistic tradition. She had known every republican leader from Michael Collins and Eamonn de Valera and was quite used to generations of IRA men passing through her house with their guns. I admired her greatly and we got on extremely well.

That Sunday at Mai's there were around forty IRA men drawn from all over Kerry. Some I knew; others were complete strangers. It was my first real introduction to what was in effect the Kerry organization and I wasn't sure what to expect. Training was of a very rudimentary nature, but some of those present were experienced and keen to pass on useful hints. At sixteen I was still much the youngest but there were a half-dozen or so in their late teens or early twenties who all came from other parts of the county. At that time modern weapons were in short supply. The best available were Second World War US Garands and Carbines. Although the first consignment of Armalite rifles was on its way from America to Ireland it would be some time before any could be spared for training.

We spent the morning divided into small groups for weapons and explosives training. In the early afternoon we set off on foot towards the mountains. We walked for several hours until we had reached a deep glen cut into the flanks of one of the peaks through which ran a fast-flowing mountain stream. We walked into the glen until it was possible to go no further and there we engaged in shooting practice. Improvised targets made from sheets of cardboard were placed at varying distances from us, and in small groups of five or six we stepped forward to shoot, using the various weapons available. The targets were changed regularly and those in charge kept a tally of how we were scoring. Even though I was used to guns and gunfire I had never experienced the level of noise produced by five or six people firing high-velocity weapons at the same time in a relatively confined space. The smell of cordite and the noise can be overwhelming at first and you have to force yourself to stay calm and pick your shots. I knew that I had done quite well but was surprised and pleased when the Kerry officer in charge said to me, 'Top of the class.' We were not far from where the FCA, the Irish Army Territorials, had their rifle range and practised on Sundays. If anyone heard our shooting, unlikely as that was in such a deep and remote glen, they would most likely assume that it was the FCA. Over the coming months there were many Sundays like that.

It was the spring of 1971 and the IRA campaign in

Northern Ireland was moving into overdrive. Kerry had long been a prime IRA training area and now recruits from Northern Ireland were being sent there. By the summer of that year, Joe O'Connell from County Clare, who was later captured by British police after the Balcombe Street siege in London, and I were training many IRA people in weekend and week-long camps, which usually took place at Mai Dalaigh's. I was still only sixteen and very young to be doing such a job, but I was keen and had the confidence of the Kerry OC. More importantly, I was available – something which should not be overlooked – and was also pretty confident, unaffected by the knowledge that the people I was training were, almost without exception, older than me.

Joe O'Connell was a quiet, pensive man in his early twenties. He had been a radio operator and electronics trainee at Marconi in Cork and was just the type of dedicated, intelligent man the Provisional IRA needed at that time. Mainly through O'Connell's prompting, I spent a lot of time studying explosives. I had no particular interest in such matters; I just thought that I should become competent in as many areas as possible. I was surprised to find how much information was available in the local library. I also studied the old IRA and British Army training manuals. I was active in Sinn Fein and sold the IRA newspaper door-to-door in the housing estates near my home. One of my regular customers turned out to be a former British Army sapper. We would have occasional conversations at his door about how the 'war' was going, but it was some time before he told me about his background in the British Army. I knew that he had a heart condition and couldn't work, but the rest was a mystery. He was sounding me out, weighing me up, no doubt a little reluctant to trust a sixteen-year-old. He was married with a young family, all at school, and his wife worked. I would go to his house during the day and over a cup of tea or two he would draw sketches of different booby traps, explaining the properties of different explosives. Updated IRA training manuals were now available; I would show these to him and he would scribble notes and make comments on any errors or deficiencies. I worked hard and soon had an extensive knowledge of the subject. By now I was, in effect, the IRA's training officer in Kerry and was often O'Connell's assistant, dealing mainly with explosives training in larger training camps organized by the IRA's General Headquarters staff.

The young IRA recruits from Northern Ireland who were sent to Kerry for training were by and large the type of ordinary young men you would find in any British or Irish city. They listened to the same music, wore similar fashionable clothes and often followed the same English soccer clubs. They all had their youth and their anger. They saw their primary duty as protecting their own areas: the Provisional IRA was born and forged in the white heat of sectarian warfare. The vast majority of the recruits had no coherent political outlook. In fact, they mainly despised politics. A youthful fascination with guns and bombs and a desire to get even with Prods was all the motivation they needed. Ill-educated and ill-equipped, they were vulnerable to republican propaganda. The hard leadership of the Provisional IRA, mainly older and embittered men who had waited all their lives for such an opportunity, plied them with guns and turned their hatred into a lifelong commitment to violence.

They had been ground down by bigotry, starved of hope. In other cities they might have rioted and returned to normal life, but the IRA gave them a sense of purpose and a cause to kill and die for. Many had seen their communities laid waste by sectarian attack; now they were hitting back, to restore their pride and dignity. Without doubt some of the new recruits would in time carry out the most awful acts of violence. But the real blame lies with their leadership, the old republicans, the Northern equivalents of the old IRA leadership in Kerry, who taught them discipline and obedience, inculcating reverence for a tradition that sanctified murder, even the murder of friends for some minor transgression of the republican code.

There was still a steady flow of refugees from the burned-out areas of Belfast and Derry to temporary housing or refugee centres in Kerry and other parts of the South. Stories of the atrocities suffered by the nationalist communities at the hands of the British Army circulated freely. For the first time I began to question the integrity of the briefings that the leadership was giving to us.

Garret Cotter, an elderly republican who had been active in the IRA bombing campaign in England in 1939–40, had a gym in a large shed beside his house. The gym was used by various sports clubs from the town. Garret was a strange man, a lifelong IRA member who had planted bombs and perhaps killed people. Yet I remember a conversation with him on a summer's evening as we looked out on the fields backing on to his home. He pointed at a couple of rabbits and said, 'I can't understand how anyone could kill one of God's creatures.' That same evening he also said that he felt that young IRA volunteers were expected by the present leadership to sell their lives too cheaply. Garret was a well-known republican and it was pretty much common knowledge that the IRA sometimes met in his gym, but the Garda never bothered us. On this particular occasion, a priest from the North had just returned from a brief holiday there. He was a close friend of the local

IRA leader, who considered him an adviser and asked him to address us on his experiences there.

The thirty or so IRA men present heard the priest tell us how, on his trip to the North, he had discovered that British soldiers were regularly raping Catholic women in Belfast and Derry. While this seemed improbable to me – not even a hint of it had appeared in the Irish media – I was too unsure of myself to voice my doubts to the leadership, who looked as if they wanted to believe it. It was of course in the IRA's interest to create scare stories like this to demonize the British soldiers; it hyped up the volunteers and justified the bloody acts of terror they were engaged in.

For all that, though, it took the IRA some time actually to kill a British solider. Gunner Robert Curtis was the first to die, machine-gunned on North Belfast's New Lodge Road, at the beginning of February 1971. Then, on 9 March, the campaign against the British Army took a new and murderous twist. Three off-duty soldiers from the Royal Highland Fusiliers, two of them brothers aged seventeen and eighteen, were lured from Mooney's bar in the city centre, a neutral area where they would have a chance of a good night out away from the routine of security patrols. They met up with two attractive young women in the bar and thought that they were on to a good thing, as one of the girls promised them a party on the outskirts of Belfast.

After the women had gained the trust of the Scottish soldiers, they called on the assistance of the 3rd Battalion of the Belfast Brigade of the IRA, who sent down three men from Ardoyne to meet them, ostensibly to drive them to the party. The soldiers never reached their destination. As they drove out of Belfast that night, the three soldiers were let out of the car when they needed to urinate at the roadside, each still holding a beer glass in one hand. They were shot in the back of the head and left where they fell. It was a shocking event for many people, including those who had a more romantic view of the cause.

Around this time a new recruit joined the IRA in Kerry. Brendan Dowd, from Ballymaceligott, about five miles outside Tralee, was a tall, strongly built, good-looking man in his mid-twenties, who had spent most of his working life in England, first going there when he was fourteen. Intelligent, with a wide range of technical skills, Dowd was undoubtedly a cut about the average IRA volunteer of the period.

Dowd came up with the idea of stealing explosives from a quarry where he worked. It was a simple plan. Security was lax and the explosives were stored in a tin hut, the only impediment a cheap lock and bolt on the outside. We broke into the quarry at night and forced our way into the hut, stealing explosives and several large rolls of cordex – a detonating cord in short supply and much prized by the IRA. We also stole a large number of electric detonators. It was my first real IRA operation. Breaking into a tin hut late at night hardly qualified as an operation, but we did get priceless explosives. I recall little sense of fear or excitement. I was more worried about the fact that events had moved very quickly and I hadn't cleared things beforehand with the Kerry OC. But I needn't have worried; he was delighted and congratulated me at the next meeting. Shortly afterwards the material was collected from where we'd hidden it at Tom McCarthy's farm and sent to the IRA in Northern Ireland.

In August 1971 internment without trial was introduced in Northern Ireland by the unionist Stormont administration, in an attempt to smash the developing Provisional IRA campaign. It was a disaster. A combination of poor intelligence – many of the people arrested had no republican connections – and ill-treatment of some of those detained gave the IRA campaign a major boost, attracting popular support with many new followers.

During this period IRA units in the South, including Kerry, were placed on standby. The OC drove four of us to a house in the village of Doon in East Limerick, where we hung around for a few days watching the television reports of gun battles and rioting in Northern Ireland, hoping for a call that never came. After a couple of days we were driven back to Kerry.

By early 1972 I was spending most of my time training IRA recruits from different parts of Ireland. After one local Sunday training session I returned to my parents' house along with my explosives training kit: timing units, booby traps, watches, clocks, detonators, gelignite and material for manufacturing homemade explosives. While I was mixing up a batch of explosive in the garden shed some sulphuric acid, which must have leaked or spilled from its container, came in contact with an inflammable mixture of weedkiller and sugar, which immediately burst into flames. The fire spread quickly; I ran from the shed and reached the back door of the house when a huge explosion rocked the building. I was blown into the hallway in a cloud of dust and smoke. When I got to my feet I stumbled to the front door and ran blindly from the scene of the explosion. I was unhurt but probably in a state of shock. I kept running until I reached the McCarthy farm. I had no idea of how much damage had been done. Only later did I discover that the concrete shed was completely demolished, the kitchen and rear of the house badly damaged and all of the windows blown out. Many of the windows of neighbouring houses were also broken. My parents had not, thank God, been at home – though I would not have been mixing the explosives had they been in!

Tom and I walked across the fields to a small, local hotel a short distance away, used for weddings and work functions and the like and quite often by Sinn Fein for meetings and social events. It was a place that would feature much in my IRA career in later years. I phoned the local IRA leader who came immediately. He obviously wasn't very pleased when I told him what had happened. He instructed me to make myself available to the local police, telling me that as a juvenile and first offender I would get off lightly. I didn't like the idea of it but had no choice: orders were orders. Just weeks before, a Kerryman charged with possession of several guns had been fined and given a suspended sentence. Even senior republicans convicted of IRA membership, which didn't happen too often in those days, received only minor punishment – fines or very short periods of imprisonment.

On returning to the house I found it swarming with policemen. My mother looked shaken but was obviously glad to know that I was unhurt – although as usual she displayed little in the way of emotion. She had returned to find her home in ruins and her son in trouble. I was arrested and taken to the local police station. The biggest concern the police had was that there might be more explosives in a dangerous condition in the rubble. I assured them that there weren't and then refused to answer any more questions.

I was remanded in custody to Limerick prison, an unusual course of action. At seventeen I was under-age for prison and should have been sent to St Patrick's, a Dublin Borstal for young offenders.

Limerick prison was an awful institution. The food was poor: small bowls of stew that was little more than soggy potato and minuscule pieces of fat and carrot, supplemented mainly by bread and porridge. The conditions were primitive and unhygienic; squalid, in fact, with overflowing toilets and chamber pots that often couldn't be emptied. On my first day prison warders tried to make me wear prison clothes but I insisted that I was a political prisoner and therefore entitled to wear my own clothes. This was something that republican prisoners had fought hard for over the years and there was no way that I was prepared to compromise. The prison was simply trying it on because I was so young. Eventually they gave in, much, I'm sure, to the disgust of the other prisoners, who were forced to wear the uniform. Much of my time in Limerick was spent studying for my Leaving Certificate ('A' level equivalent), which I had completely neglected up to this point. I had missed many months of school over the previous couple of years, either due to my IRA activities or because I was bored by it and couldn't be bothered to go. The prison authorities gave permission for my course books to be allowed in, and arrangements were made for a prison officer to supervise the exams. There were no study facilities or teachers available, so it was a matter of getting on with it myself. I spent many hours studying alone in my cell. I did quite well under the circumstances, particularly in English and history, and although I failed Irish I retook it a number of months later in a school in Limerick and passed. The results would have qualified me to go to university but at that stage I had no interest in anything beyond the IRA and the cause. My father and other relatives visited regularly while I was in jail and I wrote and received letters from friends in Tralee. My mother never came. She wrote regularly and explained that she just couldn't bear to see me in prison. I understood her feelings entirely and had known from the start that she wouldn't be able to cope with it.

While I was in jail a handful of other republicans were remanded there, among them members of a small republican splinter group called Saor Eire. A tiny, ultra-leftist group, Saor Eire had split from the IRA in the sixties and usually confined themselves to carrying out bank robberies in the Republic. These men had been caught in Cork with detailed plans of an army barracks. One day in the prison yard they told me that they had an escape planned for that day and wanted me to help them. They explained that at midday, when chapel bells in the city rang for the Angelus, a rope would be thrown over the wall. As soon as the first bell went they wanted me to run towards the part of the wall furthest away from the rope to draw the two prison guards in the yard after me, allowing them vital seconds to make their escape. I had no intention of helping Saor Eire. They were seriously tainted with accusations of gangsterism and were lining their own pockets from the proceeds of the bank robberies. When the first bell rang out I ran towards the inner wall and by way of the adjoining wood store clambered on to it. I ran along the wall towards the rope but by then the alarm was up; the rope had been spotted by kitchen staff whose window looked out onto the space between the inner and outer walls and a couple of the kitchen staff had already cut off my route. I stayed on the wall for a while, refusing to come down but eventually, of course, I had no choice and was frogmarched off to a punishment cell. I received a couple of thumps along the way but there was no malice in them: they were just something that was expected in the circumstances. The Saor Eire people had also tried to escape but without success. No charges were made and the incident seemed to be quickly forgotten. I had indeed run towards a part of the wall away from the rope, as requested, but this was only because it was much easier to get on to the woodshed from there and I was still quick enough to make it to the rope before the others. The Saor Eire faction seemed to believe that I had played my part and were quite happy. It was a hopelessly badly planned attempt anyway, with no real chance of success.

One other incident while I was in Limerick scared the wits out of me. Half asleep in my cell one night, I had a sense of something else in the cell. It was very dark with just a little light coming through the window. I sat up in the bed and something scurried away. I picked up the prison mug and threw it in the direction of the noise. My heart was pounding as I stood on the bed – naked. My eyes were getting used to the dark. I knew now it was a rat or a mouse but I didn't know which. I knelt down and groped for my shoes, throwing one towards where I thought it was. There was another quick scurry and I let fly with the other shoe. I knew that I had hit it. I grabbed the chamber pot and lashed out blindly, feeling something squelch. I kept on battering with the chamber pot, hysterical with fear. It was too big to be a mouse. It had to be a rat. I picked up a shoe and hit it with the pot and the shoe, both hands flailing. I don't know how long it took but eventually I stopped – trembling and thinking I was going to be sick. I backed away and sat up on the bed. There was no doubt the rat was dead, but it still took me some time to get the courage to approach it. I managed to push the crushed body into the chamber pot, using the shoe as a shovel, and threw it out of the cell window. Shortly afterwards the light was switched on as the prison guard did his hourly check. He was surprised to see me sitting up and asked if everything was okay. I told him that I had got up to go to the toilet and was going back to bed. I couldn't be bothered to explain. I told one of the staff in the morning but he just shrugged his shoulders. There wasn't much facility for complaint in Limerick in those days and not much point in it anyway.

While I was on remand the Irish government, in response to growing opposition to the IRA campaign, introduced Special Criminal Courts. These were non-jury courts where the evidence was heard by only three judges. I was charged with possession of explosives and instructed, like every IRA volunteer of that period, to refuse to recognize the authority of the court. I did so and received a six-month prison sentence for my pains. Had I complied, I might easily have got away with a suspended sentence.

After the hearing I was transferred to Mountjoy prison, in Dublin, a much bigger prison than Limerick, with far more experience of dealing with IRA prisoners. There were other Provisional IRA prisoners there but not as many as usual, since, following a riot, some of them had been transferred to the Curragh. Here we were treated as political prisoners. We held classes in Irish and republican history and generally operated as a unit. I cannot remember how many of us were there – probably about a dozen. Most of the others were a good deal older than me and while I remember some of their names I can recollect little detail of my time there. I never again met any of my fellow prisoners, either from Limerick or Mountjoy. Being in the company of other IRA prisoners from different parts of Ireland undoubtedly gave me a sense of the organization's being bigger and more structured than I had realized until then. But what I really remember is the smell of sweat and urine and the dirt. It was dirtier even than Limerick.

One day in July, when I was three months into my sentence, I was called in to see the prison governor, who told me that my grandmother was dead. I applied for parole to attend her funeral but it was refused. I felt really sad about her death. I suppose I knew that she would have made a fuss of me when I was released and would have wanted to hear all my stories about jail. I had less than two months left of my sentence and felt angry that I had not been given parole.

While I was in Mountjoy several major events of the early years of the 'troubles' took place. On 7 July 1972 the IRA had unprecedented talks with William Whitelaw, the Secretary of State for Northern Ireland, at the home of Paul Channon, another senior Conservative, in Chelsea. The IRA delegation included the top men: Seamus Twomey, Sean MacStiofain, Daithi O'Connaill, Gerry Adams, Ivor Bell and Martin McGuinness. I knew some of Adams's younger brothers slightly, due to the fact that they had been evacuated from Belfast to Kerry during the worst of the troubles and had stayed period-ically with the Ferrises at Churchill or sometimes with the O'Shea family at Curaheen on the Dingle peninsula. Just before the talks were to take place Adams was released from internment on the insistence of the IRA leadership. They saw his release as a gesture of good faith on the part of the government, but, more im-portantly, people like Seamus Twomey had quickly recognized that the twenty-three-year-old Adams was already an unusually gifted and astute political analyst and strategist and they figured that his presence at the talks would lend the IRA credence.

Gerry Adams had joined the old IRA in 1965 at the age of seventeen. His father, known as Old Gerry, had served a long period in prison during the forties after being wounded by the RUC in Belfast; he had drawn a revolver on them when they called on him to halt during a period of heightened IRA activity in the area. Adams's mother was a Hannaway, one of the oldest and most respected republican families in Belfast. He is extremely proud of his family tradition.

During the late sixties Adams was active in street agitation and demands for better housing in Belfast. Surprisingly, until 1969 there was no overt IRA activity in the city; much of the leadership of the movement was committed to pursuing a political agenda, relying heavily on street protest and building broad fronts with other groups whenever their interests converged. After the IRA split, however, Adams chose to side with the more militaristic Provisionals, becoming a battalion quarter-master, responsible for weapons. At twenty-two he became Officer Commanding the Second Battalion, Belfast Brigade, one of the biggest and most active battalions, based at his home in the Ballymurphy housing estate in the west of the city. I might have met Adams when he came to visit his brothers in Kerry during that period, but if I did I don't remember, and I certainly have no impression of him from that time. Had we met it is doubtful that I, a seventeen-year-old IRA volunteer from Kerry, would have made much of an impact on him.

The talks with the British never got off the ground. Afterwards, Adams was not returned to internment, but went on the run and resumed his previous position as adjutant of the Belfast Brigade, under the command of Seamus Twomey. Twomey, a former manager of a bookie's shop, had invented the car-bomb earlier that year, and this was to revolutionize IRA operations. Soon afterwards, in March 1972, he sent a unit driving two cars packed with explosives into the centre of Belfast. One of the cars exploded in a crowd, which had been moved away from another suspected bomb, and six people, including two policemen, were killed.

Twomey was a hard-headed West Belfast man,

sectarian without a political bone in his body. Inside the movement he was known as 'Thumper', because of his habit of hitting the table to get his way at meetings. After the failure of the talks with the British, two weeks earlier, he and Adams struck again with a series of car-bombs in Belfast city centre. That day – 21 July 1972 – is now known as Bloody Friday. It was a savage attack. Nineteen bombs were exploded, six without warning. Nine people were killed, 130 maimed and injured.

Taking advantage of the disgust that the Provisionals' actions had aroused among decent nationalists north and south of the border, the British Army launched Operation Motorman and regained control of national-ist areas of Northern Ireland such as the Bogside in Derry, places under IRA control that had become no-go areas for the RUC and the army. The only law previously existing in these areas was that of the Provisionals. The IRA made no attempt to resist the army's massive show of strength and simply faded away, often across the border to the relative safety of the Irish Republic.

Watching these events unfolding while I was in Mountjoy, I knew that the loss of these no-go or 'free areas' was a huge blow to the IRA. No matter how brave a face they put on it, they were never again – with the possible exception of South Armagh – able to enjoy the same degree of operational freedom in Northern Ireland. Only one other young prisoner agreed with me. All were of the belief that the IRA had made the correct decision and that to attempt to take on the army in open battle would have been suicidal. In retrospect I realize that the IRA leadership was right. It was in no position to make any sort of stand.

I was released from Mountjoy in September 1972 and was met at the gate by my brother Donie. He had married while I was inside and of course I had not been able to attend the wedding. He had no interest in politics and believed that the IRA and anybody associated with them was either mad or bad, or both. He tried to talk to me about why I was involved and sought to persuade me that I should have no more to do with it, but I wouldn't listen and we dropped the subject before it turned into a heated argument. My mother came out to meet me when I got home and fussed around, cooking and making me try on clothes she had bought for my return. She quietly said that she hoped I had learned my lesson and wouldn't get involved in any more trouble, but true to form she never pushed it: she had said her piece and I could make my own decision. I immediately reported back to the IRA.

A couple of weeks afterwards I was instructed, along with other local volunteers, to present myself at Mai Dalaigh's one evening and to expect to be away for a few days at least. When we arrived twenty people were already crammed into Mai's house. It was obvious that something very big was going on. Some of the people in the house were important figures in the IRA: Tom Sullivan, from Doon in East Limerick, who would, briefly, be the IRA's Chief of Staff and whom I had met before at IRA training camps, and Sean Garvey, from South Kerry, who had long been a member of the GHQ staff.

It was obvious on this evening who was in charge. As it transpired, there was no need for most of us to stay away from home overnight. In a pattern that was to be repeated several times over the next few days, we climbed into the back of a cattle-truck along with generators, spotlights, walkie-talkies and a radio set and drove the short distance to Farranfore airport. Today a thriving local airport with regular flights to England and other parts of Ireland, in 1972 Farranfore had neither runway nor facilities. The airport was hardly used and was certainly not manned at night. The security was non-existent. Along with most of the other locals, I had no idea what was happening, but by the time we reached the airport our purpose was pretty clear. The generator was started up and lights placed at either end and at the sides of the runway. It was explained that we were waiting for a plane that was carrying weaponry for the IRA. The sense of excitement and tension was overwhelming. No one present had ever been involved in such an important mission. I was told by the Kerry IRA leader that the plane had taken off from Algeria and that the pilot was Yugoslavian. I have no idea how much of that is true. We waited for hours, talking quietly between taking turns at watch on the gate. There was a sense of anti-climax when nothing happened that night. At about 4 a.m. we withdrew to Mai's. Locals such as myself went home, while Sullivan and others stayed there. We assembled the next night: same procedure, but again nothing happened. We were beginning to wonder if something had gone seriously wrong, but we possessed so little detail that our chat was just idle speculation.

On the third night the entire operation degenerated into farce. Though the plane did arrive, it turned out that the runway was too short for it to land. That certainly didn't inspire much faith in the ability of those who had planned the operation. After much heated discussion Sullivan rushed from Farranfore, leaving those remaining completely bemused. I remember thinking that the whole thing was a complete disaster. Not until later did I find out that the operation had been rescued and that the first RPG7 rocket launchers to reach the Provisional IRA had been successfully landed at Shannon airport instead. Whether contingency plans had been made I

69

don't know, but using either bribery or sympathizers an unscheduled flight managed to land at Shannon and had its cargo of RPG7s safely removed. We were not aware of any of this at the time.

Some weeks later those of us who had been at the airport were called to a meeting at Garret Cotter's gym. We had been there a few minutes when the Kerry IRA leader entered. He was accompanied by the legendary Joe Cahill, who was carrying what turned out to be one of the rocket launchers landed at Shannon. He explained that it was an RPG7 anti-tank weapon. Everyone at the meeting was very excited and the RPG and missiles were passed around with much comment. At last the IRA was getting hold of the type of sophisticated equipment that it had previously lacked.

Very soon afterwards, in October 1972, the IRA used their new weapons in a series of attacks along the border. Despite much initial excitement the attacks were largely unsuccessful due to lack of proper training and poor storage facilities, which often had a detrimental effect on the weapons' batteries and firing pack. It was typical of the IRA's inefficiency during this time.

At this stage I was still living at home with my parents but my involvement in the IRA took me away for long periods. Whether I was training new recruits, attending meetings or generally helping with organizational work or the movement and storage of weapons and explosives, my life was dominated entirely by the republican movement. There was also Sinn Fein work to do when IRA business was slack. For a brief spell I worked in a local factory that made brass tubing for export, but I was bored to tears by it. I had no interest in such humdrum work. I only took the job because I had no money and my mother, for all her easiness, wasn't too pleased with an unemployed eighteen-year-old who contributed nothing to the household. The IRA does not pay volunteers unless they are regarded as full time and then only a basic pittance. I was not yet in that position so money was very scarce. Even had I wanted or had the time to go out and socialize I couldn't have afforded it.

Throughout the early months of 1973 it was becoming clear that a large number of IRA men in Kerry were unhappy with the conservatism and caution of the local leadership. They had joined looking for action and were getting precious little of it. The leadership had been in charge, almost unchanged, for many years and was very set in its ways. The leaders had also become arrogant and were intolerant and dismissive of criticism.

A local man called Maurice Pendergast had been promoted to a senior position in the IRA's finance department. A radical socialist who despised the local IRA leadership, he, along with other young Turks like Brendan Dowd, was pushing for the sanctioning of armed robberies to raise finance. Up to that point money had been raised on an ad hoc basis, but pressure from the new Northern leadership for the South to pay its share was mounting, and they didn't mind how the money was got. The local leadership in Kerry and other areas of the South was totally opposed to this new initiative. They cited the experience of the 1940s when the IRA had engaged in armed robberies in the South. It had brought them into open conflict with the state and had almost led to the destruction of the IRA when de Valera's government reacted strongly, executing several IRA men and leaving others to die on hunger strike. It also gave rise to charges of gangsterism, which the IRA found very hard to live down.

Subsequently, during the reorganization of the IRA in the 1950s, the IRA leadership had introduced what became known as General Army Order Number 8, which explicitly forbade any overt or aggressive IRA activity in the twenty-six counties. In early 1973 that edict was still in place. However, an IRA leadership desperately strapped for cash is rarely in the mood for quibbling. In May 1973 an order finally went out from the North that money was to be raised from armed robberies to be carried out in the South. A team was put together under the control of the IRA leadership and led by a man called Brendan Hughes, from Coalisland in County Tyrone. In Kerry Maurice Pendergast had already been in contact with a group, and through him the IRA leadership had already laid plans for the armed robbery of a post office van.

Brendan Hughes was sent to Kerry, where he met with the local leadership. They refused to obey his instructions and ordered him to leave the county within twenty-four hours. But it was too late: the local leadership, traditionalists to a man, had lost their authority. Within hours of Hughes's reporting back, a delegation from the IRA leadership was on its way to Kerry. The leaders included Seamus Twomey, who was by now Chief of Staff of the IRA and not the kind of man whose wishes were defied; J. B. O'Hagan, from Armagh, a veteran of the border campaign of the fifties, was Twomey's adjutant. Very much a traditional conservative himself, O'Hagan was nevertheless totally in favour of the new policy. Brian Keenan, originally from South Derry but long resident in Belfast, has often been described as the IRA's most efficient military operator. In my opinion this is correct. A hardline doctrinaire Marxist, when Keenan joined the Provisionals his capabilities quickly impressed the leadership. By this period in 1973 he was already one of the leading contacts between the IRA and the Libyan government. The fourth member of the delegation was Kevin Mallon, another veteran of the fifties campaign. In August 1957, RUC Sergeant Arthur Ovens kicked open the door of an unused cottage near Mallon's home town of Coalisland, County Tyrone. He was instantly blown to bits by a mine that Mallon had planted earlier. Mallon was found not guilty on that charge but shortly afterwards was convicted of conspiracy to cause an explosion and of possessing explosives; he received a fourteen-year sentence.

The four men formed a close and formidable team, but they met with organized opposition in Kerry, Dublin, Cork and Wexford, where the local leaderships contained strong traditionalist elements from the 1940s and 1950s. The local leaders feared that their easy lives might now be disrupted by shoot-outs with the Garda, accusations of gangsterism, loss of respectability and, last but not least, the breaking of ties with members of Fianna Fail, the most strongly nationalist party, who might be inclined to help with the North but would run a mile from armed robberies and the like.

Mallon, Keenan, Twomey and O'Hagan were in no mood to take any nonsense. By the time they reached Kerry their reputation had preceded them. They dismissed the old leadership, with the exception of Brendan Dowd and me, and replaced them with people ready to carry out the new policy. I remained as training officer. I was much the youngest person to be involved in the local leadership but it should not be supposed that being the IRA's training officer in Kerry was in any way a senior position. Brendan was appointed the new OC. He had made a big impression on Pendergast, who pushed hard for him to be given the job, partly because Pendergast believed he could control him. Within days the mail-van robbery that had been planned quietly in advance was carried out by Brendan Hughes and his team. I played no part in it, even though I was aware of the details. Brendan Dowd drove the getaway car.

In June of that year, a couple of weeks after the mail-van robbery, the annual republican pilgrimage to Bodenstown took place. We left Kerry early in the morning by train. The mood was different from previous years; the old traditionalists were largely gone, dismissed or disappeared into semi-retirement. Brendan Dowd was now in regular contact with Twomey and Keenan. On the journey he called me aside. 'Would you be interested in becoming a full-time volunteer?' he said. Interested! I would have eaten his hand off for the opportunity. It was what I had always wanted. Now I was to be a full-time revolutionary. I knew that what had gone before was simply preparation. In my mind the best was yet to come.

4

Within a week of becoming a full-time member of the IRA I was sent to Donegal along with Martin Ferris and another man from Kerry. Ferris was over three years older than me but we knew each other fairly well. He too came from a republican family and I knew some of his relations. He was a gifted athlete and played Gaelic football for Kerry. He had never been popular with the old leadership and had a reputation locally as a hardman. He was often in the headlines for drinking and brawling and had played only a peripheral role in IRA activity in the area up to that point. Now that the old, somewhat respectable leadership had been displaced by younger militants, Ferris's hour had come. I knew that Brendan Dowd had read him the riot act about his drinking and general behaviour, but Dowd needed men like Ferris for armed robberies and similar activities. Ferris feared little, was ready for any risk and was prepared to do whatever was asked of him. He was capable on the one hand of extreme, irrational and violent behaviour, but on the other possessed qualities like loyalty and generosity towards friends. We saw little of each other in those years but always got on well when we met.

Donegal is the most northern of all Irish counties,

sharing a frontier with Counties Derry, Tyrone and Fermanagh in Northern Ireland. Like all border counties in the Republic, it is a frontline recruiting ground and an operational and logistical base for the IRA. Organizationally it falls under the IRA's Northern Command. Brendan Dowd drove the three of us there, to a hotel called the Carrigart near the village of the same name, where we were awaited by Pat Doherty. Pat was to feature heavily in my life in later years. At this stage quartermaster for the IRA in Donegal, he was responsible for training camps and bomb factories. He was admired hugely, and was closely associated with Martin McGuinness, then in charge of the IRA in Derry.

Doherty was quiet, with a fixed smile which later earned him the nickname 'Smiler'. The darker side of his character can be judged from his other nickname, 'Papa Doc', after Papa Doc Duvalier, the infamous Haitian dictator. Ponderous and cautious, Doherty bore more resemblance to a civil servant than to a terrorist leader. Slow to make enemies, loath to take decisions, his rise through the ranks of the IRA was gradual, careful and consistent.

Pat and his brother Hugh had been born in Scotland after their parents had followed the thousands of other Donegal folk who had travelled to Scotland in search of work. For years the Dohertys had lived in a tough, inner-city council estate in Glasgow and Pat still spoke in a mixture of Donegal and Glasgow accents.

A short ferry-ride from Northern Ireland and with a large Irish emigrant population, Scotland was so valuable to the IRA that they excluded the country from military operations. Instead it was used as a kind of Ho Chi Minh Trail, an arsenal and jumping-off base for active service members en route to bomb the rest of Britain. From the early 1970s to the present day the security forces have regularly discovered IRA stores, active service units and proof of IRA planning and preparation in Scotland, but there hasn't been a single IRA operation there since the start of the campaign.

We spent our first week in Donegal at a training camp run by a Derryman. I learned little or nothing new there, but here on the border we were regarded as relatively inexperienced people. The next two weeks were spent in a bomb factory near Carrigart, learning how to make explosives from Net nitrate fertilizer. Once trained, the idea was that we would use the expertise to establish similar bomb factories in the South. In our fourth and last week we spent a number of days in the company of a border active service unit led by a man from Donegal. The ASU had positioned a large landmine under a culvert on a narrow road just over the border. A command wire ran from the landmine to a firing point on the southern side of the border. We took it in turns to man the landmine. The three of us and our commander would man it at night and the other two men would take over before daylight. It was explained to us that a landmine should never be left unattended in case the army discovered it and lay in wait for the volunteers to return. A few days later the two who manned the daytime shift were caught by the army. We heard that they had behaved badly, failing to take the security precautions they had been instructed to observe. It is believed that the army forced them, at gunpoint, to defuse the landmine.

It was also in Donegal that I had my first conversation with Daithi O'Connaill, then perhaps the Provisional IRA's best-known leader, who came to visit us in the house near the border that we were using as a jump-off base for the landmine. A tall, angular man with a hawkish face, he had achieved near-legendary status within the IRA. Shot six times during the IRA border campaign of the 1950s, he loved to tell the tale and tell it he did, at every opportunity and at great length.

Our four weeks in Donegal over, we were collected by Brendan Dowd and returned to Kerry. Ferris and the other man were detailed to instruct other people on how to design and run a bomb factory; I was to take charge of a new GHQ training camp. It was strongly felt by the leadership that there was a need for a large facility well away from the border area where volunteers could receive a good solid training with little fear of detection, and at this stage I was the only one of the three of us who was a full-time IRA volunteer. Once back in Kerry, I travelled with Brendan Dowd to the remote southern part of the county. There we met with a local republican from south Kerry who brought us to an isolated farmyard in the Glencar valley, an area of incredible natural beauty. Set amongst the highest mountains in Ireland, its abundance of lakes and rivers and its scope for hill walking make it an area very popular with tourists, fishermen and climbers. We were determined to establish the most efficient training camp the IRA had organized in modern times.

It was an ambitious project and both Dowd and I were conscious of the need for maximum security. The land was owned by a man called McGillicuddy, who had in fact been interned with my father and uncle in the 1940s. After Garvey had introduced us we let him go as there was no need for him to know the detail of our business, although no doubt he suspected. We explained to McGillicuddy what we required and he said that he would be delighted to help. First of all he took us to a small, one-storey cottage on the shores of Caragh Lake. It had no running water, no electricity but it did have an open fireplace and a small gas cooker as well as a bed and some oil lamps. Access was via a rough track from his farmyard through heavy woods. While it was ideal as a place for me to stay when there was no camp on, it wasn't suitable for what we had in mind. It was far too small and sat feet from the edge of the lake. Completely without cover at the front, it was exposed to view from the road that ran along the far side of the lake.

McGillicuddy then introduced us to his young son, Joe. He explained that even though Joe was only thirteen he knew the area as well as anyone and was completely trustworthy. Glencar had long been regarded as a solid republican area and the McGillicuddy land had seen many training camps over the years. Kids like Joe brought up in such a tradition in remote rural areas were often older than their years in such matters. Joe led us off in the opposite direction from the cottage into the foothills of a mountain covered in dense ferns and scrub. Before too long we came to the place that Joe thought was ideal. He was right. At the top of a narrow rock-strewn track, almost hidden by bracken and fern, we came to a dip in the mountain where there was a small clearing about fifteen yards in width and roughly the same in length, surrounded by dense vegetation. There was a small natural spring near by which would provide plenty of water and we could use gas bottles for cooking. We thanked Joe and drove to Killorglin, a town about twelve miles away. There we bought a large assortment of pots, pans, cutlery and a couple of gas bottles and some rings. The only thing we had in abundance was sleeping bags. We also bought several rolls of the black plastic farmers use to cover silage, some timber stakes about twelve feet long, rope and tools.

We drove back to the McGillicuddys' and, parking the car in their farmyard, set off on foot for the campsite. We soon realized Joe was following us, keen to help. We let him stay and he turned out to be very useful. Over the course of the next two days we built a structure rather like a marquee, using long sheets of the black plastic which we then camouflaged with sacking covered with twigs, branches and fern. From a distance it would pass unobserved and blended into the background quite well. Once we had the camp established we brought the weapons in. We had quite a collection: Armalites, Garands, Carbines, Springfields, sub-machine-guns, pistols, an RPG7 rocket launcher and dummy warhead and mortars as well as the explosive kit needed for training. We had to find a number of safe dumps for this equipment and again it was Joe to whom we turned. Only he and I were ever aware of where the weapons were dumped when no activity was taking place. Joe seemed to know every potential hiding place, from gaps in the rock to small caves and disused animal hides. Like any boy his age, he was excited at being able to help and we took advantage of that. As far as he was concerned, the politics of the situation were neither here nor there and he never had any further involvement with the IRA.

The camp ran till the end of 1973. The permanent staff were me and a man called Dermot from Lurgan, with occasional GHQ staff passing through. In those few months we trained around 200 volunteers from the North. Most of them were young boys in their teens, although there were some notable exceptions. The IRA man John Francis Green, from Monaghan, spent a while at the camp with me after escaping from Long Kesh – now the Maze – that year. Green was later found shot dead in a farmhouse on the border, allegedly ambushed by Captain Robert Nairac, the British military intelligence officer who was himself tortured and murdered by the IRA in 1977.

Jim Monaghan and an electronics engineer, both from Dublin, were occasional visitors to Glencar. At that time they were both heavily involved in the IRA's engineering department, Monaghan concentrating on mortar development and the electronics engineer on the development of a remote-control device for landmines that would eliminate the need for command wires and thus make the mines harder to detect while increasing the distance from which they could be detonated. He had used his spare time in the electrical repair shop where he worked developing the prototype for the IRA's first remote-controlled device. At Glencar he had the time and space to perfect it and was happy working on his own.

We normally took volunteers for five days, with Sundays being changeover day. The volunteers left home by various routes. At a central rendezvous point they would be put into the back of a cattle truck or van with its windows blacked out and driven to Glencar. The journeys to and from the camp were always made at night. Once they were at the camp every effort was made to ensure that they would see no local newspaper or product that would reveal the location of the camp.

Only material essential to a particular training session was brought from the dump and at night only two weapons were kept for guard duty. I was the one person armed at all times. It was also my job, with Joe's help, to point out escape routes for use after a raid, and to select the spot where volunteers were to rendezvous after they had completed their getaway.

Volunteers slept in sleeping bags on the ground, with two at a time on all-night staggered watches, or 'stags'. After breakfast the day would begin with intensive training in the characteristics and capabilities of a number of weapons – their range, length and weight, how the firing action worked, and their ammunition. Theory was followed by the tedious but potentially life-saving procedure of field-stripping guns, which gives familiarity with the weapons and demystifies them. We explained how to clean the weapons, a routine carried out repeatedly. One of the most frequent causes of a gun jamming is dirt and excess oil and I was always amazed at how little the IRA cared about this. It was a sign of a good operator if he cared as much about looking after the material on which his life might depend as he did about finding a target. Safety procedures and firing techniques followed, and the day's lectures were rounded off with anti-interrogation sessions or a talk on the constitution or orders that governed the organization. At Glencar we concentrated quite a lot on firing practice, mostly using the lighter weapons – .22 rifles, pistols and a couple of converted .22 sub-machine-guns. We could afford to spend hours doing this most days as the likelihood of discovery in such a remote area using the quieter .22 calibre ammunition was negligible, and this type of ammunition was cheap and easily available. Such freedom gave us a great opportunity to monitor development and to correct bad habits. Only those we felt had reached the required standard were allowed a short firing session with heavier weapons at a location deeper in the mountains.

Some people were sent to the camp to learn particular skills or because their local OC thought that they had an aptitude in a particular area. One of these skills was bomb-making, so from time to time we ran a rudimentary course. IRA bombs at that stage were fairly crude devices, using clocks or watches as simple timers. By now I was something of an expert in this area and conscious that preparation was the key to success.

Failure to test circuitry was not the only cause of premature explosions – or 'own goals', as the British Army called them. It was commonplace to work at bombs with bare hands instead of wearing rubber gloves, and a lot of the young married volunteers wore gold rings; we later discovered that these sometimes made a contact where the two wires crossed the ring, completing the circuit and detonating the bomb. Problems with static electricity were another reason for premature explosions.

While I enjoyed training the Belfast people, I was depressed by their insularity and sectarianism. They were city lads who were often unused to the countryside and this caused problems as well as the odd amusing moment. On occasions at night the entire camp would be awakened after some Belfast man had mistaken a fox or a wild goat for hordes of Special Branch men. Many of them had never been out of their own areas before travelling down to Kerry. They bragged of fighting the Brits with stones and petrol bombs and competed with horror stories of what the 'Orangies' would do if they saw you walking towards them down the street. Belfast men often seemed to believe that the IRA began and ended in Belfast, which occasionally caused problems, but usually they were never at the same camp with men from other areas. Personal tragedy and bitterness often lay behind the men's decisions to join the IRA. Many of them had enlisted after a close relative, sometimes a father or older brother, had been killed on active service by the army or the police. Some had either been interned themselves or had had relatives in Long Kesh. These stories were occasionally hard to listen to and mostly I simply got on with the job in hand. I had much more in common with the older and more experienced men on the border. They were hard, efficient and dedicated and I admired their sense of purpose.

In the middle of August a team was sent down from East Tyrone after they had taken part in a failed attack on Pomeroy army and RUC base. Twenty-seven-year-old Daniel McAnallen and eighteen-year-old Patrick Quinn had been killed when the mortar bomb they were firing exploded prematurely. Kevin McKenna, the unit's leader, had looked on helplessly as Quinn and McAnallen, who was his best friend, died. He and the other survivors were now on the run. They had been sent to Glencar, where they would be able to train properly in the use of mortars to prevent a recurrence of the problem that had led to the premature explosion. Jim Monaghan, the designer of the first IRA homemade mortars and a sometime attender at mortar-training sessions, had identified the problem and devised a solution to it.

The first IRA mortars were primitive but effective. The mortar barrel itself was made from hydraulic tubing, which was stabilized by a base plate and bipod; distance was gauged by adjusting the angle of the barrel accordingly: a ratchet on the side allowed the barrel to be adjusted right or left. At the bottom of the barrel a 'firing' pin was welded in place. The mortar shell itself consisted of two pieces of tubing: one holding the main charge, the other tube containing the propulsion unit screwed into the section holding the main charge. The propulsion unit had a series of perforations to allow gas to escape. A standard number of J-cloths which had been previously soaked in sodium chlorate were packed into the propulsion unit, into the end of which a firing cap was pushed. A length of black fuse extended to a detonator in the main charge.

In theory when the shell was dropped into the mortar the firing cap at the base of the shell struck the firing pin in the tube. This in turn activated the J-cloths, causing the build-up of gas which propelled the shell from the tube. By that time the cloths would have also ignited the black fusewire. The length of time it took the flame from the fusewire to reach the detonator was theoretically more than the maximum amount of time the mortar could possibly remain in flight. As a result the mortar shell would explode only after it had reached its target. The bomb at Pomeroy had contained no effective seal between the propulsion unit and the main charge or shell. Once the J-cloths had ignited, the flame jumped the gap, bypassing the black fuse and the detonator, and the bomb had exploded prematurely in the mortar tube.

Understandably, McKenna and the rest of the squad from East Tyrone were upset by the events at Pomeroy. McKenna was determined to have it proved to his satisfaction that the problem had been sorted. 'We don't want any volunteers dying because of bad workmanship or lousy training.' He was mainly getting at Jim Monaghan but occasionally he would glance over at Brendan Dowd and me. 'Ye had better be right about this. Someone will carry the can if it goes wrong again.' I believed the threat.

I got on well with McKenna and the rest of that team while they were in Kerry. McKenna never had a lot to say but he did instil a quiet confidence. There was no doubt that he was very much the person in charge. He was not a man to waste time and was difficult to get close to. We established enough of a relationship that first time for things between us to be quite easy but he could obviously be a very difficult man who expected things to be done properly. He was also noticeably more concerned about security than anyone I had ever met, a concern that was to have ramifications later in our relationship.

Mortar-firing using dummy shells usually took place at Inch Strand on the inner side of the Dingle peninsula – a six- to seven-mile spit of firm white sand backed by dunes which was, in those days, out of the tourist season, a quiet and remote area. It was ideal for mortar training. You had a straight line of vision and could recover the dummy shells quite easily. The shells would also be undamaged from landing on the soft sand.

During this period I was on the run from the Irish police, who had been raiding local houses looking for me since I had gone full time in June. At the time the Irish police had been making full use of a law which allowed them to charge a person with IRA membership on the say-so of a Garda superintendent. As the IRA refused to recognize the authority of the Irish courts the word of the superintendent was enough to convict. No further evidence was required.

Occasionally I would travel from Glencar and slip into my parents' house for a few hours. I could never really give notice that I was coming. By now my sister was training to be a psychiatric nurse and was studying in Cork, so often only my mother was at home. She would never question me about what I was doing but she would invariably ask, 'When are you going to get sense?' She was always glad to see me and would fuss around looking after me, muttering that I couldn't be getting enough to eat. And, as always, there would be new clothes she had bought for me since my last visit.

I saw my father only once during 1973 after I had become full time. Brendan Dowd brought him to meet me in a pub outside Tralee. We had a few drinks and chatted for a few hours but inevitably the conversation lacked something. He never asked me exactly what I was doing. Even if he had I couldn't have told him. He was relaxed, just concerned that I should look after myself. Perhaps that sounds strange, but to my father being in the IRA was perfectly normal and he seemed content to meet me just once that year.

Glencar was exposed to strong, driving winds and heavy rain and when the weather started to get bad towards the end of '73 we moved the camp closer to Tralee, to an empty house owned by an elderly republican. It was a house I knew quite well because I had first used it for meetings in the early days and I recommended it as a good winter alternative. We had nothing like the facilities available at Glencar and the camp was a much smaller affair, concentrating mainly on explosives training. We left much of the equipment in dumps at Glencar.

Around that time Martin Ferris, a relative of his and another man from Fenit came to the camp for explosives training. They were preparing to take part in the bombing campaign in England now under the control of Brian Keenan. All three of them later operated there, where they were at least partly responsible for some of the worst atrocities of the IRA campaign. There was quite a change in Ferris by now. He appeared much more mature and committed. We had always got on well and that week we often sat up late talking about the campaign, football or just different people that we knew. I had no doubt that Brendan Dowd's tough approach was largely responsible for Ferris's different attitude.

I spent Christmas 1973 in the company of an old republican from Cork called Jerry McCarthy, at a farmhouse outside Tralee. McCarthy had converted the farm's milking parlour into a mortar-manufacturing plant and was busy turning out large quantities of shells, most of which are probably lying rusting in hedges to this day. McCarthy had been involved in the IRA all of his life and had been one of the main people involved in its reorganization after it had been virtually destroyed during the 1940s. He was tall and gangling and one of the ugliest men I have ever seen. An electrician by trade, he had spent most of his working life in the Cork dockyards and was very gifted technically. McCarthy and the owner of the farm, Paul Barry, a mountain of a man and a ferociously militant republican, got on extremely well. Sometimes, though, late at night around the fire after a whiskey or two, Barry would wind McCarthy up by asking deliberately stupid questions about the mechanics of some explosive device. He would act the part of the local yokel until McCarthy, a man of little patience, would storm off to bed muttering about stupid people. As soon as he was gone Barry would collapse in laughter and then begin to think of another way of winding him up the following day. I enjoyed Christmas there and Barry was always plotting some harebrained scheme or eager to discuss a mad plan.

Shortly after Christmas I travelled to Doon in East Limerick, where I met with Tom Sullivan for the first time since the Farranfore airport episode. Sullivan was now Chief of Staff of the Provisional IRA, a position he held for a very brief period. I stayed overnight in Doon and the next day Sullivan drove me to Ballinamore in County Leitrim, to a pub owned by the veteran republican John Joe McGirl, where Maurice Pendergast, now the IRA's director of finance, was waiting. After having something to eat and a short conversation I was driven by a local man to a semi-derelict cottage in a remote area outside of Ballinamore. Sacking covered the gaps where once there had been windows and doors, and the only lighting was by way of oil lamps. The two men living there were unshaven and scruffily dressed. A small gas stove and some pots, pans and cutlery which had seen better days seemed to make up the primitive cooking and eating arrangements.

One of the men was Kevin Coen, from Riverstown in County Sligo. A small, stocky farm labourer, he was a few years older than me. The other man was also from

County Sligo but he left within a few days and I never got to know him. Kevin Coen and I became close friends in the days and weeks that followed. It was the beginning of 1974, I was nineteen years old and living in a cold, dank shack on an exposed hillside without television or radio, running the risk of spending years in jail if I was caught by the police. By now I was a travelling IRA man who could be sent anywhere to do what was required at the time. I was happy enough to accept that. Whatever the IRA asked of me I would attempt to do to the best of my ability.

Our job at Ballinamore was essentially to produce two tons of fertilizer-based explosives every week. This involved first placing four bags of Net nitrate fertilizer in a forty-gallon barrel raised from the floor on concrete blocks, combining it with several gallons of water and heating it. Without wanting to go into too much detail, our aim was to produce ammonium nitrate, which, when mixed with diesel oil, was the primary ingredient of IRA bombs. Four hundredweight of Net nitrate produced approximately one hundredweight of ammonium nitrate explosive. The bomb factory I was responsible for running supplied the Mid-Ulster Brigade of the IRA: South Derry, East Tyrone, South Fermanagh, North Antrim, North Armagh and West Fermanagh. I got on very well with Kevin Coen who was a happy-go-lucky, hard-working, ferociously healthy man. There were supposed to be three people working in the factory at all times but most of those who were sent there couldn't stick it for longer than a week or two because of the stench.

I stayed at Ballinamore until Easter 1974. It was a popular base for IRA men operating along the West Fermanagh border running from Bundoran in County Donegal to Blacklion on the Fermanagh border, and during this period I got to know the members of an ASU located near by. Kevin Coen knew all of them quite well and introduced me to them in a sympathizer's house not far from the bomb factory. Afterwards we would meet there occasionally. The leader of the group was Pat Dalton, from County Waterford, a close associate of Brian Keenan.

Harry Duggan, from Feakle in County Clare in the Republic, was another member of the group who operated on the border, with Eddie Butler from County Limerick. Along with Joe O'Connell and Hugh Doherty, the brother of Pat Doherty, now vice-president of Sinn Fein, they would now go on, under Brendan Dowd's direct leadership and Brian Keenan's overall control, to conduct a ruthless terror campaign in England.

Duggan, O'Connell, Butler and Doherty would later be captured in London after what became known as the Balcombe Street Siege. Pat Dalton's whereabouts are currently unknown. Another member of that border active service unit, Francie McGirl, would later be charged and acquitted of the murder of Lord Mountbatten. He also took part in a gun battle in County Leitrim in 1983 following the kidnap and rescue of Don Tidey, when a young Irish soldier and policeman were shot dead. Kevin Coen was later killed by the SAS while hijacking a minibus at Cassidy's Cross in County Fermanagh, and Brendan Dowd was caught after a shootout with police in Manchester. He too is still in jail at the time of writing. Dalton knew that I had trained a lot of people in the use of mortars and he was interested in trying to organize an attack on one of the border barracks with me handling the mortars. We discussed several options but nothing ever came of it.

The bomb factory was not a pleasant place to work. The smell from the boiling of fertilizer was utterly nauseating. We had to cook and eat in the middle of the fumes and heat and were often physically sick as a result. At night we usually slept in a piggery owned by the farmer whose land adjoined the bomb factory. We worked Monday to Friday from early in the morning until late at night. On Friday nights the two tons of explosive were collected by local men. Kevin Coen and I usually spent the weekend in Riverstown at his mother's home. County Leitrim on a wet day in January is one of the most miserable, lonesome places it is possible to imagine. Decades of migration had drained the life from it; a wet, boggy tapestry of deserted cottages, small uneconomic farms and a sparse and mainly elderly population gave the place an air of gloom.

I was not sorry to leave it.

5

I finally returned to Kerry at Easter 1974. I saw my family, mother and father and sister, who was home on holiday, but I stayed with friends who lived near my parents. It was by now much too dangerous for me even to visit them. The police had stepped up the search for me and my parents' home was being raided regularly. After a few days I received word that I was to go to Monaghan Town near the border with Northern Ireland. On 1 May, along with another volunteer from County Cork, I was driven to Monaghan, to a house in Park Street, a well-known IRA centre and home of Fergal O'Hanlon, who had been shot dead by the RUC during an attack on a police station during the IRA border campaign of the 1950s.

We were introduced to a man sitting alone in the living room. Eddie Collins, from Cork, recently released from jail in the Irish Republic, was OC of the IRA's Mid Ulster Brigade – the same group for whom I had been providing the explosives during my time in charge of the bomb factory. The man from Cork was told that he was being sent to the South Fermanagh border area; I was told that I was going into mid Ulster as training officer.

I sat for some hours with Collins as he instructed me on the nature of what he required from me. In the early evening the door opened and a huge man entered. I recognized him immediately; Stan Corrigan, from County Tyrone, had been one of the Tyrone men along with Kevin McKenna who had been at the training camp in Kerry the previous year. He took one look at me and said, 'The answer to my problem has just arrived.'

I could detect an air of tension between him and Collins but didn't have an idea of the cause of it. Corrigan explained to Collins that he had just come from the police station, having been released after several hours' detention under the Offences against the State Act. He had met with a Dublin IRA man, a mortar 'expert' who, having been sent to help the East Tyrone IRA carry out an attack on an army base at Clogher in County Tyrone, was still under detention. Collins gave Corrigan permission to use me instead. At this stage I had no idea that I was about to be involved in my first big operation.

Later that evening Corrigan and I were driven to a house very close to the border. There were a couple of teenage girls in the house along with a man who was obviously their brother. It was clear that they and Corrigan knew each other very well. There was lots of good-natured joking and flirting and I formed the impression that the man was central to Corrigan's plans that evening. I stayed in the background, knowing that here I was very much a stranger. The two girls cooked us food and I realized that I was ravenously hungry. I would later learn that this was caused by nervous tension, something I became used to experiencing before most operations. Although I knew the job we were about to do was important, I still didn't know what it was. At the time hunger was all I felt. Along with the man who

93

lived in the house and a local man who acted as guide, we set off on foot across the mountain which straddles the Monaghan/Tyrone border before sloping into the Clogher valley in County Tyrone. I hadn't had time to be nervous, and it was only after our guide cautioned us to be quiet, announcing that we had now crossed the border into Northern Ireland, that I felt the tension beginning to grow. After a couple of hours of heavy going over rough terrain in the dark, bent low and avoiding open ground, whispering to each other only when it couldn't be avoided, we saw what appeared to be a bonfire burning on a hillside. As we drew closer I realized that the 'bonfire' was in fact a burning tyre in front of a house.

In the house was a group of heavily armed men that included the entire East Tyrone contingent that had trained in Kerry, except for Kevin McKenna. Henry Louis McNally, from Dungannon, was a quiet, introspective and highly dangerous killer who was finally jailed in 1988 for the attempted murder of a busload of soldiers in County Antrim. I would see a lot of Henry Louis over the coming months. Barry McHugh, also from Dungannon, was a quiet and unconvincingly committed IRA man. Pierce McAleer, from Ardboe in County Tyrone, was a short-sighted, rather jolly man who fitted uneasily with the usual hardcases. And Brian McGowan, from County Offaly in the Irish Republic, was quiet to the extent of being withdrawn. He very rarely said anything and his long silences tended to make people uneasy. There were also several other people I did not know.

The house was a hive of activity, of last-minute discussion and organization. Because I was out of my area and didn't know the team well I felt somewhat excluded from the hustle and bustle. I would merely follow instructions, when the time came.

I was given the mortar and shells to inspect and was assigned a helper, a Dublin man who turned out to be worse than useless that night. A group of us climbed into the back of a hijacked Northern Ireland Carriers lorry and shot off along the back roads to the army base at Clogher. Others, including Corrigan, made their way by different routes.

We arrived and parked on a narrow track, where a steep, low bank rose between us and the base. We were quickly joined by Corrigan and the others. All roads in the area had been blocked by vehicles hijacked by local volunteers. Up to forty IRA men were involved in what was later described as the biggest set-piece IRA operation to take place up to that time.

Stan Corrigan was armed with a belt-fed American Second World War heavy machine-gun; one of the others had an RPG7 rocket launcher. The others bore a selection of small arms, mainly of American origin, Armalites, Garands, M1 carbines. McNally had possession of the one AK47 available. I set up the mortar on the roadside. The base plate was anchored in place with sandbags. My helper had a walkie-talkie. A man positioned on top of the bank would see the shells exploding and would instruct him to tell me what adjustments needed to be made to ensure accuracy. That was the theory, anyhow.

The attack was to begin with the firing of an RPG7 warhead. We waited expectantly but nervously for the signal. When it came the flashback from the rocket lit up the area. I dropped the first of the mortar bombs in the tube. All round there was the sharp crackle of rifle fire and the heavier sound of Corrigan's machine-gun. I looked to my helper for instructions but he was nowhere to be seen. I thought, 'Fuck it,' because I knew that without his advice I was firing blind. The noise of the mortars was deafening. The security forces in the base were returning heavy fire. A stream of brightly lit tracer bullets flashed through the sky like a shower of brilliant hailstones, some hitting the roadside beside me but many going over our heads. Browning machine-guns mounted on army Ferret armoured cars started firing wildly.

Some of the shells exploded in the high trees surrounding the base. Not one hit the base directly, although some detonated in the grounds. Several of them failed to explode. An army foot-patrol slipped out of the base and opened fire on us from the west side. It was complete pandemonium. I kept on firing the mortars, hoping that someone on the bank would come and give me directions if they saw that the mortars weren't hitting the base. I shouted several times but nothing could be heard above the noise of gunfire. When I saw the others running towards the lorry I realized the attack was over and there were shouts and calls as people scrambled for the lorry, which had been badly shot up in the gunfight, mostly from the army foot-patrol. The gun-battle had lasted for about twenty-five minutes.

I carried the mortar-launcher and base plate to the lorry but was told to leave them behind. Somebody fired a Sten gun from the back of the lorry as we drove off. One of our contingent decided to fire an RPG7 warhead but was quickly stopped: the blow-back from it would have fried everyone in the confined space in the lorry. Everybody was excited and there was lots of shouting and a general impression of chaos. I remember hoping that if anything went wrong I'd be able to find my way across the border on foot. I felt curiously calm the whole time as if everything was happening in slow motion.

We abandoned the lorry a couple of miles from the border and walked across the mountain on foot. It was a long way to safety. We could see helicopters with large spotlights lighting up the countryside, getting ever closer to us. At one stage consideration was given to trying to shoot down one of the helicopters, but Henry Louis McNally and I both pointed out that it would be an act of madness. We weren't equipped to bring down a helicopter and would only succeed in giving our position away.

Once over the border we waited at a prearranged place for Corrigan and the others to meet us, but the army foot-patrol had cut off their escape route. One of them had been shot twice in the thigh. They turned up hours late, having made their way on foot. We were driven to an unoccupied, newly built house in County Monaghan. Everybody was on a high. Even Brian McGowan was more chatty than normal. The one exception was McNally, who seemed completely unperturbed by the night's incidents. He sat unobtrusively drinking tea, but I noticed that distant though he appeared to be he was in fact alert and totally aware of what was going on. He was simply not a man to get carried away by events.

We lay awake listening to the late news on the radio. The local Northern Ireland station led with a story about a bomb attack by loyalists on a Catholic pub in Belfast in which six people had been killed. Then came the news report we were all waiting for: 'A UDR Greenfinch has been killed during a rocket and mortar attack on the UDR base at the Deanery in Clogher.' Cheers and hand-clapping. 'Got one stiff anyway,' someone said. Everybody had been happy with the operation and now there was near euphoria. 'Greenfinch' was the name given to female soldiers in the Ulster Defence Regiment, the locally recruited part-time regiment set up in 1970 to replace the discredited B Specials.

I don't know how I felt and I'd be lying if I said

otherwise. I'm sure that I felt no remorse, but neither did I glory in Eva Martin's death, or take satisfaction from it. At the time I was highly motivated; I believed that I was a soldier in an army fighting in a just cause and that people being killed was an inevitable consequence, and I had no doubts that the attack had been a success. Martin was a part-time member of a mainly Protestant militia set up to deal with the IRA, particularly in border areas. The UDR had a bad reputation amongst nationalists, who saw it as little more than the hated B Specials reassembled under another name – and it has to be said that there was an element of truth in such allegations. Though the vast majority of members of the UDR have behaved honourably, and many have been killed and injured, far too many members have also been convicted of murders and other crimes committed by loyalist terror groups.

Eva Martin was killed by an RPG7 warhead but it was to be many years before I discovered the particularly horrific circumstances of her murder on what her husband Richard, many years later, described to me as 'an awful, dark, black night'. She was only twenty-eight. Her young husband, who was a clerical officer on the base, had stumbled over her body on a rubble-strewn staircase as the personnel ran for cover. The power had gone, there were no lights, but he recognized her by touch. She was the first female member of the security forces to be killed in the IRA campaign. Eva Martin was not the faceless military target I had imagined. She was an intelligent, attractive woman, head of the modern languages department of Fivemiletown High School. She had studied at Trinity College, Dublin. The Martins had been having a quiet drink with friends in the base after getting identity photographs taken. I have no doubt that the Martins were respectable and decent people who were simply doing their duty by their community.

However, at the time I had very little leisure to think through the consequences of Eva Martin's death. Stan Corrigan had decided that I was far more useful as an IRA active service volunteer than as a training officer, and I was very pleased to go along with that. Within twenty-four hours I was on my way back into Northern Ireland along with Brian McGowan. Our job was to rob and then blow up the post office in Cookstown. A man who worked in Monaghan but lived near Donamore outside Cookstown collected us and drove us to his house. It was my first view of Northern Ireland in daylight. I was struck immediately by the better roads: even the signposts were of a superior quality to those at home. Many of the farms and hedgerows appeared better-tended than those in the South. Certainly in those days the difference was quite amazing.

We stayed overnight in Donamore and then drove to the parochial house in Cookstown for a meeting. I don't believe that the local priest knew anything about our planned operation. Those present included the local OC and his adjutant, both middle-aged men of the traditional republican type. Jimmy McGivern was a street-level operator from Dungannon, and there was another full-time activist at a senior level, who would not have been part of such an operation had he not been a local man.

As we sat putting the final touches to the plan local men cut a gap in the wire fence surrounding the post office. At about 1 a.m. one of them came to the house to confirm that the fence was cut and that there was no sign of security activity. Three of us slipped out of the house and walked the short distance to the post office. We crawled through the hole in the fence and made our way across the yard to an open shed. There we waited until the clerk with the keys to the safe turned up. We knew that he was due about midday. Sleep was not an option. We were in a very exposed position near the town centre and had to keep alert at all times. Armed with only one revolver, we had no chance of escape if the security forces became aware of our presence. We also had a small 5lb bomb and two hot-water bottles containing petrol. The shed we were in was so small there wasn't even room to sit down. It was difficult to control McGivern, who was cocky and couldn't appear to see the need to stop talking. Once it was daylight we began to make up the bomb but we didn't yet prime it. As midday approached we kept our eyes on the gate, waiting for the clerk to appear.

Eventually we saw him come through the main gate, locking it behind him. He crossed the yard and opened the door to the sorting office, where we knew the money was held. Before he could close the door I crept across the yard and put the gun to his head. 'Keep very quiet and don't try anything and you won't be hurt.' He never spoke a word as I took the keys from his hand and walked him into the office. The other two were right behind me, McGivern carrying the bomb which he proceeded to prime and plant where the resulting explosion and fire would do most damage. I covered the clerk at gunpoint while the other man stood over him and made him open the safe. He knew exactly where the alarms were and how the system operated and made it clear to the clerk that if he tried any funny business I was under instructions to shoot him. The safe was emptied of its contents and the clerk instructed to remain where he was until the first post office vans arrived. They were due within minutes to collect pension money and mail for distribution to rural post offices in the area.

Then we went back through the gap in the fence and walked the short distance to a house that had been taken over by McGowan earlier that morning. As we turned into the pathway leading to the house McGowan emerged with the keys to the owner's car. We got in and he drove us to the village of Cappagh, a notorious IRA stronghold. Within an hour the firebomb exploded, gutting the sorting office. No one was hurt and we had stolen about ten thousand pounds – a fairly substantial sum in those days.

I remained in East Tyrone for a number of months, based mainly around the village of Carrickmore in the heart of one of the staunchest republican areas in Northern Ireland. This was the area known as the 2nd Battalion of the East Tyrone Brigade, a rather grandiose title bearing little relationship to what is understood as a battalion in a regular army. Stretching from and including the town of Omagh in the south and Cookstown to the north, Pomeroy/Cappagh to the east and running west to Plumbridge, it was then and has consistently remained a centre of high IRA activity. At the time the leadership in the area was composed mostly of traditional types who would have been familiar to me from my background in Kerry. Their method of operation was quite simple and carried little risk. Using a strong network of local sympathizers, they would gather the necessary intelligence and then send a request to Monaghan for an ASU to carry out the operation, if one was not already in the area. They would provide the houses, the transport, the necessary infrastructure, but would play little or no part in the actual operation. There were almost no young activists in the area because the leadership was very cautious, preferring to work only with people they knew and trusted well.

There was little normal policing in Carrickmore and the surrounding countryside. Occasionally a police patrol escorted by a large number of soldiers with helicopter back-up would venture into the area but it was a rare event and we enjoyed a great degree of freedom of movement. I stayed in different houses in the area, mainly farmhouses and the new bungalows that seemed to be sprouting up everywhere. For most of that summer I was the only active service volunteer there, but sometimes I would be joined by McNally or Pierce McAleer. I built up a good relationship with the locals and followed instructions from Corrigan. The old leadership's low-risk policies were considered too cautious and I was quietly putting together a network of young activists who were themselves keen to get involved in operations.

Using my new network we carried out a number of successful operations that summer, bombing attacks in Omagh and Cookstown, mainly aimed at government buildings, police or army barracks and financial institutions. I was anxious that there should be no civilian casualties and put a lot of planning into the detail of them. Thankfully it paid off and no civilians were injured. Out in the countryside around Carrickmore we concentrated on trying to entice the army or police into ambush situations where we could attack them with landmines or by shooting or booby traps. They were understandably cautious, so this was very difficult. If someone reported a burglary, for example, it could take the police several days to turn up and then in a helicopter with the army in attendance. We would sit in houses with a hijacked car near by while locals scouted the area for army or police patrols or checkpoints. If they saw one they would rush back and we would career off in the hijacked car. Encounters were brief. We didn't have the firepower to engage in prolonged gun-battles; we'd loose off a dozen or so shots in the direction of patrol or checkpoint and then abandon the car and make our way on foot across the rough, hilly countryside to one of our safe houses or spend the night lying out in the fields watching the searchlights of the helicopters as they searched for clues to our whereabouts. As far as everybody was concerned a successful operation was one where damage was inflicted and everybody escaped unscathed. It was an exciting time. I was nineteen, sleeping in ditches, outbuildings or safe houses, always with my clothes on, always armed. The older leadership seemed more and more content to allow me to do as I wished and I enjoyed almost complete operational control. For every job that came off many more were aborted, having been thwarted at the discussion stage or simply failing because of faulty equipment. Once, watching a huge landmine which was under a culvert on the main Omagh to Cookstown road near Creggan crossroad, I was amazed to see a joint army/police patrol set up a checkpoint right above it. I waited until there was no civilian car in sight and pressed the switch attached to the firing pack. Nothing happened. I pressed again and again – nothing. Either the detonator was faulty or had got damp, or the firing pack was not of sufficent voltage to detonate the bomb from where I lay about one hundred and fifty yards from the patrol. Had it exploded, there would have been multiple deaths and injuries, for which I would have been responsible.

Although I was frustrated at the time, I was later enormously grateful that the bomb had not gone off.

On 23 August 1974 for the second time I was involved in a murder. RUC Special Branch Detective Inspector Peter Flanagan, stationed in Omagh, was particularly unpopular with republicans. A Catholic, he had been born in the police station at Beragh, not far from Omagh, where his father had been the local sergeant. He followed in his father's footsteps, joining the RUC as soon as he was old enough to do so. For a number of years he had been a member of Special Branch – the section of the RUC responsible for gathering intelligence on republican and loyalist terror groups. He was an outcast among outcasts and had long been of interest to the IRA.

Peter Flanagan had acquired a reputation among republicans for being heavily implicated in the abuse and ill-treatment of prisoners in Castlereagh Palace Barracks and other detention centres. I am completely satisfied now that there was no basis for this belief but then it was widely accepted by republicans and I, of course, needed little convincing. As far as both I and the IRA were concerned, any Special Branch officer was a prime target.

Flanagan's movements had been monitored for some time by a man whom I shall call Scott; by 1974 he had become a key figure in the IRA's intelligence network. Scott informed senior IRA figures in Belfast that it would be relatively easy to kill Flanagan as he appeared to have no awareness that he was a target. Word came from the IRA leadership via Scott: the murder of Peter Flanagan was to be prioritized and the 'hit' to be carried out as quickly as possible. At that time, I was the only full-time active service operator in the area and consequently the job fell to me – it was as coincidental as that.

Scott told me that Flanagan visited Broderick's public house in Omagh almost every weekday lunchtime, usually parking his blue VW Beetle in George Street beside the pub. I went to Omagh and stayed with republican sympathizers in a house not far from Broderick's. For four days I checked out Flanagan's movements. I was happy enough to see his car there but I still had to check that he was in the pub. Omagh was a heavily garrisoned town with a large security presence. I could not afford to rule out the possibility that Flanagan's apparently very relaxed attitude might be a plan to flush out an IRA unit. Equally I couldn't afford to run the risk of alerting Flanagan by staying too long in the bar or by allowing him to pick up on my southern accent. On the day I finally went into Broderick's, he was sitting on a bar stool at the furthest end of the bar from the door, exactly where Scott had told me he would be. I walked to the opposite end of the bar and quietly, in a passable Tyrone accent, ordered a half-pint of Guinness. I drank it fairly quickly and then left. I wanted to make certain that nothing I did or said would arouse the suspicion of a man who was, after all, a trained observer.

I needed an accomplice and Paul Norney – a sixteen- or seventeen-year-old IRA volunteer from Belfast who was on the run having escaped from St Patrick's Institute in Belfast where he was on remand charged with the murder of a soldier – had been assigned to East Tyrone and more specifically to me. He was in the area at the time and was brought into the operation. Acting together we would murder Peter Flanagan. We also needed a driver. Locals could not be used for fear that they might be recognized by someone passing. It was also felt that a woman would arouse less suspicion sitting in a parked car in the commercial centre of a town that had seen many IRA bomb attacks. Scott went to Belfast and the IRA provided him with a young woman who had a reputation as a useful driver. I nicknamed her Lulu; we didn't need to know each other's name anyway, and she bore a passing resemblance to the singer.

The team was assembled. I made Lulu drive the getaway route with me – I had heard of one Belfast 'driver' who couldn't even change gear. In such operations planning was all. Lulu could drive all right, but I had a slight doubt about her ability to remain calm. A safe house also had to be arranged for after the operation. Would we steal or hijack a car? Where would we abandon the car after the murder? Who would collect and bring us to the safe house? All of these questions were thrashed out at a series of meetings in a local house.

The guns arrived a couple of days before the operation was due to take place. The IRA had sent brand-new snub-nose Magnum .357 revolvers. I had specifically asked for revolvers rather than pistols, which often jammed or malfunctioned. Pistols have many more working parts than revolvers, requiring them to be kept in suitable conditions, and often this was not possible. Immediately after the murder the weapons would be transferred out of the area. Eventually they would be recovered by police in London after the capture of the Balcombe Street siege gang.

The night before the operation we stayed in the house in Carrickmore, which had become our base. We didn't go to bed until after 4 a.m. – not unusual in itself as the early hours of the morning were a favourite time for army and police raids. The owner of the house and his sister, herself an IRA volunteer, stayed up quite late with us. They knew what we were about to do as they had been present at some of the meetings during the planning stage. It was a tense night, not made easier by Lulu's persistent teasing of Paul about his youth and inexperience, which he took badly. I knew that nerves were beginning to fray and a few times I had to tell her to be quiet. Eventually I had to speak to her outside the room, telling her rather sharply to drop it. Everybody was nervous; it was a prestige operation and we wanted it to go well.

In the morning the three of us were dropped at a

nearby garage by a local volunteer who then went on to 'scout' the road to Omagh to make sure that no security force roadblocks were in place.

I approached the owner of the garage, identified myself as a volunteer and told him we were 'borrowing' one of his cars. He was too frightened to resist. We filled the car with petrol and warned him that he was not to report this to the police for several hours. We knew that he would do as he was told. It would take an extremely foolhardy person to face down the IRA in such a strong republican community. We set off for Omagh with another volunteer, who drove as far ahead of us as was possible while remaining in our view. He would repeatedly flash his brake lights if a random security patrol had set up a 'spot' checkpoint. On the way into Omagh the scout who had driven ahead to the town came driving back against us, flashing his lights to give us the all-clear. He then drove to a prearranged spot where we would abandon the hijacked car after the murder and where he would pick us up to drive us to the safe house.

Broderick's lay inside the security zone. Large concrete obstacles known as 'dragon's teeth' blocked off the road. Lulu parked the car on double yellow lines around the corner, and Paul and I left the car and walked as casually as possible towards the pub. We checked to see if Flanagan's car was in its usual spot. It was.

There was now nothing to stop us. We walked into the hallway leading to the pub door. I told Paul to check Flanagan was there and in the usual place. He opened the door and looked. 'Yes, he's there.' 'You sure?' I asked. 'Yes.' 'OK, let's go.' I was first through the door; Peter Flanagan was at the bar reading the *Irish Independent*.

He understood what was happening and began to move from his stool: 'No, please no!' I steadied, took aim and fired. He was still moving, trying to escape. He stumbled to the door leading to the toilets and fell through it. I fired eight times in total and knew that most of, if not all, my shots had hit him. I remember looking at him as he lay face down on the floor of the toilet. I have no recollection of blood, or anything else, really, beyond the certain knowledge that he was dead. I knew that I had to keep calm and that the most important thing was to stay in control. I reloaded the gun just in case. This also reinforced control and discipline, allowing me to think ahead. We left the toilet and walked through the pub. The other customers and the barman were stunned, in shock. One woman said something. I told her to be quiet: 'Just sit down, shut up and nothing will happen to you.' Most of the faces were frozen; the murder had taken only seconds and it looked as though no one had moved. The owner was still standing with an empty glass and a towel in his hands.

We walked out of the pub. I was willing myself to be calm, to act as normally as possible. We strolled across the road and passed the security barrier to the car. Paul got there first and as I opened the door the car took off. I was literally pulled along for a second or two: I shouted to Lulu to calm down. I knew that Paul had not reloaded his gun and told him to do so now.

Suddenly I realized that Lulu was driving the wrong way: we were going up a one-way street against the traffic. She was also driving far too fast. We had to go back to where she had been parked to return to the right route. I had suspected that she might not be the calmest person under pressure, but she had to get her act together immediately. I talked to her in a calm voice: 'Slow down. Keep it nice and steady.' 'Is he dead?' she asked. 'Yes, he's dead all right,' I said. 'Dead, course he's fucking dead,' said Paul, giggling like the teenager he was. Lulu was steadying, slowing down and keeping within the speed limit. I began to relax a little. We were clear of the town, no one was following and we were only minutes from abandoning the car. We turned into a narrow country lane hemmed in with high, over-grown hedges. The van was waiting for us. I instructed Lulu to drive the car tight in against the hedge where it would be difficult for the helicopter to see it.

We climbed into the back of the van. More questions. 'Did it go all right?' 'Did you get the right man?' Keeping alert was what interested me – not answering questions. We pulled up in front of a fairly typical country cottage. The only person there, a young woman in her late twenties, was expecting us but had no idea of what we had just done. Paul was in a state of near-euphoric excitement and I had to keep telling him to calm down and wise up.

At 1.30 p.m. the three of us crowded around the radio in the spare bedroom to listen to the RTE news. 'A police inspector has been shot dead in a public house in Omagh, County Tyrone.' The newsreader also disclosed that Peter Flanagan had an elderly widowed mother. 'I feel sorry for his mother,' said Lulu. 'Well, I fucking don't. Couldn't give a shit about any of them,' shot back Paul. It was what I had come to expect of him.

At that moment, one clear thought flashed through my mind, the memory of which has never left me: 'You're going to have to pay for this some day.' Then, the notion seemed ridiculous. As far as I was concerned I had done no wrong. I had not committed a crime, a sin. I had no reason to feel guilty. After all, I was fighting for a righteous cause. So why? I don't know. But there was no mistaking the doubt. I pushed that troublesome thought away. 'Get your act together, you halfwit,' I told myself. I could not comprehend how such a thought could have even entered my head. Perhaps already something about the nature of what I was doing was beginning to get through to me. It was the first and only time that I have killed someone deliberately, in cold blood, and maybe the enormity triggered some religious or moral response from childhood.

After the news broadcast ended I walked into the living room. It was immediately obvious that the woman in the house had also heard the news. Her face portrayed shock, disbelief and fear as the reality of having a murderer and his accomplices in her home became clear. An awkward and uncomfortable silence followed. She clearly didn't want us. I could sense that, but there was nowhere else for us to go. We could hear a helicopter in the distance. It would be searching for an abandoned car. Scott was due to appear any moment. In fact he was already late. Shortly after 3 p.m. his company-owned car pulled up in front of the house. I was incredibly relieved to see him; I had seriously considered having to take the woman hostage since there was no doubt that she was on the edge of going completely to pieces.

I took him aside and explained the situation. He had anticipated in any case that it might be best if we were moved. We piled into his car and set off along back roads, using the route he had just travelled. Along the way a couple of local sympathizers scouted the road ahead. I knew where we were going.

Eventually we pulled into a driveway leading to a house a couple of miles from Carrickmore. We drove round the back. As the car came to a halt the back door opened. A middle-aged priest was standing there. I knew him quite well, as I, along with other people like McNally, had often stayed with him. The IRA had regularly used this house for meetings, for the induction of recruits and as a general safe house and base in the area. The priest was an active IRA sympathizer with influence at the highest levels of the republican movement. He was as good as regarded as a senior IRA activist.

There was another priest in the house. Home on extended leave from a stint in the foreign missions, he was nowhere nearly as shrewd as the first priest and was regarded locally as a friendly, irresponsible simpleton. He was a 'groupie' who liked to spend time in local republican safe houses where he would try to get people like me to talk about operations. 'That was a good job,' he would say with a sly, cunning look on his round, simple face. He would sit for hours by the fire in one house I often stayed in. Once he was there he was happy. I never regarded him as more than an idiot, useful at times but mostly tiresome and irritating.

As the four of us entered the house the senior priest insisted on blessing us with holy water from the little font inside the door. It was something he always did. Neither of the two priests could cook very well: a half-done steak and a burned chop or two was not unusual at breakfast time. Their freezer was packed full and there was a large stock of wine and spirits. After a short period Scott left with Paul. Lulu and I sat down along with the two priests for a meal that had obviously been prepared in advance by the housekeeper. Over dinner and more holy water, having listened to more radio and TV reports of the day's events, the senior priest said to me, 'Flanagan was an abominable man who sold his soul to the devil.'

The whole business left me feeling uneasy. Regarding myself as an atheist and socialist, I had little time for priests. I knew that what was motivating these men had nothing to do with secular republicanism and was simply ethnic Catholic nationalism of the most primitive kind.

But I had known from early on that the Provisional IRA contained sections of the worst elements within Irish nationalism. Hatred of Protestants and unionists was a large part of the motivation.

Later on that evening Scott came back. We got into his car and were blessed again. The two priests along with other sympathizers scouted the road to about fifteen miles away. It was coming on to dusk and I can still remember that there must have been up to fifteen cars involved in a well-organized operation to ensure that we reached Cookstown without a hitch. It was obvious that we had become local heroes. Republicans in that part of the world would always have a soft spot in their hearts for those who murdered Peter Flanagan.

I knew the couple who owned the safe house in Cookstown. By now I was familiar with most of the sympathizers and safe houses in the area; people were beginning to say that I knew Tyrone better than the Tyrone men. The couple in the house were devout Catholics and teetotal, but Lulu had somehow managed to get hold of a small bottle of vodka. We sat in the spare bedroom and had a drink or two. We didn't really talk about what we had done. Lulu just wanted to get back to Belfast as quickly as possible. I slept on the floor in the living room and Lulu used the spare bedroom. Early in the afternoon the following day Scott came and drove her back to Belfast. I never saw her again and never even got to know her first name. Just as well for Lulu, some would say. The murder of Peter Flanagan greatly increased my standing within the organization and while very few people ever mentioned it to me again it was commonly known that I had done it. That didn't stop the odd IRA man from Tyrone later letting on, with a nod and a wink, that they had been involved.

My accomplice Paul Norney was later sent to take

part in the 'war' in England. He was caught after a drunken escapade when he and a group of IRA men fired shots in a restaurant in Manchester because they were unhappy with the service. Their arrest was to lead directly to that of Brendan Dowd, who was then OC of the IRA's England department. I think Paul is out now, but not before he spent twenty-odd years in jail in England.

6

Within a few days I was back in County Tyrone where life continued as what we regarded as normal: occasional bomb and shooting attacks, training and recruiting new volunteers. By this stage I had been put in charge of the area I was operating in. Eddie Collins was gone and the Mid-Ulster Brigade was broken up into smaller, more secure sections.

The East Tyrone area was now described as a 'brigade' with three battalions. The area I was in charge of was the '2nd Battalion'. These were grandiose titles that never meant much in reality. The source of the tension I had noticed between Corrigan and Collins on my first evening in Monaghan was now clear: the East Tyrone IRA wished to be free of control from southern republicans. They resented Collins's position and influence and lobbied to get rid of him. They succeeded. It was one of the first signs that the old southern domination of the Provisionals was giving way to young, harder, pragmatic northerners.

I was now directly in control of eight IRA units, each of which consisted of between four and eight people depending on local circumstances, and had a hard core of four other full-time volunteers in the area. Like me, the four full-timers were all on the run. The old local leadership had been completely pushed out by now and we ran the area. Our lives alternated between periods of utter boredom, perhaps stuck in a safe house for weeks, and frantic bouts of activity. I was much busier than the others because my job also entailed organizational work – building up the republican base in the area, attending brigade meetings and seeing to the daily business of running an organization. Like any organized group there were personality clashes and squabbles but mostly people got on and worked together. They had no choice: very often their lives or freedom depended on it. There was a very good spirit at that time and we were busy preparing plans for a number of major attacks on security-force bases in Pomeroy and Plumbridge.

Then, in December 1974, there were dramatic developments. Contacts between the British government and the IRA resulted in a ceasefire. As part of the agreement, IRA prisoners were freed from internment but the situation was confused. A procedure was devised by the negotiating teams to monitor the ceasefire. The IRA was provided with buildings and facilities for 'incident centres'; British civil servants manned corresponding offices. I can remember driving around County Tyrone with the number of a British civil servant in my pocket. The British Army/RUC were no longer allowed to stop cars, arrest IRA men or raid houses; such incidents were considered breaches of the ceasefire. Instructions were sent by the leadership that sympathizers, owners of safe houses and so on were to be encouraged to join Sinn Fein. Rumours swept the organization, one of which concerned a declaration of intent by the British government to withdraw from Northern Ireland which, it was said, was to be signed any day. Yet it was obvious to anybody on the ground that surveillance had increased, army and police bases were being fortified and new ones built.

By Easter 1975, the ceasefire was still nominally in place but in Belfast in particular the IRA and loyalists were waging an intermittent but brutal war between themselves. There was considerable confusion about what exactly the ceasefire was intended to achieve. Daithi O'Connaill, the IRA's leading political strategist, came to Tyrone to address the annual Easter Sunday Commemoration at Carrickmore, having been guaranteed immunity from arrest by the British authorities. The IRA was out in force that Easter in Carrickmore. Kevin McKenna, recently released from jail in the Irish Republic, was in the area recuperating after a long hunger strike.

McKenna and I went on a tour of the pubs in the town to check that they had followed IRA instructions and closed for the day. Only one was open. It was a pub often frequented by members of the Official IRA. They were told in no uncertain terms to close immediately and did so. Armed IRA men were on the streets; others were based in houses ready to move if the RUC or army even attempted to enter the area. In the event it all passed off peacefully except for one very ugly incident. As the republican ceremony was taking place an IRA man approached me, and, pointing to a person in the crowd, said: 'He's a Prod from the Bush,' a small Protestant enclave a couple of miles from Carrickmore. I approached the man but it quickly became clear that he was harmless, with the mentality of a child. I told the local IRA man to let him be. Later that evening it was reported to me that Brendan Hughes – the same man who had been sent to rob the post office mail-van in Kerry two years earlier – had taken the man into a field and was beating him.

Armed with a Browning I went in search of Hughes. As I walked into the field I could see that he and another well-known IRA figure were standing over a man kneeling on the ground. I told them to leave him alone. 'Fuck off,' said Hughes's friend. I fired one shot over their heads and they stepped back, shocked. I walked nearer and fired again. They began to back off quickly, making for the gate. A couple of young volunteers from the area looked after the Protestant man, who fortunately wasn't badly hurt. The entire incident left a sour taste in my mouth. It was obvious to anyone that the man was incapable of being a threat and it was one of several incidents that led me to have serious doubts on a number of levels about what I was involved with.

Nor was I impressed with Daithi O'Connaill, who for me had been a living legend but who turned out to be an ego-driven man whose intellect did not live up to its reputation. While he was in the area he said he wished to speak to local volunteers. The meeting was arranged. Everybody was gathered at the meeting place when O'Connaill appeared. Most of the people in the room were fairly experienced IRA operators. The meeting had not begun when O'Connaill said to me, 'Sean, people normally stand up when I enter a room.' Clearly he had begun to believe his own propaganda. Though this seems a small point, it struck home that it was on the instructions of such people that men and women should murder, die or go to prison. These, and other events, caused me to think about the murders of Peter Flanagan and Eva Martin and to wonder whether their deaths had achieved anything – and whether our actions were doing anything to further the cause.

Inevitably the conversations I had with local IRA men and sympathizers centred around 'the Prods' or 'the Orangies' and it was becoming clear to me that the

Provisional IRA were in reality representative of the Catholic 'defender' tradition. In rural areas of Tyrone, Fermanagh and Armagh the relationship between militant Irish nationalism and Irish Catholicism was deep and complex. There was a deep and ugly hatred, centuries old, behind it all.

To stand with an old farmer on a hillside in Pomeroy in County Tyrone while he pointed out Protestant farms, 'stolen from us by them black bastards', is to understand the emotive power of blood and earth. No matter how I looked at it the reality stared me full in the face: this was a war between Catholics and Protestants, not against the British. I might want to attack a British Army patrol or barracks, but the local IRA men would rather shoot a Protestant neighbour who was in the UDR or police reserve.

Republicanism traditionally spoke of uniting Catholic, Protestant and dissenter under the common name of Irishmen, yet the Provisional IRA used a parochial house to induct local men into the IRA. Young, largely un-educated country lads were brought to their priest's house at night to be sworn in (even though there was no oath the term 'sworn in' was always used). The local priest was more than likely the same priest who heard their confession, whose Mass they attended, and all the while they knew that their priest actively supported the IRA. What kind of effect did this have on them? Could they really be expected to believe their Church's de-nunciation of the IRA was without ambiguity?

I wasn't from Northern Ireland and wasn't soaked in the pathological hatreds and half-truths about the 'other side'. I believed that I had joined the IRA – with some misgivings about its ugly, ethnic nationalism – to fight a war against British imperialism. But it was hard to main-tain the illusion that Northern Ireland was in a colonial situation. The truth is that I had come to Northern Ireland abysmally ignorant of the realities and yet prepared to kill and bomb.

The Provisional IRA was a Catholic defence organization and I wasn't even a practising Catholic! I remember reading an anti-nationalist analysis by Conor Cruise O'Brien and flinging it away in disgust – but always coming back to it. I can and always will understand why young men and women in Northern Ireland join the IRA, the UVF, or whatever: sectarian hatreds, peer and community pressure, a belief that you must fight to defend your people. But at its heart's core it remains a bitter form of tribalism and no amount of fancy words or window-dressing will make it something noble or decent.

While all of this was going round in my mind these weren't necessarily the dominant thoughts. I was worried, yes, but all of my friends and comrades were in the Provisional IRA. I knew no other life. Throughout the early summer of 1975 the ceasefire remained to some degree intact, if shaky. By now serious opposition to it and to the leadership of O'Bradaigh and O'Connaill had emerged. Brian Keenan in particular led a campaign against them, undermining their leadership at every opportunity. Kevin McKenna was opposed to the leadership too, albeit more cautiously than Keenan. I was not senior enough to understand the details or the background to the power struggle now taking place, but I could see what was developing. Gerry Adams and Martin McGuinness were also opposed to the cease-fire, but they were in prison during some of this period, as was Keenan. Certainly by the end of the summer the ceasefire had all but collapsed. For me, though, the tide had already been turned by an earlier exchange that dramatically crystallized my fears and doubts about my role in the struggle.

It had been in the middle of April 1975 and I was in the Monaghan Town flat, a bolt-hole for active East Tyrone operatives on the run from Northern Ireland. Present were Kevin McKenna, by then adjutant-general of the IRA, Henry Louis McNally, Pierce McAleer, Barry McHugh and James Fox. I was making tea when a television news report announced that a policewoman had been killed in a bomb explosion in Bangor. McKenna turned his head slightly in my direction and said, 'Maybe she was pregnant and we got two for the price of one.' It was an off-the-cuff remark which said it all. McKenna wouldn't have known who had killed the policewoman, even though he was adjutant-general. He simply didn't care. Some of the others laughed or grinned. McHugh, who was out of McKenna's line of vision, grimaced, looked at me and mouthed, 'Fuck'.

I walked from the room towards the bedrooms. I just wanted to get away from McKenna. This was the man I respected so much, the man who was to become my boss. To whom I was going to bring my worries and doubts. How the fuck could anyone hate so blindly? And this man was second in command of the Provisional IRA. I burst into tears and lay down on one of the mattresses on the bedroom floor. I don't know what went through my mind – remarks like that were not altogether uncommon among the footsoldiers, but you could take most of it as black humour or empty macho rhetoric. The shock of its coming from McKenna – a disciplined man of few words who carried a great deal of authority – is difficult to explain. I know I didn't want anyone to see me crying. Maybe I thought it was weak. Maybe I was too afraid to answer questions – I don't know. I did know that there was nowhere to go now. McKenna had answered all my questions. I remember getting up and washing my face and going out later for a drink with

James Fox. McKenna called out to me as I left: 'Be careful of where you're going. The Branch are busy out there tonight.'

Shortly after that McKenna called me to one side. He was sending me to take charge of West Fermanagh. My job would consist of reorganizing the area and sidelining the old leadership, who were regarded both as ineffectual and loyal to O'Bradaigh and O'Connaill. During this period I met Brian Keenan on a couple of occasions, usually in McKenna's company. It was obvious that he had enormous ability and charisma, energy and absolute ruthlessness. He and McKenna made an unlikely team but they were in some respects a microcosm of militant republicanism: the dour Catholic nationalist McKenna and the charismatic quasi-nationalist, Marxist, militarist Keenan. A belief in physical force, gut nationalism and a hatred of Brits and unionists gave them plenty of common ground.

In August 1975 James Fox drove me to Bundoran in County Donegal. I was now working directly for McKenna but in reality I would see much less of him than I had in Monaghan. I was glad to be out of East Tyrone. I knew that there would be much less pressure in West Fermanagh and fewer men on the run. The area was less central to the IRA in real terms than Monaghan. I was the only full-time operator in the area, though there was supposed to be a nucleus of solid young volunteers available. I still had to be very careful, as the Irish police were constantly questioning volunteers and sympathizers about me and were very keen to put me in jail.

We went first to Joe O'Neill's pub in Bundoran. I knew O'Neill slightly. His pub was a mecca for northern republicans, particularly from Derry and Tyrone but also from Belfast. He was firmly identified with O'Bradaigh and O'Connaill. There was also a deep suspicion that O'Neill did not want much IRA activity in his area. He was doing very well out of the troubles, thank you very much, and too much IRA activity meant the likelihood of a Garda crackdown and falling takings.

I had been told to expect that O'Neill would be far from helpful, if not indeed downright hostile. I wasn't disappointed. I stayed upstairs in his pub for a couple of days, during which time he made little or no attempt to communicate. After a couple of days he reluctantly introduced me to some local volunteers. I made arrangements to move to a farmhouse close to the border, where I stayed for a few weeks, meeting with IRA men and sympathizers from across the border in Fermanagh. To be honest, I couldn't have cared less whether I met them or not. I knew now that I was getting out. I was twenty years old and sick to the back teeth with the whole squalid murderous nonsense.

At the beginning of October I went back to O'Neill's pub and told him I was heading home for a couple of days. I didn't have much money – just a few pounds. Full-time IRA volunteers were given an allowance of £7 a week in those days. Many weeks it never arrived. I hitchhiked home to Kerry. Once there I stayed in a friend's house near my parents. After a week or so I handed a letter of resignation from the IRA to a local volunteer. The note simply said that I was leaving for 'personal reasons'. A few weeks later it was apparent that the police had lost interest in me because surveillance around my parents' home slackened noticeably. I ventured out socially a couple of times, knowing that local police would get to hear of it. They displayed no interest whatsoever. I was later to discover that my resignation was known to the police within days. It may seem strange, but little attention was paid to my departure from within the IRA itself. There is a fundamental misapprehension that membership of the IRA is for life. In fact, people came and went all the time, and sometimes their absence was not even noticed, such was the level of internal chaos.

I moved into my parents' home. There were no questions asked and I don't think that my father knew anything about my resignation, even though he was still involved locally, at least in Sinn Fein. It was a pretty dark time for me. For the first time I knew that I had devoted five years of my life to something that was evil. My twenty-first birthday was coming up and that gave me pause for thought. I had no idea what I wanted to do with my life. I had always wanted to write – poetry in particular – but just couldn't summon up the motivation. I had been writing and reading poetry from a very young age. The poets I read in those days were almost invariably Irish, along with some Shakespeare, Wordsworth, Keats and Shelley. Anything I wrote then was worthless, little more than doggerel. Patrick Kavanagh, the Irish peasant poet from County Monaghan, fascinated me and he still does today. I was dislocated, rudderless – simply passing the time. I knew I had to leave Ireland, at least for a while. I was too old to be hanging about home without regular work. I worked a couple of days a week with my father, went fishing often and read a lot. I lived a very quiet existence, spending most of my time on my own.

I realized that joining the Provisional IRA had been the biggest mistake of my life. One way or another the disgustingly stupid things I had been involved in would haunt me for years to come. It was the end of a very important part of my life and I felt sad about the mistakes of the past and worried for the first time about the future.

In May 1976 my mother's young sister Emily came home on holiday from England. I hadn't seen her for years but we got on very well. She suggested that I come to England, and offered to let me stay at her home until I sorted things out. I went back with her when her holiday was over. I knew that I probably featured on some security file in England and couldn't rule out the possibility of arrest, but I gave it little consideration. I had to get out of Ireland. So far as I was concerned, Emily's offer was a godsend and I had no intention of turning it down. I had never been out of Ireland before, so it was like an adventure. We travelled by train to Dun Laoghaire, by boat to Holyhead and afterwards by train to Milton Keynes, where she lived. Her husband, Dublin-born Billy Costello, who worked for British Rail, met us at the station. They had three children, two sons, Billy and Joe, and a daughter also called Emily, and they lived in a nice suburban semi-detached house almost in the countryside.

Billy Costello was a warm, gentle man who was easy to get along with. Sometimes I used to go to the local British Legion club with him, though I hardly drank at all in those days. He was being sociable and I didn't like to refuse. He was also good company, full of jokes and mischief. I didn't get on too well with his eldest son, Billy, who was just a year or so younger than me. But his younger son, Joe, with whom I shared a bedroom, was a much easier proposition.

A couple of days after arriving I found work as an apprentice cabinet-maker in a local factory. The work was uninteresting and repetitive, but it was a job. I trained quite a bit, running at least once a day and going to the gym at the local sports centre in the evening.

I worked overtime on most Saturday mornings. One Saturday, when I arrived back from work, I noticed that

Emily was very quiet. After a while she showed me a copy of the *Daily Mail*. There was a story in it about an IRA man named Sean O'Callaghan. It said that British police were looking for him in connection with bomb attacks in Britain. Obviously Emily knew about my IRA background, almost certainly from my mother or relatives in Tralee. But this story had nothing to do with me. It referred to another man, from Ardoyne in North Belfast. The problem was that Billy, Emily's son, had read it and was convinced that it was about me. She said that if neighbours ever found out about my IRA involvement the family would be burned out. Such was the fear in sections of the Irish community at that time.

Although I didn't have enough money to rent a flat of my own I had been considering moving to London for some time anyway. Emily's husband suggested I look for a job with accommodation, in a pub, perhaps. I looked up the London *Evening Standard* and discovered that there were plenty of such vacancies. I phoned one and a man with an Irish accent answered.

The man's name was Pat Quinn. I made an appointment to see him a couple of days later in the pub he managed, the Wellington, at the corner of Turnpike Lane and Wood Green High Road. I walked in on the agreed evening and asked to see Mr Quinn. A large, balding man behind the bar said, 'That's me.' I explained who I was. He took one look at me. 'When can you start?' 'Saturday.' '£25 a week plus food and accommodation.' 'OK,' I said. 'Be here Saturday at five,' he grunted. I gathered Pat Quinn was not a man who indulged his employees too much.

I enjoyed working at the Wellington. It was a big pub with a mixed clientele. Youngsters mainly sat in the large lounge, with a corner reserved for Pat Quinn's small favoured group of Irish drinking companions, but the public bar was almost exclusively Irish, mainly middle-aged, heavy-drinking men from the West of Ireland. There was a restaurant and bar plus a little annex where snacks were served. I kept much to myself and was far too busy exploring London to get caught up in the trivia around the bar.

Around this time I met my future wife. I had got to know her father who managed a snooker club next door to the Wellington, and occasionally Liz would come into the bar, usually with her father. Originally from Glasgow, she had lived in Hertfordshire since she was thirteen and had recently moved to London, where she rented a flat and worked at the Victoria Coach Company. At this stage we had no relationship beyond the odd joke and bit of flirting.

Shortly after Christmas 1976 I went to Dublin to get a passport, as I hadn't needed one to travel to Great Britain and I had made up my mind to go to Australia. I stayed with my brother and his wife for a few days while waiting to collect it. When I came back to London I met Liz again and put all ideas of Australia out of my mind. Before very long I had moved into her flat.

She had blond hair, blue eyes and a large, dramatic personality. Her great sense of humour made life with her seem to be one mad escapade after another. From a rough, working-class area of Glasgow, she was blunt, and quick to give her viewpoint and to argue it vehemently. She was from a Scottish Protestant back-ground, with a brother who was a member of the Orange Order. Neither of us, though, had any interest in religion. I liked her father, who was a big jovial character, but I couldn't stand her mother, a brisk woman who thought of her daughter being involved with an Irish Catholic as a calamity for the family.

I started work at a Rowntree Mackintosh warehouse

in Wood Green. The work involved going round the warehouse with an order sheet and a trolley, loading up the different items and bringing them to the loading bay where they were packed on to lorries for distribution to shops. I didn't last long: the words 'boring' and 'repetitive' are an adequate description but don't convey the full tedium of the experience. Liz and I decided to go to France, and we hitchhiked down to the south from Paris and generally enjoyed ourselves. It was a real contrast for me from life in the IRA which for a while seemed far away. I was in love and we had a lot of fun together. Some time around this period I told Liz about my past involvement in the IRA. Because of her background in Scotland this was not as strange to her as it might have been to most British people. I didn't go into much detail, for obvious reasons, and she assumed that it was something distant that I had been involved in before meeting her. We spoke about it once or twice and then it was more or less forgotten about. On a couple of occasions after a few drinks Liz sang the odd 'Orange' song that she had learned in Glasgow, but it was just a bit of a laugh.

On our return I was keen to start up a business. I decided to go into contract cleaning for the simple reason that it took little start-up money. If I was to have any chance of borrowing what I needed to start the business, I had at least to open a bank account and save some money, so I got a job in a plant hire company in Southgate in North London. After a while I went to see my bank manager to tell him what I intended to do and ask if I could borrow money to buy a van. He was extremely reluctant to entertain the idea, but with the arrogance of youth I insisted and eventually he lent me the money.

After a few months and a lot of hard work and some good luck the business began to take off and over the next couple of years it became quite successful. It often meant working round the clock, getting up at two in the morning and sometimes working nonstop for thirty-six hours. Eventually there were twenty people working part-time for me and a couple full-time. Elizabeth joined me in the business and proved exceptionally good at getting new contracts at top prices. Throughout this time I kept in touch with events in Ireland, even though I hardly knew a single Irish person well in London. I read the Irish papers regularly and phoned my family and friends. In truth there seemed to be no escape from Ireland. At the strangest of times I would find myself reliving the events of my years in the IRA. As time went on it became more clear to me that the Provisional IRA was the greatest enemy of democracy and decency in Ireland.

My mother had always been opposed to violence, although she rarely said much unless provoked by some particularly savage world event. She had little interest in politics beyond the rather common simple belief, prevalent in those days, of the innate goodness of a united Ireland. I remember once in 1972 I was sitting at home with her when a report of a horrific IRA bombing came on the television. She just looked at me and said, 'No good will come from killing and bombing.' Other times she would say quietly, 'Before this is all over no one will know or care who started it.' Needless to say, I hadn't taken much notice of her at the time. Now it was her words, along with those of writers and columnists like Con Houlihan and Conor Cruise O'Brien, that were pushing me towards doing something about it. I had been brought up to believe that you had to take responsibility for your own actions. If you did something wrong then you made amends. I came to believe that individuals taking responsibility for their own actions is the basis of civilization. Without that safety net we have nothing.

Liz and I were married in May 1978 in Wood Green Register Office. My mother came over for the wedding but none of the rest of the family could make it. Liz's mother refused to attend because her daughter was marrying a Catholic. Her father didn't come either, though I suspect he would have liked to. I had no strong feelings about marriage. I would have been quite happy for us to go on living together, but Liz wanted us to marry. I explained that I didn't regard marriage as some kind of contract binding me for life. If I felt it was right to go I would go, marriage or not.

I was becoming keen on the idea that I should somehow play a part in fighting the IRA. But how? I could write or speak out against the IRA, but that had all been done before to little or no effect. I could go to MI5 or Scotland Yard and offer help, but I didn't particularly want to line up on the British side. I wanted to be on the side of Irish democracy. For me that meant working with the government of the Irish Republic. It also meant going back to Ireland. I couldn't tell Liz what I intended to do, even though I might be endangering her life as well as my own. I was in love with her and selfishly didn't want to give her up, despite the fact that we were arguing much of the time. The business had expanded to the point where decisions had to be taken that would tie me up financially for years to come, but I didn't want to run a cleaning company in London for the rest of my life. Eventually I decided to sell the business. Liz was keen to go to Ireland but I told her nothing of my real plans.

In early 1979 my sister and her husband came to visit us. They had been going out together since they were sixteen and had married in Southampton in 1975 while I was still in the IRA and on the run. There was no way I could have gone to the wedding. My brother-in-law told me that he had been approached by a local IRA man in Tralee on a number of occasions. The IRA were trying to contact me; Daithi O'Connaill's name was mentioned. I knew now for sure that I would have no difficulty rejoining. We sold the business after Easter 1979 and set off for Kerry.

7

Liz was excited about Ireland and immediately entranced by its landscape and colour. We stopped first at my parents' home. My mother already knew Liz, having been at our wedding. My father, I could tell, disliked her on sight, but he made an effort to conceal this and be friendly. For her part she seemed unaware of his feelings. We stayed with my sister and her husband and two small children, and while Liz got to know my friends and relatives I took stock. Dotted around the roadsides of Kerry are monuments, large and small, in memory of Irish republicans killed or executed by the British or Free State government. I realized now, for the first time, that there was nothing to commemorate all those Kerrymen who had died in the First and Second World Wars. Glancing through copies of old newspapers in the local library it was obvious that infinitely more Kerrymen had died in the uniform of the British Army than had ever died for an Irish republic. They had been written out of history, as if they had never existed. Irish nationalists had recreated history to suit their own ends and were determined that nothing would upset their smug myths.

I started work in a fruit and vegetable wholesaler's, with the intention of quickly starting my own business; I've never had much interest in working for someone else. I chatted occasionally with local republicans but made no effort to make serious contact. Surprisingly, the local police displayed intense interest in me. I discovered from talking to one or two republican sympathizers that this was because of rumours that had circulated saying that I was still active in the IRA and that my resignation had been a ploy. One rumour placed me in Libya. There was no truth whatsoever in any of this but the republican movement is inevitably, because of its conspiratorial nature, a large, industrious and bungling rumour-factory.

In August that year, 1979, Lord Mountbatten was murdered on his yacht by the IRA, along with a number of others including the boatman and his son. These murders had a profound impact on me. Not only had the IRA cynically targeted a man who had been visiting that area for many years and was the softest of soft targets, they had exploded the bomb knowing that other people who were not remotely associated with the royal family would also be killed. They had also carried out the operation in the Irish Republic in direct contravention of their own orders. This had to be a decision taken at Army Council level. It was to be several years before I learned what lay behind it. For me, though, it was the final straw.

In the aftermath of the bombing I contacted a Special Branch officer whom I had known for a long time. He had been active against the IRA for many years and had questioned me several times during my early involvement. Though he came from a republican background, he was implacably opposed to the Provisional IRA and to the whole notion of the romantic revolutionary. He had passionately tried to persuade me that my decision to become involved was morally wrong and that I would come to regret it. I knew that he was sharp and efficient and I believed now that I could trust him to keep his mouth shut.

Talking to him was a frightening decision for me to make; the implications were enormous. My decision had been coming for a long time and for more than two years now I had known that it was inevitable. There was simply no more effective way for me to damage the IRA than by informing from the inside, and that is what I wanted to do. I knew what I was getting into and I did it voluntarily, with the full knowledge of what would happen if I was caught: interrogation and torture, followed by a bullet in the back of the head in a ditch on some quiet road.

I phoned the officer at the local police station and said that I wanted to meet him. I could tell that he was very intrigued – but suspicious. We arranged to meet in the graveyard near my mother's home where I had played as a child. There was always an excuse for my being in that area and there were two separate entrances from two roads divided by the width of the graveyard, about two hundred and fifty yards. I would approach by crossing the road in front of my parents' house. Opposite the ruined abbey in a dark area a set of steps led down to a tomb; we would meet there. I arrived early and stood close to the abbey, where I was completely invisible. I watched him walk in the far entrance and make his way along the central pathway to the tomb. He was wearing an anorak with the hood pulled tight over his face.

I waited until he descended the steps before walking over to meet him. I had no doubts about what I was doing but I was as tense as I have ever been in my life. I had been brought up to believe that the worst thing anybody could do was to become a police informer. Better by far to be a rapist, a murderer, anything but an informer – the decision was mine and mine alone.

'What do you want to see me for?' he asked. I explained. We talked for several hours. I believe that he quickly realized that I was serious. I laid down a number of ground rules. I would talk to him and no one else. Only the most limited number of people at Garda headquarters must know my identity. I would take no money and if anyone attempted dirty tricks, blackmail or tried to force me to do something I considered to be wrong, I would walk. I would give voluntarily but no one would take from me. I hoped that he was listening because I meant what I said and felt under no obligation to reinforce it.

We parted, agreeing that I would make contact again after I had rejoined the IRA. He gave me his home number. I knew I had taken a major and probably irreversible step in my life. If one word of this got out I would have little chance of surviving. I let him leave first and watched him walk away with a mixture of satisfaction and apprehension. I had turned against everything I had once believed in. Against friends, relatives, community: all of the things that meant so much to me.

A day or two later I bumped into Martin Ferris on the street in Tralee. He seemed surprised to see me, although I am sure he had heard that I was back. We spoke for a few minutes. We hadn't met since 1973, and in the intervening six years Ferris had built himself a reputation locally and within the IRA at the highest level. He had already been jailed twice in the Republic for IRA membership, had been acquitted of armed robbery and had taken part in numerous IRA operations, including some in England. He and several others had also undertaken a long prison hunger strike in Portlaoise in the late seventies, which had damaged his health. He was now married and was living with his wife and children in a mobile home near the village of Ardfert, about five miles from Tralee.

Neither of us had the time to talk so we agreed to meet a few evenings later at his home. I knew that Ferris could be by turns extraordinarily erratic, suspicious and yet trusting of people he hardly knew. He could be hugely impressed by people on first meeting them; often, interestingly, not by what they did but by what they said.

On the appointed evening I drove to Ardfert. As I approached the mobile home I could see Ferris kicking a football about with a young lad. The boy turned out to be Ferris's wife's son by her first husband, an Australian. Marie, Ferris's wife, had been born in Australia but had Irish parents. After her separation she had come to Ireland with her young son. Her family were republican and as soon as she arrived in Ireland Marie joined Sinn Fein. She came to know Ferris through writing and visiting him when he was in jail. Once Ferris was released they moved in together and married shortly afterwards.

Ferris introduced me to Marie and he and I left to go to one of the local pubs. I quickly made it clear to him that I wanted to rejoin the IRA. He told me that at that time he was involved only locally. He had only recently married, had taken on a large debt with a new fishing boat and worked on an off-shore oilrig for six months of the year. He was also on bail facing conspiracy-to-murder charges arising from the sinking of a fishing trawler after a dispute over fishing rights on a local oyster bed.

We had a very friendly conversation, catching up on old times. During the conversation I asked Ferris about the reaction to 'bad' IRA operations, citing the La Mon restaurant atrocity in particular. The La Mon restaurant in County Down had been the target of an IRA firebomb attack in 1978, on the occasion of a dinner for dog breeders and owners. No warning was given, because, I think, of bad planning on the part of the bombers rather than deliberate design. Twelve people were burned to death in the resulting inferno. Ferris said to me, 'I don't know what all the squealing was about. They were only Orangies anyway.'

How could a man from Kerry with no experience of Northern Ireland's Protestants have such a deep hatred? The answer lay somewhere in folk memory, a bastardized and hate-filled version of Irish history imbibed at home and school, and the psyche of a man who needed to dedicate himself absolutely, unquestioningly, to a 'cause'. I knew that I had never hated like that, yet we came from similar republican families and we had both murdered for the cause. I left Ferris that evening knowing that the only place such evil belonged was in jail for a long, long time. Such a man would never change.

A couple of weeks later I attended my first IRA meeting since October 1975. Where else could the meeting take place but at Tom McCarthy's farm, where I had played as a boy and where I had first hidden IRA guns? Present at the meeting were Martin Ferris, Maurice Pendergast – the one-time IRA director of finance, now confined to local activity because of a heart condition. Pendergast none the less remained in contact with the leadership of the IRA and was still close to people like Martin McGuinness.

I had heard of but had never met the fourth man present at the meeting. He was from a remote part of

South Kerry and was the OC of the Kerry IRA. He possessed nothing like the track record or experience of the others present, but with people like Pendergast, Ferris and me either in jail or away, he had been the only choice to take control of a much-weakened organization.

Kerry was the strongest republican area outside Northern Ireland and the border counties, and men like Pendergast and Ferris were influential in the highest councils of the IRA. But the organization in the county was in a poor state. This meeting had been called to begin the business of reconstruction. We discussed things in general and agreed to meet again on a regular basis.

I was immediately in touch with my Garda contact by phone. 'We're in,' I said and told him about the meeting. He was clearly surprised, but delighted that events had moved so quickly. The IRA in Kerry was part of the Munster Command of the IRA, which in turn was linked to Southern Command, the IRA structure responsible for the organization of the IRA south of Drogheda.

Southern Command's brief from the Army Council of the IRA was twofold: to act as a back-up to the 'war effort', by supplying money – usually from armed robberies – and also training sites, bomb factories, safe houses and so on, and to consolidate and expand the republican base.

Over the next few months plans to carry out various armed robberies were put together by the local IRA. It was relatively easy for me to foil those attempts; an occasional Garda car or roadblock at the 'wrong time'; the routine arrest of Ferris or myself; or simple 'bad planning', such as a car arriving late – a whole series of random stratagems. Being arrested myself was no big deal. The Garda would 'notice' a little flurry of activity and would decide to bring me and perhaps some others in for routine questioning. This was done by means of section 30 of the Offences against the State Act, which allowed the police to detain a person for twenty-four hours with an option of an extension for a similar period if it was felt there was justifiable reason. The local police did not believe for one minute that they were going to get any admission from people like Ferris and me: it was simply a disruption tactic and was treated almost as a joke. Occasionally a young enthusiastic detective would get a bit carried away and try to force a confession from one of us. Older and more senior detectives present would enjoy this hugely. I remember once a senior detective bringing two young colleagues into the room where I was being questioned and saying to them, 'Now sit down here, ask him some questions and you'll learn more in a couple of hours than we could teach you in years.' As he was leaving he said to me, 'Go easy on them, Sean,' with a big smile on his face. The IRA was well used to the fact that most of its operations never came to anything anyway. Everybody knew that for one operation that came to fruition many others were aborted. It was also fairly easy for me to divert people from armed robberies that might have been successful to plans that looked more lucrative but were guaranteed to come to nothing.

In the summer of 1980 I was sent word to meet the Kerry OC at a farmhouse near Milltown in Kerry. I was also asked to collect Pat Doherty, the man from Donegal, at the train station and bring him to the meeting. Present at the farmhouse when we got there was Seamus Hogan, from Tipperary, the adjutant of Munster Command, and the Kerry OC.

The purpose of the gathering was soon made clear. Pat Doherty was the OC of the IRA's Southern Command, replacing Daithi O'Connaill, who was increasingly out of favour as men like Adams, McGuinness and Doherty himself consolidated their control over the organization. The Munster Command was viewed by the leadership as sympathetic to O'Connaill and O'Bradaigh and was keen to import northerners loyal to the new leadership to oversee each section. There would be a new OC in charge in Munster – Robert McNamara, recently released from Portlaoise prison after serving a term for armed robbery. Gerry Fitzgerald, an experienced IRA operator from Ballymurphy, was made adjutant of Southern Command; from the same Belfast housing estate as Adams, Fitzgerald had worked for Pat Doherty for the past couple of years and there was no doubt as to where his loyalties lay. Kerry and Cork were to be combined into one area. Phil O'Donnell, a former British soldier, would nominally oversee developments there. The Kerry OC's responsibility was limited to South Kerry.

Before any of this could take effect I received a visit from John Joe Donnelly. Donnelly, from Ardloe in County Tyrone, was now the IRA's director of training. He had been promoted to his job when Pat Doherty, his former boss there, had been made OC of Southern Command.

Donnelly didn't know of me personally but had heard of my activities in County Tyrone. He had a big problem on his hands. The IRA training department had for a number of years based itself in Counties Mayo and Galway and had been organized locally by a man whom I shall call 'Jimmy Jones', who was very well connected. Local farmers, hotel owners and businessmen across a wide spectrum – though usually Fianna Fail supporters or members – helped discreetly with training camps and meetings and by putting up IRA men on the run from Northern Ireland.

Donnelly explained to me that a couple of weeks previously a car containing members of the IRA's training department had been stopped by a Garda roadblock at Maam Cross in County Galway. The men in the car had escaped but had left documents behind that showed clearly that the area was a major IRA training base. As a result it had been decided to move the training department out of Galway and Mayo, to Kerry, which from now would be the central area of IRA training. I would work as Donnelly's assistant. No other IRA activity would be permitted to take place in the vicinity.

I had a long conversation with Donnelly in which he outlined his requirements. Eventually he said he wanted at least six different training sites for both weapons and explosives training. The weapons-training sites would need facilities for firing practice, which had always in the past proved difficult to find.

There was also the little matter of finding billets or safe houses for his complement of up to eight full-time training officers, who would now be based in the area. From a standing start, I suddenly had my hands full with IRA business.

8

Over the next couple of weeks Donnelly dispatched his training officers to Kerry. All non-locals, they were sent to stay with sympathizers in areas where there were likely to be suitable sites. There the officers would work with local members, most of whom were experienced in this type of work. Once they had found a suitable site they would prepare 'dumps' for the weapons. The training officers knew what was required and it was up to the locals to co-operate with them. Donnelly and I would keep a constant check on developments but most of it was down to them. The biggest part of our job was transporting the volunteers who came for training to and from the camps without compromising the location.

Donnelly always dressed well in a suit and tie and drove a nice car. He had taken on the identity of a commercial traveller and I arranged a place for him to stay with a sympathetic hotelier. With such a cover, it was very unlikely that he would come to the attention of the police.

Once the training camps and personnel were in place, Donnelly and I travelled to Castlebar in County Mayo to collect the equipment – a large variety of guns, training manuals, cooking utensils, sleeping bags, and so on. We drove a van borrowed from a new recruit called Mick Brassil, who, together with two other men, had joined the Kerry IRA a month previously. He was a local businessman, if one of rather dubious background. Brassil and his two friends would all go on to play key roles in the IRA. At this stage, however, they were new and while they undoubtedly had potential they were being handled very carefully.

The van we borrowed from Brassil belonged to a company he owned, the name of which was printed on its side. Work vans like this were always less likely to be stopped randomly by the police. We drove to Jimmy Jones's home, where we stopped for something to eat and a chat with Jones and his wife.

From there we drove out into remote countryside, eventually arriving at a semi-derelict cottage in the mountains. The last remaining member of Donnelly's Mayo team was there to meet us. The equipment was already packed into boxes and plastic bags ready to be moved. We loaded the equipment into the van and then waited for daylight before setting off back to Kerry – a drive of about two hundred miles. It was uneventful, though we both sat in the front armed with pistols in case we ran into a police patrol or checkpoint. It was always risky moving equipment long distance without scout cars, but in this case we had no alternative. It was vital that as few people as possible had an inkling of what was happening. We had to remain alert all the time because we knew that we would have only seconds to react if anything went wrong. We passed the odd police car and there were always a few moments of tension until they were out of sight.

It was early evening when we reached Hogan's farmhouse near Milltown. We dumped the equipment there and I returned the van to Brassil while Donnelly drove back to the hotel, to resume his cover as a commercial traveller.

Towards the end of September 1980 the first training camp took place at a derelict house in North Kerry, owned by a republican sympathizer who used it for storing potatoes and grain. He was a keen clay-pigeon shooter and we often used his land for practising. So long as he himself was shooting, and we used only low-velocity weapons, we would be unlikely to attract attention from outside.

I had kept my Garda contact fully aware of what was happening. We decided at an early stage to let the training relocation go ahead, as it provided the Garda, through me, with a comprehensive picture of the IRA's training department – its structure, personnel and method of operation. It also left the gardai free to strike when they chose.

The first camp was to last for a weekend. Three of Donnelly's full-time training officers were present, and five volunteers who were part of a Southern Command team under the control of a very senior Belfast IRA man. They were to be the core of an active service unit that was to carry out large-scale armed robberies in the Irish Republic.

The camp was to finish late on Sunday evening, after firing practice. The gardai decided to raid it. I advised that the right time to do so would be after the shooting, so that the raid could be put down to the shooting having been heard in the locality and reported.

The raid began at 5 p.m. that Sunday. The man in charge was my Garda contact. Also in the party were members of the newly established Garda Task Force, helped by local gardai and Special Branch. During the raid six of the people in the camp were arrested and one was shot and slightly wounded whilst attempting to get away.

Two people managed to escape. One was a woman volunteer from Belfast called Geraldine and the other was a full-time member of Donnelly's staff, Seamus, from County Sligo. Still in the fields collecting empty bullet casings when the raid began, they had managed to stay outside of the cordon. Later, under the cover of darkness, they made their way across the field, and after some time they stepped out on to a roadway and began to try to hitch a lift to Tralee. Luckily for them, they were picked up by a taxi driver from Tralee who was sympathetic to republicans. They had no idea of where they were going since neither was local, but the man drove them to the house in Tralee of an elderly republican called John McKenna and told them to mention my name.

The following morning I got a message to go to McKenna's to find, to my amazement – as I thought everyone had been captured – the two survivors looking pretty pleased with themselves.

The gardai were delighted with the result of the operation; not only had they captured six terrorists and seven modern weapons, but they had also dealt a blow to the IRA's capacity to train its people. Donnelly's entire plan – the result of months of work – was in ruins. In addition, before new plans could be made the IRA would have to institute and conduct an inquiry to discover what had gone wrong. Joe Cahill and Phil O'Donnell from Derry, the former British soldier, were the men chosen to carry it out, and I was assigned to help them do so.

The inquiry dragged on for months. Dozens of people were interviewed and numerous options explored. At the end of it all it found that there was no blame attached to any local people; the blame was laid firmly at the door of the training officers in charge of the camp. The firing practice had gone on too long and they had used heavier-calibre weapons than instructed. I felt pretty calm throughout the inquiry; although there were great risks involved Cahill and O'Donnell depended on me to help them and I was fairly confident that I could control and direct the nature of the inquiry. Now that I had been responsible for arrests of IRA members and for the capture of weapons, I knew, in clear, clinical terms, that my life was more at risk than ever before.

It was almost a year before the training department was able to resume normal business. But during this period I acquired other valuable nuggets of information. For instance, all of the people who came to the training camp travelled by train using forged rail passes, printed in the *An Phoblacht – Republican News –* office at the rear of Sinn Fein's National Head Office at Parnell Square in Dublin.

On 9 September 1980, a couple of weeks before the camp was raided, Liz gave birth to our son. He was born, like me, at St Catherine's Hospital in Tralee. By now she knew that I was once again involved in the IRA and she wasn't pleased. It became a constant source of friction between us, which compounded the fact that our marriage was in trouble anyway. I was away a lot and could never explain to Liz where I was or what I was doing. Liz didn't have a car and was often lonely. The rented house we lived in was in an isolated area about ten miles from Tralee, which made it very difficult for her to meet people. To my regret, I was so caught up in what I was doing that I simply didn't understand or take time to appreciate the enormity of the birth of our son. That is not a pleasant admission to have to make, but I would never lay claim to being much of a father. I think what I probably felt was fear. By this stage and even before she became pregnant Liz and I had not been getting on. Even though I was very fond of her I found I could not bear to be in the same room for long; we seemed to argue all the time and I felt completely worn down by it. I knew even then that I couldn't stay in the relationship much longer. I also knew that I could easily be murdered at any moment. Though I was overjoyed by my son's arrival and wished for him everything that a father wishes for a child, it was hardly a normal situation, and fear and gloom were just as strong as joy.

On the day our son was born I was in Tipperary. I had travelled to Nenagh to speak to Seamus Hogan, former adjutant of the Munster Command. Hogan was still a man with contacts and influence at the centre of the republican leadership.

As we chatted he told me that the Syrian government had recently given the IRA £2 million. I was amazed that he should talk so openly about such a matter. He went on to say that the money had been laundered through the PLO. I asked why the Syrians would do this and he said that it was connected to Mountbatten, Brian Keenan and GRU, the Soviet military intelligence. I knew that Keenan had extensive contacts with East Germany, GRU and Libya, but Keenan had been captured even before Mountbatten was murdered. Later I discussed this with Ferris. He told me that the murder of Mountbatten had essentially been Keenan's plan and had been pushed through by Ivor Bell, a veteran Belfast republican and – like Keenan – a Marxist. Keenan and Bell were pushing the republican movement in a Marxist direction. In his conversations with GRU and the East Germans Keenan had apparently been asked to prove that the IRA was serious about striking at the heart of imperialism.

I don't know who thought of Mountbatten, but nevertheless Keenan and Bell obviously decided, with GRU's agreement, that murdering him would establish their credentials and also gain the IRA £2 million. This was confirmed to me in substance by Pat Doherty at a later date, when I made him aware that there was a deal of 'loose talk' floating around about it. At the time GRU was virtually running the Libyan state. The IRA's connections were essentially with the East Germans and GRU, who enjoyed serious influence with the Syrians. It was never properly explained to me why the Syrians paid the money to the PLO rather than to GRU or the Libyans but I believe that it was simply a matter of laundering it. For the PLO to have given money to the IRA was one thing; for a government to have done so would have been an entirely different matter.

On 9 January 1981 I left Liz. There was no one else involved; I just had to get out. By this stage I was attending occasional Southern Command meetings along with people like Pat Doherty, Gerry Fitzgerald, Brendan Swords, Bobby McNamara, Joe Cahill, Daithi O'Connaill, John Joe Donnelly, Phil O'Donnell, Jimmy Jones, Seamus McGarrigle, and others. Activities at that time were becoming inexorably focused on the events in the H-Blocks of the Maze prison near Lisburn in Northern Ireland. Hundreds of republican prisoners in the H-Blocks had been on a blanket and dirty protest for several years – sitting in solitary confinement in their cells wearing only blankets, refusing to wash or shave and smearing their excrement on the cell walls.

Almost ignored at first, by 1980 the protest had begun to generate enormous media interest. The prisoners were taking issue with the British government's decision in 1976 to withdraw special (effectively political) status from prisoners. It was perfectly obvious to anybody who understood nationalist history that it would inevitably

147

escalate into a hunger strike. There were enough historical precedents to show that some republicans at least would be quite prepared to die rather than give in.

Sure enough, on 27 October 1980 seven republican prisoners began a hunger strike. On 18 December, by which time one of the hunger strikers, Sean McKenna, was approaching death, a compromise between the protesting prisoners and the authorities appeared to have been reached. The hunger strike was ended, but there was serious misunderstanding on both sides about the nature of the agreement. The hunger strike demonstrated that there was a dangerous emotional core both in Irish nationalism and in Irish America, which was too easily angered by latent anti-British feeling evoked by the hunger strike.

On 1 March 1981 Bobby Sands, the IRA OC imprisoned in the Maze since 1977, began another hunger strike. He died on 5 May, but not before he had been elected as a Westminster MP for the Northern Ireland constituency of Fermanagh/South Tyrone. His death was followed by those of nine others, winning widespread popular support and admiration for the republican cause both in Ireland and internationally. If a British government had been asked to devise a plan to rescue the IRA and hand it financial, political and military support on a scale undreamed of by its leaders, it could not have come up with a better one. The hunger strike episode was a major victory for the IRA and a disastrous failure on the part of the British government. There is no clearer example of how completely some senior British officials failed to understand the extreme nationalist movement in Ireland.

However, despite the success of the hunger strikers in gaining support for the republicans, Sands' death heralded a period of frantic incoherence for the IRA. For several months the hunger-strike support groups had been the focus of its activity and the day-to-day infrastructure of the organization had collapsed in the interim. Serious rioting and anarchy prevailed in republican areas of Northern Ireland throughout the summer of 1981. In truth, the IRA was in no position to take advantage of the situation immediately; it simply did not possess the type of material and weaponry required to make the necessary impact.

Towards the end of 1980 I had taken on a job as full-time co-ordinator for the H-Block pressure group based in Kerry. In effect I could carry out my IRA duties under the cover of anti-H-Block activity while also being financed by them. Away from the border counties, the hunger strikers had more support in Kerry than anywhere else in the Irish Republic, due largely to the strong republican tradition in the county. Also during this period senior members of the IRA's England department were in regular contact with Mick Brassil and me, plotting how to get material into Britain for the bombing campaign that would inevitably follow the end of the hunger strike.

In June 1981, eight IRA prisoners escaped from Belfast's Crumlin Road jail. Within weeks five of them had made their way to Kerry. After a hunger strike protest meeting in Tralee I was approached by a brother-in-law of one of the escapees – Joe Doherty from Belfast – who had lived in Tralee for a number of years. Doherty was in town and eager to get in touch. I met him and Mick Brassil that evening at a hotel outside Tralee to make the necessary arrangements. Within weeks Doherty, Paul Dingus Magee, Gerry Sloan, Angelo Fusco – all from Belfast – and Peter Ryan from Tyrone were in safe houses in the Tralee area.

Peter Ryan's parents and his sister were also living in Tralee at the time. Magee's and Fusco's wives and children came to join them shortly afterwards. But Ryan and Sloan had never intended to stay in the area. Sloan spent much of his time in Dundalk and was subsequently seriously injured in a car crash. Ryan returned to Monaghan and his IRA activities. He was a particularly vicious man who relished violence and murder. Utterly ruthless, with a bullying sadistic streak, he was responsible for many murders in County Tyrone. Even in Tralee he attempted to rape a German female guest in a house he was staying in. He was eventually shot dead in the early 1990s by the British Army at Coagh in Tyrone.

Joe Doherty was given a job in a shop owned by a wealthy IRA sympathizer and respected member of the local business community. He also began an affair with Mick Brassil's wife, which caused complications: Brassil threatened to have no more to do with the England operation unless the situation was resolved. It was, in an unexpected way.

Doherty was also having an affair with a local woman to whom he boasted of his prison escape and IRA activities. Word of this got back to local detectives, who decided to investigate by peering in through the windows of Doherty's workplace. Doherty was glad to be given an excuse to take off. He was no longer active in the IRA: it was obvious that he had no further interest in involving himself in anything dangerous. For some time he had expressed an interest in going to America. Following a meeting with Pat Doherty this was agreed, and Joe Doherty took leave of absence from the IRA. Effectively he resigned. Everyone knew he was not coming back; nor would he have been very welcome.

Doherty went on to become a celebrity of sorts in the United States, after the British government fought a nine-year legal battle to have him extradited. Ultimately he was brought back to face the life sentence imposed in his absence for his part in the murder of SAS Captain Westmacott in Belfast. Doherty won enormous support among the Irish-American community for his battle against the British government. Once again a little-known IRA volunteer had been elevated to hero status and another major propaganda victory had been won, for the IRA.

Angelo Fusco and Paul Magee had also been serving life sentences for their parts in the murder of Westmacott before their escape from Crumlin Road. Both were now living with their families in houses in Tralee rented through an estate agent with republican sympathies. Fusco and Magee were experienced operatives. Fusco – controlled and somewhat introspective if at times rather boastful – liked to describe himself as a 'killing machine'. Magee, on the other hand, was outgoing and friendly on the surface but did not appear to me to possess Fusco's cunning or control.

At that time the level of operational effectiveness in the Southern Command was poor. In August 1981, two small armed robberies had taken place during the annual Rose of Tralee International Festival. At that time of the year both targets – a hotel and a restaurant – would have been awash with cash. In each case, however, an in-experienced IRA team had done the job, leaving behind large amounts of undiscovered money. There was a clear need for a skilled active service unit tasked with carrying out armed robberies in the area: Fusco and Magee were briefed to man the team. In October/November, they carried out a wages snatch at the local railway station in Tralee. Under a little-known and little-used piece of inter-governmental legislation, known as the Criminal Law Jurisdiction Act, it was legally possible for Fusco

151

and Magee to be arrested in the Republic of Ireland and charged with escaping from lawful custody in Northern Ireland. As a result I had been pushing my Garda contact for some time to arrest both men, but the gardai were curiously slow to act. In this period, just after the hunger strikes, there was still a great deal of nationalist bitterness at what was seen as the British government's attitude towards the protesting prisoners. I cannot say with certainty if a lack of political will played a part in the slowness of the gardai to act, but other events that took place around that time lend credence to that view.

It was only after I threatened to tell journalists anonymously of their whereabouts that Fusco and Magee were later arrested at home: both were subsequently sentenced to eight years' imprisonment. Fusco later took part in a failed escape bid and was sentenced to a further three years. After Magee was released, he returned to Tralee but the British government filed an extradition warrant against him. He was released on bail and went on the run. He later turned up in England as part of an IRA active service unit. Following a police chase in Yorkshire he shot dead an unarmed special constable. He was arrested after a huge police hunt and sentenced to life imprisonment for that murder.

9

Nineteen eighty-one, the year of Sands' hunger strike, was incredibly busy for me. My marriage had broken up, my IRA duties were increasing and I had also to throw myself entirely into hunger strike support activity.

In June a general election was held in the Irish Republic. Inevitably the Maze hunger strike was a central issue. In Kerry the H-Block committee's nominated candidate was Sean McKenna, one of the survivors of the first and unsuccessful hunger strike.

Although nominally the person in charge of finance for the election campaign, I found myself responsible for running large sections of it. Gerry Adams, then vice president of Sinn Fein and adjutant-general of the IRA, came to Tralee and we addressed a public meeting from the same platform. The fact that McKenna came very close to getting elected shocked me and clearly shocked the local political establishment. In the border counties two of the hunger strikers succeeded in getting elected to the Irish parliament. It was a quite staggering illustration of just how much anger there was among supposedly moderate southern nationalists. Not one of the candidates would ever be able to represent their constituencies, since they were all in jail and some would go on to die on hunger strikes, yet thousands of people were prepared to 'waste' their votes on them.

In the middle of all this activity came a further complication. A local trade union support committee had been formed in Tralee and was loosely affiliated to the H-Block committee. At one of their meetings in July the two most prominent members – neither of whom was a member of the IRA or of Sinn Fein – announced that they were going on a hunger strike in support of the prisoners. What was already emotional and ugly was likely to become more so.

There appeared to be no way of stopping the two men, Liam Hutchinson and Jimmy Brosnan, from proceeding with their hunger strike. Hutchinson was a particularly determined and clever man with a long background of trade union agitation in both Ireland and Britain. I had no doubt that he would stick with it at least until emotion had been raised to a dangerous level in the Irish Republic. Brosnan was not made of the same stuff and I was sure thirty to forty days without food would knock the romance out of him. Hutchinson, however, had made plans for other trade unionists to join their hunger strike at regular intervals.

I had no desire for massive gains to be made by successful hunger strikers. How to stop them before the whole affair escalated out of control was my problem. I could not order them to stop because they were not members of the IRA. I decided that the only way to derail the plan was to join their hunger strike, knowing that this would be the last thing that the leadership of the IRA wanted at the time. Any volunteer must get permission from the Army Council before he or she commences a hunger strike; it was absolutely certain that I would be ordered off the strike by the leadership before it progressed too far as it would distract from the Maze protest. My only hope was that my hunger strike would undermine Hutchinson's plan in the process – since Hutchinson and Brosnan would both have to end their strikes if I were to do so. The whole business would do some harm to my credibility with the IRA leadership as it would show a degree of indiscipline, but it would also prove my commitment to the cause and it would be understood in the context of the emotion created by the hunger strike and the frustration of republicans as they stood helplessly by while their comrades starved to death.

The hunger strike was announced to a crowd of about a thousand people at an open-air rally in Tralee in mid-July. There were two demands. The first was that Ireland's largest trade union, the Irish Transport and General Workers' Union – to which Hutchinson and Brosnan belonged – should immediately ballot all of its members to establish whether or not they supported the demands of the hunger strikers in the Maze. It appeared certain that the result would be overwhelmingly in favour of the hunger strikers and would force Ireland's largest trade union to back the prisoners' demands officially. More rioting and more deaths would result as the Provisionals exploited this development. The second demand was for the Irish government to issue a clear, unambiguous statement supporting the demands of the hunger strikers.

Within days of our hunger strike beginning, trade unionists in Limerick and Waterford announced plans to join us. A Capuchin monk in Dublin was also prepared to commence a hunger strike in front of the Irish parliament. The situation was rapidly running out of control. I was still satisfied that the innate caution of the IRA leadership would lead them to oppose the venture. After about two weeks – with support gaining momentum –

Pat Doherty came to Kerry for an IRA meeting. By this time I was beginning to feel the effects of fourteen days without food – nauseous and weak with occasional headaches – but I was fit and healthy and wasn't experiencing any great problems. I knew that I would begin to deteriorate after the third week.

I collected Doherty from the local railway station. His first words to me were, 'I thought you were on hunger strike.' 'I am,' I said. He seemed surprised that I should be driving after fourteen days without food. I drove him out of Tralee to a farmhouse where the meeting took place. There were about fifteen people there – all of them well known to me.

Doherty began by asking them if they supported me in the hunger strike: all replied yes. We then had a general discussion about the state of the local organization. Afterwards I drove Doherty back to the house where he was staying. After a brief discussion about the rights and wrongs of the hunger strike Doherty unveiled his plan. He had already communicated with the prisoners' leaders in the Maze. Tomorrow, he assured me, they would be issuing a statement to the media thanking us for our support and asking us to call off the hunger strike on the grounds that it detracted from their campaign.

That was it. There was no way the hunger strike could continue in the face of opposition from the Maze hunger strikers. I reported back to Hutchinson and Brosnan. I suspect that Brosnan, who was already suffering health problems, was secretly glad. Hutchinson knew that he was snookered and reluctantly agreed that there was no alternative but to abandon the protest on receipt of the statement from the Maze prisoners. The statement came the following day and we made the announcement in a Tralee hotel. I am convinced that taking control of that hunger strike and thereby allowing it to be ended before it escalated was one of my most important achievements. Over the next couple of years several senior members of the IRA confessed to me that they had got it wrong and that the hunger strike could have radicalized nationalist sentiment in the Republic, just as the Maze hunger strike did in Northern Ireland. The sight of people dying in the Republic because the Irish government refused to support the hunger strikers in Northern Ireland would have provoked widespread anger and resentment.

Our strike over, I was now able to attend to more standard IRA business. And on 3 October 1981 the Maze hunger strike was called off. Ten prisoners had died – over half of those who had participated. It looked like a defeat for the prisoners, but in fact they were very quickly granted all of their demands.

Throughout the strike the IRA's England department had been assiduously preparing for the moment when they would move into action. During the summer of 1981 Mick Hayes, quartermaster to the England department, had been a regular visitor to Kerry and to Mick Brassil in particular. I had introduced Brassil to Mick Hayes several months before in Limerick. I knew that Hayes would immediately see that Brassil could be extremely useful in transporting explosives and weapons to England.

Mick Hayes was one of the primary culprits in the Birmingham bomb atrocity of 1974, when twenty-two innocent civilians were killed in bomb explosions in two Birmingham pubs. He escaped to Ireland and in 1977 was jailed for three years in Portlaoise for arms offences. Along with Owen Coogan, from Belfast, he was one of the senior members of the most secretive IRA department. The IRA's England department was responsible for all operations on the British mainland. In practice it often played a leading role in the IRA's occasional continental escapades, with operatives switching from England to Germany or Holland in particular, as required.

Once it was obvious that the hunger strike was drawing to an end, the IRA was desperate to begin bombing prestige targets in England. For the sake of both morale on the ground and its own credibility, the leadership needed 'spectaculars' in England.

Mick Brassil was a big rumbustious character from a wealthy family who had long been associated with oil and petrol distribution: he and his father, William, had systematically defrauded Esso Oil Ireland over many years. This eventually came to light in the late 1970s and early 1980s when they were the subject of a major fraud investigation. The family also had an interest in the haulage trade and Brassil had recently bought an old established pub called Brassil's in Tralee from another uncle, which he refurbished at great cost.

It was the haulage business that interested Mick Hayes and the IRA. For a number of years Brassil had had a regular contract to deliver mussels from Cromane in Kerry to Billingsgate Market in London. Hayes recognized that it would be relatively easy to hide explosives and guns in amongst the mussels and transport them to the active service unit in England.

Several meetings were arranged in Tralee and Dublin involving Jerry Tuite, an IRA man from County Cavan who had recently escaped from Brixton prison in London, Mick Hayes, Owen Coogan and Albert Flynn. I was aware from Brassil of almost every single detail of the operation and passed on all of those details to my Garda contact. Brassil consistently came to me for advice and reassurance. He was not supposed to do this and in a subsequent inquiry said nothing about our relationship to the England department.

Angelo Fusco, who had struck up a very friendly relationship with Brassil, was brought in to help, and Brassil also had an assistant with him on his journey – a local IRA man who sometimes worked for him.

Early in October 1981 Hayes travelled to Kerry with the explosives and guns. They were brought to Brassil's pub, where, upstairs, Fusco and Brassil packed the material and weighed it. Because Brassil's documents would show a specific weight of mussels it was necessary to make sure that the weight of the crates remained the same when the explosives were substituted for mussels.

The night that Brassil and his helper were due to leave for Rosslare in County Wexford to take the ferry to Fishguard, I got a phone call from Bobby McNamara, who needed a man for an armed robbery at a post office in Cork City. I was spending a lot of time in McNamara's company and was effectively helping him to run the IRA in Munster. I had been in Cork with Bobby and Gerry Fitzgerald a couple of weeks before and knew in general terms that an armed robbery was being planned.

I found a local volunteer who was in position to travel and a sympathizer drove him to Cork. I phoned my Garda contact and alerted him to the robbery. I had no specific details, and he appeared reluctant to involve Cork police in anything to do with me, saying that it could cause 'problems'. I had no idea what he meant. The following morning armed gardai arrested three armed robbers at the scene after they had raided Togher Post Office in the city. It didn't take a genius to work out that the Cork Garda had their own source of information.

By this time we had much bigger things on our minds. I told my Garda contact that Brassil's lorry was on its way. I had suggested to him on a number of occasions during the build-up that the sensible thing to do would be to let the lorry proceed to the service station on the M4 where it would be met by the active service unit, which comprised, among others, Tommy Quigley and Paul Kavanagh – later jailed for their involvement in IRA bombings in England. The lorry alone would lead police to at least two members of the ASU, who could then be tailed to the rest of its members.

Brassil returned to Tralee to report that everything had gone perfectly. So far as I was aware everything was under control – the right information was in the right hands, or so I thought.

On Saturday 10 October, 1981, a remote-control bomb in a van at Chelsea Barracks in London killed an elderly woman and a teenager and injured twenty-three soldiers and sixteen policemen, some seriously. On the following Saturday Sir Stewart Pringle, Commandant-General of the Royal Marines, lost a leg when a Provisional IRA bomb exploded in his car in London.

I could not understand what was happening. I spoke to my Garda contact and arranged to meet him. By now we had begun to rotate meeting places – sometimes in the graveyard, sometimes near a corner of the town park which was shrouded in darkness. I would get into the park through a gap in the railings and when he drew up in his car I would quickly slip into the back seat and lie there.

'What's going on?' I asked. 'What do you mean?' he said. 'About England,' I said, a little pissed off at this stage. 'Oh, we'd never trust the English police with that sort of information. Now if it was the RUC that would be different.' I simply could not believe what I was hearing. I had deliberately infiltrated Brassil into the IRA's England department. Months of work, at no little risk, had gone into ensuring that everything planned by

160

Brassil, Hayes and Coogan was known to Garda Special Branch. The IRA's entire active service organization on the ground in England could have been wiped out in one stroke. Instead the Garda appeared to have allowed their plans to develop and had done nothing about it.

I could not understand it. Either they doubted the efficiency or security of the English police – which judging from my own experience I can understand – or bitterness about the hunger strike at the highest level meant that bombs in England were acceptable at that time. Another possibility – remote, I think – is that my Garda contact never passed the information on.

There is something that should be clearly understood here. Whether I had existed or not Brassil would have joined the IRA. His access to or ownership of lorries travelling regularly to England meant that sooner or later people like Hayes would have developed an interest in him. I simply moved to take control of the situation, judging that I could then remain in a position to help to inflict maximum damage on IRA plans. That was the theory, at least.

I played no part in the planning of IRA operations in England at that time. I introduced Brassil to the England department, knowing that he would come to me for advice and make me aware of all that developed. He behaved as expected and I passed all of the information on.

For the majority of people in Ireland, 1981 was undoubtedly a disastrous year, and one which had profoundly positive implications for the republican movement. The fact that ten IRA prisoners were prepared to starve themselves to death rather than be classified as criminals could not be ignored. Foreign journalists, TV crews and the merely curious flocked into

Belfast. There, for the first time in many cases, they met articulate republican spokesmen. People like Gerry Adams and Danny Morrison became household names in Ireland and elsewhere.

The republican movement was awash with new funds – particularly from America – new-found respectability and new recruits. Sinn Fein's political fortunes were revitalized and given a new sense of direction by the election of Sands and the hunger-strike candidates in the Irish Republic.

The beneficiaries of this respectability and wealth were the younger radical northerners like Adams, McGuinness and Morrison. The old guard – represented by southerners like O'Bradaigh and O'Connaill – though still powerful, were gradually becoming yesterday's men. The battle that had been fought from 1976 was approaching its end and it was obvious by now that the faction represented by Adams and McGuinness would win.

In his highly developed, individual style, Adams moved slowly and carefully. While others such as Morrison and Tom Hartley were impatient to be rid of the old guard or at least to have their influence considerably reduced, Adams acted only when he was certain that a significant split between the old and new guard could be avoided. The hunger strike galvanized support in Northern Ireland for the republican movement and now more than ever before it was a northern nationalist movement controlled by northern nationalists. Daithi O'Connaill might later claim that the Adams/McGuinness leadership was not representative of the movement as a whole. The problem for him and O'Bradaigh was that this was far more true of them. For nationalists in Northern Ireland and for the republican movement nothing would ever be the same again.

The IRA still had a difficult job on its hands. Internal security demands meant that it had to vet the influx of new entrants carefully because there was a danger that the Special Branch would attempt to exploit the flood of would-be recruits. Nineteen eighty-one changed everything. In Tralee and the surrounding area a new generation was introduced to militant republicanism. The hunger strike proved that in some areas of the South an emotional ambivalence towards the IRA lay just under the surface.

In August 1981 I started to go out with an English woman living in Tralee. Originally from Buckinghamshire, Louise had lived in Tralee for about two years. She had come to visit in Kerry a couple of times and had fallen in love with it. She was a big, bright, athletic woman with a wonderful, gentle personality. She could be the life and soul of the party, and she possessed a compassionate, non-judgemental quality that was wholly natural. We had mutual friends and occasionally we ended up in each other's company. After a while we began to see a lot of each other.

Our affair quickly turned into a serious relationship. By October of that year we were living together in a rented flat in Tralee. Louise knew that I was involved in the republican movement: living in Kerry she could not but have known. The hunger strike meant that my name and face were now well known in the area. She had no interest in politics, however, and made it very clear from early on that she wanted to know as little as possible about my activities and certainly wanted nothing to do with them.

I knew, I suppose, that by establishing a relationship with an Englishwoman I was exposing her to possible danger. If my role as a Garda agent were uncovered by the IRA it would be likely that some at least in the IRA might believe that Louise was a British agent. At the very least it was likely that in such circumstances she would endure a pretty rough time. But the truth is that by the time we began to live together I was too much in love and too weak or selfish to face up to it. She was to know nothing of my role as a Garda agent until many years later.

10

As 1981 drew to a close I was asked to help organize the IRA in the west of Ireland. In the wake of the hunger strikes, areas where republicanism had lain dormant for many years were beginning to show potential. In January 1982 I moved with Louise to County Galway, where we rented a house in a remote area on the edge of Connemara, called Cloonabinia. The brief I was given by Pat Doherty – still OC of Southern Command – was to reorganize Counties Galway, Clare, Mayo and Roscommon, with a view to recruiting young volunteers and organizing armed robberies in the area. The area had always been used extensively by the IRA's training and engineering departments and for senior IRA meetings, but it had played almost no role in providing finance.

Jimmy Jones was still the leading figure in the area. But he wanted to continue the work he had been doing for years rather than follow a new direction, which he felt would undermine the very effective support network he had built and maintained, in Mayo in particular.

Far from wanting to organize the area or carry out armed robberies, my main interest was to learn as much as possible about Jones's network and pass whatever information I could to the Garda. Jones was an extremely cautious man who wouldn't readily tell anyone anything he felt they didn't need to know. In spite of this, I spent a fair amount of time in his house, where there was a constant stream of people like Adams, McGuinness, Doherty, John Joe Donnelly – now in charge of the engineering department – and a Dublin man in charge of the training department which was once again based in the area. One of my tasks was to liaise with the training department, which I usually did by having weekly meetings in restaurants or cafés in Galway City.

Over the coming months I discovered quite a lot about Jones's network and the activity taking place in the area. I quickly realized that his work was of such importance to the IRA – running training camps, bomb factories, large weapons dumps and many important meetings in an area with little or no Garda surveillance – that there was little possibility that the Chief of Staff, Martin McGuinness, would actually sanction an armed robbery there, unless this were for a vast sum. Certainly he would not sanction anything against Jones's advice. Doherty wanted reorganization and finance raised because he was OC of Southern Command and under pressure, but he would never overtly criticize Jones or find himself in opposition to a decision taken by Martin McGuinness. Jones, for his part, would play the game but would always ensure that now was never the right moment to carry out an armed robbery. There was always something of greater importance going on.

None of this bothered me in the least. I wished to maintain a good relationship with all of them and gather as much information as possible. During this time I made frequent trips back to Kerry. I wanted to keep up with everything that was happening there and the people themselves, in particular Mick Hayes, the England department quartermaster who was still in touch with Mick Brassil.

By this stage I had introduced Hayes to another Kerryman. Michael Browne, from Fenit, about five miles from Tralee, had became involved in activities during the hunger strike. He was of particular interest to Hayes because he owned a fishing trawler and was an experienced sailor. Browne would sometimes visit me in Galway and keep me up to date with his contacts with Hayes. Around this time, too, Mick Brassil approached me and told me that he had a new man willing to transport explosives and weapons to England. The man, a coach driver for a Tralee-based coach company which ran a weekly passenger service from Tralee to London, had told Brassil he was prepared to hide material in the luggage bays. I went to see him with Brassil and he confirmed his offer. I communicated that information to Hayes. Both Brassil and Browne travelled to Dublin several times to meet with Hayes and Albert Flynn. Hayes's original plan was for Browne to ferry an active service unit and equipment to England, dropping them at an isolated area in Cornwall – an area of coast with which Browne was very familiar.

Just before I went to Galway I had been called to a meeting involving Adams and McGuinness. Bobby McNamara, Gerry Fitzgerald and Martin Ferris also attended the meeting, which was held at a farmhouse near Middleton in County Cork. Driving to and from the meeting was slow and hazardous as there was heavy snow on the mountain road crossing the Kerry/Cork border. We sat around a table in a small kitchen at the rear of the farmhouse.

Adams was extremely pushy at the meeting and made it quite clear that he believed that Southern Command was not pulling its weight. The primary purpose of Southern Command was to provide back-up to GHQ and Northern Command, particularly by raising finance through armed robberies. In this task it was failing lamentably – thank God, so far as I was concerned. Sensing his anger I goaded him to see if I could make his deep reserve crack a little. I caught a glimpse of controlled anger when I said that many volunteers were unhappy with the failure of the leadership to inflict serious damage on the 'Brits' in the wake of the hunger strike. He reacted by attacking Southern Command's record. Eventually, McGuinness calmed the situation by saying that if any of us wanted to meet with IRA commanders from Northern Ireland to discuss the problems on the ground it could be arranged. Together they made it clear that they believed that we in the room were the people who had to make it happen. My being asked to move to Galway after this meeting was as a direct result of Pat Doherty being told by Adams and McGuinness to deliver on armed robberies; they had stressed that message forcefully at a GHQ meeting and Doherty was hoping that I would be able to come up with the goods. There was certainly tension between Adams and me that evening, but it suited me to appear militant, and the fact that I was willing to face Adams publicly did me no harm. But wherever armed robberies were going to happen it certainly wasn't where Jimmy Jones held control and where much valuable and secret work took place away from the eyes of Special Branch.

In March 1982 a Belfast republican called Pat Currie was released from Portlaoise prison and moved to Tralee, where it was felt another full-time experienced operative would be useful. Currie was stockily built, edging towards fat, and rather fond of the good life but, unusually for a Belfast man, he fitted in well in the area.

By the summer of 1982 I was moving frequently between Galway and Mayo, as well as Kerry and Cork and Waterford – the area that Martin Ferris and Pat Currie were now responsible for. I was also liaising between Brassil, Browne, the coach driver and Mick Hayes. That summer Ferris was working on an oilrig off the west coast. For two weeks out of every four he was absent from the area, which effectively meant that his responsibilities fell to me. By this stage the Garda had taken to arresting me quite regularly under the Offences Against the State Act, which allowed them to hold people for a maximum of forty-eight hours for questioning. They knew that I was active: my name or my face was coming up quite regularly in reports from different parts of the country. With the exception of my contact and two senior gardai in head office, other policemen saw Ferris and me as the two most active and senior southern IRA men, and arrested us merely to disrupt our activities.

Nineteen eighty-two was a year of widespread IRA activity in Kerry and dozens of new members were recruited. Sinn Fein's office in Tralee was partially converted into a bookshop selling republican literature. Sales of *An Phoblacht* increased considerably in the Tralee area from several hundred to over two thousand weekly.

After the armed robbery at Tralee railway station and the subsequent arrest of Fusco and Magee in late 1981, the following year saw a rash of armed robberies and raids for weapons – particularly in the Tralee area. At that time the IRA had access to a lot of inside information. There was also an almost endless supply of people prepared to help in a variety of ways. On the surface there appeared to be so much support that one day, walking through Tralee, Pat Currie said to me, 'This place is like Andersonstown in 1972.' A post office van was hijacked and robbed, a frozen-food depot's weekly takings stolen; armed robberies became a regular occurrence. Houses were raided for guns, as was a gun dealer in Castleisland, a small town outside Tralee, from where over seventy guns were taken. Most of these were recovered in a graveyard near the Ferris family farm within forty-eight hours, after I told the Garda where they were. Because of the recent raid on the training camp, the arrest of Fusco and Magee and the fact that I was providing high-grade intelligence, it was necessary to allow some small armed robberies to go ahead without interruption.

Throughout this period I kept my Garda contact informed of all of my activities. I was constantly diverting the IRA's attention from potentially very large robberies to ones where the rewards were much lower. It was not too difficult for me to do this in my position – most decisions were not questioned – but there had to be some good results to justify the amount of activity. I could not afford the slightest amount of suspicion. Equally, of course, I was able to prevent many robberies from ever leaving the drawing board.

For example, for some time gardai had undertaken 'random' escorts of post office vans delivering money, pensions, children's allowances and so on from the central post office to outlying rural post offices. These vans could sometimes carry considerable sums of money. IRA orders expressly forbade any overt aggressive actions towards the Garda, so all that was necessary to prevent a robbery was a Garda escort for the van the IRA intended to rob. The system was so random that it was unlikely to arouse suspicion among either the IRA or the local gardai.

Unfortunately there were exceptions. On one occasion the IRA planned to rob a bank in Foynes in west Limerick. The information came to me from a long-standing IRA member who had worked on a huge building project at Aughenish in County Limerick. The building company's wages – a large sum – were held in the bank before being collected by clerical staff from the plant. Sometimes there was a Garda escort, sometimes not. I told my Garda contact that the raid was planned for a certain day and all that was needed was for a Garda escort to be present. Unfortunately the IRA team chosen to carry out the robbery included a couple of people who took a rather cavalier view of certain orders. One of them, Hugh Hehir, from County Clare, had been released from the Maze prison in 1981 after serving a long sentence for possession of explosives in Belfast in 1974. The other was later involved in the 1996 murder of Garda Gerry McCabe during a bungled IRA robbery in the same area.

When Hehir and the others realized there was a Garda escort they decided to take the initiative. They over-powered the two Garda officers, disarmed them and locked them in the local police station before making off with the money. One of the gardai, who somehow suspected that his superiors had reason to believe a robbery might take place, attempted to bring a case against the Garda commissioner for wilfully placing his life in danger. I never heard how that finished.

From my point of view the danger lay in the fact that Bobby McNamara eventually discovered what had happened and wondered how the gardai could have known that a raid was planned for that day. Luckily for me, Bobby was a particularly slow-witted man whom most people didn't take too seriously. Neither did he possess the fortitude or tenacity to turn his suspicions into a real issue. At a meeting in Limerick shortly after-wards, however, Pat Doherty asked me to keep an eye on the situation. I had to agree with him that it was likely that there was an informer somewhere in the vicinity, but the 'evidence' available seemed to point towards the Limerick area. I told Doherty that I would sift through what we knew and see where it led. Not surprisingly, the IRA is paranoid about informers and hardly a week goes by without some scare, so I wasn't particularly bothered, even though I could have done without it. The two Uzi sub-machine-guns taken from the two Garda officers were later discovered in an IRA arms dump in England, which shows the organizational links that extend from rural Ireland to IRA operations in England.

The summer of 1982 also saw a most bizarre incident involving Mick Brassil, Pat Currie, Martin Ferris, a Norwegian and, to a small degree, myself. Brassil was introduced to the Norwegian by a woman in Tralee with whom the Norwegian had come to stay as a guest while supposedly in Kerry on business. The Norwegian dis-covered that Brassil had republican sympathies and told him he was in possession of a large number of assault rifles stolen from a Nato base in Norway. It was later confirmed that such a raid had in fact taken place. Brassil told Currie who in turn informed Ferris. I was out of the area at the time, in Galway. On my return to Tralee Ferris and Currie told me their story. Apparently the weapons were in sealed containers, dumped in fairly deep water off the coast of Norway. I wasn't just sus-picious: I was incredulous. When I was told that the Norwegian wanted a hefty deposit to hire a boat and diving equipment to recover the weapons I was even more sceptical.

Ferris asked me to go to Joe Cahill to see what the IRA leadership made of it all and I agreed, but only on the basis that I was reporting this, was not involved and was highly dubious about the Norwegian's entire story. As I expected, when I met Cahill at Sinn Fein headquarters in Dublin he too was extremely doubtful. When I mentioned that the Norwegian was looking for money upfront, Cahill nearly had a heart attack. 'No, no, no!' he was shouting. 'Fuck's sake, Joe,' I said. 'Calm down. I don't want you giving him any money either.'

As we were talking, Gerry Adams came down the stairs. Cahill explained the substance of the story to Adams, who listened intently before replying. He asked me to monitor the situation and to decide if it was worth going any further. The conversation then turned to other IRA matters. Adams wanted to know what things were like on the ground, the state of morale, and so on. Then he asked how people felt the SDLP and John Hume in particular could best be dealt with. 'What about killing Hume?' he asked. I replied that I thought it would be madness: even though in theory loyalists would be blamed for it, if a couple of IRA men were caught after killing or attempting to kill Hume, the consequences for the republican movement would be catastrophic.

I knew that the IRA had seriously considered 'wiping out' Hume and much of the SDLP leadership in the 1970s. It was commonly believed by people such as former Chief of Staff Seamus Twomey that the biggest mistake ever made by the IRA leadership was to allow the SDLP to achieve a dominant position in northern nationalism. Twomey and others, like Kevin McKenna and Ivor Bell from Belfast – perhaps Adams's closest associate – still held that view. But it was much too late. In time I would discover how Adams and others would 'deal' with John Hume.

Did Adams believe at the time when Sinn Fein had begun to contest elections that it was feasible, useful or worth the gamble to kill Hume? I don't know. He didn't make his own position clear that day; he was simply taking soundings and not just from me. Around that period there was a 'general' revival in the debate about the failure to deal with the SDLP in the early 1970s. Sinn Fein were now contesting elections for the first time but the SDLP were firmly entrenched in electoral terms as the undisputed voice of northern nationalism and a serious rival to Sinn Fein on the ground.

As usual, details of this conversation were passed on to my Garda contact.

11

I spent much of the latter part of 1982 engaged in organizational work or planning armed robberies in the Midlands and in South Leinster – Wexford, Carlow and Kilkenny – as well as keeping an eye on events in Kerry. My work had to appear to bear fruit while at the same time damaging the organization from within. It was a difficult balancing act but entirely possible with the right application.

The Norwegian escapade ended, as I had thought it would, in pure farce. Brassil said that he would be prepared to guarantee £3,000 as an initial down payment if the money could be raised elsewhere in the short term. A local businessman guaranteed a loan for me at a bank. The businessman and the bank official both knew the money was for the IRA, but that was no problem for either of them. However, I found out from my Garda contact that the local police were aware of the transaction. I handed the money over to Ferris, who gave it to the Norwegian, who of course promptly disappeared. The Norwegian told Scotland Yard his story and then tried to sell it to the *News of the World*. Brassil eventually repaid the loan in full – including interest.

Throughout 1982 I regularly attended Southern

Command meetings. Under Doherty's control Southern Command had been greatly slimmed down from its early days. Meetings now consisted of about fifteen rather than up to thirty people; they were held at different venues – sometimes County Kildare, Meath, North Tipperary or County Mayo – and followed a familiar pattern. We travelled to meetings from our different areas to central pick-up points, maybe a hotel carpark or a sympathizer's home, where our transport was left, and were then taken, usually in the back of a van, to the meeting place. There was a nominal military or para-military dimension to meetings, in that those attending 'fell in' before every session and stood to attention before being 'dismissed'. Pat Doherty chaired them efficiently and smoothly. We all knew each other quite well and the atmosphere was usually relaxed with a degree of friendly rivalry between the different areas. If one area had recently carried out a successful armed robbery they would try to goad the others. The local area OCs gave verbal reports on the state of affairs on their patch and there was general discussion about the organization, or specific requests from Northern Command or GHQ. Afterwards there would be discussions between individuals who perhaps required help or co-operation from one or more of the others present. For security reasons operations were discussed individually with Doherty.

If the training, engineering and finance departments from GHQ had an urgent or important request to make they would be represented. Martin McGuinness or Gerry Adams occasionally put in an appearance, but they would rarely have much to say. Both were always guarded and were more or less content to sit and listen, contributing no more than one or two comments or questions. Meetings usually lasted two days, beginning in the evening and continuing through the following day until late. Food was usually sandwiches made up previously by locals; sleeping arrangements depended on what was available and were often sleeping-bags on the floor. The local people looked after the security. There was always a scanner switched on so that police messages in the area could be listened to. From my point of view they were particularly dangerous meetings: while I had to gather as much information as possible I had to behave and involve myself as if I were a dedicated IRA man. I used to let the detail of the meeting wash over me without any attempt at evaluation, and then once it was over run it through my mind to formulate a full report for my Garda contact. I have always had a good memory and didn't need to concentrate to remember detail.

Even though so-called supergrasses previously existed, 1982 saw their expansion into a full-blown 'system' and one of the main weapons in the state's armoury against the terrorist organizations. In November 1981 Christopher Black, an IRA volunteer from Ardoyne, who had previously served a five-year sentence, was arrested by the RUC. Black was twenty-seven years old and understandably did not want to go back to jail. After a couple of days' detention in Castlereagh he offered to co-operate with the RUC in return for a guarantee of his own and his family's safety and immunity from prosecution. Black's decision to turn supergrass produced blind panic in the IRA. No one really knew how much information he had, but it transpired that he was unable to damage the higher echelons of the IRA.

It would appear that like all but one of the super-grasses who followed Black, he was motivated by selfish interests, the exception being Kevin McGrady from the nationalist Short Strand enclave in East Belfast. Throughout 1982 further supergrasses popped up regularly in both republican and loyalist terror organizations. The republican INLA and the loyalist UVF were particularly damaged by such people and neither organization ever really recovered.

One of the supergrasses, Raymond Gilmour, had been an RUC agent for a number of years before deciding that he wished to give evidence in court. His father, an elderly man living in Derry, wanting to thwart his son's efforts, co-operated with the IRA in staging his own 'kidnapping' and thus putting pressure on his son to withdraw his evidence.

I learned about this in October 1982, when I, along with Pat Doherty, Martin McGuinness and Martin Ferris, attended a Sinn Fein dinner dance in Tralee. I arrived late, having travelled from Wexford where I had been scuppering a post office robbery. Eventually Doherty, McGuinness and Ferris came to join me in a small bar outside the function. McGuinness and Doherty could hardly be described as great socializers and certainly in those days they both had a strong puritanical streak in their make-up. They were here to do business, not to party.

I had an initial chat with Doherty about what I had been doing over the previous couple of weeks. Then Doherty said to Ferris, 'Explain the situation about Gilmour to Sean.' Gilmour senior, I was told, was to be brought to Kerry in the next couple of days, where he would be 'held' until his son 'retracted'. McGuinness then told me and Ferris that he and Gerry Adams were standing down as Chief of Staff and adjutant-general respectively, to be replaced by McKenna and Doherty. The reason given was that both Adams and McGuinness had been chosen by Sinn Fein to contest assembly elections in Northern Ireland, which had been called by Jim Prior, the secretary of state for Northern Ireland.

There is no doubt, however, that the supergrass system, an exclusively Northern Ireland phenomenon, also played a part in their decision, for nobody knew where the next supergrass would come from. It was no co-incidence that both McKenna and Doherty lived in the Republic and were safe from compromise by a new supergrass.

Adams and McGuinness would both remain on the IRA Army Council but would no longer be exposed to the daily risk of having to oversee operational decisions on the ground in Northern Ireland. Ivor Bell, Adams's close associate, was to take control of Northern Command, and though Doherty would remain OC of Southern Command both Ferris and I would play increasingly prominent roles.

Effectively, under Adams's influence in particular, the IRA was moving firmly towards the principle of collective leadership, though Adams and McGuinness remained the two central players in the republican move-ment. Long gone were the days when a Chief of Staff like Seamus Twomey could behave as the 'boss of bosses'. The role and importance of the Chief of Staff was much reduced as the IRA slowly but inexorably came under political control.

It should not be thought that 'political control' meant moderation. On the contrary. At this stage the IRA was flirting with Marxism in a way they had never done before. The 'armalite and ballot box' strategy was about to be infamously introduced to the outside world by Danny Morrison at a Sinn Fein ard fheis – the annual party convention.

Gilmour senior was duly brought to south Kerry, where he stayed for many months, being minded by relays of local IRA volunteers. I took almost no part in the affair beyond occasionally arranging for photographs of him to be taken in which he would hold up a copy of a recent *Irish News*, Northern Ireland's nationalist newspaper. This was intended to reassure Gilmour that his father was alive and also of course to remind him of what his father was 'enduring' and what might happen to him. I kept the gardai informed at all times of these events, but they were curiously uninterested in Gilmour senior. In spite of the threat to his father, Gilmour gave evidence and since there was no point in holding on to Gilmour senior any longer, in September 1983 he was released and returned to his home in Derry. The IRA never had any intention of killing him because it would not have gone down well with nationalists who hated Gilmour but saw his father as an innocent victim.

In December 1982, a man who was slightly drunk came into a small gambling arcade near the Sinn Fein centre in Tralee. He made a nuisance of himself with some youngsters who were playing on the slot machines. One of the kids – a young girl whom I knew by sight – came walking by the centre crying. I asked her what was wrong and she said that a man in the arcade had frightened her. She pointed him out to me and I told him to go away and leave the kids alone. He went off quietly and to my mind seemed relatively harmless. It wasn't until he was gone that the owner of the arcade told me that he had been asking questions about me and the Sinn Fein centre.

I thought this strange but for obvious reasons didn't want to pursue the matter. That same night Pat Currie was drinking in a pub in Tralee when he overheard the same man asking questions about me. Currie managed to get the man from the pub to his car and drove him from there to the Ferrises' farm at Churchill near Fenit – about five miles away. The man was moved to a derelict house in the area, where another local IRA man stayed in charge of their captive while Currie returned to Tralee to find me.

I was at home when Currie came and told me what had happened. I went with him immediately to the house where the man was being held and took over: Currie had to leave early that night because he was on his way to Waterford City to plan an armed robbery, and I dismissed the other IRA man.

When I removed the hood covering the prisoner's head it was immediately obvious that he was very frightened. The story that emerged over the next couple of hours was sad in the extreme. He was a Corkman, an alcoholic who, several months before, had spent some time in a treatment clinic for people with dependency problems. While there he had met and become friendly with a fellow alcoholic, a detective based in Tralee who invited him to visit him if ever he was in the area. The man foolishly told the detective that he had spied on republicans in Cork for a detective there when he was desperate for money for drink.

A few months after leaving the clinic the man began to drink again, eventually turning up in Tralee, where he called at the local police station to see his friend in the hope of getting some money from him. In the police station his 'friend' gave him a small amount of money and told him he would give him more if he would travel around the local bars and pick up any gossip or information about local republicans – especially me.

I spent the night talking to the Corkman, essentially trying to put the most sympathetic interpretation on the story that I could. With the aid of a tape recorder I questioned him, all the while slanting the questions to make him appear a pathetic victim of Garda pressure. I reasoned that the IRA would much prefer to equate

Garda methods with the perceived nationalist view of RUC and military intelligence methods. There was also the possibility that disclosure would force the Irish government to put pressure on Special Branch to pull its horns in.

The following morning Martin Ferris and another IRA man turned up. After some discussion we decided to release the Corkman and to hand the tape over to a local priest, who would simply hand it to a senior policeman. We would wait to see what, if anything, happened. This man was not a member of the republican movement and even though he had spied on republicans for the police it hadn't resulted in any damage done: no one went to jail, no weapons were captured.

Meanwhile, Pat Currie had gone to Waterford to finalize plans for a wages robbery at the leather factory at Portlaw near the River Suire in County Waterford. So far, he and Ferris had failed to pull off even one successful armed robbery in Counties Cork and Waterford. I told Ferris that I would co-operate with him on this robbery if afterwards he would help me with a post office robbery in Wexford. I was now in substance, if not formally, responsible for operations in much of Southern Command. It was very much in my interests that Ferris and Currie should remain in charge of that area as it meant I knew everything that was going on there without going near it. I also knew that there was a possibility – slight though it might be – that I could be in trouble. My Garda contact and his superior knew about this robbery: we had stopped and foiled so much IRA activity by this stage that it was agreed that something I was directly involved in be allowed to go ahead.

We set off for County Limerick. In the back of the car we had an inflatable rubber dinghy and an outboard motor, both stolen. We were driven by a man from

South Kerry to a little village in west Limerick called Ballyhahill.

Cars used in armed robberies right across the Irish Republic were often stolen in Kerry and looked after by a sympathizer in Ballyhahill. One such car had recently been delivered there but when we arrived we discovered that an IRA unit from Limerick City had moved it earlier that same evening. As a result we decided to steal a car in Ballyhahill and drive on to Waterford, where we were to meet up with Currie. We eventually found a car and transferred the dinghy and outboard motor to it. It was now very late at night and we were driving in a stolen car without replacement numberplates. At this stage I had had no sleep for almost forty-eight hours, since before the interrogation of the Corkman, and I was very tired.

We reached Waterford City after one in the morning and drove straight to a flat owned by Raymond Cody, a local IRA man and former British soldier. Everything was chaotic; Currie had even failed to get the weapons. Cody said that he could borrow a sawn-off shotgun from some Irish National Liberation Army people he knew.

In preparation for the day ahead I lay down on the floor and went to sleep. All my life I have been able to sleep soundly in almost any circumstances. Irrespective of how tense the situation was, once I put my head down I was usually asleep almost immediately. If the thing was on, it was on: if it wasn't, it wasn't. At this stage I couldn't have cared less. When I woke up in the morning Cody and Currie were there complete with a sawn-off shotgun that didn't actually work, which suited me fine.

Ferris, Currie and I got in the car. Ferris drove. We knew that we were breaking every rule in the book by driving a stolen car without a change of numberplates. Undoubtedly the car was reported stolen; all it needed was one alert policeman and we were in trouble. We drove to the bank of the Suire, where we left the dinghy and the outboard motor, and then on to the leather factory, which was set in an old estate surrounded by high walls. We parked at the rear of the factory on a quiet road. Ferris and I knew that Currie was always nervous when something was about to happen and we kept winding him up, knowing also that he could be generally relied upon not to panic. Currie and I got out of the car, climbed over the wall and hid in some bushes not far from the wall. From there we had a clear view of the pathway along which the wages clerks would walk as they brought the money from the offices to the factory. We knew they were due to come any minute now. We had to crouch down in the bushes so that no one could see us.

When we saw the two wages clerks walking by we rushed out and confronted them. They handed over the money straight away, even though in the process some of the notes were scattered on the ground and we had to scramble around collecting them, which delayed us. One of the clerks was very nervous and I had to keep re-assuring him that he would not be harmed. When everything is happening so quickly there is no time to be conscious of nerves or tension and at times like these I have always felt at my calmest.

We ran back to the wall and climbed over; Currie was already breathless and had difficulty getting over. Ferris was almost a nervous wreck by the time we reached the car. Drivers in these situations have the worst job. You don't know what's happening; you just have to wait and wait. Minutes can seem like hours. Ferris drove off and and I busied myself by calling Currie 'a fat bastard'. He in turn was close to throwing up because he was so unfit. Ferris drove for several miles while we made fun of Currie's discomfort. We parked the car then walked across a short patch of swampy ground to where we had left the dinghy. Crossing the river was the only way to get out of the area without going back through Waterford City, which would have been madness. Ferris was far and away the most knowledgeable about boats and he took charge. He started the outboard engine and we piled into the boat, Currie almost capsizing it. Halfway across the river the motor cut out and it took several minutes for Ferris to get it restarted.

On the other side of the river we had to cross some boggy land until we reached a little road where a car driven by a local IRA woman from Waterford was waiting for us. We got into the car and drove for a couple of miles until we came to another car parked off a narrow road. We were all wearing boiler suits and hoods which we now took off and packed in a bag along with the money. Currie got out of the car, taking the bag with him. He had already prepared a dump in the area and would leave the bag there until it could be safely collected.

The plan was that the woman would drive Ferris and me to Kilkenny, where we would catch a train to Dublin. It was intended that that night, assisted by the brother of a well-known Dublin Sinn Fein figure, we would carry out another robbery.

However, for all our planning we had forgotten that the railway station lay on the far side of a bridge, over which travelled all traffic coming from our direction. Sure enough there was a police roadblock on the bridge. We were in a long line of traffic and decided to get out of the car and cross over the bridge on foot. I was first out. As luck would have it, an off-duty policeman out shopping was walking by. He was still wearing his policeman's trousers, which I spotted immediately. As I turned to whisper to Ferris the policeman, who had walked on a step or two, asked us to hold. We could certainly have escaped, as the young policeman was rather nervous and unsure of what to do.

I could see that the woman's car had already been waved through the Garda roadblock. By now, attracted by signals from the young policeman, a couple more policemen on the roadblock had come down. We quickly found ourselves in the back of a police car heading for the nearest police station in Kilkenny. Even though we had been wearing boiler suits, my clothes in particular were soaked.

We were searched and put in separate cells after being informed that we were being held under the usual mechanism: section 30 of the Offences against the State Act 1939. Our clothes were taken from us and taken for forensic examination to see if fibres from them could be connected to fibres from the seats in the stolen car.

I decided to take a chance when the local detective inspector in charge of the investigation – who had just seen Ferris – came into my cell on his own. I told him that I needed to make a telephone call and that it would be in everyone's interest if he allowed me to do so with only him present and aware of it. Something in my manner must have got through to him. 'I'll be back in a while,' he said. After he left I was brought up for questioning by a couple of local detectives. They were a bit confrontational but no more than I was used to by now.

Later that evening the detective inspector returned and let me out of the cell. I followed him to an office where he closed the door, and, pointing to the phone, said, 'This had better be good.' I phoned my Garda contact at home; even before the phone was answered the detective inspector said, 'You've done that before.'

When the garda answered I explained the situation. It

turned out he was already aware that I was under arrest. He told me that he had been in contact with 'Dublin' and to say nothing more: everything was under control. I told him that the detective inspector was with me and he asked me to pass the phone to him. There was a short conversation consisting of 'yes' and 'no' answers on the part of the detective inspector. When he put the phone down he said, 'We're not going to recover the money, are we?' 'No,' I replied. He just grunted and took me back to the cell.

The following day, Saturday, a team of detectives regarded as specialist interrogators came from Dublin. I knew some of them because they had questioned me on previous occasions and even though they persisted for a long time it was all rather halfhearted: they did not expect to get an admission of guilt. The local detectives from Waterford and Kilkenny were much more aggressive.

Ferris and I were released at about lunchtime on Sunday, with much black humour all round. The Dublin-based detectives lined up near the door and began to sing 'Michael, row the boat ashore' and there was much talk of 'Be careful how ye spend the money' and 'We'll see you again, no doubt.' 'Cheerio now,' we said, 'and thanks for the new clothes.'

Ferris and I were both chewed out a little by Pat Doherty for doing the robbery ourselves; we were supposed to plan and delegate rather than actually take a direct part. Doherty, who had little or no experience of direct involvement in IRA operations himself, thought it extremely foolish when there was plenty of cannon fodder available to do the dirty work. If memory serves me correctly, we had stolen just under £30,000.

12

In November 1982 Kevin McKenna, who was in charge of Northern Command and as such 'oversaw' the England department for the Army Council, asked me if I was interested in going to England on active service. I said yes without hesitation. Shortly afterwards I had a meeting with Mick Hayes in the Red Lion pub in Cornmarket in Dublin, and we decided that, because of the need to keep a low profile when engaged in such high-risk operations, I would drop out of Southern Command. Pat Doherty was to be informed by McKenna that I would give the impression of no longer being too active. I told Ferris what was happening: it would have been impossible to carry it off otherwise.

As a result, in the early part of 1983 I saw much less of Ferris and Currie and gave the impression of devoting my time to Sinn Fein rather than to IRA activities. Between January and March I had a series of meetings in Dublin with different members of the IRA's England department. Owen Coogan from Belfast, a friend of Adams's, was now the head of the department and Mick Hayes, Albert Flynn, Pat Murray and Pat Magee were also major players.

Pat Murray, originally from Glasgow but with family

connections in County Mayo, was a former member of the British Army – a brutal man who was in my opinion a classic sociopath. Murray had a long and violent record in England, on the Continent and in the Irish Republic, and was heavily involved in the wave of IRA operations in England that had followed the end of the hunger strike. A tall, strong man with reddish hair, he was nicknamed 'Pope' and had a large cross tattooed on his chest. He had all the political motivation of a typical Glasgow Celtic supporter.

Pat Magee, from Belfast, was an altogether different type of character. Small, dark and swarthy, he was essentially a loner. He too had a lot of experience, dating back to the late seventies, of operating on the British mainland. Highly intelligent and cool, but a strange, moody individual, he and Murray made an unlikely but effective team.

Hayes, although quartermaster, was best described by Pat Doherty as 'that idiot running around the country', but he was completely dedicated and would unquestioningly do as he was told by the IRA. An incurable romantic, he saw the republican movement as his family. If ever arrested by the police, he would 'communicate' with them only by singing republican songs. He may have been an idiot but he was a dangerous and ruthless one.

Albert Flynn was essentially Hayes's sidekick. Studious and careful, he said little and acted in different capacities, often fulfilling the job of recruitment officer.

At about that time I also had a meeting with Martin McGuinness. I had recently been introduced to a businessman who had an import/export firm and business dealings in Libya, from where he imported large rolls of black plastic, used for silage covering, in which it appeared possible to hide weapons or explosives. I explained the situation to McGuinness, who appeared very interested. He arranged for me to meet a man at a pub near Dublin, in Naas, County Kildare, whom he described as quite elderly, in his late sixties; the man would be in the company of a woman his own age. When I went into the bar it was quiet and there was only one elderly couple sitting in a corner. I approached and it was clear they were expecting me.

I filled him in on the circumstances and he listened carefully but said very little. He told me that he was shortly going into hospital for an operation but that he would be in touch as soon as possible. As normal, I informed the Garda of this. Though I never heard from that man again, it is entirely possible that this inform-ation formed a part of an already existing conduit between Libya and the IRA.

Ivor Bell, Gerry Adams's old friend, had been appointed Chief of Staff – a position he had wanted to hold for many years. Bell was a veteran of the 1950s IRA and had been interned during that period. He was a Marxist and had been very close to Brian Keenan, now of course in jail in England.

Even though Owen Coogan was the man in charge of the IRA's England department and attended GHQ meet-ings in that capacity, the department was so important to the IRA that both the OC of Northern Command and the IRA Chief of Staff kept a very close watch on it. My Garda contact was delighted that I had penetrated right to the heart of the IRA's most prestigious and secretive division.

The department was organized in Dublin out of Ballymun, a large corporation estate of ugly low tower-blocks with a population of about sixty thousand people. Magee and Murray both lived there, and Coogan often stayed in different houses and flats on the estate.

In some ways Ballymun was an ideal place to operate from: it was large, populous and anonymous. Except thanks to me, of course, the gardai were now aware of its role and a specialist surveillance team based in Harcourt Street Garda station was now devoting most of its resources to monitoring Coogan, Murray and Hayes. I had also been able to give names and addresses of other houses and flats in the area that were being used as safe houses.

A pub on the edge of Ballymun was a favourite meeting place. Opposite the pub was a park in which Coogan met me on a number of occasions. It was clearly a place he used regularly.

On the surface the early months of 1983 were very quiet. Michael Browne – the boat owner from Fenit – was now working with the IRA's arms-smuggling team based in Europe and made several trips to the Continent to meet the people involved in that network. The IRA had acquired from Middle Eastern sources weapons and explosives valued at just over £2 million. Currently this material was hidden near Milan in northern Italy, but the plan was to move the gear to Le Havre, from where Browne and his boat would then ship it to Ireland. Browne kept me informed of all that was going on there and I in turn told the Garda.

Ferris and Currie were still responsible for Kerry, Cork and Waterford and both were attending Southern Command meetings. I was extremely close to the decision-making process. Not only did they trust me, they both relied heavily on my judgement and would do almost nothing before they consulted with me. Ferris certainly regarded me as his closest friend in the IRA and there were times when we were constantly together. We were regarded by both the IRA and the police as a team, policemen routinely referring to us as the 'terrible twins'.

191

Even though I was now working exclusively for the England department I was very well aware of much that was going on in the republican movement at different levels.

In February/March 1983 the IRA put together a plan to flood the Irish Republic with forged English £20 notes. The notes had been bought from English criminals and were of good quality. It was hoped that co-ordinated groups of IRA volunteers would successfully get rid of £5 million worth of notes in one weekend, changing them in pubs, bookmakers, hotels, and so on. Though for an operation of this nature the IRA could enlist perhaps 200 volunteers and sympathizers, I still thought that the target of £5 million in a weekend was impossible; even half that would be extremely difficult. But not everybody was happy with the plan. In a republican area like Tralee such an operation would inevitably hit some business people who were sympathetic to the 'cause'. If it became known that the plot was the work of the IRA – which it almost certainly would – their judgement would not be favourable.

In the event the scheme never really got off the ground. The evening before the plan was due to take effect, a Garda raid in Dublin uncovered £10,000-worth of notes. I was in Dublin when this happened. Mick Hayes brought a man I didn't know to the house I was in. He asked me what I knew about the counterfeit money plan and I told him. He was clearly horrified and said that he was going immediately to see Ivor Bell to protest about what he regarded as madness. All I know for certain about this man is that he worked for a government department. Hayes obviously regarded him as important. He also knew that I was going to England. I have no idea who he was or where he was coming from but he seemed to have some authority.

On hearing what had happened in Dublin, Ferris decided that it was too dangerous to proceed. Some areas – notably Wexford and Limerick – did in fact launder a little of the currency, but overall the operation was patchy and a number of people were arrested. Months later instructions were issued that all the remaining notes were to be destroyed. Though on this occasion the plan had failed, laundering counterfeit money was a fundraising tactic the IRA would return to on a number of occasions.

This operation did not involve me at all but I knew that it was part of a concerted drive towards large-scale fundraising. Also to that end, during this period the leadership sanctioned a number of kidnappings in the Irish Republic. Kevin McKenna had long been of the opinion that occasional kidnappings where huge ransoms could be extracted were a far more effective way of raising finance than the low-level post office and bank robberies usually undertaken by Southern Command.

Kevin Mallon – recently released from prison in Portlaoise – had had much time to think long and hard about kidnappings. It was his idea to kidnap Shergar, the Derby winner then retired to stud at Ballymany. Mallon's thinking was in some respects quite clever. Kidnapping a horse would never be viewed by the general public in Ireland as equivalent to kidnapping a person. There would be no father, mother, husband or wife tearfully begging for a loved one's release. In this Mallon was, I think, substantially correct. Even though there was a real fear that the kidnapping of Shergar would fatally damage the very valuable Irish bloodstock industry, many ordinary people in Ireland had an ambivalent attitude towards the kidnap.

Mallon successfully sold his idea to McKenna. Ivor Bell was also keen. Mallon was given permission to recruit a team from Southern Command to carry out the kidnap. Among them were Gerry Fitzgerald and a handful of Dublin-based volunteers who were no longer involved in Southern Command but who were working for Mallon on 'special projects'. I did not know the nature of those 'special projects'; nor did anyone in my orbit with the exception of Pat Doherty, who was a member of the Army Council.

Bobby McNamara, who had been in jail with Mallon, was asked to find out details about the stud at Ballymany. I remember his making some remark to me about Shergar's trainer when I met him in Dublin early that year. I knew that McNamara was in Dublin to see Mallon and wondered briefly what interest they could have in the trainer.

On 8 February 1983 Shergar was kidnapped from Ballymany by an armed IRA gang that included Gerry Fitzgerald, Paul Stewart from Belfast, Rab Butler and Nicky Keogh. Shergar was loaded into a horsebox and driven off towards north County Leitrim. Things started to go wrong almost immediately. To handle Shergar, the IRA recruited a man who had once 'worked with horses'. Working with horses is one thing: dealing with a thoroughbred stallion, which can be a difficult, highly strung creature at the best of times, is another story altogether. The horse threw itself into a frenzy in the horsebox, damaging a leg and proving impossible for the team to control. He was killed within days, even though the IRA kept up the pretence that he was alive and demanded a £5 million ransom for his safe return.

Shergar was owned by a syndicate of forty, the Aga Khan being the largest shareholder. If Mallon had had any insight into the mindset of the Aga Khan, he wouldn't have bothered kidnapping Shergar. On being informed that Shergar had been kidnapped, the Aga Khan immediately said that he would not pay one penny for his safe return. Although under pressure from other shareholders, he refused even to discuss the matter.

I was told the bare bones of the story of the Shergar kidnapping by Gerry Fitzgerald about two weeks or so after the event. We were sitting on a bench in Dublin's Garden of Remembrance. Fitzgerald had asked to meet me; Paddy Burke, a well-known republican, had told him that he had seen me with Mick Hayes and Fitzgerald was anxious to deliver a friendly warning.

Some weeks before, while in Donegal, Fitzgerald had come across Owen Coogan talking to Sean Meehan – brother of the Belfast republican Martin Meehan. As far as Fitzgerald and many other IRA men were concerned, Sean Meehan was regarded as 'bad news'. Fitzgerald warned me that in his opinion I should have nothing to do with the England department if they were using Sean Meehan. This warning would turn out to be fully justified, though by now I was already fully committed.

Since the end of the hunger strike there had been a renewed bombing campaign on the British mainland – always very popular with republican supporters. Until now the campaign had been effective: two innocent civilians were killed in an explosion at Ebury Bridge near Chelsea Barracks on 10 October 1981; one week later Royal Marines Commandant-General Stewart Pringle lost a leg; on 26 October Ken Howarth, a bomb-disposal expert, was killed at an Oxford Street Wimpy Bar when the bomb he was attempting to defuse exploded; and in November a bomb exploded at the home of Sir Michael Havers, the Attorney-General, although no one was injured. A number of other operations were attempted, without success. But on 20 July 1982 two bombs in London killed eleven soldiers of the Household Cavalry and the Band of the Royal Marines, as well as several horses. Though it was the most spectacular result the IRA had achieved in this phase of its mainland campaign, it still wasn't enough.

All of these operations took place while Owen Coogan was in charge of the England department. Clustered around him was a group ranging from back-up people like Mick Hayes to frontline operators such as Tommy Quigley and Paul Kavanagh from Belfast, John Downey from Clare, and Murray and Magee.

My purpose in going to England in 1983 was twofold. First, I was to plant sixteen bombs on English beaches. The plan was borrowed from the Basque terrorist group ETA, which had tried a similar tactic, bringing havoc to the Spanish tourist industry. The links between ETA and the IRA run deep; the two organizations have often co-operated and pooled ideas, technology and training. As far back as 1972, ETA supplied the IRA with weapons. The accounts of what was supplied differ but not the fact of it. Just before I rejoined the IRA in 1979, ETA terrorists came to Ireland for training in the use of the Provisionals' homemade mortars.

Basques and republicans shared an enthusiasm for Celtic culture and the old leadership of O'Connaill and O'Bradaigh had long held to the idea of a pan-Celtic federation of Scots, Welsh, Irish, Bretons and Basques. It was a notion as bizarre as the IRA's refusal to recognize the legitimacy of the Irish Republic. After the hunger strikes of 1981, contact between ETA and republicans increased considerably, particularly on a political level. ETA supporters regularly visited Ireland for tours, speaking engagements, conferences, and so on, and republicans did likewise in the Basque country.

The beach bombs I was to plant were small – one and a half pounds of Frangex (a gelignite-type explosive used mainly for quarrying) and a timer, all contained in a plastic lunchbox. They would be staggered to explode over an extended period of time. Before the first was due to go off a warning would be given of the time and location; the warning would go on to state that all English beaches had been 'mined' and that there would be no more warnings. The bombs were to be planted on the beaches of major holiday resorts from Scarborough to Blackpool, but leaving out Wales. If it had succeeded, the plan would probably have caused death and injury: certainly it would have meant financial disaster for many of Britain's best-known holiday resorts.

The second part of the plan, however, was much more worrying, and potentially the most dangerous scheme ever devised by the Provisional IRA. On 20 July, a Royal Gala to raise money for the Prince's Trust was due to take place at the Dominion Theatre in London's Tottenham Court Road. The Prince and Princess of Wales were certain to be in attendance. Among the groups performing were Duran Duran and Dire Straits, two of the Princess's favourites. My instructions were to murder the royal couple. I was to achieve this by planting a bomb in a public toilet directly behind the royal box – behind the walltiles if possible – just as was later done in the successful bombing of the Conservative Party Conference in Brighton the following year. It was a brilliant and horrific plan. The IRA leadership was still desperate to strike at the heart of the British Establishment in revenge for the death of the hunger strikers. If Charles and Diana had been murdered by the IRA, Anglo-Irish relations would sink to a new low. The fall-out for the Irish community, particularly in London, can only be guessed at, something the IRA leadership would have regarded as a bonus. Men like Ivor Bell and Kevin McKenna had little appreciation of the political implications of such an act. They just wanted to push the issue of Northern Ireland to the top of British politics and get even.

I would travel to England using false papers. Once I had established a base, Hayes would deliver to the coach driver in Kerry fifty pounds of Frangex and seventeen long-delay timers, which had a capacity for a thirty-two-day-delay system. The driver would put the consignment in the luggage compartment. The package would carry no name, no forwarding address. The coach travelled from Tralee every Friday, finally stopping at a hotel in Highgate the next day. There the driver would hand the material over to me.

One day in April I travelled to Dublin by train with Martin Ferris. He was on his way to a Southern Command meeting and I was on my way to see Hayes and Coogan. At this stage the gardai were getting very jittery about the prospect of my actually going to England. It was obvious they had little trust in Scotland Yard's Special Branch or the anti-terrorist section based there, and it would be difficult for the gardai to keep control of the situation once I was in England. How far could they allow the situation to develop before notifying the British authorities? These questions were worrying the two senior Garda officers based at Dublin Castle who were aware of my situation.

My Garda contact and I decided that at this stage the sensible thing to do was to find a way of aborting the plan before I left Ireland. On the day Ferris and I travelled to Dublin the Garda surveillance unit based at Harcourt Street station was ready. Ferris and I were followed from the station. We walked to a little café off O'Connell Street, where we had something to eat, and then split up – Ferris to go to the Southern Command meeting and me to meet Mick Hayes in the Red Lion pub in Cornmarket. The plan was for the Garda surveillance team to follow Ferris to the Southern Command meeting and with luck find some incriminating material there and charge and convict everyone present of IRA membership. With the entire Southern Command staff, at least one member of the Army Council and several members of GHQ removed at one go, it would then have been impossible for the IRA to have allowed me to go to England.

Because I was aware that we were being followed, it was fairly easy to spot the people from the surveillance unit. Ferris, however, noticed nothing unusual. I was on edge because Ferris is very sharp, and I couldn't help feeling that the surveillance team were just a little too obvious. I was glad when we split up. I took a taxi to the Red Lion where Hayes was already waiting. As we left the pub I noticed that a man dressed as a down-and-out had picked up the tail. I was really worried; if Hayes realized we were being followed he might become suspicious. He had the sort of mind that made all kinds of unconnected leaps, and he saw informers around every corner. To preserve my safety it had been necessary to tell the surveillance unit to follow us both. But now I had to shake him off without Hayes becoming aware of it.

Cornmarket was quiet, with few people on the streets. I was worried that Hayes might have noticed the 'tramp'. So was the tramp, because he was staying quite a way back. As we turned a corner a taxi drove past. We jumped in. The last I saw of the tramp was him standing on the street, looking bemused, to see where we had gone. Though with my experience you have to limit the danger of exposure by covering every possibility, luck is a vital element. Hayes and I then travelled to Ballymun to meet Coogan. We discussed the plan at some length and I stayed in a house there that night, having arranged to meet Hayes the following morning to go over some details. After leaving me, Ferris linked up with Pat Doherty and they went to a flat on Drumcondra Road, rented by a 'runner' from South Derry and general messenger for Doherty.

Later that evening, as the entire IRA's Southern Command sat discussing business, the Irish Special Branch raided the building. Heavily armed police broke down the front door and charged up the stairs, banging on the door to the room before eventually smashing their way in. It doesn't appear to have occurred to them that keys would have been useful and even if they'd been unable to find keys at such short notice they could at least have entered quietly before smashing their way into the room. In the event, the people at the meeting had time to burn any incriminating papers. Although everybody at the meeting was arrested and later charged with IRA membership, it was clear that without some corroborating evidence they would walk free. With the exception of Doherty and Dickie O'Neill from Belfast, a former England operator now in charge of the Dublin IRA, who did not apply, all were immediately granted bail – a sure sign that the State had little expectation of conviction.

The bungling of that particular plan meant that it was now almost impossible for me to avoid going to England. To attempt another ruse to avoid it would be simply too dangerous in the circumstances.

Around the middle of May everything was finally in place for my trip to England. My Garda contact told me that Pat Murray and Pat Magee were in the Preston/Blackpool area and were under surveillance by the English police, and under no circumstances was I to link up with them. It was later revealed that they had planned to blow up an army barracks in Blackpool but realized they were being followed, managed to escape and made their way back to Ireland. One local man in Blackpool was charged with conspiracy to cause explosions.

I travelled first to Dublin, driven by my Garda contact. I had got on the Dublin train in Killarney, about twenty miles from Tralee, but had got off at Mallow in County Cork to meet him and we drove to Dublin all the while going through the options and pitfalls. 'This is the first time I have driven an IRA man who is about to kill the Prince and Princess of Wales,' he joked.

I had already supplied a wealth of information about how the England department operated. The gardai were now aware that a travel agency in Dublin was used extensively by Hayes and Coogan. They knew about Murray's and Magee's roles as well as that of Albert Flynn, and about the locations of at least six houses and flats in Dublin used extensively by the England department – known to other IRA people as the 'flat caps'. They were also aware of a sympathizer to whom Coogan had introduced me who worked as a steward on the Dun Laoghaire–Holyhead ferry and carried messages, money, passports and so on to active service units in England. In fact, thanks to me there was now little that the Garda didn't know about the England department's operations.

As we drove to Dublin I could not help but reflect on all that had happened since 1979. Now here I was in the company of a senior Garda officer being driven to meet Owen Coogan on the way to carrying out the most spectacular IRA operation to date. 'If they only knew,' I thought to myself. 'If they only knew.'

Once in Dublin I got out of the car at the bottom of Griffith Avenue and walked to a local pub to meet Hayes, having arranged that I would keep in near-daily contact with the Garda. He and I left after a few minutes and went to a house in Ballymun, where Coogan was waiting. Hayes left and Coogan gave me a false passport with a photograph I had taken some time previously and a stolen Irish driving licence in the name of Patrick O'Sullivan, of Patrickswell in County Limerick. He also gave me £2,000 in sterling and a photograph of a man who worked as a ship steward on the ferry from Dover to Calais. This man lived at an address in Priory Road, Dover. If I got into real trouble I could go to him, show him the photograph and he would, apparently, be able to get me out of the country.

I also had a name and phone number of the travel agency. Coogan told me that the man there could get a message to him or Hayes very quickly using an elementary code. Because it was a travel agency it was possible to say things like: 'I want to know if there is a three o'clock flight to Paris on a Thursday,' indicating that I needed to speak to Coogan at three o'clock on the Thursday. It was simple and it worked.

That night I stayed in Pat Murray's house in Ballymun, a ludicrously slack arrangement bearing in mind that at that stage Murray and Magee were on the run from the British police. Coogan, of course, had no inkling that I knew that Murray and Magee were in England.

That evening I met the woman who would travel to England with me. She was a small, thin woman in her late twenties with shoulder-length dark hair. I would cross with her and her two children – one little more than a baby and the other a youngster of five or six. We would to all intents and purposes have the appearance of an ordinary couple travelling to Leeds to visit relatives.

13

The following day, a Friday, my 'wife and family' and I got up early and took the train to Rosslare in County Wexford from where we would catch a ferry to Fishguard in Wales. We had a few hours to wait before catching the late sailing. As we neared the ferry I was horrified to see parked a coach from the company in Tralee where the IRA sympathizer worked, and by bad luck the driver was indeed the sympathizer. This left me with a problem. It was quite possible that there were people from Tralee on the coach and that they might recognize me. I phoned the travel agency and spoke to Coogan within the hour. I explained the situation and asked for advice. 'Up to you,' he said. 'You're on your own now, the decision is yours.'

In one sense phoning Coogan was useful for me. If I were to travel alongside the coach passengers, I would always be able to claim subsequently that someone from the coach had recognized me and had talked about it. I put the thought to the back of my mind, knowing that it might yet be used to my advantage.

The crossing was uneventful. We had booked a berth and we stayed out of the way. It was about one o'clock in the morning when we docked at Fishguard. I had to fill in an 'anti-terrorist' form, routine for Irish people travelling to Britain, under the bored eyes of two Special Branch officers. That completed, we walked to a large pub which had a special licence to cater for late-night boat passengers. I was worried that the coach passengers might go to the pub as well but there was no sign of them; they had obviously travelled straight on to London. We had something to eat and tried to be as unobtrusive as possible, avoiding conversation with people or doing or saying anything that would give anyone reason to remember us. We had to forget the implications of who we were and what we were doing, and be that very ordinary Irish family on our way on a routine journey. There was always a possibility that Special Branch had someone in the pub weighing up the passengers. If not, the owners of the pub would certainly have had regular visits from them and would co-operate when asked.

Early that morning we took a bus to Carmarthen and booked into a guesthouse. Later the young woman and her two children returned to Ireland by a different route. She wasn't the brightest by any means but she did what she was asked to do without fuss or bother, in many ways typical of the low-level operator who was content to follow orders and ask no questions. Her lack of curiosity and her willingness to use her children made her very useful for the England department.

I was on my own now. I headed for Liverpool, a city I had only been to once before. The man who worked on the Dublin–Liverpool boat and to whom Coogan had introduced me would meet me there in a couple of days.

Once in Liverpool I booked into the Central Hotel, not far from Lime Street railway station. I phoned my Garda contact to let him know that everything was proceeding according to plan. Over the next couple of days

I stayed in my hotel room as much as possible, going out only for newspapers or something to eat. The fewer people who saw me the better. I had to wait a nerve-racking three days for Coogan's messenger to show. It had been arranged before I left Ireland that we would meet in front of the YMCA, a short walk from the hotel. I was to go there each day at 3 p.m. until he showed. I didn't want to be standing in front of the YMCA for longer than about fifteen minutes at any one time.

A couple of days later, as I waited outside the YMCA, I saw the messenger walking towards me. He walked past me without acknowledgement or indication that I should follow. I waited until he had gone quite a way up the street and then followed. He walked towards a shopping centre where he went into WH Smith's and began to browse through some books. I walked up beside him and did the same. He was extremely nervous; there was always a possibility that he had been followed. He told me that the equipment would be at the hotel in Highgate, North London, on Saturday week at three o'clock. As soon as he delivered his message he turned and walked away without another word. I looked through some books for perhaps thirty minutes more and then left. I walked around for a while to check if I was being followed. Anti-surveillance is not an exact science and I tend to rely on my instincts rather than on specific techniques. Once I was reasonably satisfied, I returned to the hotel and phoned the garda to let him know. The following day I travelled to London and booked into the Russell Court Hotel.

Around nine the following morning I went to the Dominion Theatre on Tottenham Court Road. Some science fiction film like *Return of the Jedi* was playing, as I remember. The cleaners were at work and I simply walked in through the open door. It really was as simple as that. No one took a single bit of notice of me. Checking out the theatre like this was the perfect opportunity: if I was stopped I would simply say that the doors were open and I didn't think there was any harm in looking around. I would have been told to leave, but there was no reason why my being there should be associated with a plot to kill Charles and Diana. I felt confident about my ability to talk my way out without arousing suspicion. The interior was just as Coogan had described it. I walked up the stairs to the royal box and stepped inside. It was a small, flimsy wood-constructed balcony on the left-hand side of the stage – and about fifteen feet away, separated from it by two doors, was the men's toilet. A bomb containing twenty-five pounds of Frangex would kill or injure anybody within a radius of about sixty feet. Although I had no intention of planting any such bomb I had to familiarize myself thoroughly with the layout in case of questions later. I knew that it was possible to plant the bomb, either in the toilet or in the area of the royal box itself. I knew that it was possible to kill Charles and Diana and that were I to do so many other people would die too.

I left the theatre, walking past a cleaner at the bottom of the stairs. She didn't even glance at me. I spent most of the rest of the day in Hyde Park, trying to think ahead and work out a way of aborting the plan without leaving myself open to suspicion. The weather was very warm and it was pleasant lying on the grass in the warm sun.

I was going to have to talk face to face with my Garda contact soon. The telephone could only be used to keep him up to date – our conversations were inevitably fairly cryptic and short. After some effort I persuaded him that he was simply going to have to come to England and meet me. But first he had to get clearance from his superiors.

I travelled back to Liverpool and the following Tuesday evening the Garda contact flew from Dublin. We met at a Greek restaurant near Lime Street, not far from the Central Hotel, where I was again staying. He was travelling under a false name because his superiors had not yet notified the British of the situation and they weren't going to until they had to. He was in a delicate position and was clearly nervous. He said that Special Branch at the airport had taken more than normal interest in him. At that time it was only what a single Irishman travelling to England could expect.

Eventually he settled down and we talked. The British general election campaign was in full swing and I thought that this gave us an opportunity. Fairly consistently over the years the British press – particularly the tabloids – carried rather lurid stories about the latest IRA man believed to be at large in England planning all kinds of mayhem. The kindest thing to say about most of those stories is that they were usually related with great enthusiasm. People involved were always criminal genuises, expert bomb makers, masters of disguise, and so on.

It would not be unusual, I argued, for the tabloids to run a similar IRA scare story during the general election campaign about me. I told him that it would prove far more difficult to solve my problem once the explosives arrived in Highgate in five days' time. Even now if I was arrested by police I would find it difficult to explain the false passport and the stolen driving licence, but at least these were non-threatening. The possession of explosives and timers would be a very clear sign of intent and clearing me then would involve strings being pulled and sensibilities smoothed all over the place, with the very real possibility that the truth would leak out in time. Then he said something which greatly disturbed me and still does today: 'There's no reason why you can't go ahead with the beach bombings. The bombs are very small and you can put them in out-of-the-way parts of the beaches.' I could not believe what I was hearing. 'Are you completely out of your mind?' I asked him. 'I've no intention of planting any bombs anywhere. What happens if a child wanders near one of those bombs before it explodes?'

I really don't know whether his proposal was serious or whether it was more a question of thinking out loud. It certainly didn't solve the Charles and Diana problem. I wondered what his superiors would say if the bombs were to explode. Anyway, I was having nothing to do with it. I was convinced that my idea was the best way out and that it had to be done quickly. If a story was to be leaked to newspapers in England, Scotland Yard were the only people to do it. The plan would have to be cleared at the highest level and it was essential that only those who absolutely needed to know were made aware of the situation. We went to my hotel bedroom and talked late into the night. I had a sense that he was out of his depth. Always very confident in Ireland, he seemed unsure of himself in England, relying on me to sort out the problem. It was strange sitting with him in a hotel room in England. All our meetings in Ireland took place under cover of darkness, and most of the time we'd hardly seen each other's face. Now, for the first time, I had a sense of his body language and facial expressions. Our meeting was also a chance to catch up on much of what was happening in Ireland. Ordinarily most of our talks were hurried, but here we had a chance to sit down and discuss things properly. We were both happy with the general situation. By now I had been working with him for nearly four years and it was obvious that the IRA had no suspicions about me. He was so tense that night that I found myself having to work to relax him. Every sound made him twitch and he kept warning me about the need to be careful. I think he would have felt a degree of responsibility had anything happened to me.

We met again the following morning. It looked as if he had decided that my plan could work, but he was going to have to discuss it with his superiors. He returned to Ireland that day and I went back to London.

The next day – Wednesday – I phoned as arranged. The plan had been given the green light. Scotland Yard would call a press conference late on Thursday evening and my name and photograph would be released to the media. They would be told that I was in England to carry out an IRA assassination during the run-up to the general election. Within a day or two they would also release the name and description of John Downey – the Clareman who had been active periodically in England – which would deflect some attention from me.

I had asked my Garda contact to do one other thing: to ensure that Dublin contacted the police in Tralee to enquire about my whereabouts, asking them to check if I was now in Kerry. I knew that once the Garda started asking questions word would quickly filter back to the local IRA. At least then there was a possibility that the IRA would believe that it was the Garda who had notified British police that I was not at home. There was also the chance that I could have been seen in Dublin with Hayes or Coogan at any time in recent months. Of course, I could not be sure that they would swallow either explanation, but when it came down to it, this was my only option.

On Thursday morning I went to Victoria station and bought an inclusive train and boat ticket to Paris. I had to be out of the country before the story broke. On the train I spoke to a young woman and her mother who were from Bolton and were going to Paris for the week-end. Both were very friendly and I chatted freely with them, knowing that I would attract less attention travelling in a group than if I were alone. I had a feeling they would be useful when we got to Dover. When the train reached the port I carried some of their luggage for them to the boat. Passing through passport control with my Irish passport I was once again stopped and questioned by two detectives. The young woman returned when she realized what was happening. She was strikingly attractive and she had a bit of a good-natured go at the detectives for holding me up.

One of them handed me back the passport, smiled and wished me good luck with a knowing look, thinking the girl and I were set for a romantic weekend in Paris. The three of us travelled together to Paris, where we met a friend of theirs – a nurse based in Saudi Arabia who was holidaying in Paris for a couple of weeks. The mother, daughter and I booked into the same hotel. The following morning I went out to get the English newspapers. At a newspaper stall my heart almost stopped when I saw the *Daily Mirror*: the story was all over the front page. Somewhat comically, they had nicknamed me 'the Jackal'.

I went and phoned my Garda contact straight away. The story was also in some of the Irish papers and of course the subject was of lively debate locally. He wanted me to stay away for at least a week or two, which had been my intention all along, but there was a more pressing problem that we had not foreseen. My passport had been stamped when I left England and the date clearly proved that I had done so the day before the story appeared. If the IRA ever saw that passport I would be in big trouble, and I needed the passport to get back to Ireland. Until now I had made no attempt to contact Hayes or Coogan, and the longer I remained in Paris the more difficult it would be not to make contact. I had to get back to Ireland and destroy the passport as fast as possible.

The following day, a Saturday, I flew from Paris to Dublin. Once through controls I went to a toilet, destroyed the passport and flushed it away. I wanted to burn it but that proved impossible.

I then took a taxi to Kerry, telling the taxi driver that my grandmother had died and I was rushing for the funeral. I got him to drop me at a sympathizer's house in Castleisland, about ten miles from Tralee. I left my travel bag and French money there and he drove me to Tralee.

By now it was about seven o'clock on Saturday evening. The first person I met in Tralee was Pat Currie, who was drinking in Mac's Bar, a place frequented by local republicans. He told me that there were a number of journalists and photographers from British news-papers in town trying to follow up the story. Their interest now seemed to be focusing on my girlfriend, in part because she was English and also because they couldn't find me. She must have been suffering, but any form of contact between us was too dangerous. A local journalist with whom I was quite friendly came into the bar. He had been contacted by a number of colleagues eager for his help. He told me that in his opinion some of the journalists would not leave things alone until they had spoken to me – even though the local police had advised English journalists that their safety could not be guaranteed in certain bars in the town.

The local reporter had heard that I was around and had a journalist from the *Mail* waiting in another bar not too far away. I decided that the best thing to do was to give a short interview denying the story and poking fun at the 'Brits' and that's what I did. During the interview he asked me who I would vote for if I was in Britain and I said, 'Thatcher,' at which stage the local journalist said, 'C'mon, Sean, try to take the thing seriously.' Years later I learned that William Hucklesby – then commander of the anti-terrorist branch of Scotland Yard and the man who named me – was not happy that I had reappeared so soon. It certainly made him look foolish, but there was nothing else I could have done to protect myself.

For a couple of weeks I kept my head down and made no attempt to contact anyone, although I knew that the operation must have been giving senior levels of the IRA grave cause for concern. It turned out that Pat Doherty was in Kerry to see Ferris. I went to the meeting and asked Doherty to pass on a message to Coogan, giving a telephone number and a time when I would be there.

I couldn't tell anything about the level of internal investigation from Doherty's attitude towards me. He knew I was working with the England department, and would have known about the plot to kill Charles and Diana, but he would not necessarily have been aware that I was the person asked to carry it out. He was a little cool, but since he was never the warmest of people it was difficult to judge. It was a dangerous period for me. Men like Ivor Bell and Kevin McKenna weren't much given to fairy stories and it was difficult to know if they had been taken in.

That June I travelled to Dublin for the annual Bodenstown commemoration for Wolfe Tone and whilst there went to Joe Cahill and gave him the money left over from the England operation, asking him to return it to Coogan. One evening, in a republican drinking club, I was approached by the wife of a Belfast republican and friend of Hayes. She told me to go outside, where a man was waiting on a motorbike. He was to drive me to a city-centre pub to meet Hayes. Once I saw the bike I was nervous. I don't know why. Irrationally, I really did not want to get on that bike. For some reason I had a bad feeling about what would happen next. I didn't know where I was going. I didn't know who was driving the bike and at that stage I had no idea what the IRA really thought about me. There was no time for considered evaluation: did I get on the bike or run for it? I remember thinking as I got on the bike that I had made a fatal error and had to restrain the urge to jump off. Strangely, once we began to move, the fear lessened considerably and I felt much more in control.

We parked near the rear entrance to the pub. The rider led the way, up some stairs to a separate bar and there was Hayes sitting in a corner. I sat down beside him with some relief – had my real role been uncovered we would not be having this meeting in a public bar, surrounded by other drinkers. He still had some questions. 'Who in Kerry knew or suspected about the Dominion Theatre?' They were questions I could handle confidently. We spoke for an hour or so and there seemed to be no suspicion in Hayes's mind. Not that the danger was over yet. This was just the first interrogation; within days Coogan too would be looking for a meeting.

The fact that my photograph had appeared in the papers was a cause for some concern and had ramifications for the rest of the organization. Some of the safe houses Hayes and Coogan used in Dublin had had no idea that they were involved in the England department. The sympathizers obviously knew that they were helping the IRA but not which specific section. Since I had stayed in those houses this was no longer the case. Hayes would have to find new houses and he wasn't too happy about it.

We made arrangements for me to see Coogan in a few

days. Knowing how the IRA operated and also that Hayes was not important at leadership level, I knew that I wasn't yet in the clear.

A couple of days later I met Coogan in the park opposite a pub in Ballymun. He was in an upbeat mood and told me there had been a heated argument at a GHQ meeting when the subject of my aborted campaign came up. Ivor Bell was instinctively suspicious but McKenna and Coogan had backed me wholeheartedly – especially, apparently, McKenna. This did not really surprise me. As far as he was concerned, it had been his operation and he wouldn't want to be seen as incompetent. What he thought privately was another matter. He trusted me more than most but he almost never said anything that he shouldn't. I knew that in his heart McKenna trusted no one and would readily believe his mother could be an informer.

If anything, surprisingly, the incident upgraded my profile. Most people were impressed that I had managed to escape and had done so without contacting and possibly compromising anyone else. Coogan asked me if I was prepared to return to England and I said I would. He also urged me to try to get the local police used to the fact that I was sometimes away for periods of time. It was strange that he didn't know this was already the case. The England department was often so isolated from the rest of the IRA and so arrogant that they had little concept of how things worked in the mainstream.

Several times following this I bumped into Magee and Murray in Dublin. Pat Murray really was a head case. He once headbutted a woman because she failed to step aside quickly enough for him. On one occasion I was in their company after both of them had been drinking heavily. Margaret Thatcher's name was mentioned. While they had been in Blackpool attempting and failing to blow up the army barracks they had become aware that the Conservative Party Conference was due to take place there. After that fiasco in Blackpool further operations there that year were out of the question, but Murray said, 'You always know one place where Thatcher has to be at the same time every year. That's the place to get her.' The following year the Grand Hotel in Brighton was ripped apart by an IRA bomb. Five people were killed and the prime minister was lucky to escape with her life.

14

While I was immersed in the England department an increasingly bitter power struggle was being played out between the younger northern radicals, represented by men like Gerry Adams, Martin McGuinness, Danny Morrison, Ivor Bell and Pat Doherty, and the old traditionalist southerners led by Ruairi O'Bradaigh and Daithi O'Connaill.

In the general election in June 1983 Adams was elected MP for West Belfast. In line with republican policy, he refused to take his seat at Westminster, but his election was a huge propaganda boost and cemented his position as the leading republican figure of his generation.

One of the major problems faced by Adams, Bell and McGuinness was that the IRA Executive – a twelve-person body elected at the last IRA convention in 1970 – was split evenly between those loyal to the Adams and those loyal to the O'Bradaigh faction. The traditionalists might no longer have been representative of the movement as a whole – certainly not in areas like West Belfast and Derry – but they could be replaced only by calling a new IRA convention and electing an Executive.

The Executive was a constant thorn in the side of the

leadership and there were whole areas of policy in which it could not move without the Executive's agreement. The drain on IRA funds needed to pay for Sinn Fein's increased political role – and bungled attempts at raising money, not least the failure of the Shergar kidnapping – meant that money was still a major problem. There was muttering on the ground – much of it quietly inspired by O'Bradaigh and company – that too much IRA money was being diverted into politics, which inevitably restricted the IRA's operational capacity.

Once again the IRA turned to kidnapping. By August 1983 the core of the team responsible for Shergar's kidnapping were ready, under Mallon's control and direction, to try again. I had kept the gardai informed that the team taken from Southern Command for 'special operations' still existed. None of them had returned to normal duties and that could only mean another operation to raise huge funds – almost certainly another kidnapping. I also knew the team's 'fixer' in Dublin – the man who provided safe houses and back-up – and had made the Garda aware of his involvement. But I had no idea who they were targeting.

Later that month a seven-man IRA unit under the direct control of Kevin Mallon approached the luxury home of Canadian multi-millionaire Galen Weston at Roundwood in County Wicklow. Weston's multi-national business chain included holdings in Britain and Ireland, Fortnum & Mason and the supermarket chain Quinnsworth amongst them.

The operation was to fail miserably. Due to intensive surveillance of the team members and a phone tap on the 'base' provided by the Dublin 'fixer', the Garda were ready and waiting. When called upon to surrender, some of the unit opened fire and there was a wild gun-battle during which Mallon and a close associate of his escaped. Five of the would-be kidnappers were captured: Gerry Fitzgerald, Paul Stewart and Rab Butler – all on the run from Northern Ireland and based in Dublin – Nicky Keogh, a native Dubliner, and Peter Lynch, from South Derry.

Galen Weston hadn't been at home at the time of the attempted kidnapping, but every effort had been made to ensure that the gang believed he was. He had in fact been in England playing polo with Prince Charles.

Once again the IRA's attempts to raise large amounts of cash had ended in disaster. Mallon's credibility was coming under strain and if it had not been for a subsequent event in Belfast, on 9 September, he would not have survived for one more try. On that day, acting on information from a new supergrass, Robert Lean, the RUC arrested twenty-eight people in Belfast. Among those arrested was Ivor Bell, Adams's main ally and Chief of Staff of the IRA. Once Bell was arrested Kevin McKenna once again became Chief of Staff and he at least, in spite of Mallon's previous form, still had faith in the latter's ability to deliver.

Bell and the others were in custody for just over a month, until Robert Lean 'escaped' from the top-security Palace Barracks in Hollywood, County Down, where he was being protected by the RUC after being given immunity from prosecution. Under pressure from his family, he had decided to retract his evidence and one night, when his minder had conveniently fallen asleep, Lean took the car keys and drove out of the base without being questioned. He drove straight to West Belfast and placed himself at the mercy of the IRA. Because he had already been offered an IRA amnesty for retracting his evidence, Lean knew that the IRA would not kill him. To do so would fatally undermine the best strategy they had for dealing with the supergrass system. Lean publicly withdrew his evidence at a hastily arranged Sinn Fein press conference and was promptly rearrested by the RUC who discovered, because he had been given immunity, that they could not now charge him with anything. But the damage was already done: the fallout from Bell's arrest and his removal as Chief of Staff would later cause him to create serious problems for the IRA.

The bungled kidnap attempt had lost Mallon his special operations team. His lack of knowledge of IRA personnel in Southern Command led him to turn to Pat Currie, with whom he had been in jail. Even though he was still a frequent visitor to Kerry, Currie was now mostly based in Dublin.

Southern Command had been reorganized in June of that year. Martin Ferris and Dickie O'Neill were now joint adjutants, Dickie taking particular responsibility for Dublin, where the IRA had previously failed to take advantage of the financial opportunities available, and where its organization was in a shambles.

I had pushed hard for over two years for Ferris to be given a more senior role, and it was known that the Army Council was keen for Doherty to move on from Southern Command. Every time the opportunity arose I mentioned to senior republicans that Ferris was ready to take over from Doherty. After all, Ferris was popular with the grass-roots element and now that he had left his wild days behind he was much more thoughtful and would attempt to weigh up situations instead of diving in blind. For almost a year before Doherty announced it I had been sure he would be given the job. I was delighted, since it provided me with the perfect cover. Ferris trusted me implicitly and our working in different areas meant that Ferris would attend meetings that I didn't, and would brief me privately and fully on those meetings. I was asked to take responsibility for Kerry, Cork and

Waterford and to be jointly responsible for IRA operations with Ferris in the Southern Command area outside Dublin.

Though Ferris had run a relatively effective operation in Kerry, he knew that he had failed miserably in Cork and Waterford and apologized for handing over an area that was largely in a mess. In Waterford there were about a dozen people who could be trusted and little in the way of support, except for a couple of tiny pockets around the Dungarven area. I knew the engineering department spent a lot of time in Waterford and obviously had reliable contacts but these were not available to Ferris or me. Cork had also been a disappointment for the IRA in this campaign. There was never the sort of support there that the IRA in Kerry had at various times enjoyed. For whatever reasons – personality clashes, poor leadership, and the fear of a local informer stronger than ever among the old hands after the fiasco of the attempted post office robbery in Togher in 1981 when the police had been lying in wait – the organization in Cork was in a poor state. When the IRA had established an inquiry to discover the truth about Togher several of the older volunteers had refused to co-operate. They had been saying for years that there was an informer inside the organization and they were fed up that it wasn't being taken seriously. Cork had a lot of potential but no one had been able to harness it. The situation was dangerous but it suited me down to the ground.

Pat Currie was placed in charge of internal security for Southern Command. Both Ferris and I had recommended him for the job; his appointment was useful to me as it meant that the person responsible for winkling out informers was someone who would, in most circumstances, do exactly as I told him and who would keep me up to date with whatever he was working on.

Once again I now attended Southern Command meetings, having taken leave of absence during the England period. Some of the personnel had changed. John McCallion, a Belfast man based in Dublin, was now quartermaster – although not a very efficient one, it has to be said. Bobby McNamara had fallen out of favour and had been replaced by the younger, more militant Kieran Dwyer, from Limerick. Recently released prisoners such as Sean Finn and Jimmy Kavanagh, from Wexford, were playing more important roles, and Jimmy Jones was also contributing more to Southern Command than he had previously. Gone were the days when people like Daithi O'Connaill pulled the strings at Southern Command level. It was now a tighter, more focused and more militant organization.

At this stage I was in receipt of huge amounts of information. I knew through Ferris most of what was going on at GHQ meetings and about security matters through Pat Currie, who was working with the former Chief of Staff, Seamus Twomey, now GHQ director of security. I had also been asked by the England department to vet potential recruits from Southern Command. From my base in Kerry I was in fact aware of many more operational details than would have been apparent to the IRA leadership. This is not to suggest, though, that the golden rule of 'need to know' did not sometimes apply, even with Ferris and Currie.

By November 1982 Mallon was ready to regroup his special operations team. Currie came to Kerry and asked me if I could supply men for another kidnapping operation. He was ambitious and saw his involvement with Mallon as a means of furthering his own career within the organization. This was Currie's big opportunity to deliver. I couldn't ask who was going to be kidnapped and he was clearly under strict instructions from Mallon not to disclose details. Everything Mallon had touched since his release had ended in failure and he knew that the next one had to work. I agreed to supply a car and teams: Michael Burke, from Cork, Hugh Hehir, from Clare, and two other men from Tralee. There were already two stolen cars garaged just outside Tralee. Currie also wanted a hired car, which he assured me would not be used in the actual operation. Once the team was assembled, they set off for a meeting place in County Offaly, none of them knowing exactly what they were being asked to do.

The operation did not go altogether to plan. Burke and one other man were in the hired car and the other two in one of the stolen cars, when they ran into a 'routine' Garda roadblock near the small village of Rathheale in County Limerick. The hired car went first and was let through, but the stolen car, in a panic, crashed the checkpoint; Hehir and the other man abandoned the car in a forest a few miles away. Hehir made his way to Limerick and the other man returned to Tralee. Burke and his accomplice continued to their meeting place in Offaly. The next day Mallon and Currie turned up in Kerry and together we found Hehir's companion and went back for the abandoned car. I thought that they were mad to do that, but it was Mallon's show. I brought a new set of numberplates and we exchanged them for the old ones. We had some difficulty getting the car out of its hiding place, as the ground was boggy and it was a job to make the tyres grip. After a lot of pushing we got it going. They headed off to Offaly with the Kerryman driving the stolen car, and I returned to Tralee. The gardai were informed of everything I knew, but it wasn't enough. I did not have the vital piece of information: the name of the target.

The following day Don Tidey, an executive in Galen

Weston's company, was kidnapped as he drove his thirteen-year-old daughter to school from their home in Rathfarnham, County Dublin. Disguised as a Garda officer, Michael Burke had flagged down Tidey's car and bundled him away before driving to a prearranged spot where a van with a new team awaited them, to transport Tidey to Leitrim. Currie was supposed to have been at the same spot in the hired car, to take the kidnappers back to Kerry. Unfortunately, at this point the operation descended into farce. Currie had in the meantime crashed the hired car, and the kidnappers were forced to go on with Tidey and the new team to Leitrim.

Currie eventually made his way back to Dublin after retracing his steps and unsuccessfully trying to burn out the crashed hired car. The man who had hired the car – Billy Kelly, an IRA sympathizer from Tralee – was obviously in trouble. Later that evening, when he heard the news of Tidey's abduction, and with no sign of the hired car returning, he called at my flat. Both the police and the car-hire firm had already been to his home, but he had managed to avoid them. I tried to calm him down by telling him that if he reported the car as stolen and refused to say anything else it would be difficult for the police to press charges. Kelly was a weak man and I did not have much faith in his ability to keep quiet. I don't believe he would have hired the car for the IRA had he known it was to be used in a kidnap.

As we left the flat we were both arrested by local police. I was held only until the morning and they hardly bothered questioning me. They were convinced, however, that Tidey was being held in Kerry. With some forethought, Mallon had deliberately chosen to use cars stolen in Kerry and to spirit Tidey off in the opposite direction, towards North Leitrim, near the border. Because Kerry was regarded as a centre of republican activity, Mallon had judged correctly that the Garda might think, at least initially, that Tidey was there. In their follow-up inquiries the Garda discovered that Mick Burke from Cork and two Tralee men – all known IRA operatives – were missing from their homes.

The subsequent Garda search was widespread, taking in the area around North Leitrim, particularly Ballinamore, which had long been an IRA stronghold. It being too dangerous to be out and about, Burke and one of the Tralee men were trapped there, though Hehir and the other Tralee man did manage to get out of the area and make their way to Dublin. That Tralee man returned to Kerry a couple of days later. From his description I knew that Tidey was being held near Ballinamore, not far, in fact, from where I had operated my bomb factory in 1974.

I immediately informed the gardai, who had already scaled down their search in that area. It took a couple of days for me to convince them, but they resumed the search and eventually found Tidey in a makeshift hide in a wood. He was released unharmed, but a young Irish soldier and a Garda officer were both shot dead in a gun-battle with the kidnappers, who escaped in the confusion. Among them was Francie McGirl, who had been acquitted of the murder of Lord Mountbatten in 1979. There were also several of the nineteen IRA prisoners who had escaped from the Maze six weeks before. Mick Burke and the other Kerryman were not there. They were several miles away in a safe house and had spent no time with Tidey. Two brothers, both of whom I knew from my days at the bomb factory in the area, were later charged and convicted for their involvement in the kidnapping.

For months before the Maze escape I had been aware that Northern Command was looking for six .25 Derringers, almost the smallest revolver imaginable. The

.25s were of little practical use, but their size made them easy to smuggle; the demand for them almost certainly heralded a planned prison escape, and a massed one at that. It was unlikely in the extreme that an escape was planned for Portlaoise prison, as its position in Southern Command area would have brought the plan to my attention. A jail escape from England was a possibility, but Northern Command, not the England department, was looking for the guns. At least one such weapon was provided by Kerry as I tried to track down the exact purpose. I was pretty sure that they were to be used in an escape from Crumlin Road jail, in Belfast, or in the Maze, as there were no other alternatives. I passed the information on to my contact, but for whatever reason it doesn't appear to have been acted on. Such plans and schemes are, of course, continually in preparation. On this occasion, of course, the price paid was the successful escape of nineteen prisoners.

After the gun-battle and Tidey's release, Mick Burke and the other Tralee man made their way back to Kerry, but it was deemed too dangerous for them to return home. I knew from the Garda that there was a witness who could identify Burke from the kidnap scene, but had to keep such information to myself.

I put Burke and the other man to work in South Kerry, training volunteers from Southern Command. Normally this would have been done by the training department, but it gave me an opportunity to monitor the quality of new recruits coming through from the South. Burke and the other man were capable training officers, the sites were available in South Kerry, and the training department was under pressure and only too glad to offload some work. I, of course, immediately passed the names and details of almost every new IRA recruit from the Republic to the Garda.

By the end of 1983 I felt that we had done well. All of the kidnappings had failed except in the case of Tidey, where in fact there was good reason to believe that a sum in the region of £2 million had already been paid over out of the country. Though I have no proof, it is also commonly believed that some large multinationals, worried about the kidnap threat in Ireland, paid money to the IRA as a form of insurance. The kidnappings, even though they were hardly a spectacular success, had frightened people. Few in the IRA or the security forces are in any doubt that money was paid. How much and by whom I do not know but from that time money appeared to be less of a problem than previously.

A year or two earlier, between late 1980 and early 1981, I had attended a meeting in an upstairs room over a bar in Bundoran, to discuss IRA finance. Among those who attended the meeting were Gerry Adams, then the adjutant-general of the IRA, Pat Doherty of Southern Command, and Tom Cahill, a brother of veteran IRA leader Joe Cahill and recently appointed IRA director of finance. Also at the meeting was Gerry Fitzgerald, then Pat Doherty's adjutant on Southern Command, and a couple of others from Northern Ireland whom I did not know.

The meeting was chaired by Gerry Adams, who baldly stated that the IRA was in serious financial difficulties. He described how it cost £2 million a year to keep the organization functioning at its present level, and that it currently fell to Belfast to provide the major part of the funds required, money raised from the IRA's interests in its many drinking clubs – some of which made over £150,000 a year – and gaming machines in West Belfast. The Falls Taxi Association's two hundred or so black taxis – London cabs imported at the height of the troubles to replace West Belfast's defunct bus service – each yielded a weekly levy of £15, which also found its way to the IRA coffers. In addition, money came from less obvious sources – extortion, tax swindles and social-security fraud.

The only other self-financing region was South Armagh, and that was because of its position on the border and the smuggling opportunities that that afforded. Almost everybody in South Armagh smuggled – since the establishment of the Irish State it had become a way of life – but the IRA were far more organized than individual operators. The local IRA dealt in everything that could be smuggled, from petrol to cattle.

By contrast, Southern Command, which in theory could provide large amounts of finance, raised barely enough to cover its own running costs. Clearly there were areas of potential that were not being exploited.

Adams explained that Tom Cahill had been taken out of an 'important position' in Belfast Brigade in order to take responsibility for putting the IRA's finances on a professional level. I was unimpressed by Tom Cahill and could not see why the IRA leadership believed that this was the man to transform IRA finances. The job demanded energy and imagination and Cahill seemed to possess little of either. But he had been around for a long time and was regarded as solid and reliable. More importantly, he was a staunch supporter of the new leadership, and control over the money was important. Adams and McGuinness were still being openly challenged by O'Bradaigh and the old leadership, and though it wasn't all-out war there was a good deal of sniping.

The meeting continued into the early evening and discussed many possible means of raising finance: everything from rock concerts to providing outlets for gaming machines; if we could find the outlets, Cahill would arrange the machines. It is doubtful if today there is a town in Ireland that does not contain a gaming machine or two providing the IRA/Sinn Fein with finance. As was so often the case, the meeting was inconclusive, but it was apparent even to me that if the IRA was to survive it needed a huge amount of money – £5–10 million – to allow it to invest and plan for the years ahead.

One thing was clear, though. After that day we were to see a slow but steady and noticeable 'professionalization' of the IRA's handling of its finances, to the point where the IRA in Northern Ireland now employs its own homegrown lawyers, accountants and computer experts. Within a couple of years of this meeting, South Armagh had stepped up its earning power and was supplying serious finance to the IRA, the proceeds of straightforward smuggling of all kinds of consumer goods as well as grain and cattle frauds involving the EEC and the smuggling of petrol and diesel to the South, where it was much more expensive. At one stage the Secretary of State for Northern Ireland was forced to issue an order forbidding petrol tankers to be driven on certain roads in South Armagh, such was the scale of IRA-controlled petrol smuggling in the area. It is a very different organization from the days when Joe Cahill kept the money in biscuit tins in sympathizers' houses.

15

With Christmas 1983 approaching, Mick Burke introduced me to an IRA sympathizer from the Munster area, who had a most remarkable story to tell.

The man was friendly with an active INLA member operating in the area. Close to or during the period of the 1981 hunger strike, the son of a prominent politician had apparently gained access to a quantity of explosives and passed them to him. I did not know what to make of this story when I first heard it. There was no proof whatsoever, and nothing to suggest, that the politician knew anything of it.

I had met the sympathizer a few times and he had always returned to this story. Because Burke was aware of it, I knew I would have to pass it on. If the story was true then the dangers were immense for the politician, and for me. I told my Garda contact about the story, but at that stage there was nothing to back it up.

If the politician's son was sympathetic enough to republican terrorists to pass on explosives, would he also pass on sensitive information to which he might have access? How much use could the IRA make of this? It was a dangerous situation and I knew that I had to keep control. I told Pat Doherty the substance of the story and said that I would try to verify it. Doherty was happy enough to leave it with me for the moment. I discussed the subject with Maurice Pendergast, and we set out to discover if there was anything in it. I introduced him to the sympathizer who had originally brought the story to my attention, and Pendergast – a shrewd and cunning character – was almost immediately convinced that the man was telling the truth. He decided to take things further.

He quickly contacted a local councillor who knew the politician and his family, and organized a meeting with the son. Pendergast collected me early on St Stephen's Day and we drove to a local hotel where we had arranged to meet. We sat and talked with the son in his bedroom. I simply told him that the IRA had a very high-ranking informer in the Irish Special Branch, who had passed on that there was an investigation going on into his relationship with the INLA, to whom some in Special Branch believed that he had supplied explosives.

It was obvious that he was an extremely worried young man and he quickly admitted that he had in fact provided them with explosives. He seemed to be very concerned about what his father would do or say. He also deeply regretted his actions. He professed to believe in a united Ireland but only one achieved by peaceful means. I cautioned him that he must never say anything to anyone and that we were trying to help him. I told him that we could keep him informed of the state of the Special Branch inquiry – which, of course, did not exist. He agreed to do this and I told him that we would meet again at the hotel in about a week's time. I kept my Garda contact informed of what we were doing at all times, as whatever else happened we couldn't allow the young man to fall under the control of the IRA, or permit the INLA to have a valuable bargaining tool.

When I next met him – without Pendergast – he was in an awful state. In spite of my instructions he had gone to a Special Branch officer who was a friend of the family and had blurted out his story. He should have known that the Special Branch man's friendship with the family would mean that he would tell his father immediately – which, of course, is what he did.

Some of the explosives supplied by the young man were used in an attack on a radio mast at Schull, in West Cork, which the INLA described as a NATO listening-post. The INLA rarely had access to explosives, and the fact that they were able to claim credit for an explosion implies that it was the same material responsible.

I could have met the son again after that, but I didn't. Indeed, the IRA never officially knew that I had met him a second time. Pendergast did, but he trusted me sufficiently to believe me that I was handling this myself for good reasons. He knew that information had been exchanged and that I wanted to keep it very tight. Doherty asked me about the situation, but I said that, although the son had handed over explosives, he was now very nervous and it was impossible to know how he would react if we tried to pressurize him. I cautioned that time was on our side, and that the information could prove useful but it had to be handled very carefully. I told the Garda contact all about this, but there seemed little else I could do. The irony of the situation was that the Garda Special Branch officer, to whom the politician's son had confided, was one of the very few Garda officers who knew about me. I often wondered what he must have thought when he realized that I was aware of all of the intricacies of the whole messy business.

It had always been the case in Ireland that in matters of politics and bombs it isn't what you do but who you know that matters. Whoever you are, information is a valuable commodity. At least in this instance if the IRA wanted to make use of what they knew, they would have to go through me, and I in turn would be able to inform the Garda. There were political dangers on both sides. If the politician found out that an attempt was made to extract sensitive information from his son, which would have ramifications for his own career, he might instigate measures that would have severe consequences for the IRA in the South. As a result, the information was effectively put into cold storage and thankfully never used.

On the broader front, the 1983 Sinn Fein ard fheis, which opened in Dublin on 11 November, saw the Adams/McGuinness faction gain its most decisive victory yet over the old guard of O'Bradaigh and O'Connaill. O'Bradaigh and O'Connaill stood down as president and deputy president of Sinn Fein respectively and several of their supporters on the National Executive followed suit. They knew that they would have lost an election. Adams's election as president went unopposed. The National Executive was now firmly under the control of the young, militant but pragmatic northerners, who would decide the future direction of Sinn Fein. O'Bradaigh and O'Connaill looked increasingly old and out of touch. Many of their principles – such as refusing to recognize the authority of the Irish government, believing the IRA to be the legitimate government – were just plain daft and were seen as such by a vast majority of people in the Republic. O'Connaill had been largely responsible for the 1971 Provisional policy of Eire Nua, a federal solution proposing four regional parliaments including a nine-county Ulster, and the old leadership had promoted this heavily over the years. Adams and company had long been opposed to Eire Nua on the grounds that it made too many allowances for unionists, and a vote at the ard fheis sounded its death knell in Sinn Fein. O'Bradaigh and O'Connaill had been consistently and comprehensively outflanked. All that remained of the old guard was the traditional Sinn Fein stance of refusing, if elected, to take seats in the Irish parliament. Adams was determined that this too would change, but it was an emotional issue for many republicans and he moved characteristically cautiously on the subject.

The Adams/McGuinness group had left nothing to chance. Even at Southern Command meetings before the annual ard fheis a list of eight names for positive candidature had been circulated by them. O'Bradaigh and O'Connaill never had a hope. They were considered past their sell-by date, middle-aged southerners who had no active record since the fifties. At a stroke the republican movement was now dominated by northern radicals who had been involved at every level since 1970.

In a few weeks, by the end of 1983, Adams and McGuinness were in complete charge of the republican movement, with the exception of the IRA Executive, a twelve-person body that acted in an advisory capacity to the Army Council. The Executive had been elected at the first convention of the Provisional IRA, in 1970, and had remained in place ever since. One of its functions was to appoint the Army Council, who in turn selected a Chief of Staff. When the 1970 Executive was elected the Provisionals were dominated by traditionalists, and its current membership reflected that. Of the twelve people on the Executive six were still loyal to O'Bradaigh. The problem for the new leadership of Adams and McGuinness was that the only way they could have an Executive more reflective of the new membership was to call a convention of representatives from every level and section of the organization. They had little to fear from such a meeting, but a man as cautious as Adams moved only when he was certain of victory. The convention would take place, but only when it suited him.

Instead Adams began to expand an idea that he and Ivor Bell in particular had begun to develop during the latter's brief tenure as Chief of Staff. The idea was to create a 'revolutionary council' – a thinktank that would encompass as many shades of republican thought as possible – which would in effect circumvent the existing traditional structures. The Army Council, where Adams and his allies held sway, was immediately interested. O'Bradaigh smelt a rat and knew instinctively that the grand scheme was to replace the existing traditional Executive and Army Council. In the short term he knew that he would be able to use the Executive to make problems or to slow down the speed of change, but ultimately he knew that he could not stop the juggernaut of the new leadership.

Adams, Bell and McGuinness were simply feeling their way. Meanwhile a new language was evolving to deal with 'armed propaganda' which is how Adams now chose to describe what was previously known as the IRA's 'armed struggle'. Questioned by a journalist about the Don Tidey kidnapping, Adams said that he would neither 'condone' nor 'condemn', and yet every senior security and political individual in these islands knew that as a member of the IRA Army Council he was one of the people who had to sanction any operation that was a departure from the norm.

The Revolutionary Council was set up in 1983. Its membership fluctuated, according to its needs. Not all of the people who attended were members of the IRA, and some were brought in just for one meeting. Sinn Fein members who were senior republicans would never – because they had no real IRA experience – end up on the

Army Council or on GHQ or even Northern Command, but the Revolutionary Council allowed them to promulgate their views – which were similar to those of Adams – at the highest levels of the IRA. The initiative allowed Adams and Ivor Bell and their allies to swamp the old guard on the Executive by demonstrating that their views were not representative of the movement as a whole.

Nineteen eighty-three was a year when the kidnappings – particularly that of Don Tidey – rebounded politically on the republican movement. Intelligence available to the IRA suggested that the Irish government was seriously contemplating the introduction of internment without trial. The IRA was convinced that it was only as a result of powerful political pressure from the British government that the Irish were persuaded to stay their hand. Presumably if the Irish had introduced internment in the Republic the pressure on the British to do the same would have been strong. The British, with their memories of their last experience in Northern Ireland in the 1970s, were petrified at the very suggestion.

That year, however, Sinn Fein faced other problems: while they were flying high in nationalist Northern Ireland, the party was a political irrelevance in the Irish Republic. The IRA Army Council devoted much of its resources and time to trying to change that.

The main stumbling block was that Sinn Fein/IRA were wedded constitutionally to the principle of abstentionism which meant that because they refused to recognize the legal or moral right of the British government to rule in Northern Ireland and since they also believed the government of the Irish Republic was an illegal assembly, in the event of being elected they would abstain from taking their seats at Westminster and Dublin.

However, almost every Irish citizen recognized

absolutely the legitimacy of the Dublin parliament. If Sinn Fein was to make any progress politically in the Irish Republic it would have to take account of the political realities. If Sinn Fein wanted an official voice there was a certain pointlessness in contesting seats in parliamentary elections and then refusing to take them. It resulted only in derisory votes and lost deposits.

Adams, McGuinness and Doherty understood this quite clearly. Indeed, Doherty made his position clear privately to me at the time and also told me that the leadership was strongly in favour of scrapping abstentionism but that they had to move carefully. Their difficulty was that IRA and Sinn Fein rules forbade, under pain of dismissal, a member even raising the subject of abstentionism for discussion. In addition, they were aware of the quite widespread feeling in the republican movement that too much emphasis on politics would inevitably lead to a reduction in the primacy of armed struggle. So even though by the end of 1983 Adams and company were riding high, they still had to be very careful. They were determined to turn the republican movement into a ruthless, pragmatic and politically astute vehicle for the establishment of a united Ireland. As Tom Hartley, the general secretary of Sinn Fein, said at the time: 'riding above all principles is the principle of winning'. But there were suspicions, not just among the old guard, that Adams was too clever by half and too inclined to play the politician. There was dissension but more importantly a vague sense of unease about where the leadership was taking the organization. By the end of 1983 Adams was pushing hard in other quarters in British politics – notably left-wing politicians Ken Livingstone, Tony Benn and Jeremy Corbyn. But this was mere window-dressing. On Saturday 16 December an IRA unit based in London bombed Harrods department store in London's Knightsbridge. The half-hour warning issued was worse than useless in an area filled with Christmas shoppers. Eight people were killed.

Such were the shock and anger both in the United Kingdom and in the Irish Republic that the IRA was reluctant to take responsibility: suggestions were leaked to the media saying that the bombing had not been authorized by the IRA leadership. These were untrue. The subsequent inquiry within the IRA – the results of which I heard from Doherty – found that specific permission had been given to bomb Harrods, which was seen as a symbol of the British establishment. However, the leadership knew that civilian casualties on that scale did not advance their cause, and privately criticized the lack of planning and foresight by the bombers.

This was not necessarily the view of every senior IRA person. At a Southern Command meeting shortly afterwards, Kieran Dwyer from Limerick suggested that he was very unhappy with the bombing, suggesting that they should have driven a lorry loaded with explosives up to the building and issued no warning, thereby 'killing a few hundred and really giving the Brits something to whine about'. Such comments were not unusual.

16

Nineteen eighty-four opened quietly for Southern Command. During 1983 the area command had been slimmed down and now comprised about twelve people, who ran the various sections. Martin Ferris was now OC of the whole region, which in turn was divided into seven geographical or command areas, each with an OC who represented it at Southern Command meetings. Pat Currie was quartermaster and finance officer. I was in charge of operations – in other words trying to make sure that there were none. All in all there were about twenty full-time people and about five hundred active volunteers or sympathizers who could help in smaller ways: in fact some of the sympathizers were more useful and active than many of the volunteers.

It is difficult to say with hindsight how much the pressure of living a double existence was getting to me. My girlfriend Louise and I got on very well, but I could share nothing of my activities with her and so the biggest part of my life remained a secret from the woman I loved. I had seen a lot of my son over the past couple of years, as he came to stay with us regularly in Tralee. He was four and growing up quickly, but I had little in the way of a personal life; everything was dominated by the IRA, and there was no escape. I was always aware that my life was constantly in danger but in some curious way I accepted that. What was worse was the fact that I could not tell my girlfriend or indeed anyone what I was really doing. On the surface I was a committed and senior republican – that is how I was known and that is what people saw when they looked at me. But I spent almost all of my time in the company of people I despised, had little or no respect for or even on occasion felt some pity for – the weak or inadequate who were always cynically used and exploited.

I had to live a constant lie, every second of the day and night. I couldn't even choose which books I read. I remember when Pat Currie, who was staying in my house, came across a book of poems by Paul Durcan, a well-known Irish poet with well-publicized anti-IRA views. 'I'm surprised at you reading that, Sean,' he said. 'Durcan's politics stink.' Poetry and literature had been important to me all of my life and now I was deprived of even them. At the time I never clearly thought out the implications of living such a life, but then I could not afford to let such realities become too intrusive.

Experienced republicans such as Kevin McKenna and Pat Doherty were not stupid and after years of experience their instincts were finely honed. One careless remark – no matter how insignificant it might have appeared – could have set alarm bells ringing. I had to be constantly disciplined whilst not appearing to be so.

Sometimes I wanted to scream in frustration – to tell Doherty or McKenna just what I thought of all their squalid machinations and their ruthless disregard for the lives of ordinary people. The world of the IRA, certainly in those days, was small, incestuous and paranoid, ever inward-looking and obsessed with conspiracies, both real and imaginary. To survive, and get the job done, I had to be that IRA man – dedicated, ruthless, always willing to obey orders and to promote the republican cause.

Gerry Adams and his supporters were slowly but surely establishing a tight control over both the IRA and Sinn Fein. Anybody whose face did not fit or who was regarded as unsound was badmouthed or simply moved aside in a very manipulative manner. Adams was preparing to take the republican movement down a much more pragmatic road and nothing was going to get in his way. Though it was now obvious that the old guard would split and form a new organization, not all of the people worried about the new direction were from the old guard.

A perfect example of this was Brian Keenan, still in jail in England but a man whose influence could be troublesome for any leadership should he choose to use it against them. It was no secret that Keenan was keen to get rid of abstentionism and build a political base in the Republic. Equally he was unhappy about the upgrading of political activity to what he perceived as the detriment of the 'armed struggle'. Ivor Bell, Adams's old friend and a member of the Army Council, was also beginning to worry. Bell thought that the IRA was directing too much of its money to Sinn Fein's electoral contests and not enough to the 'armed struggle'. But such was the scale of change that Pat Doherty, now adjutant-general, who would have been frightened out of his wits to say anything bad about Keenan were he about, was now sufficiently confident to talk openly about 'Brian's erratic decisions'.

He used the term to describe an episode in 1976 when Keenan formed a secret squad – including Mick Hayes and Pat Currie – and had them bomb hotels in the Republic and then claim the attacks on behalf of the

UFF, the intention being to heighten anti-unionist feeling in the Republic. Keenan told no one about it, and the leadership only learned the truth in the late seventies, when Mick Hayes unwillingly told Daithi O'Connaill about it in Portlaoise jail.

In March 1984 Gerry Adams and three other republicans were shot and wounded by the loyalist UFF after a court appearance in Belfast. It is a measure of how important Adams had become to the republican movement – or of how successful he had been at making himself indispensable – that, had he been killed, there would have been no one to replace him. He and he alone was responsible for instigating the changes that were bringing the IRA out into the real political world.

Even Martin McGuinness, Adams's most important ally in the reinvention of the IRA, could not have fulfilled the role, trusted though he was by hardliners in a way that the more political Adams could never be. For many militarists it was McGuinness's involvement in the new direction that clinched their support. Quite simply, if it was good enough for McGuinness it was good enough for them.

Within a couple of weeks of being shot Adams had recovered sufficiently to tour the country as Sinn Fein contested the European elections. This time agreement had been reached that if a candidate were to be elected he would take his seat in the European Parliament. It was a small step, but taken against the wishes of most of the old guard, who rightly saw it as the slippery slope towards the abandonment of their cherished principle of abstentionism.

I spent the early part of 1984 quietly monitoring a plan to smuggle in a huge shipment of weapons from America. The plan was being engineered by Ivor Bell, who had enlisted the help of Michael Browne, the skipper and owner of a fishing trawler called the *Marita Ann*. The weapons for the shipment had been put together in America by the 'Murray gang', a notorious group of Boston criminals involved in drugs, prostitution, extortion and anything else from which money could be made. Although the Murray gang were of Irish-American extraction, their interest in the operation was purely selfish. The IRA was well aware of this and had insisted the gang provide hostages, who were to remain in Dublin while the operation took place. This would ensure that if the Murrays even thought about selling out the IRA they risked two of their leaders being murdered. Apart from financial gain, the gang was aware that being able to boast about its transactions with the IRA back in Boston would greatly add to its prestige and the sense of fear it could create.

The IRA had travelled a long way from the days in the early seventies when the ultra-conservative Catholic leadership would have balked at the thought of even employing a car thief in Belfast to steal a car for use in an IRA operation.

Ivor Bell also had working for him a Belfast republican called Tony Bradley, recently released from Portlaoise prison, and Bradley made contact with me to see if I could provide large, secure dumps to store weaponry. He was looking for large, purpose-built underground bunkers. I told him that I could provide what he wanted and he told me to wait until he got back in touch. He made no mention of when or from where the arms were coming. But unknown to Tony Bradley, the skipper Michael Browne had already told me as much as he knew at that stage. Browne, in fact, had a serious drink problem and could not be relied upon to keep his mouth shut when on a binge. I became his 'minder' and during the planning of the operation he lived in our house for long periods. A lot of information was to come my way over the next few months, most importantly the sheer scale of the operation. Throughout the summer plans for what became known as the '*Marita Ann* affair' progressed. I went with Browne a couple of times to examine likely spots on the southwest coast where an arms shipment could be safely landed.

That summer generally saw a distinct absence of urgency in IRA business in the Republic. This was in part because the top-level investigation into the kidnappings, covering the security lapses, the political fallout and Mallon's planning, was still taking place inside the organization. No one was keen to come up with new proposals and operations until the kidnapping saga was over and a verdict reached. In addition, the leadership had no intention of engaging in anything in the Republic that might provoke the government into taking strong action against the IRA. There was a feeling among some of the leadership that the IRA had lost its way, had almost committed political suicide by carrying out badly planned kidnappings that had brought them into direct confrontation with the Irish State over the murder of the young Garda officer and soldier during the Tidey rescue.

Politically, however, Adams and McGuinness were slowly but steadily increasing their influence and control, cannily recruiting younger IRA activists, many of them recently released from the Maze, to positions of influence. Educated politically in the prison and hardened by their involvement in prison protest, these men were in the main formidable operators with minds that knew almost nothing beyond their commitment to republicanism.

As the *Marita Ann* operation moved closer to its climax, Michael Browne's behaviour became increasingly erratic. It was obvious that he was both a loose cannon and under great pressure. I continually reported my fears about him and what I felt was his lack of security consciousness. When drinking and in the company of local IRA men he rarely missed the opportunity to tell them that he was working for GHQ. The truth is that had he not been a boat-owner no one would have paid any attention to him. Of course, his behaviour suited me; if a leak were sprung on this operation Browne would be the first suspect.

In August Browne was sent to a clinic for the treatment of alcoholics, in Killarney, about twenty miles from Tralee. Martin Ferris suggested that we might have to kidnap him from the clinic in order to push forward with the operation. Browne had already agreed on co-ordination points with a former US marine, John Crawley, who was working with the Murrays at the Boston end but who was now refusing to disclose the details to anyone in Ireland. Ferris, who was to be in charge on the *Marita Ann,* was not amused. Eventually I persuaded Browne to give me the co-ordinates, which kept Ferris happy. The operation could continue.

As September approached plans were firmed up. Transport had to be arranged and radio communication between both boats and landfall. It was decided that the cargo would be moved out of the immediate area as soon as it was landed. After that Bell would take charge of it. Inevitably it would end up in bunkers in County Meath, where much of the IRA's back-up weaponry was stored. Some of these bunkers were sophisticated hiding places, often concealed beneath farm buildings. From there material would feed the different units in Northern Command as and when required.

Mick Burke, the Corkman still on the run following the Don Tidey kidnapping, was based in South Kerry and would be charged with manning the radio. A major communications link was set up in West Clare in case the *Valhalla*, the gang's boat carrying the weapons from Boston to Ireland, or the *Marita Ann* had to divert to that area.

By the third week in September all of the details were in place. I continued to make it very clear that I believed it quite likely that the operation was compromised, because of Browne's inability to keep his mouth shut. It was a very fine line for me. While I didn't want the operation cancelled, I wanted to make it clear for any follow-up inquiry that there had been leaks and general bad security. It was fortunate for me that Browne was considered to be an excellent skipper, and irreplaceable for this job.

I took little part in the operation itself beyond, ironically, looking after the monitoring of the police force. Conveniently, I was able to tell my Garda contact the nature and range of our monitoring so that they could take the necessary steps needed to avoid detection.

The *Marita Ann* was due to leave under cover of darkness, carrying a crew of four men: John McCarthy, Gavin Mortimer, Martin Ferris and the skipper, Michael Browne. I spent the hours before the appointed departure time with Ferris. Food and fuel had to be bought for the *Marita Ann* and for the *Valhalla*'s return journey, most of it at a supermarket owned by a republican. We had done this many times before and he would assume it was for another training camp. Knowing that the Garda was in full possession of the plans and was poised to intercept the *Marita Ann*, I realized that it was unlikely that I would see Ferris in similar circumstances again. If convicted he would go down for many years. However closely we had worked, I can't say I felt any sympathy for him. He was about to smuggle seven tons of guns and bullets into the country, which would be used to murder and maim in Northern Ireland while he was safely tucked up in his bed in Kerry. I also believed that Ferris was motivated more by a desire to advance himself within the IRA because of his own psycho-pathological make-up than out of any sense of genuine political belief. I had come to know him extremely well and had seen the way he enjoyed people being afraid of him.

As Ferris was taking leave of me in a café near the Sinn Fein centre in Tralee he looked at me with a slightly pleading expression that said, 'Why don't you come with me?' It was a measure of Ferris's often carefully disguised but all too real lack of genuine self-confidence in his own ability. I ignored it and after Ferris had left phoned my contact to tell him that everything was going ahead as planned. Now I could only wait.

A couple of days later when I switched on the radio early in the morning I heard the news I had been expecting: 'Garda and naval personnel have intercepted a boat carrying a large amount of weapons believed to be intended for the IRA off the coast of Kerry.' Though I had not known it, I was almost sixty miles from where the weapons were to be landed. I had stopped pretending to monitor the local police some time before as I had known that they were under instructions not to use their radios. I felt a sense of both relief and euphoria but still I had to maintain the image of the concerned 'comrade'.

I was just leaving to go into Tralee to find out what was happening when a car containing two local republicans drove up. They reported that all five men on the *Marita Ann* had been captured: Ferris, Browne, Mortimer and McCarthy and John Crawley, the former US marine who had travelled in the *Valhalla* and had transferred to the *Marita Ann* at sea. The *Valhalla* was by now heading back for Boston, where its crew would eventually be picked up and arrested. We drove into Tralee where gardai at a roadblock attempted to wave us down. We ignored them and drove on to Ferris's house. We had been there only seconds when local detectives arrived and arrested me and one other man.

At the station the Garda did not appear to be interested in questioning me about anything. They assumed that I knew all about the *Marita Ann*, but they had no evidence of my involvement and they knew that I wasn't going to admit anything. Some of them were gloating about the capture of the weapons, although most of them seemed happier with the capture of Ferris than with that of the huge arsenal on board.

I was held in the police station in Tralee for the maximum forty-eight hours and then released. Part of the reason for keeping me there was because that weekend there were plans to unveil a statue of Roger Casement, a national hero who had been captured in a German U-boat in 1916, trying to land weapons for the Irish Volunteers – forerunners of the IRA. With emotions running high the Garda probably believed that I was better out of the way.

Within days the internal investigation and recriminations began. I had several meetings with Pat Doherty going over the background to the entire venture. Because the operation had been under the overall control of Ivor Bell, and because his opposition to the direction the movement was taking and to the leadership of Adams, McGuinness and Doherty was hardly a secret, this was a hot potato for Doherty.

Doherty also harboured a strong personal dislike of Bell. When Bell had been made Chief of Staff he had inherited Doherty as his adjutant. Bell had not been happy with the situation and had lost no opportunity not just to make this clear but to humiliate Doherty whenever possible. Doherty actually told me in the clearest possible terms that if Bell had not been arrested in 1983 on Robert Lean's information and removed as Chief of Staff, he, Doherty, would have been prepared to resign from the republican movement.

It is not surprising, therefore, that Doherty was anxious that Bell should not emerge well from the inquiry. In the early stages of the investigation, Doherty discovered that when Bell and some of his supporters had seen the TV coverage of the capture of the *Marita Ann*, Bell was overheard to say, 'The others will be well pleased about this.' 'Others' was taken to be a reference to Adams, McGuinness, Doherty and company. It suited my purpose that Doherty's investigation was completely coloured by this bias. Again internal machinations within the IRA were playing to my advantage. The inquiry dragged on over many months against the background of increasing hostility between Bell and much of the leadership.

Within days of the capture of the *Marita Ann* stories began to circulate in the media about how the *Valhalla* had been monitored by the FBI from the start and had been followed by satellite across the Atlantic. The IRA leadership never swallowed these stories for one moment. Pat Doherty said to me, 'No one in their right mind would believe that the FBI would be prepared to allow a criminal gang in Boston amass a huge arsenal for the IRA and then stand by while it sailed off into the Atlantic.' First, the FBI would have wanted to claim the credit for the arrests and, second, the risk of something going wrong was simply too great. The IRA leadership knew that the source that led to the capture of the *Marita Ann* was in Ireland. Doherty was so blinded by his hatred of Bell that he was determined to prove that the capture was the result of a 'leak' near Bell or of Bell's incompetence.

Even after Bell was dismissed from the IRA, much later in 1985 for attempting to overthrow Adams and McGuinness in a coup, Doherty was still determined to pursue him to the extent that in the summer of 1985 he asked me if I would be prepared to kidnap and interrogate Robert Lean, who was now living in Tramore in County Waterford. This of course would be unsanctioned and I would be personally responsible. Doherty was convinced that either Bell's common-law wife or a source close to her was an RUC or MI5 agent and he believed that Lean might hold the key to this. He was suspicious of Lean's 'escape' from Palace Barracks and thought that it had been 'facilitated' by a section of the security services that was furious about Bell's arrest because it had deprived them of a contact close to the then Chief of Staff. I thought the request was a bit fanciful and that it had more to do with Doherty's personal feud with Bell than with any hard evidence. I declined to take him up on it.

17

Following the capture of the *Marita Ann* and the arrest of Ferris, Southern Command was not surprisingly in a state of disarray, and morale was very low. Doherty assumed the reins for a couple of weeks before asking me if I would take over from Ferris as OC of Southern Command. I tried to decline, saying that I felt that Dickie O'Neill, based as he was in Dublin, would be a better choice, but eventually Doherty insisted that I take the job, with Dickie remaining as adjutant with special responsibility for Dublin. I made it clear that I considered O'Neill joint OC, but in reality I was the senior partner.

The removal of Ferris meant that I had much more work to do and more meetings to attend, and was consequently much more exposed than I had been before. I spent a great deal of time in the everyday running of Southern Command, liaising with the training, engineering and finance departments in the North. I was also responsible at this stage for the vetting of new operatives from Southern Command area for the England department – which in effect allowed me to reject the most suitable candidates in favour of those I thought would be no danger to anyone but themselves. But from my point of view, the difficulties often arose from the timing and minute details of sabotaging my own work and that of other people.

One of the first such tasks I faced was to engineer the escape of Ferris and the others who had been on board the *Marita Ann*. The plan was to use the opportunity of the reading of their bail applications at Dublin's High Court. In such a high-profile case there was a fifty–fifty chance that they would be produced in court. Dublin's High Court is essentially a public building, with few of the security measures that appertain at the Special Criminal Court, where terrorist trials always take place. If Ferris and the others were to escape, doing so from here would be their best chance. The bare bones of such a plan had been in existence for a number of years. It was decided that this case was sufficiently high profile to justify using it.

The general public and prisoners share the same toilets in the High Court. Ordinarily prisoners were handcuffed while urinating, but if they wished to use one of the cubicles, they were uncuffed. We planned to put a small revolver under the rear of the toilet seat, which one of our men – probably Ferris – would retrieve and then force the guards to release the others. Then, using the guards as hostages, they would move quickly to the front of the building, where two stolen vans with armed IRA men would be waiting. Plans were also made for stolen motorbikes and cars to be left in various other places, with the keys in place, in case they were needed.

I told my Garda contact about the plan for the escape. Obviously the simplest solution was simply not to produce the men in court, and he agreed to that. Weeks of IRA time, not to mention money, had been spent planning the operation, which came to nothing. In fact, several years later Tommy McMahon, convicted of the murder of Lord Mountbatten, reactivated the same escape plan only to be overpowered by a detective when he produced the gun he had collected from the toilet. The plan wasn't necessarily foolproof.

From November 1984 life became increasingly awkward and busy. Around that period I also became a member of Sinn Fein's National Executive. I had been asked a couple of years before if I was interested in joining the National Executive, and had declined, but when I related this to my Garda contact he was disappointed and said that it was something they would be very interested in. As a result I went to the Sinn Fein regional area council – comprising Cork, Kerry and Waterford – and told the sitting delegate, Don O'Leary, from Cork, that the IRA had decided that I would now represent the area on the National Executive and that he, O'Leary, would propose me for the position. I told him that in return I would ensure he was later co-opted on to the Executive. It was enough to mention that this was the will of the IRA, and it was extraordinary proof, if any were needed, that Sinn Fein and the IRA are by no means separate entities.

Once on board, I found that with the exception of the contributions of a very few, the level of discussion and basic comprehension was abysmal. The agenda was a curious mixture of political debate and the tedious minutiae of general house-keeping. Such gatherings tended to be dominated by the same handful of people – Adams, McGuinness, Doherty, Morrison and Hartley – who maintained control by a mixture of manipulation and doctrinaire singularity of purpose. Other members were usually overawed and bullied by Tom Hartley, then general secretary, who 'policed' the meetings for the leadership, especially Adams.

At that time four of the roughly twenty-five members

of the National Executive were also members of the IRA Army Council: Adams, McGuinness, Doherty and Joe Cahill, who was joint national treasurer of Sinn Fein and also bursar for the Army Council. As a result Sinn Fein and the IRA were and are inextricably linked. Bearing in mind the very nature of the movement it would be impossible to do business in any other way.

Around this period the Army Council decided that it was once again time to have a detailed look at IRA/Sinn Fein in the Irish Republic. It wanted a complete evaluation of the movement and to develop a strategy to help the IRA/Sinn Fein progress in the Republic. Up to that point the IRA had lacked a coherent focus to its existence in the South. As far as Adams and McGuinness were concerned, it was more important to divert surplus personnel and resources towards establishing a serious political base for Sinn Fein. This would lend credibility to the party. Pat Doherty was given the responsibility for drawing up this policy report, but much of the work fell to me, which made sense. Though Doherty oversaw it for the Army Council, the area was my responsibility. Other people were also involved, but I did the lion's share.

Naturally the issue of abstentionism was never far from the debate. Most southern republicans recognized the state in one way or another, whether by paying taxes, drawing the dole or working for government bodies. The problem for Adams and McGuinness was historical and entrenched. While a significant section of Northern Ireland's nationalists denied the legitimacy of British rule there, the overwhelming majority could not see one sensible reason why their southern counterparts did not recognize the Irish Republic. All Irish republicans who came to accept the reality of the existence of the Irish State eventually became fully constitutional and abandoned physical force. Such was the case with Fianna Fail in the 1920s and Sinn Fein/The Workers' Party in the 1970s. Could Adams and McGuinness balance involvement in constitutional politics with the traditional role of the IRA as an instrument of terror? If so, could they persuade the organization that this was possible and the correct winning formula? Many traditionalists were still deeply suspicious.

No nationalist group in Irish history has been in rebellion against the British presence in Ireland for as long as the Provisionals. No group has ever had their long-term cohesion or hard-edged street experience born out of sectarianism. If any group could balance an Armalite-and-ballot-box strategy, it was the current leadership of the Provisionals.

Adams, McGuinness and their supporters were just about ready to take on the traditionalists within the organization. They would do so for one reason and one reason only: efficiency. They would do whatever it took to advance their cause. They were and are a different breed – almost a race apart – possessing a hardness that is almost beyond the comprehension of most British politicians and southern Irish nationalists.

This period – when I was juggling important allegiances to different masters – was one of the most incredibly difficult and dangerous of my life. There seemed to be no end to meetings and travel, while all the time I was passing on the information to halt IRA plans – often my own – in their infancy or to help the Irish government to understand IRA strategy. It was desperately lonely working inside my own head, being unable to confide in anyone, always having to be another person – even when I wanted to scream and say, 'Here I am, this is me.' Being busy helped in that there wasn't a lot of time to sit around, worrying, but worry I did. How long could this continue? One mistake was all it would take to be the end of me.

Around this time another incident occurred that showed the potential of the IRA to influence southern politics. The son of a leading Irish politician was working in a local hotel. He approached a middle-aged, once fairly senior republican, who had come to live in the area. The young man said he wanted to join the IRA, and the other man came to see me with this news. The night he called at my house Dickie O'Neill was also there and heard what the man had to say, and fortunately I was able to say to O'Neill at the time that I would handle the matter myself. Not long before, the IRA, under the direction of Pat Doherty, who was director of intelligence, had decided to establish a 'black propaganda department'. They were aware that there was a large degree of cynicism about Irish politicians among the Republic's population. The 'black propaganda' department, operating in the classic communist party manner, would plant stories about politicians in the media, bug telephones in ministers' holiday homes, and so on. The aim was to encourage electors to lose faith in the established political system and parties. Because this department was entirely southern based and directed, I obviously knew a lot about it and so, of course, did the Garda. This young man's background obviously made him potentially very useful, and one senior republican did suggest that the best use might be to take him to the border and shoot him, and then blame his murder on the SAS. I was able to make sure that the only instructions he ever got were to do nothing until I got in contact, which of course I never did. What O'Neill said or did about this after I left I can't say; but I knew that the Garda were aware of the dangers of the situation.

* * *

In early 1985 Ivor Bell made his push to take control of the republican movement. He had been trying to build a power base for some time and had been hindered in this by his common-law wife's suspension from the IRA on the fairly dubious grounds of spreading dissent about the leadership. She was to be court-martialled and Bell sought out Seamus Twomey to act in her defence. But he did not tell the entire story to Twomey – that he was planning a coup. Though Twomey's and Bell's anxieties about politics displacing armed struggle were the same, Twomey was also close to Gerry Adams, who owed his position in the IRA in some measure to Twomey's patronage in his younger days.

Although Bell had genuinely wanted Twomey's support for his wife, it was also a way of creating the illusion, for Northern Command, that he supported Bell's leadership ambitions. When Twomey discovered Bell's deceit, he was furious. Though Twomey was no longer of real influence, the fact that even the most militaristic of the old-timers was not prepared to back him should have made Bell realize that he was in no position to win a contest against Adams and McGuinness.

Bell had succeeded in persuading some influential people in Belfast to support him but none was a national figure within the movement. Martin McGuinness, realizing what was happening, moved decisively to take control of the situation and Bell and his three closest associates were quickly suspended pending court-martial. Anyone within Northern Command who had been approached by Bell for support was asked to give evidence at the court-martial; those who refused were dismissed.

The most damning evidence against Bell came from the veteran Belfast-born IRA leader Joe Cahill. In 1973

Cahill had been arrested on board the *Claudia* with five tons of weaponry supplied by the Libyan government, for which he was sentenced to three years' imprisonment. After his release he maintained good relations with the Libyans, who in early 1985 made contact again. They were delighted to hear the news about the new 'radical leadership' of the IRA. Casual conversation soon revealed that they believed Bell to be that same new radical leader. Bell had realized that if he could get control of Libyan arms then his chances of pulling off a coup would be much improved and had opened negotiations along those lines, but now, facing court-martial, his entire plan was in chaos. His arrogance, his personal unpopularity with many and his relative isolation outside Belfast were all factors that militated against him. Whether Cahill approached the Libyans because he got wind of some plan of Bell's or whether the Libyans approached Cahill because they were unsure of what was happening is not clear.

Bell's court-martial was organized on traditional IRA lines. A court-martial is a rare event, particularly of a former Chief of Staff and member of the Army Council along with three senior Belfast republicans. There were three 'judges', all of whom had to be at least members of the GHQ staff, an IRA-appointed prosecutor and a member of the IRA selected by the defendant to act as his defence. The IRA would play by the rulebook, on the surface at least, but would make sure that the people chosen to be judges would return the result the leadership wanted.

The judges chosen in this instance were Owen Coogan, who hated Bell, Seamus Twomey, who felt betrayed by his old comrade, and me. I had been privately briefed by Pat Doherty, who had made it quite clear that the leadership wanted only one result: Bell's dismissal.

I in fact managed to duck the court-martial, arranging for Dickie O'Neill to go instead. The last thing I needed to do in my position was to make enemies – and Bell and his supporters would have been particularly dangerous opponents. Even though it looked like the leadership had won the battle, you could never be sure, and I didn't want to take the risk.

In fact, Bell solved the problem for me by simply refusing to attend his court-martial, which went ahead without him. He obviously knew that it was comprehensively loaded against him. He and the three others were duly dismissed and warned that they would be shot if they attempted to set up a rival group or joined an existing one such as the INLA.

Bell sent back a message to the IRA to say that their own actions proved how soft they had become. 'If it was the other way around and any of you refused to attend the court-martial, you would be dead by now,' he said. But Bell did not understand that Adams, McGuinness and Kevin McKenna were not softer, just cleverer. Killing Bell would have been an option only in the most extreme of circumstances. In the event Adams was 'kind', insinuating that poor old Ivor had been led astray, manipulated and made a fool of by his much younger common-law wife. After the court-martial Adams went around saying with a concerned shake of the head, 'Whatever happened to my good friend? This is not the Ivor Bell I know. It must be that woman's fault.' This finished off Bell far more effectively than killing him. His murder might at least have led his supporters to rise up and retaliate.

Bell had hoped to gain the backing of the old guard, and subsequently bring about a convention, which the leadership had opposed. But now that he was well and truly out of the way they backed the idea, convinced that they would win the backing of the convention emphatically. Pat Doherty spoke to me a number of times during 1985 about the mechanics of such a convention – once suggesting that it could be held in France – but there was no detailed proposal. One of the major problems of such a gathering was security; every single IRA person of any importance or influence would wish to be there. It would be the first convention since 1970, when the Provisional IRA had been formed.

From late 1984 to the summer of 1985 I attended a number of GHQ meetings in my capacity as OC of Southern Command. GHQ is the section of the IRA with operational control over all IRA activity, running the IRA on a daily basis. It is appointed by the Chief of Staff and is subordinate to the Army Council, which decides overall strategy for the republican movement. Among those present at the meeting were the major IRA players: Kevin McKenna, the Chief of Staff; Pat Doherty, the adjutant-general (Doherty was also director of intelligence and represented the training department at GHQ meetings); Martin McGuinness, roving but in effect OC of Northern Command; Danny Morrison, director of publicity; Gabriel Cleary, director of engineering; Kieran Conway, director of research; Owen Coogan, director of the England department; Seamus Twomey, director of security, and a couple of others.

The meetings usually started in the evening and continued the next day, and routine was fairly standard. For obvious security reasons, people travelled by arrangement to a pick-up point where they were met, had their transport garaged, and were driven to the meeting. The meetings were different from Southern Command meetings, more high powered and tense. Each department would be required to provide an update of its activities since the last session. We would get away with nothing and often had to fight our corner. Southern Command usually came in for some justified criticism. While I certainly had no intention of making the type of improvements that would make the IRA's killing machine more effective, I still had to try to create the illusion of enhancing efficiency and resources.

A man like Kevin McKenna – who often communicated in a series of near grunts – was not easy to hoodwink. He is not known for patiently listening to explanations or showing understanding of any difficulties. What he wanted was results – proof that he could see and understand – not fancy words and promises. McGuinness spoke little but listened and watched intently. His contributions when they came were always sharp and incisive and he commanded instant attention.

Much of the real business at these meetings took place out of session between individuals who needed each other's co-operation. I had to be careful that Pat Doherty did not see me as a threat. Doherty was long regarded as the expert on southern affairs – not just of Southern Command – and was the person in the leadership with the best grasp and understanding of southern politics and mindset. I had seen how he had turned on Bell and I had no wish to create more problems for myself.

The conspiratorial nature of the IRA meant that there were always mutterings about 'sell-outs'. McKenna was a particularly suspicious man who worried about security to the point of irrationality. When McKenna was first made Chief of Staff, Brendan Swords, a well-known IRA man, said to me, 'Now we have a Chief of Staff who will send scouts out in the morning before he goes for the milk.' McKenna claimed that scrupulous attention to his own security had led to his rarely being the focus of Garda attention, unlike many less significant others. I can remember instances of meeting McKenna in County Monaghan when he would drive out to a lake in the countryside, produce fishing rods and we would pretend to fish. Only then would he talk and even then he would glance round constantly to make sure he was not being observed. If ever he had occasion to go to the Sinn Fein head office in Dublin he would arrive head down, cap on and collar pulled up, and throughout his visit would constantly be asking people to check whether Special Branch were watching the building.

As a result, McKenna was very successful in hiding much of his activity from the security forces, and indeed from other republicans. When Sid Walsh – then OC of the IRA prisoners in the Maze – was released from prison in 1984, he had no idea that McKenna was Chief of Staff. Having barely heard of him, he was convinced the job was held by Adams or McGuinness. Some members of the security forces even believed that McKenna was semi-retired. He was a serious operator and not a man to play games with.

Yet such was the extent of his paranoia that it had its amusing side, as demonstrated by the following episode.

In the summer of 1985, an IRA man called Benny Green from Lurgan in County Armagh was on the run in the south after a post office robbery. Benny was having an affair with the wife of another IRA prisoner, who was in jail awaiting trial on charges related to the same robbery and who had learned about the affair. He threatened to co-operate fully with the authorities unless the IRA made Benny finish the relationship. Benny was spoken to and he agreed, but within hours of making his promise he was back in the woman's house in Dundalk.

McKenna decided that Benny Green would have to be 'arrested' – in other words kidnapped – by the IRA. And he would be held . . . where else but in Kerry? He was duly 'arrested' and spent many months in Kerry being guarded by local young IRA men. Benny managed to gain the sympathy not only of his guards but also of some of the people in the houses where he was being held. Eventually one of his 'jailers' gave him the money for the train fare back to Dundalk and drove him to the nearest train station. I was in Dublin when I heard the news. Through a friend Benny sent word that he was quite prepared to attend a court-martial but only if J. B. O'Hagan, the veteran republican and friend of his family, was allowed to defend him.

When I told McKenna the news he went ballistic; we were at the back of the Sinn Fein head office in Dublin and we had a fierce argument about how Benny had come to escape. In spite of my real situation I found myself getting angry with McKenna, and had to remind myself that I couldn't care less about Green, McKenna or this petty problem.

Eventually Benny's court-martial took place in a housing estate in Dundalk. A local IRA unit was present – and armed. A senior republican figure from Belfast, who worked in Sinn Fein head office, was the convenor; I was the prosecutor; J. B. O'Hagan defended Benny and the three judges – effectively the jury – were Mick Burke from Cork, Sean Finn and Jimmy Kavanagh. Finn and Kavanagh had spent a long period in prison with O'Hagan and worshipped him. Burke also knew him and held him in similar high regard. Benny was smart and knew that with O'Hagan on his side there was little chance of anything too bad happening to him. Everyone else involved was aware of this.

One of the most absurd moments came when Seamus Twomey – one of the principal witnesses against Benny – had to be physically restrained from attacking him. The whole farce ended with Benny's being found guilty of a secondary offence and being ordered to leave the country. Because he was wanted by the police the IRA had to make the arrangements; Benny was sent to America and provided with a job and was probably better off than at any time in his entire life. Twomey was incensed that Benny had got off so lightly: 'Call yourself a fucking prosecutor,' he said to me. One of my abiding memories of that night is Twomey banging on a table and saying again and again, 'If I could just be Chief of Staff again – just for five fucking minutes.' No one had any doubt what Benny's fate would have been had that been possible.

After Benny's court-martial, Mick Burke, who was still on the run following the Tidey kidnapping, decided to hand himself in to the police in the mistaken belief that they would be unable to charge him. I knew differently, for the Garda had told me that there was a witness able and ready to identify him as the bogus Garda officer who had stopped Tidey's car on the morning of the kidnapping. Of course I could say nothing of this to him. I drove him to a solicitor's office in Tralee and the solicitor accompanied him to the local police station. The witness, who was on holiday in Britain at the time, returned and picked Burke out at an identity parade. Despite IRA attempts to intimidate the witness, which included an arson attack on his Dublin car-showroom, he stuck to his story and refused to be frightened off. Burke was granted bail but was later convicted and sentenced to ten years' imprisonment.

It would be impossible to detail all of my activities during this period. I was extraordinarily busy and the flow of information to the Garda was at its zenith. I was regularly meeting many of the most senior republicans in Ireland; I was OC of the IRA's Southern Command, a member of the GHQ staff and of Sinn Fein's National

Executive. I was also incredibly stressed, and the pressure showed no signs of abating. In November 1984 Louise – with whom I had now been living for over three years – became pregnant. She still acknowledged nothing of my real activities. Had she known the whole truth she would have run a mile – and justifiably so.

I was always conscious of the fact that she was English. If any suspicion fell on me it was also likely, to some degree, to fall on her. I didn't really believe that she would come to any serious harm, but if the truth ever came out about me – and I was murdered – the effect on her and also on the child would be catastrophic. All these things I knew and yet I went on doing what I was doing, primarily because I felt I had no other choice but to continue doing the job I had started. I was also in love with her and unwilling to end the relationship. At any moment she could have been dragged into a nightmare world that she knew nothing about, and it would all have been my fault. Fortunately, close associates such as Ferris knew that she had no interest in politics and that she steered clear of asking questions, so she was, at least for the moment, safe.

18

Towards the end of 1983 I had become aware of a man called Sean Corcoran, from Cork, who was to become the subject of perhaps one of the shoddiest passages in the history of the IRA and of the Irish state. Certainly it was and has continued to be a matter of great concern and sadness for me. I have endured many attacks in the Irish media and much ignominy, a great deal of it understandable because, for reasons that will emerge, I admitted in print to being responsible for his murder.

I am now glad to be able finally to explain the entire circumstances behind the story of Sean Corcoran's life as an informer for the Irish police and his eventual murder. It is a long and sad story, and one that is difficult to tell, but in the interests of the truth that must now be done.

During the seventies Sean Corcoran was an IRA supporter and sympathizer, though never what might be described as heavily involved in any direct activity. Arrested in the seventies, he admitted under questioning that he was a member of the IRA, though even this was not strictly true. The police told him that he would be charged with IRA membership unless he agreed to work for them. He did so and was released. For the next couple of years he supplied low-level information to the gardai about republicans in Cork. Then, because he was scared, he drifted out of contact with republicans, some of whom had already begun to suspect in an unfocused way that he was not a man to be fully trusted.

It was not until the hunger strikes of 1981 that Sean Corcoran reappeared on the republican scene in Cork City during an attempted robbery there. The night before, I had sent a man to Cork to take part in the robbery but I did not know which post office was to be robbed. Sean Corcoran, it later transpired, told the Cork gardai about the robbery, and the would-be robbers were arrested leaving the post office while Sean Corcoran was 'waiting' for them a couple of miles away where they planned to abandon the stolen car.

An investigation was called into what had happened. Seamus Twomey came to Cork to handle the inquiry and promptly put everyone's nose out of joint with his blunt, aggressive manner. Several local IRA men refused to co-operate. It was thought that the robbery had been rushed and badly planned – which was true – and the results of the inquiry were consequently inconclusive.

Sean Corcoran drifted away again and was not involved with the IRA in Cork after that until 1983, when Mick Burke took charge. Burke began to use Corcoran as a driver because it was believed that after their questioning of him in the seventies the Garda had lost interest and that he was therefore relatively clean.

Some time in late 1983 I met Sean Corcoran for the first time. I was in Cork at an IRA meeting and Mick Burke said that he would provide a man to drive me to the house where I was staying that night. The man was Sean Corcoran. I had been in the car for less than five minutes when I became convinced that something was not as it should be. By the end of the journey I knew for no rational reason and without one shred of proof that

Sean Corcoran was working for the gardai. How? Why? I don't know. Perhaps I saw something of myself in him. I can give no satisfactory reason even now: I just knew.

When I next met my Garda contact I asked him straight out if he knew whether Sean Corcoran was a police informer. The look on his face told me all I needed to know. He couldn't understand how I could have guessed so quickly. I warned him that Sean Corcoran would be in extreme danger and could be murdered. The phrase 'There was just something about him' is an anodyne one and perhaps does not make real sense to many people, but in Corcoran's case it was true, and it was to be his death warrant.

Over the following months I met Corcoran several times and each time I became more concerned about him. At one stage he drove me to a house and then made an excuse to leave, saying that he needed petrol when the indicator showed that the tank was more than half full. I think he was under instructions to report back to the gardai when he knew where the house was. If he were to do anything like that in the company of other experienced IRA people he would almost certainly create instant suspicion. A clandestine investigation would have followed, usually involving passing some bogus information to the person involved and then monitoring the police reaction.

I warned my contact repeatedly over many months that I believed Corcoran's life was in danger. He was being used more and more by the IRA in Cork and it was, I felt, only a question of time. All of this took on an added urgency when Pat Walsh – an experienced IRA man from Cork who now played only a small part in the organization – heard that Corcoran was once again active. He approached me and asked me whether I was aware that Corcoran had been under suspicion in the seventies and had never been properly cleared. He felt that young, inexperienced IRA men in Cork were making a great mistake in having anything to do with him.

Once again I went to my contact, telling him that they must move Corcoran and his family out of the country. I knew that he believed me, but he seemed powerless to do anything about it.

By mid-1984 I had succeeded in withdrawing Corcoran from much IRA activity in Cork. I told nobody that I suspected something, just that I felt that he was a weak man who might not stand up to police questioning and therefore was to be used only sparingly, and certainly not for anything of major importance. My reasoning was twofold. If he was producing little in the way of information the Garda in Cork would lose interest in him. Even better, they might suspect that he was not to be trusted and withdraw him.

What I really needed was another informer in Cork, one who was unaware of my position, in whom I could plant my 'deep suspicion' of Sean Corcoran. He would tell the gardai in Cork, who would then see the danger he was in and have no option but to pull him out. But of course I couldn't take the chance unless I was certain of my man. I ran the risk of telling a committed IRA man, who would wonder why nothing was being done about it.

What I did not know was that Corcoran was being put under enormous and unrelenting pressure to come up with the goods by two detectives in Cork City. Such pressure on someone who was obviously very frightened was unfair and I believe morally unjustifiable. They continued to push when it must have been obvious that, for whatever reason, Corcoran was not regarded by the IRA as someone in whom much confidence could be placed.

Quite simply, the detectives bullied and threatened him into continuing to work for them.

By the time the *Marita Ann* was captured Corcoran was essentially redundant to Cork Special Branch. Until then Special Branch had been directing him to target Martin Ferris and me. Now that Ferris was in jail their attention turned to me exclusively. It was a farce. I was working for the Garda Special Branch and supplying extensive and important information, while two junior Special Branch officers based in Cork were pressurizing Corcoran to come up with the information that would put me in jail or – as he later admitted under IRA interrogation – have me killed.

At one stage the detectives deliberately supplied him with information about a security van they knew would be travelling on a particular route and carrying currency to the value of £250,000. One of them apparently said to him that he was to give this information only to me. 'It's him we want and we're not that interested whether he ends up in jail or dead.' Corcoran was too frightened to pass the information to me at the time and it came to nothing. But after the capture of the *Marita Ann*, another plan evolved that was so grotesquely amateurish and dangerous that it beggared belief. Its origins are unclear.

Sean Corcoran began to ring the Sinn Fein centre in Tralee, leaving messages that he wished to see me urgently. I ignored the messages until one day Pat Currie – the Belfast man in charge of security for Southern Command – was in the centre and took Corcoran's message. The essence of Currie's job was to be on the look-out for informers. He wondered why Corcoran, a man supposedly under no suspicion by Special Branch, would communicate with me using a phone that was believed unsafe. He regarded it as at least a bad breach of security, which it was. Later that same evening Mick

Burke, now out on bail, turned up in Tralee. He told Currie and me that Corcoran had said he had a contact in army intelligence who knew the name of the person who had given the information about the *Marita Ann* to the authorities. He would give this name only to me.

At this stage it was obvious to Currie and Burke that Corcoran was behaving peculiarly. As for me, I could have cried. The military intelligence community in the Irish Republic is a very small organization, and highly unlikely to have had anything to do with the *Marita Ann* affair. How, in any circumstances, could a man like Corcoran meet with an army intelligence officer who would have such information and be willing to pass it on to him? The *Marita Ann* operation had obviously been handled by Garda Special Branch, who brought in the navy because they had no choice. Why would they tell army intelligence? Even if they had, Corcoran was a completely anonymous Cork republican, supposedly not suspected even by Cork gardai of IRA involvement except during that period of questioning ten years before.

All of this was bad enough, but when Burke then told Currie that some of the older but now largely inactive Cork IRA men had long harboured suspicions about Corcoran, I could see Currie's eyes lighting up.

Currie stayed in my home that night. I knew I had to report to my Garda contact, and, despite the danger, I slipped out in the early hours of the morning to see him. I told him exactly what had happened. He assured me that there was no possibility that military intelligence had my name. I suggested that perhaps Cork Special Branch were working with an army officer who would pretend to be in military intelligence, would meet me and then seek to entrap or set me up over a period of time. He agreed this was possible but felt it was unlikely; it

270

certainly had not been officially sanctioned. My advice to him was, once again, quite straightforward. 'Get Sean Corcoran and his family out of the country before this gets out of control.' As it was, I had had to agree with Mick Burke about the already existing suspicions about Corcoran. If Currie had been just a little sharper he would have wondered whether I had known about the suspicions and, if so, for how long had I known, and why I hadn't told him. I informed my Garda contact that inevitably an investigation would now take place into Corcoran and that I did not see how he could survive it.

Why did Sean Corcoran talk about his army intelligence officer? Did the officer exist – even as a Special Branch plan? Was he Corcoran's mad invention, or was Corcoran under so much pressure that he embarked on this course somehow relying on Special Branch to back him up? I didn't know, and there never has been a satisfactory answer.

Currie, of course, immediately informed Seamus Twomey, GHQ director of security; as I had suspected, the whole business was fast becoming completely unmanageable. Even as I was pleading with my Garda contact to get Corcoran and his wife to safety, he seemed to think that there was no need to panic and that I could handle the situation. I tried to explain that this time it was different.

When I next met Currie, about a fortnight later in Dublin, he had come up with a plan to test Corcoran. A Belfast republican called Micky Morgan, recently released from Portlaoise prison, would travel to Cork, where he would be met by Corcoran under Burke's instruction. The impression would be conveyed to Corcoran that Morgan was a man of some importance on the run from the gardai. Corcoran would be instructed to drive Morgan to a street where there lived two sympathetic republican families. Morgan would barely communicate with Corcoran; he would simply tell him where to stop at the entrance to the street. Morgan would then walk into the street and, unknown to Corcoran, be driven away by another IRA sympathizer.

I told my Garda contact about the plan and that under no circumstances should the known sympathizers' houses be raided. He said that he would do the best he could. The plan went ahead. Corcoran picked Morgan up and dropped him at the entrance to the street. The following morning, to my utter amazement, both of the sympathizers' houses were raided. Corcoran was now in deep trouble.

Why were the houses raided? Why had my contact not stopped it? I don't know, but I do know that usually in such instances cock-up rather than conspiracy provides the answer.

Events, already looking bad, took a turn for the worse. As far as Currie and Twomey were concerned, there was now ample justification for interrogating Corcoran and there was nothing I could do about it. If he was removed for his own safety, by the police, it would undoubtedly raise suspicion as to how they knew he was in danger, but that was preferable to allowing him to stay when there was a real chance that he was about to be murdered.

Meanwhile, it was decided internally that Sean Corcoran would be kidnapped and interrogated, and plans were laid to draw him into a trap. Mick Burke approached him and asked for a lift to a meeting in Kerry. They drove to Martin Ferris's mother's farmhouse at Churchill, about five miles outside Tralee, where three or four people including myself were waiting. Because the Garda had refused to heed my warnings, I was virtually helpless. I told my Garda contact that Sean Corcoran was to be brought to Kerry and then kidnapped and interrogated. He seemed unable to understand the urgency or the danger. Perhaps because the IRA had never before murdered an informer in the Irish Republic, he might have thought I was overreacting and that the interrogation would not lead to murder. Or perhaps my Garda officer was under instruction from his boss to protect me at all costs; by that stage I had passed on valuable early information to the Garda of possible Libyan arms shipments.

Whatever the reasons for the Garda's lack of response, and with this in the background, the fact remained that Corcoran was now in the hands of the IRA. I decided that I would conduct the interrogation – or as much of it as possible – on my own and try to steer it away from dangerous areas.

As soon as Corcoran was securely held, I left on the pretext of going to another meeting, which was indeed taking place, but in reality I needed to let the Garda know what was happening. My contact encouraged me to stay calm and direct the interrogation.

I returned within the hour. As planned, Corcoran had been moved to an empty house beside the sea, within walking distance of the Ferris farm. Currie opened the door to me. His first words were, 'We've got ourselves a tout.' I could not believe what I was hearing. I had left instructions that the interrogation of Corcoran was not to start until I returned. What had happened was startlingly simple. As they walked across the fields from the Ferris farm Currie had turned to Corcoran and said, 'If you don't tell me the name of the army officer I'm going to shoot you.' Corcoran had immediately broken down and admitted that there was no army officer. It wasn't even a serious attempt at interrogation by Currie, who could scarcely believe how easy it had been.

Corcoran could have saved the situation; all he'd had to do at that stage was to say that he would talk only to me – but he hadn't.

I went in to see him. He was lying on a bed with an eyeless hood over his head. Understandably, he was shaking with fear and I cursed the two Cork Special Branch officers who had pushed him beyond the limits of what could be reasonably expected. I took the hood off him while retaining my own. I spoke to him, knowing that he would recognize my voice. It was the first voice he would have recognized since being kidnapped, and I hoped, perhaps foolishly, that it would help to calm him a little.

There was absolutely nothing I could do except proceed with the questioning as gently as possible. In broad terms I already knew the story that would emerge. He admitted to having worked for Special Branch for a number of years. He admitted that he was the person responsible for the information that led to the capture of the three IRA men at Togher Post Office in 1981. I tried as best I could to keep the questioning away from areas that I thought might get him into even deeper trouble, if that were possible at this stage.

By the early hours of the morning he had made a taped confession, which even implicated, accidentally or otherwise, another man who had also worked for Special Branch in the past. Fortunately, that man had since left Cork and had moved to Dublin, and Corcoran had no present address for him.

The next day Corcoran was moved to a house on the Dingle peninsula and Currie and I travelled to Dublin by train with the tape. We arranged to meet Pat Doherty at Dickie O'Neill's house in Tallaght, on the outskirts of the city. I was determined – and, I have to say, very hopeful – that I could persuade Doherty that Corcoran would be best produced at a Sinn Fein press conference, where he could be used to discredit Special Branch and even the government. Anything was preferable to having him murdered. I was sure that Doherty's innate caution and political instincts would steer him in the direction of a non-violent conclusion.

After a few minutes of explanation at O'Neill's house Doherty asked to hear the tape. O'Neill produced a tape recorder and we sat and listened in silence. Doherty thought it very funny when Corcoran described how Special Branch had warned him to be careful in his deal-ings with me. 'You should put that on your CV,' he observed. When the tape had finished I told Doherty I wished to speak to him alone. I explained the idea of the press conference, for which there were many precedents. To my horror, and real surprise, Doherty was not impressed. In all likelihood he felt that he could not take such a decision himself and that he had to refer the matter to others.

He told me to see McKenna immediately. I knew for certain that I hadn't a hope in hell of influencing McKenna, who was always going to be much more difficult than Doherty to persuade of the merits of a press conference. As well as that, O'Neill and Currie were threatening to resign if the 'army' did not sanction the death penalty.

The following morning Currie and I rose early, borrowed Dickie O'Neill's car and drove to see McKenna, who was living in a mobile home in County Monaghan. It was still early in the morning when we drove into the farmyard where McKenna's home was parked. True to form, before we got out of the car I could see him pulling back a corner of a curtain to see who was there. When he opened the door for us his first question was typical McKenna. 'I hope that's a safe car you're driving.' When informed that it belonged to Dickie O'Neill, he nearly had a seizure.

I told McKenna what Doherty had said, and continued to push the idea of the press conference. He listened to what I had to say and asked me if Corcoran had children. I said yes, eight. McKenna grimaced and said, 'Kill him.' Because Corcoran was not an official IRA volunteer he was not even entitled to a court-martial.

On the way back to Dublin I managed to speak to the Garda contact. It felt as if I wasn't getting through to him, as if he didn't understand. I couldn't understand his attitude and lack of urgency. I was getting more and more worried and frustrated and every time I looked over at Currie I felt like being physically sick. I was still trying to think of a way out when we returned the car to O'Neill. Seamus Twomey was there and he insisted that 'his people' take over. Twomey's nose appeared to be somewhat out of joint because he hadn't yet been involved: he was sending two people from internal security to Kerry the following morning. Currie and I were returning by train that evening and we arranged to meet them in the carpark of a local hotel the following day.

We were met off the train by a local IRA man who drove us to the house where Corcoran was being held. I had left instructions that he was not to be harmed or ill-treated in any way, and as far as I could ascertain those instructions had been obeyed.

I left along with Currie, went home and managed to phone my contact again. For the first time he seemed to display some anxiety, as if it had finally dawned on him how serious the situation was. I told him that I would keep him up to date on every development when possible but that the situation looked as black as it could be.

Currie and I met with Twomey's people the following

morning and brought them to where Corcoran was. The men were from Belfast, and Currie certainly knew at least one of them quite well. In organizational terms, they were within their rights to take control at this stage. Technically speaking, they should have been brought in much earlier, as this was their area of responsibility. They needed a local man to work with them and they wanted to move Corcoran somewhere quieter and more remote. I gave them a man and told them where to go. Currie went along with the three of them. That was the last time I saw Sean Corcoran alive.

At the first opportunity I phoned my contact again and told him where the murder was to take place. He took details from me and I felt sure the gardai were about to intervene. Later that night, having heard no news, I was walking to a phone box in the village when Currie and the local man turned up. I was horrified – I was sure that by then they would all be in the police station being questioned about Corcoran's kidnapping. Their presence was enough to confirm that things had gone fatally wrong.

Currie stayed in my house that night and recounted in great detail the last hours of Sean Corcoran. How he was shot in the back of the head in a field, outside Milltown in County Kerry. How the body was wrapped in black plastic and a sleeping bag and put into the boot of a car. How the two Belfast men, their work done, were driven to Killarney railway station while Currie and the other man brought Corcoran's body back to Cork, where they dumped it on the side of a narrow road outside the village of Ballincollig. How they washed the blood from the ground into a small drain near by and how one of them, seeing a patch of blood on the grass, had urinated on it to much amusement. Currie was very proud of himself that night.

I just did not know what to think, never mind do. There was a filthy taste in my mouth from the whole bloody business and I believe that Corcoran's life could have been saved without great difficulty. I had done everything possible to prevent his murder, and equally the gardai had done nothing.

I still cannot understand what went wrong. Did the gardai believe me when I told them that Corcoran's life was in serious danger? I think so – but the fact remains that they did nothing about it. Was I regarded as more valuable than Corcoran and therefore to be protected even at the cost of his life? I don't know. To all of those questions I have no real answers.

The next occasion I met the Garda contact I was furious. As soon as I got into his car I brought up the subject of Sean Corcoran and was told, 'You must put this behind you. It's terrible, but these things happen.' I just didn't know where to start, what to say, whether to punch him, or what. After about five minutes I told him to stop the car and I got out and walked in the dark across the fields towards home. I was completely shattered – but already there was another problem to deal with.

Currie had by now discovered that the other man named by Corcoran as a possible informer worked in a pub in Dublin. We held a meeting in a flat in Ballymun, attended by Currie, Dickie O'Neill, Seamus Twomey, Kevin Mallon and me. Currie and O'Neill were seeing conspiracies everywhere and Twomey – never the brightest – was soaking it all up. Mallon was there at my insistence. He was my trump card if we were to save this man's life. After O'Neill and Currie had discussed why this man must be kidnapped I immediately said that this was a ridiculous way to approach the problem and that it was the most likely action to lead us straight into a Garda trap. In this instance we needed to take our time.

Mallon – more intelligent than the others and more cautious since the debacle of the kidnappings – agreed with me: it was to be put on the long finger. A debate then began about general IRA affairs. I remember opening the front door and looking out from the balcony: Ballymun was a miserable place on a summer's day. Half-starved dogs roamed around scavenging in the rubbish and here I was discussing kidnap and murder with people like Twomey and Mallon, whom I would once, a long time ago, have viewed as heroes but whom I now knew to be pathetic, ugly figures – gang leaders with not a scrap of moral fibre between them. I came back inside just in time to hear Dickie O'Neill say, 'O'Callaghan's bored because we're not talking about stiffing someone.' This was met with general amusement. I thought, 'If you only knew, you little pricks. If you only knew.' O'Neill did not know who had pulled the trigger on Corcoran but he assumed it was me, as would many other IRA men.

The Dublin man's life was safe for the time being, and I was sure that the Garda recognized that, no matter what it took, I would never tolerate a case like Corcoran's again.

I never recovered from that traumatic period. The strange thing was that after the murder of Corcoran my standing and reputation within the republican movement was at its peak. Very few people knew the details; as far as they were concerned I was OC of Southern Command and we had just had a major success. Privately, I was never more disgusted with the whole business. At a Sinn Fein ard comhairle meeting shortly afterwards, Martin McGuinness put his arm on my shoulder and whispered, 'Well done,' as he passed by.

Sadly, I felt that somehow Sean Corcoran's murder

had cast a shadow over my girlfriend's pregnancy. There were days when I just didn't know what to think, days when I could not even be bothered to try.

His murder haunted and sickened me then and has continued to do so ever since. There is no doubt that it destroyed my desire to continue as an informer. I knew that the work was important but although I could provide the necessary information I was powerless to ensure that people acted upon it. This one event not only signalled the end of my role as an informer but was to have disastrous consequences in later years.

19

In the latter part of 1984 I was asked to find eight or nine men to go to Libya. It was explained that they should be from a rural background and be comfortable handling cattle; I was not told why they were needed. From my point of view it was the first serious indication that the Libyan connection had been reactivated.

Obviously it was important to choose carefully, so I deliberately picked a fellow who was over six feet, had long very blond hair and thick-lensed glasses. I reckoned that even the dumbest policeman couldn't fail to pick him out. Some months later, in early 1985, I learned that Gabriel Cleary, IRA director of engineering, was also in Libya. Kevin McKenna – ever cautious – told me that there were expectations of 'lots of modern gear'. His grand scheme was that with such gear the IRA could create a 'free zone', running along the Clogher valley from Tyrone to Fermanagh – an area the security forces could enter only in strength and with helicopter back-up, a similar situation to that existing in South Armagh. It was a plan that had obsessed him for years.

Shortly after that, when I was up in Dublin one day, I got a message that Joe Cahill wanted to see me. I went along to the Sinn Fein offices where he normally lurked.

Cahill reminded me of a certain businessman, a keen sailor who owned a boat, and who had been an IRA sympathizer. During the seventies he had acted as liaison for Brian Keenan when Keenan was running the IRA's bombing campaign in Britain. Cahill wanted to know if he was still sound. I replied that I believed he was. Cahill asked me to arrange a meeting, so I approached the businessman, who was more than agreeable, and I arranged to see him at his home. On the agreed date I met Cahill in Dublin and we drove there together. I was more than curious to know what was going on, but Cahill wasn't going to tell me and I wasn't going to ask. I did, of course, suspect that the sudden interest in the businessman had a great deal to do with his boat – and Libyan weapons – but I could not be sure. Or not yet.

My Garda contact told me to be cautious; he was worried that, coming so soon after the *Marita Ann*, this might be a set-up. I felt that was unlikely. It was all too complicated in its way and such a set-up would not, I felt sure, be McKenna's style.

Cahill and the businessman went upstairs to talk while I remained below. When Cahill returned he looked very pleased and it was obvious that things had gone well. When we were in the car he confirmed that, saying, 'Your man is still very sound.'

A week or so after that Cahill was back in touch. He told me that McKenna wanted him to have a further meeting with the businessman within two days. For such sensitive contacts, rather than telephoning I travelled to his home, spoke to the businessman and returned to Dublin to tell Cahill the meeting was on for the next day.

On the way back Cahill told me that we were meeting a couple of people at a hotel en route and that they would be coming with us to meet the businessman. When we got to the hotel carpark there were two men sitting in a car. I recognized one of them; Malachy McCann was the IRA's director of purchasing, the man in charge of buying and importing weapons. Since Joe Cahill, the IRA's senior finance person and member of the Army Council, and Chief of Staff Kevin McKenna were both also involved, I figured there could be no doubt why they were interested in the businessman. I passed all this information on to my Garda contact, some of it before Sean Corcoran was murdered, some after.

Sinn Fein work was beginning to take up a lot of my time. Local elections loomed and the IRA insisted that I stand as a candidate in the Tralee area. Throughout this period Corcoran's murder was constantly on my mind and, though busy, I began to spend much more time at home in Kerry with my girlfriend. I felt dispirited by the terrible turn events had taken, and my previous motivation had all but disappeared.

In spite of this, some of the Sinn Fein National Executive meetings became very interesting during the period from April to June 1985. Sinn Fein and John Hume had recently had some public exchanges, as a result of which Adams proposed at a National Executive meeting that Sinn Fein publicly invite John Hume to a meeting. 'We may have nothing to say to John Hume,' he said. 'The probability is that we do not. But northern nationalists will never forgive our refusal to talk.'

Adams's proposal was carried unanimously, but immediately afterwards there was a moment of high farce. Having propelled his proposal through the meeting, Adams appeared to adopt the persona of an international statesman. He announced that he also wished to invite other groups, such as People's Democracy, at which stage Danny Morrison laughed out loud and said, 'You don't mean that bunch that fall around drunk at the Rock Bar every Saturday night?' 'Just invite them, Danny,' replied Adams. 'I'm not inviting that bunch of idiots,' retorted Morrison, before turning to his copy of the *Irish Times*. Adams was obviously very angry. I found it hard to keep a straight face. Adams finished the squabble by regaining his temper and saying in a soft voice, 'We'll talk about this later, Danny.' He knew that Morrison had poked fun at him in front of every leading member of Sinn Fein. He also knew that he looked rather silly. No invitation was ever sent to the People's Democracy.

John Hume responded publicly to the invitation by saying that there was no point in meeting with Sinn Fein as long as it was controlled by the IRA. A meeting was therefore arranged between the IRA and Hume. To my certain knowledge the IRA delegation consisted of Seamus Twomey, J. B. O'Hagan and one of the Maze escapees. On the night in question I was in Sligo to see Jimmy Jones, but that meeting was cancelled because Jones had been drafted in to help organize the Hume/ IRA summit. The meeting was a failure, in any case, ending after only a few minutes when Hume refused to allow the IRA to videotape the proceedings.

All of this was set against the backdrop of the behind-the-scenes diplomatic activity that eventually resulted in the Anglo-Irish Agreement of 1985. For years Sinn Fein/IRA had kept up a steady tirade against the SDLP, describing them variously as domestic cockroaches and the Stoop Down Low Party. But Adams was gradually coming to realize that John Hume was hugely influential within the nationalist movement – if not indeed its dominant figure – particularly in the politically influential circles of Irish America. Adams's immediate challenge was to work out ways of co-opting Hume's influence and harnessing his respectability.

The Anglo-Irish Agreement was sold to Margaret Thatcher on the basis that it would bolster support for the SDLP to the detriment of Sinn Fein, and would result in improved co-operation on security from the Irish Republic and also, it was believed, a tougher line there on the IRA. None of that materialized to any significant degree, except that in the short term the electoral rise of Sinn Fein was indeed halted, and in fact reversed.

Sinn Fein/IRA opposed the Anglo-Irish Agreement because they recognized that it was a gift to the SDLP. They also believed that it institutionalized partition. But under the surface, Adams in particular was viewing things in a different light. Though of course opposed to the Agreement, he learned two valuable lessons from it: that the British government would ignore the wishes of unionists if it suited them; and that John Hume was a much bigger political player than were the republicans. In that recognition lay the beginnings of the IRA/Sinn Fein peace strategy. Over the coming months and years IRA/Sinn Fein's outward stance towards John Hume and the SDLP began to soften. All of this was obvious to anybody attending the meetings that I was attending, particularly if, as I was, you were interested in examining the nuances of republican plotting and language.

The local elections took place on 20 June 1985, and I was elected to Tralee District Council as Sinn Fein candidate. One of the reasons why I have always distrusted most politicians is that I understand how easy and effective it is to be insincere and dishonest. I didn't want to be a Sinn Fein candidate, nor even a councillor, talking about and proposing things I did not believe in. In fact, in most cases I held the opposite view from the one which I was forced to propound. I did what I could, but it was at best faintly irritating having to go along with half-baked policies that would have been greeted with laughter at a meeting of the Flat Earth Society. The irony was that by by June 1985 I was OC of the IRA's Southern Command, a member of GHQ staff, a member of Sinn Fein's National Executive and a local councillor – as well as being a high-level informer for the Irish police. A bizarre existence, if ever there was one. And through all of this time the murder of Sean Corcoran remained uppermost in my mind. In spite of my responsibilities I still could not, at that time, summon any enthusiasm for my work.

Throughout the summer of 1985, I acted as the contact between the boat-owning businessman and the IRA. One day, after bringing him another message of yet another meeting, he asked me if I knew what was going on. I replied that I didn't, nor must he tell me. He replied that he was only prepared to go ahead if he could work with me, to which I replied that he must sort that out with Joe Cahill.

I knew that plans involving him and the IRA were steaming ahead, but I hadn't been made privy to them. I knew the idea in essence and that was enough. I was happy not to be officially involved: if it ever came to anything I would be in the clear. Although I was OC of Southern Command, this did not automatically make me aware of any or all arms shipments into the Irish Republic. Information in the IRA is compartmentalized; this was an Army Council operation, and McKenna, Gabriel Cleary and others were going to tell no one about it who did not need to know.

On 27 June our daughter was born – but I was exhausted and stressed, and felt I was beginning to lose control, as if everything was coming unglued, and I was dangerously close to not caring.

At the end of August I resigned from the Sinn Fein

National Executive and shortly afterwards stood down as OC of Southern Command, giving the excuse that I wanted to spend more time at home. There was resistance. Gerry Adams initially refused to accept my resignation from the National Executive and at one stage Pat Doherty came to my home and offered me the position of national organizer for Sinn Fein. It was an important job: the abstentionist issue still hadn't been resolved, but the leadership was determined to bring it to a head, and the Army Council had decided that making political progress in the Irish Republic was the main task facing the movement at the time. The national organizer would play a key role. I turned the offer down. From that point I dropped very much out of the public frame. I still had access to an enormous amount of information from different sources, which I always passed on, but in truth I'd had enough.

I also became aware around October that a small number of people were beginning to oppose and perhaps even distrust me. I knew for certain that Maurice Pendergast had suspicions that he could not articulate. Luckily for me he seemed unwilling to act on what was obviously a highly honed instinct. Once I ceased to be in absolute control it left a gap into which other people moved, and some began to question my way of doing things. For quite some time I had had the sort of control – certainly locally – that allowed me to set the pace and provide cover for my real activities. Once that control had gone, it was inevitable that eventually people would begin to wonder why certain things were done in certain ways.

In November I made up my mind to leave Ireland, along with Louise and our daughter. By that time all I was really doing in terms of republican activity was attending council meetings and keeping in touch with people like Pat Currie. I told my Garda contact. I think from a personal point of view he was glad to hear it. We had both known that this double life could not go on for ever. And perhaps after Corcoran's murder he understood that it was only a matter of time until I ended up the same way. But I don't think that fear was the reason I felt I had to get out. I was simply tired from the crushing emotional and mental pressure of the life I had been living. Louise wanted to return to England too. She had never really spoken about it, but I knew it was in her mind and I went along with it. The biggest sadness would be leaving my son. He was now six years old and I had seen a lot of him throughout those years.

Making arrangements to leave without anyone's knowledge was difficult. I had to tell my ex-wife that I was leaving but I told no one else except my Garda contact. The gardai made a token attempt to make me stay, but I think they knew that there was simply no point in pursuing it. My mind was made up.

20

We left Tralee under cover of darkness on the evening of 6 December 1985. With the help of a friend we had quietly sold most of our possessions. We couldn't afford to have any visitors in the last couple of days. One glance would have shown that we were moving and had word leaked out it would have been very bad news for us. It was an emotional event for me, as it was for Louise, who had by now made many friends in Ireland. I had said goodbye to my son a couple of hours before we were due to leave and he had been very upset. He didn't know exactly what was happening, of course, but he knew that I was going away and that he didn't want me to. How can you explain any of this to a six-year-old? I didn't know whether I would ever see him again, whether I would ever speak to or see my parents, brother or sister, or indeed old friends from childhood and schooldays. What would happen to Louise and our daughter? How would we live? I didn't have an answer for any of these questions. Driving out of our house, past the familiar windmill and the canal at Blennerville, I felt sadness mixed with relief. I really loved this place and I determined then that one day I would return.

We made our way to Cork, where we intended to get

a flight to Heathrow. The Garda had already asked me if I would be prepared to meet the English police once I arrived at Heathrow and I knew that someone from Special Branch would meet me at the airport.

By the time we reached Cork, however, my girlfriend had been taken very ill and was suffering from severe abdominal pain. We quickly drove to a local hospital, where she was admitted for tests. I was now in a difficult position. We had been extraordinarily lucky that no one had come to visit us at home during our last couple of days there; I couldn't push my luck by going back now. We had very little money and I could not afford to stay in a hotel for long. Most republicans in Cork would know me by sight, so it wasn't safe to hang around for very long. The tests revealed that Louise had acute appendicitis, which had gone untreated for some time; she was extremely ill and would require an operation and a longer than normal period of recuperation. She was feeling very low and I badly wanted to stay and visit her, but after a couple of days it was clear that that would be too dangerous, and that our daughter and I would have to go to England ahead of her. My daughter was just five months old at the time. I knew that the moment I disappeared the IRA rumour mill would spring into action. As the plane took off I wondered if I would ever see Ireland again.

It was a bitterly cold evening when we arrived at Heathrow. I was holding our daughter in a little carry-cot, waiting for my luggage, when a couple of stewardesses began to play with her. Suddenly I heard this voice beside me saying, 'Get rid of them! Get rid of them!' Everybody else heard him as well. It was my introduction to the policeman from Scotland Yard who had been assigned to look after me.

Over the next month or so I would learn that he was far from the best choice: he proved to be inefficient, a racist and a bigot. For now we walked to a car and drove to a guesthouse close to the airport, where we waited outside for quite a long time until the owner arrived and let us in. I didn't discuss anything with the owner, but it was obvious that he knew my escort was a policeman. I was Irish, carrying little in the way of luggage, and I had a young baby with me. It wouldn't have taken much to work out that I was in some kind of trouble.

At this stage I had only £4.04. I had left several hundred pounds with Louise, which is what remained from the sale of our possessions. My daughter and I stayed at the guesthouse for several days, during which time I met my very own policeman a number of times. Even the most simple dealings with him were nearly always pointless. Once, when I asked him to get some disposable nappies for my daughter – the smallest size available – he came back with antiseptic wipes.

Four days or so after we had left Cork, Louise signed herself out of the hospital there and flew to Heathrow, where she got a bus to where we were staying. Her condition was poor and she really should have been in hospital, but being away from our daughter in such strange circumstances had proved too much for her to handle.

Strange as it might seem, she still did not question me about my work. She obviously had an idea, though, and was glad that we were leaving Ireland. She assumed that the guesthouse owner was a friend of mine from my past.

She phoned her parents, who lived near by, and told them to expect us. That evening we took a taxi to their home. She appeared confident that we would receive a friendly reception, but I was not nearly so sure. After all, they hadn't seen their daughter for four years. They knew about their grandchild but hadn't met her, and their daughter and I weren't married. To cap all of that, we were landing at their home in a taxi in the snow, with very little luggage and even less explanation. To say that it all looked odd is hardly overstating it.

Her parents did greet us in a friendly, if reserved, manner. My girlfriend, her mother and our daughter rather quickly went upstairs, leaving me alone with her father, a quiet, somewhat withdrawn man. For perhaps an hour and thirty minutes no words were spoken. Eventually he said, 'Be careful of the shower in the morning. The water comes on very hot.' Then he went back to doing his *Daily Telegraph* crossword puzzle.

We stayed with her parents for a week or so and throughout that period they asked very little about our situation or future intentions. We told them that we were moving to Bristol, where I would work in my uncle's business. No such uncle existed, but we had to tell them something to buy time. While we were there I wrote a letter to Pat Doherty, which I sent by way of my Garda contact, to be posted in Dublin. In it I outlined my 'anger and frustration' at having been the subject of local gossip regarding my integrity and loyalty to the cause, and my decision to leave the movement rather than remain and create further problems for them. Rumours would have escalated to such a degree by the time the letter arrived with Doherty that its contents would have appeared entirely plausible. And so, to my satisfaction, it proved. I later learned that Doherty, McKenna and O'Neill would not countenance the notion that I was an informer, and though they were still keen to talk to me to clarify matters, the necessity to do so was perhaps less urgent.

By now I had also been introduced to another policeman, Graham, who was of far superior quality to his predecessor in every respect. He attempted to debrief me, but he lacked the background and it wasn't entirely successful. I was also in constant phone contact with the Garda and they were aware of my dealings with the English police.

When we left Louise's parents' home we went to stay briefly with an old schoolfriend of hers who had once visited us in Ireland. Then we moved back near her parents, where we shared a house with another of her old friends. I had no idea what I was going to do. I knew from my Garda contact that discussions were taking place between the Garda and the British security services about how best to give me a comprehensive debriefing.

Early in January I received word from Graham that 'other people' wanted to speak to me. I checked with the gardai – they knew about it and were happy for me to go ahead. Even though I was concerned that too many people might get to know about me, I realized that by this stage I had no real alternative. I went to London – to Liverpool Street station – where I reacquainted myself with my first policeman, who proceeded to get us lost as he tried to find the hotel where we were due to attend the meeting.

When we eventually found it I was introduced to a tall, fair man in his late thirties or early forties, who looked as if he had spent considerable time in the army. The policeman left as soon as very basic introductions had been completed. I turned to 'John', as he called himself, and said, 'Does this mean that I'm not going to have to deal with that halfwit any longer?' He laughed loudly and said, 'Yes, Plod is a bit tiresome, isn't he?'

Strangely, in all of my dealings with the security forces over the years, that policeman is the only person I found it impossible to deal with. But I felt that the security service's disregard, sometimes even contempt, for 'Plod' was uncalled for.

During my first conversation with 'John' I explained that the most important thing I had to tell him was about the boat-owning businessman and the Libyan connection. He listened carefully to what I had to say and then asked me if I knew where any shipments would be landed. I replied that I didn't, and he said, 'Arklow, off the coast of County Wicklow.' I didn't reply; it seemed to me that they already had the information they needed. The next thing I told him, however, produced an instant reaction. It concerned Sean Meehan, brother of well-known Ardoyne republican Martin Meehan. The IRA already knew that Sean Meehan was an RUC Special Branch and MI5 agent, because a rogue member of the security forces had fingered him. Meehan had been lucky to escape the clutches of the IRA. I had found out from Seamus Twomey that the IRA believed that Meehan was in Fort Worth in Texas. I told this to John. The look on his face told me all I needed to know. In fact I was able to tell him that the IRA had sent a man to Texas to investigate and that they believed Meehan ran a small haulage business there. John confirmed or denied nothing, but he was obviously very interested.

We arranged to meet again after lunch. Only at that point did John explain that he didn't work for the police, but for another 'agency'. I told him that I had more or less grasped that. I also said that I was in regular contact with the Garda and would be bound by what they said. The information was not too well received, but I didn't care. This was how it had to be.

John told me that they wanted to conduct a full, professional debriefing, which would be cleared at a high level with the RUC and the Garda. I was quite agreeable, especially as the Garda had already mentioned this before I left Ireland and were keen for me to comply as they lacked the facilities for such an operation outside

Ireland. He further explained that I would have to live outside Britain for this to happen – somewhere in Europe – and that I would have to leave the country within two days. I wondered why this had to be, but to be honest I didn't give it a lot of thought. I explained that I would be taking Louise and our daughter with me, but he seemed to have no opinion about this.

I really didn't know what Louise was going to make of my telling her I wanted to move to some place on the Continent, but she trusted me and had long ago taken the decision not to ask questions. Before I left, John gave me £300 to cover the cost of travel and told me that 'Plod' would give me a further £1,700 to cover relocation costs, accommodation and so on, once I had actually left the country. I went home and told Louise that we were going to live in Europe for a while. Her passport was out of date, so I would have to go first and find a place for us to live, and she would then follow with our daughter once that was sorted out. She was relatively happy and appeared to have confidence in me, which helped her to overcome her fears and uncertainties about the future.

Two days later I met with policeman 'Plod' and we travelled by train from Victoria to Dover and then by ferry to Calais. On the ferry he told me that if the police ever became aware that I was in Britain after this day they would have to arrest me. He also muttered something like, 'Maybe it will be different in a year or so.' Beyond registering that, I took little notice. Only later would I realize that what he said that day on the ferry was indeed of some importance. In effect, I was being escorted from the country and told not to come back

Once we got to Calais we had a drink and he went off back to London. Before he left he gave me the £1,700. Good riddance, I thought to myself. I stayed in Calais that night and travelled on to Paris the following morning. I spent a couple of days there but decided that Holland would suit us better, so I took the train to Amsterdam and booked into a hotel near the centre. I had a phone number for John and used it. Throughout this time I was in constant contact with Louise. After a couple of days in Amsterdam I rented a flat, or at least paid the initial deposit. It wasn't in the best position, being too central, and even though it was relatively expensive it wasn't best suited to a couple and a young baby.

I had been in Amsterdam for about a week when a further meeting was arranged with John. Like many meetings that followed, it was arranged in a tortuous, almost comical way. I would phone a number in London, which was always answered by the same woman, who then gave instructions usually on the lines of, 'Turn left, proceed eastwards for five minutes, on coming to a named landmark turn right, next left, second right.' I had some good fun trying to spot who, if anyone, was monitoring me as I followed the convoluted instructions.

Our first meeting in Amsterdam took place on the day when Louise and our daughter were due to fly in. John was quite adamant that Amsterdam was not a good place for me to live. It had a large Irish community, many of them from Belfast, and a substantial core of IRA sympathizers. I was aware of this but perhaps did not really appreciate how well organized they were there. He suggested that I move to Haarlem, a town relatively close to Amsterdam. We spoke for some time that day and he outlined how he would like the debriefing to develop. He proposed to see me at least once a month; after these meetings he would liaise with the RUC and Garda and together they would formulate the questions and follow-on for the next session. I was quite happy to help in any way I could. Helping to inform democratic governments about IRA terrorism and possibly helping to save lives seemed to me to be a decent thing to do.

Later that day I went to the airport to meet Louise and our daughter. I had given up the flat in Amsterdam, and we stayed the night in a small hotel in Haarlem. The next day we booked into fairly cheap self-catering accommodation, from where we spent a week or so investigating the area until we chanced upon Zandvoort, a seaside resort on the North Sea, a short train ride from Haarlem. Because it was still February and well out of season there was plenty of accommodation at relatively cheap rates. We rented a small house from a young married couple who lived next door. It suited us just fine and Zandvoort was a lovely place at that time of year. The people were friendly and easygoing, and we had the sea to enjoy and wonderful nature walks near by. We were happy, and for the first time since our very early days Louise and I were spending a lot of time in each other's company. I even wrote the bulk of a long novel.

On top of the initial relocation allowance of £2,000, MI5 paid me approximately £500 a month, which, after rent, meant that we lived on slightly less than £40 a week. It wasn't possible for me to work without a permit, although I was writing all of the time. The lap of luxury it was not.

Once every three or four weeks John would come over and we would spend a day together going through whatever areas were of interest to him. He handled these sessions in an extremely professional manner, asking questions that were coherent and intelligent, which meant that little time was wasted. We usually met fairly early in the morning. I would phone London from an agreed callbox and would follow the directions given.

Somewhere along the route John would appear and we would go to a hotel room that he had booked. The session would continue all day with a break for lunch in the room. Our dealings were always amicable, but we tended to stay away from our personal lives and political views. I didn't want to discuss with him my motivation, my personal views or my relationship with my girlfriend. John often asked to see a section of the novel I was writing but I always refused.

Before our meetings began John always made it clear that he did not wish me to admit to or discuss specific activities I may have been involved in in Northern Ireland. Then one day, after about four of these sessions, he said to me, 'It won't be possible to get you a pardon.' I looked at him in some amazement. The subject had never come up before and I had certainly not raised it. He went on to explain that it was impossible for someone in my position to get such a pardon. He gave the example of Anthony Blunt, who had in 1964 been granted immunity from prosecution in return for telling the security service the full story of his spying activities for the Soviet government. It had caused considerable controversy at the time and wouldn't be allowed to happen now.

John told me that the RUC believed me to be responsible for the murder of Detective Inspector Peter Flanagan, but that they had no proof. He also mentioned that Sir John Hermon, Chief Constable of the RUC, was willing to let the matter drop. Trevor Forbes, head of Special Branch, said that I should be rewarded for the work I had done, but Michael McAtamany, Deputy Chief Constable of the RUC, said I should be pursued to the ends of the earth. That is what I was told, without my asking any questions. I have no way of knowing if these stories were true.

At this stage John raised the question of whether I would be prepared to lecture to the SAS and junior intelligence officers. He also asked if I would agree to questioning by RUC officers in Holland, and told me that provided I admitted to nothing they had not one shred of evidence against me. I replied that I was quite prepared to do whatever he wanted. Neither of these matters was ever mentioned again and I can only presume that he and his agency were unable to find a way around the obvious difficulties of my situation.

We continued with the debriefing until September 1986, when it came to an end. John had told me some months previously that September was the likely cut-off date, and he made it clear to me now that if I returned to Britain, and the RUC found out, I would be arrested. He reaffirmed that there was no evidence against me. Before we finally parted he handed over £4,000 with a suggestion that Sweden might be a good place to live. I asked him two questions. 'Do you believe that I have told you the truth?' He replied that he did. I then asked him what he thought I would do next, and he said, 'I think you will return to the British mainland and that the RUC will get their claws into you.' It was a pretty prophetic answer, as things turned out.

When the time came to say goodbye I don't think that there was any sense of loss on either side. I had been more than happy to help and the relationship had remained professional. John was capable and played his part cleverly and subtly. My intention had been simply to make sure that I helped people to understand the true nature of the Provisional IRA and to that end I was prepared to work for the benefit of either the British or the Irish government.

Throughout my stay in Holland I had remained in touch with my Garda contact and had occasionally been able to help him; but now, for the first time since 1979, I was free of any official contact with anti-terrorist agencies. Misguidedly, I felt that for the first time my life was my own. I was to be quickly disabused of this assumption.

21

In November 1986 I returned to England, aware that I had to maintain a low profile to avoid attracting police or IRA attention. For financial reasons it was almost impossible for us to remain in Holland; I had no work permit and could at best get only a low-paid job in the black economy. In addition, Louise had continuing health problems which meant that she had to go to hospital in London every four weeks for tests and monitoring. To do so in Holland would have meant going private and we simply could not afford it. Consequently England seemed the only viable option for us.

We settled in Tunbridge Wells, partly because Liz, her partner and our son had moved there and it meant that I was able to see the boy again. We rented a three-bedroomed semi-detached house in a quiet part of town. I had no idea whether I could work in my own name, and thus any work I got during that period was either part-time or temporary – labouring, shelf-stacking in supermarkets, and so on, where few questions were asked. Before long Louise was well enough to return to work, at first part-time and then full time.

Life was relatively happy, and for some time I was

quite content to let the days go by in an easygoing way without dwelling too much on the past or the future. We both felt unfulfilled, though; the future seemed empty and a bit bleak. Of course, my involvement in Ireland was missing from my life, and I felt its absence. Every now and again something would happen that would push Ireland, or more specifically the IRA, into the fore-front of my mind.

In autumn 1986, just after the end of my debriefing with John, the republican movement split. An IRA convention held in Navan in October of that year – the first since they became operational in 1970 – voted by a large majority to abandon the traditional republican policy of refusing to allow Sinn Fein candidates to take their seats in the Irish parliament if elected. Once the IRA had taken such a position, Sinn Fein's rubber stamp was inevitable. The Sinn Fein ard fheis which took place soon after, on 1 November, overwhelmingly endorsed the decision of the IRA convention.

Ruari O'Bradaigh, Daithi O'Connaill and the group of traditionalists aligned to them walked out of the ard fheis in a planned move. They were supported by those IRA members who were opposed to the new policy, and together this group immediately announced the formation of Republican Sinn Fein. They were warned by the IRA that any attempt to establish a military wing would be met with an immediate and severe response.

Meetings did, however, take place across the country, and this led to the formation of the Continuity Army Council. To avoid any further split in the republican movement the IRA agreed that its members could also be members of RSF, providing they gave full allegiance to the IRA's armed struggle. Of course, as long as the IRA was engaged wholeheartedly in the armed struggle there was no real opening for the Continuity Army Council, but once the IRA moved into ceasefire mode things were rather different. Indeed, in recent times the CAC has gone on to engage in occasional bombings and attempted bombings, probably with some degree of support on the ground from disgruntled IRA supporters.

Following the emergence of Republican Sinn Fein, the Provisional IRA stepped up its campaign on the ground to prevent their support seeping away to RSF: this was, of course, facilitated by the arrival of the huge Libyan arms shipments in late 1985 and early 1986.

Of even more concern to Adams and McGuinness had been the signing of the Anglo-Irish Agreement in November 1985. They knew that if the Dublin government fulfilled its obligation under the Agreement to improve security co-operation, then the pressure on IRA logistics and planning would increase dramatically. Quite clearly, the Agreement was also designed to damage Sinn Fein in its electoral battle with the SDLP for control of northern nationalism.

But although the IRA was implacably opposed to the Agreement, with good reason, Adams – that pragmatic politician – was still examining it in terms of how republicans could turn it to advantage in the longer term. Some of the National Executive felt that it should be left to the unionists to destroy the Agreement, or if not destroy it then succeed in damaging their own credibility by engaging in confrontation with Thatcher. Since she had refused to give in to the hunger strikers, some judged it unlikely that once the Agreement was signed she would backtrack, no matter what pressure was brought to bear – especially since its political impact would be confined to Northern Ireland.

This was the political backdrop in 1986, when the Provisionals ended abstentionism. No one at the time was aware of the massive shipments of weapons that had recently been imported from Libya. I knew later from two people who were present that the call from the floor of the IRA convention was, 'Give us the gear to finish the job.' Few of them knew then that much of the 'gear' was either already available or on its way.

I had thought from my conversations with John that the security forces were well aware of the details of the Libyan connection and on top of the situation. On 1 November 1987 I learned that the French authorities had seized a massive one hundred and fifty tons of arms and ammunition, including twenty surface-to-air missiles bound from Libya to the IRA on board a coaster called the *Eskund*. My first thought was, 'Bullshit.' Surely the capture was not down to the French but was the result of intelligence co-operation and surveillance dating back to 1985? My delight was quickly to turn to disbelief and anger as it became clear that the IRA had in fact already succeeded in landing three shipments. How could this have happened after all the information I and others had provided? It is difficult to say, but I suspect that internal rivalries within the different security agencies in both jurisdictions had much to do with it. I had told the Garda, Scotland Yard and MI5 that the shipments were due and MI5 were aware of where they would be landed. And yet the historical fact remains that such shipments still successfully made their way into the country.

With such material at their disposal the IRA very probably had the military hardware to keep the campaign going for many years to come. More importantly, they had achieved a significant psychological victory. The most important function of the security forces was to try to deprive the IRA of money and material; with the Libyan connection the IRA had demonstrated its effectiveness by importing, distributing and dumping vast quantities of weaponry. It was a huge aid to the morale of the organization – it also provided the IRA with the wherewithal to continue their activities indefinitely.

I could hardly believe that such a security disaster was possible. The key person captured on the *Eskund* was Gabriel Cleary, the IRA's director of engineering and the man most responsible for its range of very effective homemade weaponry – from mortars to sophisticated long-delay timing devices. Over the coming weeks the Irish government carried out massive searches to try to find the Libyan weapons from the three previous shipments – with some success, it must be said. During that time I kept in regular touch with my Garda contact, who was certainly helpful in reminding and prompting me about individuals and areas where such amounts of weaponry might be held.

Around this time I made a momentous decision on a matter I had been thinking over since 1981. I now realized that there was only one way in which I could continue to help damage the killing capacity of the IRA: by handing myself up to the RUC and giving evidence against as many people as possible. Whereas before, my information had enabled the Garda only to entrap, now, in formal court proceedings, it could be used to put the same people away for many years. By January 1988 I was determined to follow this course. It's quite possible that had I not met Louise when I did I would have turned myself in many years before. It was now well over a year since I had finished the debrief in Holland and life had been largely uneventful during that period. My daughter was growing up, as was my son, and Louise and I had a more than friendly but increasingly detached relationship. There were so many things that I had never been able to say to her, and so many questions she had not wanted to ask, and this had inevitably come between us. I couldn't continue working indefinitely in part-time and poorly paid jobs, which was soul destroying, and I was having difficulty with my writing. To some extent I inhabited a twilight area where there was little chance of normality or permanence.

Handing yourself up to the authorities to face a certain life sentence is not an easy thing to do. It was fourteen years since the murders of Eva Martin and Peter Flanagan, and those killings were no longer in my mind daily. Time and distance do have an effect and it is pointless to pretend otherwise. But I have never been able to stop thinking about the murder of Sean Corcoran. Then and even now the circumstances surrounding his death and the failure of the Garda to intervene have not been resolved. I know that nothing can bring any of these three people back from the dead, but at least in the case of Sean Corcoran I could do something to right the wrongs of the past. One of my reasons for handing myself up was to force a proper Garda internal investigation into his death: I had plans as to how I could achieve that.

Life drifted on through the summer while I tried to work out what I must do next. No matter what, I would have to take the decision I thought was right. Something was pushing me inexorably towards handing myself in. Often the words that flashed through my mind were my own from years before, after the murder of Peter Flanagan: 'You're going to have to pay for this some day.'

One of the difficulties for me was that there was no one I could discuss things with. Louise knew nothing of what was going through my mind. How could I explain to her that I was going to walk away from her and our daughter into a life sentence? What would happen to them? And always the thought came back that my children never seemed to play the part in my considerations that they should. There always seemed to be something more 'important' to worry about.

In September I summoned up the courage to tell Louise that I was thinking of handing myself up to the police for IRA stuff I had been involved with in the 1970s, long before I had met her. At first I don't think she knew what to make of it and wasn't – to put it mildly – very keen on discussing it. She simply didn't want to know about it, even though I knew she had realized that something very serious was on my mind.

A couple of times over the next two months I walked up to the police station in Tunbridge Wells, but I wasn't yet ready to go in. Eventually, on Tuesday, 29 November 1988, at about 7.15 p.m., I walked into the police station and asked to see someone from CID. The young policeman behind the desk asked me what it was all about and I said that I wished to admit to the murder of a Special Branch detective inspector in Northern Ireland in 1974. He looked at me for a moment or two, trying to work out whether he had heard correctly or whether I was some kind of headcase.

He then asked me to sit in a room while he went to fetch someone, or possibly a straitjacket. A detective came in and asked me some questions, which I answered. I was put in a cell. A short time later a superintendent arrived and explained that I was being held at the request of another police force who wished to question me.

Though I had the support of many senior IRA people, my handing myself up would, in the immediate future, cause some panic and renewed anxiety about my intentions. My objective was to do maximum damage to the IRA and I needed to ensure that knowledge of my arrest did not precipitate an exodus of vulnerable IRA people over the border into the safety of the Irish Republic. In order to do so, I needed to persuade them I *wasn't* the kind of person who would give evidence. I had thought a lot about how to do this and I now set out to create as much confusion as possible.

To maintain the stance I had already established with Pat Doherty, I first decided to present myself to the police as someone who had been driven to the point of despair because some people back home thought I was an informer and I had been so horrified of being accused of such a terrible thing that I had left Ireland. Now I was engaged in a drastic last-ditch attempt to clear my name of that charge by giving myself up. I knew that I had the support of many senior IRA people who were so tunnel-visioned about the rightness of their cause that they could not believe that anyone would become an informer except for reasons of greed, fear or manipulation by the security services: for them it would be inconceivable that anyone might be acting on principle. The very fact that I had given myself up would negate the possibility that I was an informer. Even within the Garda only three people had known that I was an informer when active, and, even though that number might have increased since then, I believed it unlikely that rumour and specu-lation would cause the IRA to come to any conclusions. They would expect Special Branch to add fuel to the rumours that I was an informer only if I wasn't one.

The situation can be understood only if you remember that the IRA is an organization that produces people pre-pared to starve themselves to death, people prepared to spend large parts of their lives in prison. In short, it pro-duces people who are prepared to inflict death, pain and suffering on themselves as well as on others in pursuit of a cause. Being an informer, in Irish nationalist terms especially, is the worst crime you can commit, so anyone of my family background who had been involved in the republican movement at such a senior level and for such a long time could well be expected to be half mad at being thought to have betrayed the cause.

Before I gave myself up I had laid the foundations of the cover story by phoning a Tralee-based journalist called Gerald Colleran, to tell him that I was giving myself up to prove I was not an informer. I had told my girlfriend that I was going to hand myself in and she had stopped talking to me: full stop. She felt that I was letting her and our daughter down, and she was right, but the force that was propelling me into that police station left me powerless to resist it, even though I tried. I never dreamed when I was an active IRA member in my late teens that one day I would do this. I was walking into certain life imprisonment with the expectation that I would serve at least ten years, but I knew that it had to be done. Having said that, walking into that police station was the most frightening thing I have ever done: my heart had pounded and my legs had wanted to turn right round and walk away to safety.

I was held in the police cell in Tunbridge Wells until the following morning, when two RUC officers arrived from Belfast. I would get to know both of them fairly well over the following years and though at this stage I knew nothing about them, in time I would come to have a high regard for them both. They were scrupulously professional, and they were both demonstrably decent men who operated at all times within the rule of law.

They spoke to me for several hours that day. I was being fairly cagey, as were they. I am convinced that they thought that there was more to me than met the eye, but had nothing on which to base that suspicion. Early on one of them asked me if there was something here they should know, but all I could say was that I would make things clear later.

That evening the Tunbridge Wells police asked me to sign a form agreeing to return to Northern Ireland. I did so, and later we were driven to the airport. A detective from Tunbridge Wells accompanied us on the flight. We were met at City airport in Belfast by other RUC officers and driven to Gough Barracks, an RUC interrogation centre in Armagh City.

I had been suffering from a fairly severe back problem for a couple of years, and because of the night in the police cell, the drive and the plane journey, I was in serious pain. In fact I had been in hospital on a couple of occasions in England and on the day I handed myself in I was due at St Thomas's in London to see a Canadian specialist. It was one of the reasons I had chosen to act then; otherwise I might have had to put it off for several months while I had treatment. Happily, the first person I saw at Gough Barracks was a doctor. Later that night I was introduced to a senior police officer from RUC headquarters who obviously knew quite a lot about my background. I gave him the real reason why I had handed myself in and also made it clear that I was not interested in any kind of deal with them. My motives were to damage the IRA by preventing as much future activity as possible. If that meant a long prison sentence for me, so be it.

Although I had spoken in general terms about my involvement in the IRA to the RUC officers in Tunbridge Wells, it wasn't until I reached Gough Barracks that we began to go over my past life in detail. I confessed to many crimes and knew that I would be charged with those that had taken place in Northern Ireland during 1974 and 1975. However, the one thing I really wanted to talk to the RUC about was the murder of Sean

Corcoran. I knew that it was outside their jurisdiction, having taken place in the Irish Republic, but at least I could set a plan in action. I was aware that no investigation had taken place in the intervening years and that the one reason why the case might possibly be reopened was if new evidence came to light. Even when I had been considering handing myself up, I decided this was the only opportunity and indeed the only means I could think of to instigate, albeit belatedly, an inquiry into the matter. Questions needed to be asked; the Garda had to be forced to reveal why they had not intervened. I knew that I could not be charged by the RUC for that murder because Northern Ireland and the Republic of Ireland are two completely different legal jurisdictions. Any action had to come from the Garda.

Thus it was that, three years after Corcoran was killed, I made a statement to the RUC in Belfast in which I confessed to his murder. That statement was patently untrue; I knew the circumstances of his death in detail, and the people who were responsible. I needed the Garda to face up to their responsibilities. As far as I was concerned, although with hindsight such a course of action may seem foolhardy and difficult to understand, I knew that I was already facing two charges of murder and in all likelihood life sentences in Northern Ireland. I knew that my motives were well intentioned. I wanted the truth to come out. I had, after all, voluntarily given myself up and confessed to two murders for which the police had no evidence against me.

The RUC were duty bound to take any information relating to criminal activities in the Irish Republic to the Garda. I believed that once my file reached Dublin the Garda would look into what had happened. Only then would my contact be forced to reveal that it had been known where Sean Corcoran was being held, that it had been known he was about to be murdered and that the police had still not intervened. I hoped that the police hierarchy would have changed in the three years that had elapsed since the murder, and that at the very least there would be somebody there who would push for an internal inquiry to discover what had really happened.

Corcoran's death could and should have been prevented by the Garda. After all, they had been aware for a long time that his life was in grave danger. I had kept them informed every step of the way and they had failed to act. They knew that I had not killed Corcoran – I had told them so and had given names of those present. In the course of my statement to the RUC, I had included details that differed significantly from the version I had been told by Pat Currie. I stated that three bullets had been fired, when I knew that only one was used. I stated that Corcoran was kneeling when he was murdered, when I knew the forensic evidence would prove otherwise. By so doing, I hoped that there would be sufficient disparities between the two versions I had told them, and that the Garda would be forced to clarify what had really happened. I also expected that the deliberate errors in the fake confession would mean that the Director of Public Prosecutions in Dublin would be unlikely to authorize the Garda to proceed against me.

Having made my statement, I presumed that wheels would turn within the Garda and that in the fullness of time an internal inquiry would uncover the facts of the case. I was sadly mistaken: nothing happened.

It was only much later that the two RUC officers dealing with the case told me that they had taken the file concerning my activities in the south of Ireland, including the Sean Corcoran affair, to the Garda authorities in Dublin, and that the particular Garda involved had simply glanced at the file and suggested they go for a drink. I wasn't aware until quite recently that the Garda did subsequently, in June 1989, submit a file to the DPP, who decided that there was insufficient evidence to proceed with a prosecution. To all intents and purposes at that time, I was still 'guilty' of the murder of Sean Corcoran. I have never been asked for clarification by the Garda, either then or now.

In 1992 I made a terrible error, the consequences of which remain with me to this day. It was three years after my 'confession', and I had heard nothing from the Garda or the RUC on the subject. I had, of course, hoped that the truth could be revealed by an internal inquiry. No such inquiry had taken place. I certainly did not want to cause Sean Corcoran's family any more grief than they had already experienced and up to that point had had no intention of going public. I hadn't thought it would be necessary. But when it became clear that there was no movement on the matter I reluctantly decided the story must come out notwithstanding the fact that it would in all likelihood prove a significant weapon in the hands of the republicans and their media allies. In 1992, I was collaborating with Liam Clarke on a series of articles for the *Sunday Times* and I knew that Liam had excellent contacts with the RUC. He would undoubtedly be aware of the statement regarding my part in Corcoran's murder. I repeated my 'confession' to him and it was subsequently published in the *Sunday Times* and other newspapers. Surely now the story could not be ignored. The case would have to be reopened and the truth revealed.

I realize now that such a course of action was the wrong one to take. At that point I could have told the whole story, the real truth behind Sean Corcoran's death, and my subsequent efforts to instigate a full inquiry by means of my 'confession' of 1989. However, I did not and to a certain extent I cannot now think why. After thirteen years of being an informer and of living solely in my own head without recourse to advice from friends and family, I was used to making my own decisions. In this instance it didn't occur to me to deviate from the stance I had taken with the RUC. I was in prison, and was likely to remain there for a very long time. I was not used to taking the future into account. From the age of fifteen I had been a member of the IRA and had been immersed in their bizarre world of plotting and paranoia. The right way forward was never simple. In prison, a lonely labyrinth at the best of times, those tendencies became if anything more exaggerated than before and the sense of isolation was extreme. It was almost like a form of madness. False confessions are commonplace within the prison system and although mine had not been forced it was as unreliable as if it had been, but for different reasons. Some skewed logic had taken root in my brain; in my obsessive pursuit of getting the case reopened I had lost sight of how such an objective could best be achieved.

After the 1992 interview in the *Sunday Times* in which I admitted to Corcoran's murder, a number of newspapers picked up the story and carried it forward. During the following two years I was interviewed in jail by journalists from a variety of newspapers worldwide, and one in particular from the *Boston Globe,* in which the story was trotted out once more with grisly embellishments. Because the whole account was false it seemed pointless to quibble over details. Once I had repeated the lie to the *Sunday Times* it was increasingly difficult to admit to any other publication that there was no truth in the story. Incredibly, I still believed that the original confession and my reiteration of it might eventually have the intended effect. Of course by then this was extremely unlikely, but in my isolation I could not know that. After a while, and in spite of the fact that my story had not and could not be verified by the Garda, it took on the mantle of truth.

After the initial flurry of interest the story died away. It was only a couple of weeks following my release, five years later in 1997, that it again became a source of controversy. This time it was primarily at the instigation of one journalist, Vincent Browne, who pursued the case and managed to turn it into a major issue. I have no quarrel with Browne for running the story. He is a pioneer of investigative journalism, and I respect him for that, even if I find him quick to condemn and too inclined to believe those whose opinions lend weight to his angle. He insists that the murder of Sean Corcoran was a tragedy that was covered up, and he is right to do so. I only hope that in his pursuit of the gardai responsible for negligence he will remember that everyone is capable of making mistakes, whatever the motives.

Vincent Browne's highlighting of the case once again caught me in a cleft stick. I knew that the strategy I had taken was a mistake, but I did not know how I could put matters straight. I had neither confirmed nor denied that I had killed Sean Corcoran. Ironically, since the major joy of having come out publicly as an informer was being able to tell the truth, I was still caught by an old lie. I confided in a friend and ultimately we concluded that because the story was so complicated it could be explained at length only in the context of this book. As a result, since my release I have simply had to take all the allegations on the chin. Having fabricated the story and then repeated it to a number of publications, it was actually easier to perpetuate the lie than to try to explain what happened, particularly when you know you're not going to be charged with a murder you haven't committed.

Following my release and the attendant publicity, the Irish Minister for Justice has in fact instructed the Garda to conduct an official inquiry into the circumstances surrounding the murder of Sean Corcoran. At the time of writing, that inquiry is ongoing. It has been a long time coming and I can only hope that the unvarnished truth will emerge, not only to demonstrate my innocence once and for all but, more importantly, for the sake of Sean Corcoran's family who, for the past twelve years, have had to live with the consequences of this appalling tragedy.

Vincent Browne observed in an editorial in his magazine, *McGill*, in March, 'It is obvious that O'Callaghan will deny his involvement in the murder of John Corcoran, and that he will have some elaborate but ultimately unbelievable explanation of why he earlier said he was involved.' Browne believes, as others do, that I killed Corcoran to save my own skin. I should point out that I risked my life every day as an informer and when I was in real danger I simply left the country. I rejoined the IRA to save lives, not to take them.

I would also like to point out what is obvious. What possible reason could I have had, other than the one I've given, for confessing to a murder I had not been accused of and falsifying the details to ensure the gardai knew I was lying?

While I had my reasons for telling the RUC about Sean Corcoran, the case was obviously not high on their list of priorities. They were more interested in talking about the crimes I had committed in Northern Ireland. After going through my involvement in the IRA in Tyrone in 1974–5, I was formally charged with the murders of Peter Flanagan and Eva Martin and then taken by helicopter to court in Omagh, where the magistrate remanded me in custody to Crumlin Road prison in Belfast for four weeks. Immediately after the court hearing I was taken to the prison by helicopter.

Once in Crumlin Road, I was fingerprinted, photographed and brought to a cell in the basement annex, which had been used to house the paramilitary super-grasses in the earlier 1980s. At the time only one other prisoner was housed there. Michael Stone was a notorious loyalist who had attacked and killed mourners at the funeral of the IRA terrorists killed by the SAS in Gibraltar. I wondered why he was being kept there and not in the main prison, but it wasn't any of my business and I didn't really want to know. The final part of my plan to prove to the IRA that I was not an informer, or about to give evidence, involved Michael Stone. I sent word to Gerry Adams, through a friend who had visited me, that I had made plans to smuggle in a gun and I was going to kill Stone and also two RUC officers who had made it clear that they would be coming to interview me. This, I felt, would be definitive proof of my loyalties. When Adams heard about it, he took his pipe from his mouth and shook his head, muttering, 'No, no. God, no.' What I did not know, when I had dreamed up my plan, was that the IRA was plotting a major escape from Crumlin Road, and the last thing Adams wanted was any other operation that might put the whole escape in jeopardy. Word came back from him instantly that I was to drop the plan.

The routine at Crumlin Road was desperately mind-numbing. I was locked up for twenty-three hours a day, with only one hour's exercise in a small, narrow, caged-in yard. No television, no radio and little in the way of newspapers. Perhaps worst of all, there was no window in the cell and the large fluorescent light remained on the whole time. After years of being my own man, the first few months in that annex were grim and I certainly wasn't given any favours. Not that I asked for any.

22

I had several visitors in that early period in Crumlin Road. My father, brother and sister came a number of times, but I wasn't particularly keen to see them – I had to maintain the pretence with them that I was still an IRA man and I didn't like that. I managed to get word out to the IRA, who, of course, were very interested in what I was doing. They were told that I had handed myself up to prove that I wasn't an informer.

Throughout that period I had regular, sometimes all-day meetings with the two detectives who had come to Tunbridge Wells. They now knew – they had known within hours – that I had been a Garda informer. Without that knowledge it would have been impossible for me to give evidence. The meetings involved questioning about my entire life while they took copious notes. It was a long and complicated process and they were extremely thorough. Though in the early years of the troubles there is no doubt that the RUC was riddled with men whose bigotry was obvious and real, those officers I dealt with – with the exception of one man – were models of correct behaviour and decency. I have no doubt that, though there are still some RUC officers who are unfit to be in uniform, these problems must be seen in the context of Northern Ireland's troubled and divided society and that without the bravery, dedication and sacrifices made by the majority of RUC officers, Northern Ireland would have descended into an infinitely worse bloodbath years ago.

Christmas Day 1988 – my first in jail – passed by much as any other day. Effectively I was in solitary confinement, having no contact with any other prisoners and being locked up almost all the time. My visits were limited to three per week, of thirty minutes each, but I took little advantage of this. My back was still causing me a great deal of pain and some days I simply couldn't take the hour of exercise. I had no contact with my girlfriend or daughter during this period. I had written but had received no reply. I knew that it would take time for her to forgive me – if she were able to forgive me at all.

By the beginning of 1989 it was dawning on me that, for whatever reason, I was not going to be allowed to give evidence in court against my ex-colleagues. I was not to know that the 'peace process' had already spluttered into life. Charles Haughey, then Irish prime minister, had sanctioned two meetings between representatives of his government and Gerry Adams, Pat Doherty and Mitchel McLaughlin; they had taken place in March and June 1988 at a Dundalk monastery.

By the end of 1988 Sinn Fein/IRA had been in contact with the head of the Catholic Church in Ireland, the SDLP and the Dublin government. Most importantly, talks between Adams and John Hume continued in private. It is inconceivable that the British government and senior security sources were unaware of such developments, and in fact later statements by Peter Brooke, the new Secretary of State, confirmed this. I was therefore in the position of having handed myself up, hoping to give evidence against senior republicans, at a time when both governments were anxious to 'keep the door open'. Although I was unaware of specific developments, I was certainly not insensitive to the realization that events were moving ahead and I was in danger of becoming useless.

I was extremely disappointed by the current situation and therefore had to consider if there was anything else I could do. The IRA had issued a public statement saying that I was not an informer and threatening to take action against those who persisted in circulating such rumours. I was also aware from a friend that Gerry Adams had insisted strongly to some Kerry republicans that they were wrong in making such allegations.

The only way I felt I could be immediately useful was by reporting developments from within the main body of the prison – which meant I had to get myself moved there. During a visit by a republican sympathizer I mentioned that I was being held in the annex against my will and had applied to the Prison Service Head Office to be moved. Republicans would believe that the prison service was simply another weapon in the state's arsenal and would do as the RUC wished in such matters. Given their very nature and their attitude to the state, they could believe nothing else. The reality was very different.

Realizing that I had to follow my remarks through, with the agreement of the RUC I told the prison governor very forcefully that I wished to be transferred to normal prison accommodation immediately. If they failed to comply with my wishes I would begin a hunger and thirst strike. I received a reply saying that I would not be transferred, so I immediately embarked on the strike. I hoped the republicans would believe that an informer would not need to go to such lengths to be transferred – further proof that I was not an informer myself.

I had never been on a full hunger and thirst strike before and had little idea of what to expect. The first few days felt okay and of course I knew that my request would be granted before my health seriously deteriorated. Around the fifth day I began to feel very ill, not helped by the lack of exercise. My mental state was not helped by the fact of my solitary confinement.

After six days without food and water I was informed that my request had been granted, but that first I would have to go to the secure wing of Musgrave Park military hospital because of worries about damage to my kidneys. I remained at Musgrave Park for a week or so and when I was deemed well was transferred back to Crumlin Road.

At Crumlin Road I was brought to C Wing, which housed about ninety republican prisoners and a similar number of loyalists. I was put in a double cell already occupied by a prisoner from Derry, who was not actually a republican but who had been accepted by them and had therefore placed himself under their control. Minutes after my arrival it was four o'clock and time for the evening meal.

Republicans and loyalists had come to an agreement concerning meal times in the prison, which meant that they refused to be placed together in any communal areas. Consequently, republicans and loyalists used the dining area on alternate days, taking meals in their cells when the other group was in the dining area. It was a strange, indeed eerie and rather frightening experience to walk into a room occupied and controlled by about ninety IRA prisoners. While I was fairly sure that I was safe from any immediate attack, it was still a moment I knew had the potential to go seriously wrong. Crumlin Road was an old Victorian prison on the lines of Mountjoy in Dublin. The cells had no internal sanitation

– we used chamber pots and slopped out – and about twenty-one hours every day were spent locked in the cell. Quality of life depended to a large extent on who, if anyone, you were doubled up with. It was a great treat to get a couple of weeks when you didn't have to share a cell. Being locked up with someone who had a primitive attitude to hygiene or who found it particularly difficult to do time could be very difficult. The people I shared with were generally okay and I got along with them without great problems.

It took a few days for any sort of pattern to emerge from the other prisoners. It was obvious that I was a source of some discussion among them and it was hard to detect where most people stood in relation to me. The man in charge of the IRA prisoners in the jail was Sid Walsh, from Belfast. Walsh had spent much of his adult life in jail. I knew him because he had been a member of Sinn Fein's National Executive at the same time as me. He was an exceptionally intelligent, thorough and dangerous operator whom I knew would have to be handled very carefully indeed. Walsh was one of the most important and influential IRA prisoners, if not the most important of all, and was more at home plotting and planning in prison than he was in the outside world. I spent most of my association time in his company, and our conversation ranged freely over a wide area of politics, literature and, of course, the struggle which had already cost Walsh thirteen years of his life and would soon reward him with another sentence of twenty-two years. He was released in 1998.

At that time Walsh certainly did not believe that I was an informer, regardless of what he might say today. He is naturally quite embarrassed that he spent almost a year talking to me in some detail about every area of republican activity, and is bound not to want his superiors to know that he talked so freely. He is in many respects an intelligent and civilized man, but none the less one who would not hesitate to kill or maim for the cause.

One of the most interesting exchanges I had with Walsh took place on the weekend of the Hillsborough disaster. The republican prisoners were all in the canteen when the news came through on television. Like most other young people in Northern Ireland, IRA prisoners often supported English football clubs, and many of them were already gathered around the television set watching football results and news. A few minutes later Walsh, who had seen the news reports, came walking towards me. I knew by his face that something was troubling him and I thought I knew what it was. 'You'll never guess what they're saying,' he said. 'Try me,' I replied. '"Who gives a fuck about those supporters – they're only Brits."' I had guessed correctly. 'Is that what we've created?' he asked. I didn't answer. The following day during the exercise period in the prison yard Walsh returned to the subject. 'If I ever end up like some of those guys, will you promise to put a bullet in the back of my head?' he said. There was no adequate reply for that. Walsh was obviously very upset, angry and close to tears, and it made me realize once again what a horrible stinking mess extreme Irish nationalism is.

It was from Walsh that I learned about a plan to carry out a large-scale breakout from the prison. The scheme involved putting a 500 lb bomb in the bucket of a digger and blowing a hole in the main wall of the prison. Inside, smaller Semtex bombs would be used to blow open gates that would allow the prisoners to get to the hole in the main wall. As many as 180 prisoners would take part in the escape. Six stolen cars would be parked near by, to be used by those whom the IRA leadership viewed as key people. I had been earmarked to go in the same car as Walsh, primarily at his insistence. He wanted to go south immediately after the escape and did not want to make contact with the IRA, at least not in an official way, until the heat was off. He was relying on my contacts in the South and particularly in Kerry to allow him to do that.

I was faced with a serious dilemma. Could Walsh be testing me? And who, if I were to blow the whistle, could I trust in the prison service to handle the matter with the necessary tact? A few days later I asked to see the prison governor, hoping that he would be the one I needed. As it turned out, and purely by accident, I got the right man. I had no intention of giving him all the details of the plan, but I gave him enough information to pass on to one of the RUC officers I had been dealing with. The date for the escape had not yet been picked, but most of the plans were by then in place.

There was one other prisoner in the jail who spent a substantial amount of time in Walsh's and my company. Kevin McMahon, from Belfast, was the IRA commander on C Wing where we were all housed, though he was answerable to Walsh, who was the IRA's prison commander. The interesting thing about McMahon was that he was one of the people who had been captured at the IRA training camp in Kerry in 1980. It had been my information that had sent him to jail in the Republic for eight years. McMahon was nowhere near as sharp as Walsh, but he would have been aware of the rumours that I was an informer. And the fact that he had been captured at an IRA training camp in Kerry with which I had been involved made it possible that he considered me largely responsible for his arrest.

Dealing with people like Walsh and McMahon kept me on my toes. One day when talking with Walsh in the prison yard I inadvertently referred to the IRA as the 'Provos', a term never used by members of the organization and certainly not by those who have been around for some time. Most IRA members refer to it as the Army. As soon as I used the phrase I could have kicked myself, especially as I saw clearly the reaction on Walsh's face. There was a moment when he took in what I had said, before he digested it and decided that it was not important. It could have quite easily gone the other way.

During that period I also came across some of the people I had known from my days in East Tyrone in the mid-seventies. The most prominent and interesting of these was Henry Louis McNally, from Dungannon. McNally had been involved with the Provisional IRA almost from its inception and was a legend in IRA circles in the Mid Ulster area. A quiet, unassuming man then in his mid-forties, McNally was one of the IRA's most formidable and experienced operators. Unlike many men involved for such a long time, McNally had only ever spent a short period in jail. Charged with possession of a weapon in the late seventies, he had spent only a period on remand before being freed because of lack of evidence. I wondered what he was in for now.

I had spent a lot of time in McNally's company during my days in East Tyrone, and we had taken part in many operations, including the one that had led to the murder of Eva Martin. He had a strong pragmatic streak and a ruthless edge, often concealed by his air of vague indifference. One day in early 1974, near a village called Mountfield, close to Omagh, McNally and another IRA man had murdered a retired naval recruitment officer while he was walking his dog along a country road. As McNally's companion ran back to the waiting getaway car, he realized that McNally was not alongside him. As he turned to see what was happening another shot rang out. McNally had walked back and shot the dog. When they reached the car the accomplice said, 'What the fuck are you playing at?' McNally replied calmly, 'Dead dogs tell no tales.'

That was McNally. He was a man who kept his thoughts mainly to himself and allowed very few people to get close to him. This time around, though, it seemed, McNally was well and truly caught. It emerged that he had been captured, along with some very experienced operators, trying to blow up a busload of soldiers returning to their barracks in Antrim Town. When I asked McNally why he had been operating so far from his home base in East Tyrone, he replied that the security forces now had such a tight grip in that area that it was becoming increasingly difficult to operate. They were finding it necessary to move into areas with lower-grade security force activity, where the perceived danger from the IRA was regarded as substantially lower. McNally and his friends had discovered that, away from their hardcore stomping grounds, they too were more vulnerable.

I have no doubt from my conversations with McNally that he firmly believed that the security forces were on top of the IRA campaign in that period. Though he believed that the IRA campaign could continue, he was convinced that the IRA's best days were behind it. If anyone was in a position to make such a judgement it was he.

The IRA prisoners in Crumlin Road at that period represented as broad a cross-section of the membership as you could expect to find anywhere. The spectrum ranged from hard, experienced operators such as Walsh and McNally, who would never be in jail unless caught redhanded, to the young volunteers who had implicated themselves in various crimes through confessions made under questioning in holding centres such as Castlereagh and Gough Barracks. There was also a marked difference in the level of political understanding between the older, often jail-educated prisoners and the younger, sometimes semi-literate ones. The older hardcore used their time in jail to begin the political indoctrination of the younger prisoners. Most of these younger prisoners had no experience of the world outside the republican ghettos and were easy prey – sponges – for any kind of political ideology, no matter how half baked. They simply had no capacity, or desire, to resist the mix of mythology and ideology that was constantly pumped into them. One of the writers recommended to them was Tim Pat Coogan, the Irish historian and nationalist author of many books on the IRA and Irish nationalism.

Life continued fairly uneventfully in Crumlin Road throughout the summer of 1989. I had occasional visits from my solicitor, Paddy McGrory, who was a highly respected Belfast man and a close friend of Gerry Adams. He may have had the bumbling air of a down-at-heel country lawyer but he was in fact an extremely clever man. Though undoubtedly a republican, McGrory was none the less a man who I believe would never have instigated, supported or condoned violence.

I knew that one day soon I would be handed the formal depositions setting out the state's case against me and would be expected to hand those depositions over to the IRA leaders in the jail for perusal before giving them to my solicitor. I knew that if I ever did so I would be signing my death warrant. While these depositions would be a record of the charges made against me, they would also contain other material that was incriminating in the extreme.

McGrory did not visit often, and when he did the

conversation was often of a very general nature – except on one occasion. On this visit McGrory told me that the Director of Public Prosecutions in Northern Ireland had personally sent my case files to England, to Lord Mayhew, then Sir Patrick Mayhew, the Attorney-General. When I replied that I thought that all such files went to the Attorney-General's office McGrory smiled and said that he knew of only one previous case when this had happened, 'and it wasn't a case I would have been involved in'. I asked him what case that had been and he replied that it was that of Private Ian Thain. I knew that Thain had been convicted of the murder of Thomas 'Kidso' Reilly in West Belfast, had served only a couple of years in jail and on release had been allowed to rejoin his regiment. I asked McGrory what this meant and he replied that it must mean that my case had 'quasi-political implications'. I had no doubt that McGrory had a good idea of what that meant. I also believed, correctly as it transpired, that Paddy McGrory would respect client confidentiality to the letter and would play no part in anything that might result in the murder of another human being. Though McGrory could not have been certain what lay behind the events he told me about, he must have known that his revelation would place me very much on my guard. Indeed, it is possible that he was letting me know that I was in a dangerous position. There was nothing I could do except pass the information on to the police through a prison governor. When I later spoke to the police about it they were amazed and mystified about how McGrory had got hold of such information.

Autumn came and the planned day of escape drew close. It was not discussed further between Walsh and myself, which was quite normal; I wasn't involved in the planning, so there was nothing to discuss. I didn't need to know anything about it until the last moment. I was, however, well aware that on my information several of the people whom the IRA were most anxious to get out would soon face trial, be convicted, and be sent to the Maze prison. The whole purpose of the escape was to liberate experienced terrorists who would then be free to play a pivotal role in a revitalized IRA campaign, both in England and in Northern Ireland. As most of these men were currently gathered under one roof in Crumlin Road the escape had to take place before they started being transferred. The evenings were getting darker much earlier now, and that would provide valuable cover in the hours after the escape. The Belfast Brigade of the IRA intended to cause large-scale diversions, including hijackings and attacks on the security forces in West Belfast, to ensure the security forces would be cautious about carrying out searches, for fear of finding booby traps or ambushes. It would be the following day before they would be able to move into the area in strength.

I made the jail authorities aware that the escape plan was coming very close to fruition. I remember one particular Friday night in late autumn when the tension in the prison canteen was palpable. It was obvious that, much as they tried to appear nonchalant, a small group of the most senior prisoners was very edgy. One prisoner, Barney McAleer from Tyrone, not the brightest, could hardly contain his excitement. At one stage McAleer had to be spoken to by Bernard Fox, a senior Belfast IRA man. By the time lock-up arrived at 8 p.m. I was convinced that the escape was planned for the weekend. I had always understood that it would have to be on a weekend, a Saturday afternoon or a Sunday, when there would be no visitors and no chance of an unexpected solicitor's visit or a call from prison welfare about some domestic matter. On my way to my cell I delayed for a second or two just before the cell door was locked. 'Tell Governor so-and-so that it is on for tomorrow afternoon or Sunday,' I told the prison officer on duty. He looked at me a little blankly, I thought. 'Tell him I said tomorrow afternoon or Sunday,' I repeated, before turning and walking into my cell. It was a dangerous course of action, but I had no option.

My cellmate at the time was a rather harmless former IRA man from Derry who had long given up on the cause and was on remand for an offence committed many years before. Cellmates changed regularly as people came and went: for security reasons the prison authorities liked to move prisoners around as often as was practical. My cellmate would have no interest in any escape, as he knew he was only going to get a short or possibly suspended sentence. I wondered whether the prison officer would have the sense to go directly to the governor I had mentioned. You could never be sure that the IRA had not bought or intimidated officers into co-operating with them, but that was a risk I had to take.

I lay in bed wondering what tomorrow would bring. I had a good excuse for not going to the prison yard the next day as my back was beginning to trouble me again. I knew that Walsh would send for me only if the escape was on. My cell window looked out on to the yard where the prisoners would be exercising and from where they intended to escape. If Walsh called me I would ring the bell in the cell and go straight to the senior prison officer on duty and explain what was happening, but I hoped the security forces had the situation monitored and that no escape would take place.

That Saturday, as part of the usual arrangement, republican prisoners were let out to wash and shave and then locked up until 2 p.m. When the cell door was opened for exercise I said that I wouldn't be going out as my back was too sore. I could hear the other prisoners in the yard. They would be out for an hour. I had no watch – watches weren't allowed at that time – so I spent the time wondering if Walsh was going to call on me to join them. Then I heard the sound of the prisoners returning and the clanging of metal grilles. My door opened and my cellmate walked in. He had been told nothing, but he suspected something was going on as many of the prisoners had been spoken to by Walsh, Fox or McMahon, and he felt that there was an air of something about to happen. Walsh had asked him where I was and had said, 'Shit', when told that my back was giving me trouble.

We were let out later that afternoon to collect our food and then returned to our cells – it was the turn of the loyalist prisoners to eat in the canteen. Listening to the radio, we heard reports of widespread hijackings and gun-battles in West Belfast. The outside part of the plan was obviously in train. I wondered what the hell was happening. We were woken in the very early hours of the next morning by the sounds of large-scale activity within the prison. Within minutes our cell doors were opened and prison officers, some in riot gear, began to conduct a major search of the wing. We were individually stripsearched and put in spare holding cells while prison officers and sniffer dogs went through our cells. There was no sleep that night and we remained locked in our cells throughout the following day. The searches of our wing unearthed only one gun, thrown from a cell into the prison yard.

In a sense the next few days brought a rather welcome diversion from the monotony of prison life. Meals were brought in from outside caterers and police officers arrived to man the prison. Searches went on for several days and eventually about ten prisoners were charged with possession of Semtex. When things had calmed down I learned that the escape had been foiled by a number of factors. The digger that the outside IRA men were going to use to carry the bomb to the prison wall had had its tyres let down, which the team discovered only when they came to drive it to the prison. The IRA also became aware that a detachment of soldiers from the Royal Marines had been in position to prevent any escape. Obviously word of the escape had leaked to the security forces, but the source could have been within or outside the jail, the work of an informer or indeed simple surveillance, electronic or otherwise. It would be some time before an inquiry started to untangle the chain of events. I was safe enough for the moment.

There was a mood of despondency among many of the prisoners for some time after the failed escape. Close to Christmas, though, a different atmosphere prevailed. Some prisoners, especially those with young children, found the going hard at that time of year, but generally most people pitched in to help each other out. A couple of weeks before Christmas someone asked me if I would write a sketch to be produced on Christmas day. It was intended that the sketch should poke fun at one par-ticular prisoner. Sean McLaughlin was very much the prison jester and had played many practical jokes on other prisoners. It was felt that it was time he was given a dose of his own medicine.

For my part I decided to have some fun of my own. I wrote a skit poking fun not just at McLaughlin but also at Gerry Adams and a whole range of senior republicans. At one stage I had an encounter between Walsh, Bernard Fox, a senior IRA man from Belfast, a group of IRA men acting as an army foot patrol, and a young Gerry Adams in Ballymurphy, who tries to sell them some 'dirty pictures'. McLaughlin becomes a police informer recruited by the RUC after being caught stealing women's underwear from clotheslines. The men all enjoyed themselves hugely. If they had known what was going through my mind I don't think they would have enjoyed the joke one little bit.

I knew that it would not be long before the courts would reconvene after the Christmas period, when I would be served my depositions by the police and a date would be set for my trial. Around the middle of January 1990 Danny Morrison, recently charged with kidnapping an RUC informer, Sandy Lynch, who was rescued by the RUC before the IRA could murder him, was moved from the Crumlin Road's A Wing to C Wing, where I was being held. It was prison policy to divide both IRA and loyalist prisoners between A and C Wings. Before his arrest Morrison had been a senior member of the republican movement. We knew each other reasonably well from our time together on the Sinn Fein National Executive. Morrison had also served as the IRA's director of publicity and was therefore on the GHQ staff. Whilst OC of the Southern Command I had attended GHQ meetings with him.

He had sometimes struck me as too intelligent a man to see life in the black and white terms of most republicans. He also had a sense of humour, which he often directed at the IRA. In spite of this, he was still prepared to support murder and bombings in pursuit of the movement's goals. He was always friendly towards me in the prison, on one occasion telling me that there would always be a place for me in the republican movement, albeit never again at such a senior level. Though he assured me that no one of any substance believed me to be an informer, it was generally agreed that I had handled the situation badly. He told me that Pat Doherty, Dickie O'Neill and Kevin McKenna in particular had been very supportive of me at GHQ meetings.

After he had been on the wing for a week or so, Morrison told me that he wanted to have a long chat with me one evening – a general discussion about how the leadership saw things now and how, most crucially, it was developing a 'peace strategy'. A day or so later I was called out for a 'legal visit'. As I had suspected, it was the RUC, who had come to serve the depositions. I explained that Morrison and I had set aside that very evening for our chat and that I would like to go ahead with it as I was sure that Morrison, being wonderfully indiscreet, would be both interesting and useful. Once the incriminating depositions had arrived it was essential that I avoided handing them over to the IRA men; I would have to leave the wing immediately. The police handed my depositions to a senior prison officer for safe-keeping and I returned to the wing after telling them that I would pretend to be very ill in the morning and must be moved to the prison hospital without delay. While it was not an ideal solution, it would at least create the necessary confusion to perpetuate my increasingly threadbare cover. They undertook to make the necessary arrangements.

23

Danny Morrison and I spoke for nearly two hours that night in the prison canteen. He told me that the Army Council had decided that republicans must be seen to be positive about peace. Everybody knew that the republican movement was perceived to be anti-everything. The failure to make any political impact in the Irish Republic was having a devastating effect and the leadership, almost exclusively northern, were now realizing that such political progress was incompatible with the murder of off-duty policemen and soldiers and the bombing of Protestant towns. There was, said Morrison, a feeling that the republican struggle was being slowly strangled. It was time to try to form a nationalist consensus involving the Irish government, the SDLP and Irish America. The IRA had no intention of renouncing violence permanently, but it had to make nationalists believe that its intent was peaceful. It was confident that by insinuating itself into the nationalist forum it could radicalize opinion, dragging constitutional nationalists closer to its position that Northern Ireland was not reformable and that a unitary state was the only acceptable option. It was a classic Trojan horse strategy. The IRA believed that it could always rely on unionists to behave foolishly, and that it would be fairly easy to present them as the obstacle in the way of progress. The Army Council believed that it would be able to portray the British, too, as intransigent. What was perhaps not obvious was that this strategy was a direct attack on constitutional nationalism. It was the genesis of an extremely successful campaign.

Such a move undoubtedly posed risks for the IRA, but what was their alternative? American support was in decline. Since the Anglo-Irish Agreement the SDLP had more than held the line against Sinn Fein in elections in Northern Ireland, and in some areas had begun to eat into Sinn Fein's electoral support. The attempt to elect Sinn Fein candidates to parliament in the Irish Republic had ended in disaster, with many candidates losing their deposits. The RUC were, in general terms, on top of the security situation, whilst the sheer duration of the IRA campaign had produced an element of war fatigue and a dwindling interest in the world in general and, particularly and most worryingly, in the Irish Republic, where Northern Ireland was no longer one of the major political issues except during periods of heightened emotion such as the hunger strikes or at times of controversial security force actions.

In the preceding years Adams and McGuinness had looked down the road and seen slow defeat staring them in the face. They had decided to move early and make a strength of weakness. They could never in their wildest dreams have believed that other Irish nationalist leaders would rush to embrace them in the way that they undoubtedly did. Morrison had been in jail only weeks and was intimately aware of every aspect of IRA strategy. I have no reason to believe that he was telling me anything other than IRA analysis and strategy agreed by the Army Council. The following morning, as agreed,

I feigned serious illness. A bizarre element was added by the weather: it snowed that morning and the prisoners were not allowed go to the exercise yard, so I was taken by stretcher to the prison hospital whilst IRA prisoners looked on, wondering what was wrong with me. Within a couple of hours I was back in the isolation annex, and later that day the police came to see me. They were, of course, more than interested in all that Morrison had had to say.

It was now January 1990. I had been in jail just over thirteen months, and I was now back where I had started, in solitary confinement. My trial date was set for 2 May, and I spent the next three months in quiet isolation awaiting that day. One of the teachers in the jail came to see me regularly, usually bringing some books with him, and I spent most of my time in the cell reading.

My trial, when it came, was a short affair. I pleaded guilty to all of the charges but refused to apologize for any of my actions. I have always believed in playing things out to the end and I intended to keep republicans confused about me for as long as possible. I had no way of knowing precisely what they thought but I knew from the RUC that there was still a degree of confusion in their ranks.

The judge delayed sentencing for two weeks, saying that he wanted to study all of the papers in the case. He was, of course, by now aware of almost all of the background to the case. A fortnight later I was brought back to the court. The judge gave a brief summary in which he referred to the fact that I had refused to apologize. He said that in his opinion I did not appear to be unaffected by what I had done and he believed that I was bothered by conscience. Then he served me two life sentences and a total of 539 years for over forty-four other offences.

None of this came as any surprise to me. I knew before I had handed myself up that a life sentence would be the inevitable consequence. The judge had no choice but to impose those sentences. The 539 years, the total for the offences over and above the murder, have to run concurrently, which meant that twenty years, the highest fixed sentence I received, was the maximum I would have to serve in relation to those 539 years. The judge gave no recommendation of how long I should serve before being considered for release. Throughout, the courtroom was empty except for journalists, police, prison officers, my sister and brother-in-law and Barra McGrory, Paddy's son, quietly observing events. I felt no real emotion, merely a sense of anti-climax. The whole affair had lasted less than thirty minutes.

As a sentenced long-term prisoner I could not be held at Crumlin Road. There were only two alternatives: the Maze, which was used almost exclusively to house terrorist prisoners, or Maghaberry prison, which housed a mixture of former terrorist prisoners and ODCs – ordinary decent criminals. There was no way that the prison authorities were going to send me to the Maze, bearing in mind the total control that the IRA enjoyed there. Prisoners at the Maze enjoyed effective POW status, with their paramilitary structure recognized by the prison authorities. If they discovered an informer within their ranks there would be little likelihood of escape. Once paramilitary prisoners were sentenced they usually requested a transfer to the Maze, and this was nearly always granted immediately. Maghaberry was the only reasonable alternative for me, and a week or two later I found myself in the back of a prison van heading towards my new home.

Maghaberry was a new, ultra-modern prison, completely different from the old Victorian building that was

Crumlin Road. Here each prisoner had his own cell with a toilet and handbasin. The educational, gym and hospital facilities were first class. I settled in easily enough and no one bothered me. The atmosphere between staff and prisoners was generally fairly good and at that stage I saw myself sitting out the rest of my sentence writing and studying for a belated Open University degree.

In the late summer, however, another prisoner turned up in Maghaberry who was to have a wholly negative effect on my life. He was John Hanna, a former prison officer who had been convicted of helping the IRA to murder a colleague. Hanna was an extremely dangerous and irrational man who was convinced he had never done a thing wrong and who had no scruples about those with whom he worked. He had joined the prison service in 1971, and even then he was a member of the outlawed Ulster Volunteer Force. Over the years he had worked with the UVF, the UDA, the Provisional IRA, and RUC Special Branch. In the late seventies he had helped the UVF to smuggle a bomb into Crumlin Road jail in an unsuccessful attempt to kill an IRA prisoner. In 1979 he colluded with the Provisional IRA in the murder of a senior prison officer. Then, when he was working in the Maze prison he pretended to help the IRA while keeping RUC Special Branch informed of his activities – except that he omitted to tell them that he was helping to set up the murder of another prison officer.

Eventually, after that prison officer was murdered, the RUC began to realize that Hanna had his own agenda. Before the murder, they had believed that he was dealing with the IRA about a proposed prison escape, which he was. However, believing that he would never be suspected, he took the opportunity of passing to the IRA outside the address of a particular prison officer who was a hate figure among republican prisoners. He and this prison officer had fallen out some time previously and as far as he was concerned it was time to repay old scores. He was eventually arrested by the RUC and sentenced to life imprisonment.

Until now Hanna had spent all of his time in custody in solitary confinement in Crumlin Road. He was convinced that I was still involved in the IRA and started to try to associate with me whenever he could. At first I was cautious, but gradually I realized what Hanna was up to. He believed that the IRA owed him something. Of his family or former friends only his wife was in contact with him, and even then very reluctantly. He owed several thousand pounds on his mortgage and seemed to believe that if he could pay that off it would restore his wife's affections. But in spite of the fact that Hanna had lost everything and had no reserves of his own – emotional, physical or financial – he was a dangerous man.

He had a list of names and addresses of several high-ranking police officers and prison officials, and wanted to pass these on to the IRA. He was willing to do this whether money was paid or not. He gave me the list and I passed it on to the security governor, who in turn passed it on to the RUC. It transpired that one of the names on the list was that of a prison officer who was a brother of one of the policemen involved in my case, and a son of one of the prison officers Hanna had set up for murder. Once I clarified with the RUC that it was okay for me to deal with Hanna, I told him that he must under no circumstances discuss this with anyone, and he must only talk with me about it.

A short while after this, a former UVF prisoner, long gone from the organization, told me that some of the nominally loyalist prisoners were very annoyed and

341

worried that I was spending so much time in Hanna's company. They thought that he was passing information about loyalists to me. One evening, at lock-up, I made a cup of coffee and put it in my cell while I went to scrounge some fruit from another prisoner. It was quite common for prisoners to barter fruit and suchlike with each other and inevitably this traffic went on after lock-up was called as prisoners scurried in and out of each other's cells. It was a game between prisoners and staff anxious to lock up and get home, usually good natured, with most people knowing how far they could push it. I went back to my cell and sat down to write a letter. Some time later I took a sip of the coffee, thought that it didn't taste too good, and, cautiously, drank a little more. It was then that I realized that it had been tampered with.

I wasn't sure at this stage whether it was somebody playing a practical joke, or whether it was something more serious. Within thirty minutes I began to feel quite sick, but not, I thought, dangerously so. I slept most of the night but woke a couple of times feeling nauseous and uncomfortable. I'm not sure how worried I was; I still thought it was a prank, though not a very funny one. I knew that the IRA had access to poisons that were tasteless and killed almost instantly, and knew that it wasn't one of them. I went down for breakfast the following morning but still did not feel very well. Throughout the day I began to feel steadily worse. I didn't want to say anything to anyone because I still had more names to get from Hanna. If the prison realized that something like this had happened I knew I would be moved to a safer place immediately. The following day I was much worse and several prisoners remarked on how ill I looked. By now the inside of my throat was raw, my tongue was swollen, the inside of my mouth was heavily blistered and I was beginning to cough up small amounts of blood. That evening I was very sick in my cell; an officer happened to be passing by and insisted that I be taken immediately to see the prison doctor. The doctor did not know what was wrong with me and seemed to think I had a throat infection of some kind. He decided I should stay in the prison hospital for observation and tests. Over the next day or two, however, my condition worsened dramatically, and even drinking water was too much to bear; it felt like I was being force fed crushed glass. During one of the nights there pieces of flesh came away from the inside of my throat; I didn't have the strength to remove them and choked on them. I thought then that I might die. I had lost a lot of weight and was very weak. That evening I asked an officer for some milk, which I thought might help, and he refused, saying, 'As far as I'm concerned you're just another Fenian.' It was one of my few experiences of direct bigotry in the overwhelmingly Protestant and unionist Northern Ireland prison service.

That night seemed to mark a turning point and I gradually began to recover. The hospital had taken blood samples, which had been sent for analysis, and I knew that once the results came back I would not be long at Maghaberry. I was anxious to get back to the prison before someone got to Hanna and he passed on his information to them. Soon afterwards I was allowed back to the prison, but it was not long before lock-up and I didn't get much of a chance to talk to Hanna. I sensed that he was rather nervous but I told him that I would speak to him in the morning.

However, the following morning my cell door was opened early and I was told that the prison governor had ordered that I be returned to the prison hospital immediately. When I got there I found a prison doctor in a state of panic. He began to babble about the urgent need to get me to 'high-tech' facilities. I told him the bare essentials of the story and he left, saying that he would be back very shortly. I was left in the hospital and did not see him until the following day, when he returned with the two policemen who had interviewed me at Tunbridge Wells. They told me that they had talked with a leading toxicologist, who had said that he had never come across a person who had survived with such a level of that poison in their blood. Apparently the poison was closely related to paraquat and he thought it quite likely that I would die within thirty days. I found this hard to believe – I felt much better and knew that I was over the worst of it. The officers had just come from a meeting with prison officials and were both very angry with the outcome. The prison governor had accused them of interfering in the running of his prison. They had stormed out of the meeting after telling him and a representative from the Northern Ireland Office that I had been responsible for saving many lives and was doing the same thing in his prison. That short conversation was later to play a major part in my release from prison after serving just eight years.

Within a year John Hanna died in prison from cancer, a Catholic prison chaplain the only person at his bedside. The police inquiry into the poisoning was inconclusive. I have never drunk coffee since.

Soon afterwards I was again moved back to the annex in Crumlin Road and was later told by the police that this was a decision arrived at by the Northern Ireland Office, who didn't want me to die in their 'model prison'. They felt it would be much better for everyone if I died in the annex in Crumlin Road. It was now October 1990 and once again I was back in solitary confinement.

Bearing in mind that it would have been far too dangerous for me to go to the Maze, I consulted the police and it was decided that the best thing I could do was to apply for a transfer to an English prison. I was keen enough and asked the police to arrange that I be put in the prison that housed Brian Keenan, the senior IRA man still in jail in England. The reason given for my transfer on the application form was my wish to be closer to family members. But this was not the case. I knew that Keenan had only a couple of years to serve and I was keen to learn his plans for when he got out – or at least to find out about his state of mind. My reason for this was that after Keenan had been caught in 1979, he had sent word out of prison to say that he believed he had been set up by a senior member of the IRA's Army Council. His message went to four different people, through his wife, and it instructed, 'Wait till I get out.' I had always wondered who Keenan suspected.

There was little chance of my finding out, but I thought I had to try.

24

After several months my request for a transfer was granted. I signed a document agreeing to it, and then, unusually, the head of the Life Sentence Unit turned up. She asked me to change my application to make it temporary and revealed that once my transfer was permanent I would fall under Home Office control and would not be eligible even for a review of my sentence until I had served seventeen years. If I remained a Northern Ireland Office prisoner on transfer I would fall within their remit and qualify for their much more liberal review procedures. At that stage I hardly knew what was going on and asked her why she was bothering about it. She said something about not wanting to see an injustice done. I decided to do as she asked, and it was just as well that I did.

A couple of weeks later the prison governor came to see me in the isolation annex and told me that I was being transferred to England immediately. He wasn't allowed to tell me where I was going, but he warned me that he was unhappy with my new accommodation and that I should get it sorted out straight away. Of course, he was unaware that this was my initiative, but I was grateful for his concern none the less. He told me to pack my clothes and be ready to leave within the hour. A couple of prison officers and a detective, who was one of the governor's bodyguards, took me to the City airport in Belfast. Everything was very low-key, routine business for people who had twenty years' experience of dealing with a terrorist campaign.

We flew to Yeadon airport, where the scene changed dramatically. The plane was surrounded by armed police officers in a scene more reminiscent of Hollywood than Leeds on a Friday afternoon. I was soon to learn that this was normal procedure in mainland Britain for anyone convicted of terrorist offences.

We left the airport locked in the back of a prison van with up to seven police cars in convoy. 'Over the top' is an inadequate description of the situation, and the two prison officers and the policeman were falling about with laughter in the back of the van. I had no idea of where our final destination was until we pulled into Full Sutton prison, near Stamford Bridge in North Yorkshire. I knew that it was a top-security prison, one of only four permitted to hold terrorist prisoners. I also knew that my window of safety was limited. The fact that the IRA had not seen my depositions would have been sufficient to fuel their existing suspicions about me and it was only a matter of time before they decided to act.

The staff in the prison reception appeared friendly and relaxed. I was quickly led off to a cell and shown where things were. It was a new prison, built on broadly similar lines to Maghaberry. A young prisoner came into my cell and asked me if I was one of 'Brian's boys'. I said, 'You mean Brian Keenan?' and he said, 'Yes.' Then he said to me, 'Paul Holmes is just down the wing.' I'd never met Holmes but I knew exactly who he was. He'd been sentenced in 1973 for his part in the Old Bailey bombing.

Disappointed by my unwillingness to talk, the young prisoner wandered off. I walked over to the cell window and looked out into the yard. I saw a man walking in the yard whom I was convinced I recognized, but I had to look for some time until I felt sure. I walked down the corridor until I came to a cell with the name of Paul Holmes on the door. I saw a small middle-aged man sitting on the bed and asked him if he was Paul Holmes. 'Yes,' he said. I asked him if Brendan Dowd was in this jail. 'Yeah, he is,' replied Holmes. 'He's out in the yard now.' I turned and walked from his cell and went out into the prison yard. Holmes followed me to the cell door asking me who I was, but I ignored him and kept going.

It had been eighteen years since I had last seen or spoken to Brendan Dowd, and the change in his physical appearance was dramatic. A once powerful and athletic man, he seemed to have shrivelled to half his former size, and there was a frailty about him now. His movements, thought processes and speech had slowed, giving him an almost robotic aura; seventeen years in jail had left him virtually institutionalized. The last time we had met, in 1974, he was a fit, aggressive man in a hurry, eager to go to England, under Keenan's control, to take charge of the bombing campaign. He, with Joe O'Connell, had been involved in both the Woolwich and the Guildford bombings.

He got quite a shock when I walked up to him. It was quickly obvious that he was very much out of touch with the IRA and most of the events in Ireland. We went into my cell and spoke for a little while. He told me that I would see Keenan in the morning. He was on a different wing but they met every evening during the summer and every Saturday and Sunday all year round, out on the football pitch.

The following morning I went down and got my breakfast, and shortly afterwards the football pitch was opened. I walked out with Dowd. Standing near the toilets on the football pitch was a middle-aged man kicking a ball from one foot to the other. I recognized Keenan, though he too had aged quite considerably. Holmes was with him and another man called Harry Duggan, whom I had known slightly seventeen years before, when I was in Leitrim. He had been part of the active service unit based in Ballinamore, when I was running the bomb factory.

'You know this man here, Brian,' Dowd said. Keenan looked up and just said, 'Sean,' before turning on his heel and walking to the furthest part of the football pitch, where he stood with his arms folded. I walked around the pitch with Dowd until another prisoner aproached and said to him, 'Keenan wants to see you.' I didn't believe that Keenan would yet know all of the background to my case and of the mounting suspicion within the IRA. He would be aware that I had handed myself up and nervous about my transfer. Because of the limited communication between prisoners in England and those at large in Northern Ireland it would take some time for him to send and receive word from colleagues there. Dowd, I knew, would back me, and Keenan, once he started to think, would know that I wasn't a threat provided he didn't talk to me.

Keenan had told Dowd that he was expecting, before his release, someone from the organization to try to find out what he was thinking and what he intended to do. 'He thinks you're him,' was all that Dowd would comment for a minute or two when he returned. Then he said, 'He's finally flipped this time.' It became apparent over the next few days that Keenan enjoyed an enormous degree of influence among the other prisoners, particularly among certain heavyweight London gangsters such as Freddie Foreman, one-time enforcer for the Kray twins, and the younger breed of armed robbers and drug dealers.

When Keenan had been captured in 1979 the British media had described him in lurid terms as the mastermind behind everything from the IRA's Libyan connection to the British bombing campaign. There was ample justification for the hype. The RUC officers who arrested Keenan found half of a Libyan banknote in his possession, which he required for identification purposes with his Libyan contact. They also found a coded diary, which was sent to London to be deciphered. What they discovered when they cracked the code scared the wits out of the security forces. From three houses in Andersonstown in West Belfast Keenan had instituted a successful surveillance operation of RUC headquarters and other police barracks, as well as army headquarters in Lisburn. For over a year all phone messages in and out had been intercepted by the IRA. Even the GOC's personal number had been tapped: this operation was a measure of Keenan's formidable organizational skills. His value to the IRA was such that within weeks of his capture they had mounted a sophisticated attempt to free him from Brixton prison using a helicopter, which typically failed when the rescue team was arrested in London by British police. I had no doubt that Keenan's influence with other prisoners was such that he could have me killed almost when he felt like it. A group of London gangsters that Keenan was particularly friendly with served the food in the canteen, and after my experience at Maghaberry I felt that that was a high-risk area for me.

While Keenan didn't acknowledge my presence, nor did he make any sort of move against me. This was due in part to the presence of Dowd, and in part too to Keenan's own curiosity. He also had no firm evidence that I was an informer; and he was close to release and wouldn't want to take any unnecessary risks at this stage. All the republican prisoners who had spent many years in English prisons were inevitably out of touch with what had happened in the movement during their absence. In fact most of them had spent long periods in special isolation units and so were even less aware of events.

Keenan began to use Dowd to ask questions. I knew exactly what would whet his appetite. I told Dowd that Sean Meehan, the Belfast republican, had become an MI5 agent. When Dowd told Keenan this he went apoplectic. I knew that shortly before his arrest Keenan had become suspicious of Meehan and had left instructions that he was not to be used, in any circumstances, by the IRA until Keenan gave the all clear. Within a year of Keenan's arrest, however, Meehan was again being used by the England department, a role he would continue to fulfil until late 1983–early 1984, when he was finally unmasked as an MI5 agent, though not before his handlers had succeeded in getting him and his family to safety.

That episode allowed me to mention to Dowd the message that Keenan had despatched after his imprisonment. 'Does he really think he was set up?' I asked Dowd. Dowd just smiled and said, 'He thinks it was McGuinness.' 'He must be off his head,' I said, while at the same time being perfectly aware how Keenan had come to such a conclusion. Keenan had been arrested at a security force roadblock just outside Banbridge in County Down, in March 1979. McGuinness was arrested at the same roadblock, but in a different car. Keenan maintained to Dowd that shortly before his arrest McGuinness, who was driving a car that may well have been known to the security forces, waved him down to tell him something that he, Keenan, regarded as unimportant. Keenan was adamant that the car he was in was clean and unknown to the security forces. He thought it possible that McGuinness, spotting that he himself was under surveillance, decided to take the opportunity to get rid of Keenan, who he knew was wanted on specific charges relating to the British bombing campaign. Waving down Keenan's car, he maintained, could have been McGuinness's way of pointing out to the police that there was another 'interesting' car in the area. Even Keenan, paranoid and untrusting as he was, couldn't really believe that McGuinness was an informer. It simply could not be true. But that was not his point. Keenan was a Marxist in clear, ideological terms; McGuinness was a Catholic nationalist. I recalled that Keenan had once described Adams and McGuinness as 'two fine fucking Catholic boys'. At that stage Keenan's influence over the IRA was extraordinary and he was dragging it in an increasingly Marxist direction. This was not what Adams wanted.

Whether or not there is any substance in Keenan's belief that he was set up by a member of the Army Council, or in Dowd's allegation that Keenan blamed McGuinness in particular, it is certainly true that following Keenan's imprisonment Gerry Adams and Martin McGuinness assumed a degree of control over the republican movement that they could not have dreamed of while Keenan was around. With Keenan gone, never again would any individual be able to pull the movement in a direction that was essentially foreign to its nature.

If Keenan really believed that he was set up by McGuinness, he has done nothing about it since he was released from prison four years ago. Was he simply speculating, thinking out loud? But if that is the case why did he send such a definitive message out of the jail: 'I was set up by a member of the Army Council. I know who it is. Wait until I get out.' Most puzzling of all is how he could see any benefit in not acting sooner and thereby letting McGuinness accumulate influence over the twelve years of his imprisonment. In my view Keenan's suspicion is a direct result of his extreme paranoia. Perhaps the key to it lies in the fact that he automatically suspected McGuinness of the type of ruthless tactic that he himself would have no difficulty in employing had he wished to remove a rival or opponent. Keenan would regard such behaviour by McGuinness as a perfectly sensible way of getting rid of him. Personally, I believe it doubtful in the extreme that McGuinness would behave in such a fashion. It simply isn't his style. McGuinness is a strict disciplinarian who possesses nevertheless a degree of integrity in his dealings with IRA volunteers. Almost universally respected within the movement, he is a hard militant with a proven track record of operational experience. A British Army officer who served in McGuinness's home town of Derry once referred to him as 'excellent officer material'. Austere, a non-smoking teetotaller and practising Catholic, he is a fanatic almost beyond personal corruption who has been, along with people like Adams, responsible for mass murder.

Keenan was subsequently charged with conspiracy to cause explosions in England and sentenced to eighteen years in prison. The evidence against him consisted solely of fingerprints found in a flat at Crouch End in North London, which had been used as a bomb factory by the Balcombe Street gang. Yet the IRA were adamant that Keenan had never visited the flat.

It was now the summer of 1991 and I was spending much of my time in Full Sutton studying and exercising

– in the prison gym five or six days a week or circuit training and running on the football field most evenings. Physical exercise was a great help with combating the sheer monotony of prison life. Like many British prisons Full Sutton had a fairly serious drugs problem, but it had a liberal regime and provided plenty of facilities. I had also started a course provided by Leeds University which, if I passed it, would allow me to take an Open University degree course without my having to sit a foundation course. I chose to study sociology, and I can think of few things in the world less useful than that. I was simply doing it because it would allow me to move faster towards an Open University course. My time in the cell at night was taken up with writing – poetry and short stories – or reading. Full Sutton also had a well-stocked library and I had the opportunity to read many of the books I had missed out on over the years. It also gave me the opportunity to read again many old favourites including Dickens, Faulkner, Dostoevsky and Chekhov.

25

One morning that summer of 1991 I was walking to the education section when a prison officer stopped me and told me that the governor wanted to see me. I had a pretty good idea what it was about. In Full Sutton all prisoners were allowed to make monitored phone calls, and several times over the past few weeks I had phoned my sister. My mother, who was very ill, was staying with her. She had chronic emphysema as well as the residual effects of tuberculosis and was now on oxygen more or less constantly. When I phoned home she could listen to me but she was unable to speak. Even before I left Crumlin Road in Belfast my sister had told me that she would not live much longer.

As soon as the governor said, 'There's no easy way of saying this,' I knew that my mother was dead. I don't know how I felt about it. Though I'd been expecting it for some time it was a great shock finally to realize that I would never see her again. I knew there was no possibility of parole so I could not even go to her funeral. Prisons can be lonely places and never more so than at times like that. Other prisoners quickly get to hear what has happened and some will come and sympathize, but basically you're on your own. My mother had been so quiet that her influence on my life had seemed small, and yet her sheer strength of character cemented in me some deep-seated beliefs that remained submerged for many years of my life, perhaps most importantly that you have to take responsibility for your own actions. She had almost never interfered and we had been allowed to make many of our own decisions from a very young age. As far as she was concerned, my involvement with the IRA was my own business and I had to live with the consequences of that. Her own mother had died when my mother was in her mid-teens and she had been left to look after her younger brothers and sisters, her father going his own way and at best an infrequent presence. I never knew the full story, as I had never been able to get her to talk about it in any detail.

My abiding memory of my mother is sitting with her by the fire on winter evenings when I was very young, and the warm smell of homemade bread from the oven as she stirred the ashes with a poker. Often I would sit by the fire quietly reading; perhaps that's why I have always associated reading with warmth and with a sense of belonging. My mother always seemed calm, almost serene, with a simple acceptance of life. I rarely heard her speak badly of anyone, and all that ever seemed to irritate her were loud voices and people who couldn't see another point of view. I can never remember her hugging or kissing any of us as children but her calm and gentle nature carried its own soothing and loving aura.

Later that day Brendan Dowd came into my cell. He had known my mother and we talked for a little while. It was almost more than I could bear. I just did not want to discuss my mother or her death with IRA people. For some reason I never cried, though I wanted to and came close to it, but I couldn't break through some barrier. My mother was buried before I got permission to make another phone call. There wasn't a particular restriction on how many phone calls prisoners could make, but because I was convicted of terrorist offences I was automatically classified as Category A High Risk, or Double A, as it was commonly called. It meant that my requests for phone calls had to be referred to a unit in the Home Office that dealt with all aspects of terrorist prisoners, and sometimes it could take days before an answer came back.

Very shortly after my mother's death I went out into the football field one evening and saw Brian Keenan talking to a prisoner I did not know. Brendan Dowd told me that he was called Andy Russell and he had once hijacked a helicopter, which he had used to spirit a prisoner (or two) out of Long Lartin prison. Russell had been transferred from Full Sutton's special unit, where IRA prisoners sentenced by English courts who had not yet completed ten years of their sentence were normally held.

Keenan spent the whole evening deep in conversation with Russell. A few days later I discovered that the wife of an IRA prisoner called Damien McComb, who was currently being held in the special unit, was visiting him for the week. Because of the distances that families had to travel to visit prisoners in England, they often saved up their visits and came for a week, visiting the prison daily. The fact that McComb's wife spent half of her visiting time seeing his brother John, who was held in the same part of the prison as me, was particularly strange.

To my mind it could mean only one thing: that some serious messages were being passed between the SU and the main prison. John and Damien were allowed periodic visits together in the SU because they were brothers, so it wasn't as if they needed someone to act as go-between on family or personal matters. Something was going to happen before they were next entitled to one of their regular intra-prison visits, and this was their only way of communicating. I was also sure that time was running out for me with regard to Keenan. He had not had a visit from Chrissie, his wife and a trusted republican in her own right, since I had come to Full Sutton. Keenan would trust no one else, and as soon as she did come to visit he would ask her to establish exactly how the IRA viewed me, and once he found out that I had never been properly debriefed by the IRA in prison I would not last very long in Full Sutton. Every IRA prisoner, irrespective of who they are, has to be debriefed in prison about their questioning by the RUC, and their replies, if any. Keenan had asked Brendan Dowd to ask me if I had been properly debriefed and I had replied that I had been, in Crumlin Road. It would take some time for Keenan to unravel the truth, but I was getting close to the danger area. Once he could prove to Dowd and the others that I had lied, my safety would no longer be guaranteed.

Before I left Crumlin Road the governor there had given me the name of a prison governor I was to ask for if I had any problems. I didn't know whether he was in Full Sutton at this time, but I passed his name to another governor and told him that I needed to see this man urgently.

Later that evening I was taken to the punishment block and locked in a cell. The following morning the local Special Branch came to see me and I told them what I suspected – that an escape was being planned. Keenan would not be part of it as he was too close to his release date, but I believed that the escape would be from the special unit. They asked me if I had ever heard of Frankie 'Lucas' Quigley. I told them that I had and explained that he was a particularly dangerous IRA operator who had led some of the most notorious IRA squads in

Belfast, collectively known as the M60 team. They were responsible for several murders, including that of SAS Captain Westmacott. Those in the squad included Angelo Fusco and Paul Magee, who both later escaped from Crumlin Road and were recaptured in Tralee as a result of my information. The squad was run by Quigley, but it was Keenan's creation and Quigley was very much his man. The Special Branch men told me that Quigley had recently been observed on high ground overlooking Full Sutton. I warned them that they should be very careful and should take no chances. I think that they were particularly worried about it because two IRA men – Pearse McAuley and Nessan Quinlivan – had recently escaped from Brixton prison in London, and they did not want a similar catastrophe occurring here. Frankie Quigley had been questioned during his recent appearance by local police, as he sat in a car, but had satisfied them that he was on legitimate business. It was only later that Special Branch discovered who he was.

I was returned to the punishment block. The next morning the security governor showed up. He turned out to be a rather stupid man with a great sense of his own importance. He told me that I was being transferred to a new unit in the prison that was used mainly to house prisoners convicted of sex offences. I asked him how long I would be held there and he replied, 'Fifteen years or so.' I had spent time with dangerous and difficult people in prison, but I was not prepared to spend the next fifteen years of my life in that company, and said so. He told me that there was one other IRA prisoner in the unit – Willie McKane, a bricklayer from Strabane in County Tyrone who had been transferred there from Brixton, where he was on remand on weapons and explosives charges and was now in a very isolated position. After the escape from Brixton of the two IRA prisoners, the Home Office had decided to move him to this new unit, which housed a mix of sentenced and remand prisoners.

In spite of my protests, I was taken to the unit later that day. It was virtually brand new and the facilities were excellent, much better than in the regular prison. All the prisoners, with the possible exception of McKane, were classified Rule 41, a catch-all for prisoners needing protection, and were here for their own safety. Most were sex offenders. McKane was a small, squat man in his early twenties. He was wary of me at first but I wasn't sure why. Did he suspect me of being an informer or was the real reason for his presence here his own willingness to co-operate with the authorities?

That night I was called in from exercise in the yard and told that the duty governor wanted to see me. I went into the office and was greeted by an elderly man who told me that he was the governor whose name I had been given before I left Crumlin Road. He told me that the Crumlin Road governor was worried about my safety in Full Sutton and had told him unofficially that if I were to ask to see him he should take it seriously. Apparently, the two governors had worked together when they started in the prison service more than twenty years previously and had remained close friends ever since.

He explained that the only person I would have to worry about in the new unit was McKane. He also said to me, 'There are plenty of "nutters" here,' but he felt sure they would leave me alone. Whatever his dubious assurances, I was not prepared to spend the next fifteen years with these men. As the only 'IRA prisoner' there amongst a prejudiced and potentially violent population, my safety was more tenuous than in an average Category A prison. I told him quietly but firmly that I wouldn't stay there. He replied that there was no other choice. I told him that if I was not transferred within two weeks I would begin a hunger and thirst strike.

For the next two weeks I did little else but chat to McKane, train in the gym and run in the prison yard. McKane and I talked in general terms, with little specific mention of the IRA. It was obvious from his conversation that he was not a major operator. He had played a very minor role at local level in Strabane and was very much a junior member of the gang in London dominated by McAuley and Quinlivan. One day McKane came back from a legal visit and asked me to look at his depositions. After glancing through them I came to the conclusion that the anti-terrorist squad had made a pig's ear of the case and that McKane would walk free from his trial. They had panicked and moved in on him far too early, before a coherent legal case had been put together.

More quickly than I would have liked, the two-week deadline was upon me and I informed prison staff that I was beginning a hunger and thirst strike. There is really no way to prepare yourself for such a course of action, beyond constantly telling yourself, repeating it over and over again, that you must be prepared to go the distance. I had no intention of dying and didn't believe for one second that the prison service would allow a death in such circumstances. I also thought that the RUC or some section of the security forces would intervene if the situation began to get out of control. Hunger and thirst strikes are not exactly a joke. To my knowledge, the only person to die on such a protest did so after ten and a half days, when his duodenum burst. Medical authorities maintain that it is impossible to live longer than fourteen days without water.

The first day or two are okay, and without liquids you stop feeling hungry. After about five days, or one hundred and twenty hours, the body begins to feed off itself. Provided a person is in reasonable health and not exposed to extremes of heat or cold, the body at this point is in roughly the same situation to that of an athlete at the end of a marathon run. From then on one's health deteriorates very quickly, and the chances of a stroke rapidly increase. The central nervous system comes under a lot of strain, and sleep becomes more and more difficult. From around the sixth day you are either being physically sick or feeling very nauseous. What little sleep you get is interrupted by nightmares during which you believe you are choking, probably because your mouth and throat are so dry. Because the body declines so quickly, it doesn't suffer from the effects of vitamin seepage typical in long hunger strikes, which result in body sores. This also means that provided the main organs remain healthy the chances of full recovery are much greater than from a protracted hunger strike.

After five days of my hunger and thirst strike I was moved to the prison hospital. By the seventh day I was beginning to feel the effects quite badly. By the eighth day sleep was almost impossible and I was becoming weak and beginning to shake uncontrollably. I found that I was moving about a lot, pacing the floor, switching from the chair to the bed, in a state of almost constant movement as my central nervous system came under severe pressure.

By the ninth day I was beginning to hallucinate – the walls, chair or bed appeared to be swaying. On the morning of the tenth day I alternated between pacing about frantically, my mind rambling over childhood, family, parents, children – all in a crazy jumble with scraps of conversation and bits of poetry – and sitting in the chair, calm, watching the sun rise. Curiously I was beginning to feel relaxed, warm, euphoric even, enveloped by a warm cocoon. I knew that this was very dangerous and that I would have to keep a tight grip. I had no intention of giving in: the stomach cramps, the headaches, the dizziness, the nausea, the swollen tongue and lips, and every part of me screaming out for water, made it so difficult to keep focused and disciplined, but I was determined to stick with it; it had become a fight with myself.

Some time during the morning of the tenth day I remember the doctor saying to me that I would have to be taken to an outside hospital. Later, my door opened and I was surrounded by male medical staff, who must have thought that I was going to put up a struggle. But by then I was completely incapable of any such protest. I was handcuffed to a huge medical officer and led to a waiting prison van complete with police escort.

It was a scorching hot August day and because I was deemed a Category A High Risk they were not allowed to open a window or stop the van for any reason except at scheduled places. By this stage, I was semi-conscious and had got myself into a frame of mind where I had almost forgotten the reason I was doing this. I just knew that I couldn't give up. It eventually comes down to personal pride, stubbornness, determination, whatever.

The medical officer I was handcuffed to was upset about the way I was being treated. There was no doubt that I was in a lot of distress. The motion of the van and the heat was making me feel very sick, and I was beginning to cough up blood. There was a mattress in the van for me to lie on, but because I was handcuffed it was impossible to do so. By now I was unable to breathe properly and was having to fight panic attacks, forcing myself to relax, trying to remain calm. If I had known the length of the journey we were about to undertake on such a hot day I would have felt a lot worse.

We were destined for Parkhurst, on the Isle of Wight, but of course I didn't know that then. There are many hospitals between Full Sutton and the Isle of Wight, but none of them was deemed secure enough for someone who had worked for the security forces and later voluntarily handed himself up. To be forced to endure such a long journey on a blazing hot day after ten days without water, locked in the back of an enclosed van without ventilation, is not a pleasant experience, and for the first time I really began to wonder if they were going to let me die. I have little recollection of most of the journey. I do remember waiting for the ferry across to the island and realizing that there was no one else on board apart from armed police. There was also a helicopter overhead. I laughed to myself, thinking how ridiculous the whole thing was.

When I got out of the prison van inside Parkhurst my handcuffs were removed. I could hardly stand up but I was determined to walk in on my own. I refused to be helped and tottered from the van to the prison hospital. There were a number of medical staff and prison officers waiting for me. While they were carrying out a medical examination a prison governor turned up. He asked me what it was that I wanted and I simply replied that I wanted a guarantee that I would not be returned to the sexual offenders' unit in Full Sutton. He told me that he was in a position to guarantee my demand. By now I had been awake continuously for over three days. It was almost impossible to speak because my lips and tongue were so swollen. I couldn't concentrate on what the governor was saying and I wasn't sure that I was hearing him properly. I needed time to calm myself after the journey; to try to think rationally.

There followed an hour or so until I was satisfied that he was being truthful. He mentioned the names of the two RUC officers I had dealt with since giving myself up and told me that they had intervened on my behalf. Once I was convinced, I informed the doctor that my hunger and thirst strike was over. I was given minute drinks of a glucose-based drink every hour through the night. I was glad that it was over and once the mental strain of fighting to keep coherent and disciplined was gone and I had taken the first drink or two, I desperately wanted to sleep. Eventually they left me alone for a few hours; I was so exhausted that they had a great deal of difficulty waking me the next morning. A little later I had a visit from a very senior prison medical official. 'That was quite a spectacular arrival last night,' he said. 'I wasn't on duty but I saw all of the activity at the ferry. Do you think someone wants to kill you?' I couldn't help but laugh. 'It's no laughing matter,' he said sharply. 'You should never have been moved in the condition you were in. They could well have killed you. Someone obviously doesn't like you very much.'

Then he told me that he had signed an order saying that I was not to be moved without his permission. 'It's not much, but it's all I can do. I'm worried that they'll try to move you again.' I wasn't really sure how much, if anything, he knew about my case and in my condition it was hard to make a serious evaluation of such things. In retrospect I believe what happened was a combination of carelessness and bureaucratic cock-up. It probably wasn't until some security force influence was brought to bear that the situation was resolved. Until that point the prison service followed its own rulebook. Because I was a Category A High Risk there were only four prisons in England in which I could be held, and the only one of these that had a proper hospital was Parkhurst.

After my hunger and thirst strike I was not surpris- ingly completely worn out, and it took me a number of weeks to recover. I was kept in a cell in the prison hospital that had internal sanitation and running water and I was treated well by the medical staff. One of the curious side-effects of a hunger and thirst strike is that all your senses, with the exception of sight, become heightened, as if your entire system has been pushed to its limits and you break through some kind of barrier beyond which everything seems clearer and sharper. After six or seven days you can taste the moisture in the air and even a slight breeze on your face can feel like the ultimate balm. I thought that it was the last time I would have to undergo such an ordeal. Unhappily, I was wrong.

26

A couple of weeks after I had ended my strike I had a visit at Parkhurst from two policemen from the anti-terrorist squad based in London, who wanted a debrief about the situation in Full Sutton. A governor had already told me that following my conversation with the police about my recent suspicions a search of the prison had uncovered keys that had been manufactured in the prison workshop by a prisoner at Keenan's request.

I told them that I believed Willie McKane would be found not guilty and would walk free from court. The younger of the two looked at me as if he was about to explode. He had that languid, laid-back air of the university-educated policeman who thinks that he has nothing to learn from anyone about anything. After a couple of minutes of explaining why I believed the case against McKane to be so weak I gave up; either he couldn't see or didn't want to admit that they had made a mess of it. When McKane was found not guilty several months later I hoped the officer remembered our conversation and learned something from it.

Following the discovery of the keys the prison authorities moved Keenan, several other republicans and Keenan's close criminal associates to different prisons.

Keenan went to Albany, also on the Isle of Wight and generally regarded as a punishment prison for prisoners who are a source of trouble. It has a much tighter and more austere regime than more modern prisons such as Full Sutton.

The same two policemen called again a couple of weeks later. This time they were accompanied by another man, who described himself as liaison between the Home Office and the police. He thanked me for helping to stop what he said would have been a very serious escape from Full Sutton. He assured me that 'people' were doing everything possible to ensure that I was moved into a situation where it would be possible for me to serve the rest of my sentence both in relative safety and where 'people' could come to talk to me freely when they thought it might be helpful. In essence, he was proposing that I become a resource or reference point for anyone who wished to monitor long-term developments in the republican movement. He warned me, however, that there were some in the prison service, indeed at the very top of the Home Office, who were extremely anxious to avoid controversy, following the break-out from Brixton, which was understandably now a source of extreme embarrassment for the home secretary, Kenneth Baker. There were allegations that Special Branch had been working with one prison officer from Brixton who was pretending to want to help the prisoners escape. Controversy ensued when the prison service accused Special Branch of undercover interference. There were even calls for Baker's resignation. As usually happens with most of these situations, it was never resolved to anybody's satisfaction.

I knew by now that prison officials operated on the principle of 'Cover thy back in all circumstances.' The man told me that a directive had come from the top of the Home Office that I be returned to Northern Ireland, and given its source it would prove extremely difficult to do anything about it. He assured me that they would, of course, do everything possible to prevent such an outcome.

He and his colleagues were to stay on the mainland overnight and return to the prison in the morning. The next day I received a message from the prison officer I dealt with to say that they had come back to the prison and asked him to pass on that they were still doing their utmost.

Shortly after that the prison governor asked if I would move temporarily to a cell in the punishment block, until things were sorted out. I had no particular objection even though it meant in effect that I would be constantly locked up.

The punishment block in Parkhurst is not a pretty place and the atmosphere can be very intimidating. The staff there are geared for trouble all of the time and are certainly not keen on IRA prisoners. They didn't know what I was doing there as they had not been informed of any breach of prison rules, and they simply treated me as they would any prisoner on punishment.

I had been in the block for about two weeks when I was awakened at about 6.30 a.m. and told to get dressed. I was taken to reception, where the prison officer I normally dealt with was waiting. I asked him where I was going and he said that he couldn't tell me. A duty governor then came into reception and asked where I was going. He was told that there was a D Notice injunction on it and they couldn't tell him either, at which point he shook his head, shrugged and walked off.

It was impossible to work out what was happening. No one told me anything. I was handcuffed, put into the back of a prison van and driven to the far side of the island. There, on a small airstrip surrounded by armed police, sat a five-seater plane. Because of the size of the plane I was sure now that I was not going to Northern Ireland, but that assumption soon proved wrong. We had been on the plane a few minutes when I was told that I was being flown back to Northern Ireland – back to Maghaberry, in fact. I couldn't believe what was happening. Maghaberry was the last place I wanted to be. I had been poisoned there and had no idea of the reception I would get from other prisoners. There was no way of telling how quickly news from Full Sutton might have travelled there. Also, if I was housed in the general prison it would be difficult in the extreme to have the type of relationship with security forces that might have been possible in certain circumstances in England.

Once back at Maghaberry, I was brought into reception, where I heard a governor's voice: that of the governor I had dealt with before the poisoning incident. I thought that he was basically okay and he knew the score in relation to me – that I was an informer. I also heard a senior prison officer's voice. I had known this man since my time in the annex in Crumlin Road and knew that he too was aware of all the relevant details with regard to meetings with the police since I had entered prison. After a few moments in reception I was ushered up some side stairs and put into a cell which contained a television. Looking out of the window, I could tell that I was in an enclosed yard beside the punishment block. This was not a regular part of the prison, but beyond that I had no idea where I was.

Then a prisoner opened the flap on my door, looked in and introduced himself as Albert Baker. I knew who he was, even if I had never met him. Albert Baker was a former loyalist 'supergrass', who had spent almost twenty years in jail in England for three murders committed in Belfast on behalf of the UDA in the early 1970s. He had gained a reputation for violence during his years in the English prison system, which was the main reason that he had served so long there, even though he too had handed himself in to the police and admitted his crimes. He had also given evidence against his former comrades.

Everything fell into place. I was in the 'supergrass' wing in Maghaberry. I wasn't sure who else was here but I knew I would soon find out. At 2 p.m. my cell door was opened and I was told that the governor wanted to see me. I was walked to a room that contained nothing except a half-sized snooker table and a couple of chairs. Waiting for me there were the two men whose voices I had heard in reception a few hours before. I got on well with them both.

They explained the situation and gave me a run-down of who was in the unit: Harry Kirkpatrick, a former INLA man who had given evidence against many senior members of the organization and had been convicted of six murders; and Leonard Campbell, a loyalist from Derry who wanted to give evidence against other loyalists but who was completely without credibility. The governor labelled both of them as 'old women'. They had been in the unit for a long time. Both of them were institutionalized and spent much of their time in petty arguments, either with each other or with prison staff.

It was now November 1991 and I had been in prison for three years. I had mixed feelings about being on this wing. It was certainly safer for me, but it was a turning point. For the first time I was overtly labelled an informer and there was nothing I could do about it. I knew that having been brought here I would inevitably spend the rest of my sentence in this place, and while conditions were good I only had to observe Kirkpatrick to understand the effects of spending a long period in such stifling isolation: he was patently an intelligent and fairly determined man who had allowed the conditions to get the better of him. That was not going to happen to me.

The situation in the supergrass unit was unlike any I had ever known in prison. The food was bought separately by the cook in outside supermarkets and then cooked in a kitchen in the unit by one of the prison kitchen staff; this was to eliminate or at least cut down the risk of other prisoners poisoning a meal. In the main prison most of the cooking was done by inmates, under the supervision of prison staff. As a result, our food tended to be of a better quality than that served in the main prison. It also came quickly, which meant that it was both fresher and hotter, which was something of a bonus.

The main drawback of the unit was that it was very small and there was little or nothing to do. There was a small gym, only slightly better than useless, converted from an empty cell. The unit had to be cleaned and tidied every morning by the prisoners, which in reality meant that we would each be busy for an hour or so every day. Other than that there was nothing to do except play snooker and spend time in a small, enclosed concrete yard. Time passed very slowly.

I knew well from my time in jail that you had to conquer circumstances if you were to survive in any meaningful way. Time, in a somewhat eerie and frightening way, was your worst enemy. There was certainly plenty of it in jail, and particularly in that unit. But whereas on the one hand it could drive you mad with boredom, on the other it allowed you to do things that you would never find the time to do in other circumstances. I had long before determined to make the best possible use of the time available. I had seen too many prisoners idle their time away watching videos, taking drugs, generally bemoaning their lot or gossiping about or fighting with other prisoners. Though there was a small television in my cell I rarely switched it on and periodically I asked for it to be removed, which eventually it was. I was conscious of the fact that unless you were very careful the television would come to dominate the cell and life after lock-up. I read several daily and weekly newspapers, including *Republican News*, listened to the radio and generally kept up with the world outside.

My daily routine comprised breakfast, the hour or so of domestic work and then usually time voluntarily locked up until lunch. During those hours I read or wrote in longhand, having then no access to a word processor or typewriter. I had no contact with the outside world – no visitors, no letters. I had been writing for the three years before I had handed myself up and for periods in jail since, when I had the opportunity and the facilities. I had a collection of poetry, some of it crap, some of it promising, and one or two reasonably good pieces, I felt. I made some progress with my novel, and wrote rough sketches of two television scripts.

In the afternoon I trained in the gym and went for a walk in the yard, sometimes alone, sometimes with one or more of the other prisoners. I usually locked up early and went back to my reading or writing.

This was my routine for much of my first year in the unit. During that time both Albert Baker and Harry Kirkpatrick were released, and another prisoner, Bobby Harrison, a low-level loyalist from the Shankill area of Belfast, arrived at the unit. Bobby had decided to co-operate with the RUC whilst on remand in Crumlin Road. He found prison extremely difficult to cope with and often suffered from long bouts of depression. I was to spend the next five years with him, during which time there was quite a long period when there were only us two in the unit.

Life could be mind-numbingly boring, but I had no axe to grind with anyone. I had put myself in prison deliberately and would just have to take the bad with the good. Most of the staff were generally okay – ordinary guys doing their jobs. Now and again you came across the idiotic, the dysfunctional or, worst of all, the nightmare bureaucratic, but there was just as often as bad or worse among prisoners.

That year, 1992, was perhaps the most productive year I had spent in prison. My writing was going well, I felt, and though I didn't have direct access to the prison library I could give staff a list of books I wanted and they would order them for me. After a while I began to feel, for the first time, that my poetry was taking shape: that I was slowly, very slowly, discovering my own voice. I was grateful that I was able to train and managed to persuade the prison authorities to get some more equipment and to open up a second cell for use as another gym.

Towards the end of that year I had a visit from two Special Branch officers based at headquarters in Lisburn: my first visit from the RUC since I had been back to Northern Ireland. They wanted to go back over what I remembered about the Libyan arms shipments.

I told them what I knew on that first visit and they said that they would be back. About a week later they returned – this time with photographs. The Libyan government had decided to co-operate, to some degree at least, with the British government and had passed these photographs across. The problem was that they were copies of passport photographs and the names, of course, were false. Out of a dozen photographs, though, I was able to make two positive identifications.

27

It was around this time, at the end of 1992, that I first decided to go public with my story. I could do the IRA no more damage by covert means and I had to think of new courses of action. My activities in the supergrass unit were obviously limited, but I decided that with the help of the media I might be able to effect a different kind of change. I wrote to five newspapers asking if they would be interested in visiting me. Liam Clarke, the Ireland correspondent of the *Sunday Times*, was the first to reply. I knew him to be a very experienced journalist who had covered Northern Ireland for different news-papers for almost a generation. The first meeting was far from easy. Clarke was a man who had obviously heard many stories over the years and was not about to believe anything without proof. I gave him the name and phone number of my Garda contact but warned him that I doubted very much that he would talk to a journalist.

A week or so later I got another letter from Liam say-ing that he would like to visit me again and I discovered, much to my surprise, that the Garda contact, now retired, had agreed to talk to him. It appeared that he felt he owed me and that I had been badly treated. I didn't particularly agree with this view but it was only his opinion. He had verified the facts as I had told them to Liam, who was now very excited about the story.

Even though Liam was allowed to visit, he wasn't allowed to take notes or use a tape recorder. He had to rely on memory. By his third visit, prison officials appeared to be getting very nervous, and when he asked me if I would write the relevant details down I approached the governor for permission. All our letters in the unit had to be vetted by the police before they were posted. I was told that I could certainly write my account but that I would not be allowed to give it to Liam personally; it would have to be vetted by the Northern Ireland Office, who would then hand it over to him.

I started to write the material Liam wanted, unconvinced that the NIO would ever let it see the light of day. My assessment proved correct: the NIO refused to let him have what I had written, and also refused to return it to me. I had written about eighty foolscap pages setting out the main points of my early IRA activity and my life as an informer. Eventually, the Irish edition of the *Sunday Times* went ahead and published a series of articles on the strength of what I told Liam and what he had gleaned from my Garda contact. Inevitably the articles were not accurate in every detail, but they provoked a flurry of interest from individuals and from the media, which I ignored. They also changed the nature of my relationship with some of the prison staff, most of whom had not known until then exactly why I was in the unit, though they'd obviously known that my being there had something to do with the security forces.

Following the *Sunday Times* articles I was approached by a solicitor acting for a man called Stan Cosgrove. Cosgrove had owned a stake in Shergar, the Thoroughbred stallion kidnapped and killed by the IRA in 1983. All of the shareholders, including the Aga Khan, had been compensated by their insurance companies – with the exception of Cosgrove, who had insured only against death or serious injury. No one had been in a position to prove that Shergar was dead, and as a result Cosgrove's insurance company had refused to pay out. Cosgrove hoped that my testimony would help to break the logjam and I co-operated as much as I could. Although the insurance company was technically correct, I felt that it was sticking too rigidly to the letter of the law. I provided Cosgrove's solicitor with affidavits and statements, but as far as I am aware the insurance company never budged an inch from its original position.

It was now early 1993 and I had been in jail for over four years. Liam Clarke continued to visit, and life proceeded fairly uneventfully. Based on previous prisoners' experiences, had I been a straightforward supergrass I would have expected to serve eight years. However, I had always known my case to be complicated and I realized now that I would have to have it clarified. In the meantime, I began an Open University general arts degree.

In January Leonard Campbell, the loyalist and would-be supergrass who was in the unit when I first arrived, was released, much to the delight of everyone in the unit – staff and prisoners alike. He was an extremely difficult man to live with and had obviously opted to get through his time by making life intolerable for everyone around him. But for whatever reason, he'd never bothered much with me and I had been content to leave him alone.

Just before Campbell was released another prisoner returned to the unit. Jimmy Crockard was another loyalist supergrass, who in 1983 had given evidence against his former colleagues and had received two life sentences for the murder of two nationalists in Belfast. In 1992 Crockard had been released on life licence; though technically free, if it was believed that his behaviour constituted a threat to society he could be recalled to prison to continue his sentence. His licence had now indeed been revoked following suspicion that he had been involved in a serious assault. Crockard was a larger-than-life character who had spent much of his life in institutions of one kind or another. He was highly intelligent and, talking with him, I was constantly reminded of how the development of a person's life can hinge on one or two crucial factors, or on the roll of the dice. In many ways he was a welcome addition to life in the unit.

Soon afterwards I became involved in a libel case involving Central Television and a group of republicans, which centred on a web of community projects in West Belfast. A group of activists sued over allegations in *The Cook Report* and I agreed to give evidence on behalf of the programme. After a long-drawn-out legal wrangle it was agreed that I could give evidence 'in commission', a mechanism that allowed a witness who was unable to travel to the court to participate. The case was to be heard in the Irish Republic because the prosecution believed it had a better chance of success there. In essence, because I was not permitted to leave the prison, the 'court' had to come to me. My evidence and cross-examination by counsel, in front of a judge, would be video-taped and then shown to the jury in Dublin. However, days before this was due to take place, the case was settled and I never got to the bottom of the matter.

It was also in 1993 that I embarked on another hunger and thirst strike that almost cost me my life. For some time I had been aware that my position in the unit was ambiguous. The governor in Maghaberry whom I knew best had told me privately that I was not, as far as the Life Sentence Unit was concerned, in the same category

379

as the other prisoners in the unit (the Life Sentence Unit is the full-time secretariat that services the Life Review Board, which in turn decides when or if life prisoners may be released). In the case of every other prisoner in the supergrass unit the RUC had submitted a report summarizing the assistance the prisoner had given to the security forces. The reports gave the LSU the information it needed to put a case directly to the secretary of state and this often resulted in prisoners' early release. It was entirely in the gift of the RUC whether such a report was submitted. In my case no such document was put forward and until it was I remained a straightforward life prisoner who would be expected to serve out my sentence.

Soon after I learned this the governor concerned was transferred to Crumlin Road prison, and shortly after that he collapsed after a rugby match and died. After several requests to see the senior governor in the jail I was eventually able to tell him what I knew of my position and he agreed that it needed clarification. He undertook to write to the LSU and asked them to contact the RUC with a view to getting such a report. He seemed to believe that this was a simple formality, but I had my doubts about that. This was more than a simple administrative hitch. The policeman who acted as liaison officer with the unit had told me that he could have nothing to do with me; I was the only prisoner in the unit on whom he had never had a file. He regarded this as very strange but assumed that it was being handled by someone else, probably MI5, and decided that he wasn't going to interfere.

Several months went by and I heard nothing beyond confirmation that the LSU had written several times to the RUC and had not yet received a reply. There was a time when I would have got frustrated with such a long delay, but prison, and solitary confinement in particular, had taught me to have patience, even when I was really frustrated. After a few more weeks the governor came into my cell and I could tell by the look on his face that he was not bringing good news. 'Well,' he said, 'you were right. The report's come in, but it's a load of rubbish. I'm not allowed to show it to you, but the substance is: "O'Callaghan handed himself in but was never of any benefit to the security forces." Now even from what I know of your case that is obviously untrue.' I could not believe what I was hearing. I had expected some difficulty, owing in particular to the fact that I had murdered a senior Special Branch officer in cold blood, but never this. It was a complete fabrication and one which I could not leave unchallenged. Beyond speculation about turf wars between the RUC and the Garda or MI5, I simply could not think of a single reason why the RUC was taking this line.

The governor explained to me that even though the LSU knew there was something very wrong here, they had no authority to question the RUC any further. There was simply nothing that anyone could do until the RUC volunteered the information. Being in prison often renders you powerless, but I had never in my life felt more impotent than I did at that moment. When I told the governor that I would have to resort to a hunger and thirst strike he didn't try to dissuade me. He said only that I should be sure to line up any influential contacts that might be available to me before doing so. He was obviously convinced that, having committed themselves, the RUC would be reluctant to change what they had written.

I had no doubt that this time I had a real fight on my hands. My dispute was not with the prison or even with the prison administrators, but with a secret and politically sensitive procedure over which the RUC had almost complete control. I decided, against the governor's advice, to keep my action 'in house', because I reasoned that any publicity or interference from outside would further prejudice my case.

From past experience I knew how my strike would progress and knew I would be able to gauge how I was withstanding the physical and mental strain, but I was also frightened, because I knew what lay ahead. After my previous strike I had suffered a mild heart flutter, and the specialist had told me that the outer muscle around my heart had been weakened. My kidneys bore scar tissue from the earlier poisoning, and I had no idea if they had been further damaged by the strike.

I began my hunger and thirst strike the next day, 30 June 1993. The first few days were uneventful. The governor came to see me several times and I was left in no doubt that he was fully on my side, as were most of the prison authorities in Maghaberry. They could not admit to that openly, of course, but I knew that they were trying to do everything possible to resolve the matter in my favour.

After five days I was moved to the prison hospital, to a special secure ward where prison staff were on duty outside the door twenty-four hours a day. After seven days word leaked out to one of the Northern Ireland newspapers, which carried a brief story saying that I was on hunger and thirst strike. That evening, well after visiting hours, I was told that I had a visitor from the *Sunday Times*. I knew that Liam Clarke was on holiday and wondered who it could be. On the governor's insistence I agreed to see him. He was a young man called James Bethell, who was the son of a Labour peer. He had been sent over from London as a replacement for Liam

Clarke while Liam was on holiday. He was obviously new to Northern Ireland but had been in contact with Liam about the situation and was more than keen to do anything he could to help. Later that night I had a visit from the police officer who liaised on behalf of the RUC with the supergrass unit at Maghaberry. He was clearly worried but unable to do anything; it was obvious that the RUC hierarchy was taking a tough line. I could not believe, though, that the Northern Ireland Office would allow the death of a hunger striker in one of their prisons on such an issue without further investigating it.

On day nine I was moved to Musgrave Park Military Hospital. I was very weak and the medics insisted that I be taken to the ambulance by stretcher. Unusually, several prison staff and at least two governors shook hands with me and wished me all the best, which made me feel even more assured that I had a strong case. Prison staff in Northern Ireland would not normally show sympathy for a convicted IRA prisoner. At Musgrave Park I was held in Ward 18, the most secure section of the hospital. At the Maghaberry governor's insistence, two prison staff from the unit were made responsible for my security and stayed with me at all times.

On my first night there the principal governor of Maghaberry came to see me. What he had to tell me was worrying in the extreme. He had contacted the senior police officer who had dealt with my case, one of the two who had come to Tunbridge Wells after I had handed myself in, and this officer had told him that he had indeed submitted a report to his superiors after the LSU had been in touch; but, he insisted, his report bore no resemblance to the one he later learned eventually arrived there. When he went to police headquarters to ask what was going on he was told to 'Go home and have no further contact with O'Callaghan if you value your job.' He contacted the governor with this information, despite the fact that that could have left him open to disciplinary procedures. I simply could not understand what was going on.

By now I was very weak, with all the usual difficulties I had experienced before: inability to sleep, constant sickness, hallucinations, and one eye which refused to open. I was also experiencing severe muscle spasms and cramps and I felt like someone suffering from constant, unrelenting seasickness.

My prospects were looking grim. The young *Sunday Times* reporter came to see me the following day. He had been in touch with the RUC, had in fact argued with them, and was now convinced that the police were not going to change their standpoint. Although there were still periods when I was very lucid, these were becoming increasingly irregular, and shorter in duration.

That evening the head of the Board of Visitors in the prison came to the hospital. I had met him before and he had said that he would visit and also try to help. He told me he had arranged for a former moderator of the Presbyterian Church in Ireland to come and see me later and tried hard to persuade me to give up the strike. When he saw that I was determined to continue he agreed to try to speak with Sir Patrick Mayhew, the secretary of state for Northern Ireland. I had little hope that he would have any success.

By now I had gone more than ten days without food and water and was heading into a dangerous area from where it would be difficult to return. At this stage things could go seriously wrong, and I was getting to the point where it was hard to make rational decisions. Then the Catholic chaplain from Maghaberry came to see me. It was a well-established procedure for prison authorities 'in such circumstances', to use religious figures as intermediaries. He told me that the head of the Northern Ireland prison service had agreed to hold an inquiry into my case if I agreed to end the strike. I was well aware that this was a significant step forward but I was still not convinced that it was enough and I decided to hold out to see if any more could be gained.

That night I was rambling incoherently and one or two of the nurses spent most of the night with me, but I can remember little of it. The next day my condition had significantly worsened and I was completely out of it for long periods. The prison chaplain returned and reiterated what he had told me the day before. Truth be told, I was quite pleased with the guarantee of an inquiry, as I believed that it would place a lot of pressure on the RUC to rectify the situation. The chaplain asked me if I wanted the last rites and I said yes, not from religious conviction but because I was fighting for my life and anything that brought extra pressure to bear on the authorities was valuable.

I knew that if I was to survive I was going to have to settle for what was on offer, but I wanted to make it clear that I was quite prepared to go right to the edge. It appeared that the hospital staff themselves were unhappy with the situation and had made a formal protest to the Northern Ireland Office. The chaplain returned early that evening and the ritual of robes, candles and holy water brought back childhood memories of early morning Mass in the summertime in a little chapel not far from our home. I was in a relatively lucid state at that point and could see the funny side of the situation: me, the confirmed atheist, receiving the last rites. The chaplain told me that he was coming back to stay the night, which didn't sound to me like a great vote of confidence.

After he left I entered into a familiar phase. I felt cosy and content and a delicious warmth seemed to be enveloping me. I remembered this dangerous stage from my last strike and knew I had to fight hard to stop myself slipping into unconsciousness. I was going to have to make a decision very shortly. It was my last chance.

Later that night, before the chaplain returned, I was told that some visitors wanted to see me. I asked who they were and was told that they were from Families Against Intimidation and Terror, a human rights group based in Northern Ireland. They were primarily involved in combating so-called 'punishment shootings' and intimidation by terrorist groups. I knew that they had been enormously successful in highlighting human rights abuses by the IRA and loyalist groups and I had a very high regard for the work they had done. I would later learn that they had spent the day trying to get a visit after James Bethell, the *Sunday Times* journalist, had asked them to intervene. Eventually the principal governor at Maghaberry took the initiative and ordered that the visit go ahead.

A few minutes later two people came into the room. Nancy Gracey and Henry Robinson are two of the bravest and most heartwarming people I have ever met. Both have endured vilification and threats from loyalist and republican terrorists and have stood firm in spite of everything. I knew that I was approaching a crisis point. I might live through the night, but I would almost certainly have been in a coma by the morning. I asked where the prison chaplain was and was told that he would be returning shortly. At this stage I could hardly speak. My tongue and lips had swollen and my throat was red raw. I was happy with the guarantee of an inquiry and fairly sure that the prison authorities would not go back on their word to a prison chaplain, but I still wanted to hear the words said in front of independent witnesses.

The chaplain turned up shortly afterwards. It was now late at night, somewhere between eleven and twelve o'clock. He had phoned the head of the prison service again who reiterated his guarantee of an inquiry into the whole affair. To my great relief, he was prepared to repeat this in front of Nancy and Henry. In their presence I agreed to end the strike, and the medical staff were called in. I was later to discover that doctors had told the prison officers on duty that I had less than twenty-four hours to live.

28

I was shattered after my eleven-and-a-half-day hunger and thirst strike, and it was many weeks before I was well again. I remember little of the days immediately afterwards. For several days my diet consisted of flat 7-Up, which curiously is the perfect antidote to serious dehydration. After almost a week I drank a little water and progressed to soft scrambled eggs. I weighed only eight stones; I had lost about three stones in under two weeks. For months afterwards I would without warning fall asleep in the middle of the day. My concentration was almost non-existent and I don't believe it has ever fully recovered.

Two weeks or so after the strike ended, I returned to the unit. My demands were now top priority with prison officials. All I could do was wait. I was now in the middle of my first year of the degree course and was way behind with my assignments. I managed to catch up as best I could but it was extremely difficult. I sat my first year's exam towards the end of that year and did quite well in the circumstances. I forget the actual result but I recall that the marks were more than respectable.

In the autumn of 1993 I received a visit from Liam Clarke, who brought Andrew Neil, editor of the *Sunday*

Times. I was now allowed certain freedoms and access to the media that was unprecedented in the unit. I was aware that such a situation was allowed only because it suited certain people's political interests, but in this instance our purposes coincided. The media in Northern Ireland have become part of the battlefield. Their influence is keenly fought over by security forces, politicians and terrorists alike. Their representatives necessarily come into daily contact with spokespersons of the political parties allied to terrorist groups. This area of overlap is used by organizations like the IRA to gather useful intelligence or to plant stories demonizing people, prominent or otherwise, as a means of establishing prejudice in readers' minds before the subjects are eventually killed. The murder in December 1983 of Edgar Graham, an elected member of the Northern Ireland Assembly, is a graphic illustration of how this works in practice. I remember being told by Sid Walsh in Crumlin Road that Graham's growing influence and effectiveness had been drawn to Sinn Fein's attention at a private press briefing in Belfast attended by, among others, Gerry Adams. The one journalist present made it clear that in his opinion Graham was potentially the most effective political opponent facing Sinn Fein that the Ulster Unionists had yet produced and, in all likelihood, would go on to become party leader. Several months later Edgar Graham was dead, shot by the IRA outside Queen's University, where he was a lecturer in law.

Whatever the journalist's motives, the incident serves to illustrate the dangers of talking to people who are ostensibly politicians but who have direct links with terrorists. Maintaining the necessary distance between themselves and the political parties allied to terrorism is a difficult balancing act. For some people, terrorists and terrorism possess an irresistible romantic appeal. A process of seduction is the inevitable consequence. Unfortunately, quite often journalists fail to realize that they too can provide valuable intelligence to the terrorists. Information can flow both ways.

As a result of my meeting with Liam and Andrew Neil, I contributed the occasional article to the *Sunday Times* on the developing political situation in Ireland and within the republican movement. For a number of years now I had been studying every press release, speech and interview made by the principal characters, people like Gerry Adams and Martin McGuinness. I had no doubt that the IRA leadership was preparing for a truce, and, equally, that this would not last. But I knew that when it came it would last for a substantial time – anything less than a year would detract from the IRA's credibility.

I also became involved again with the *Cook Report* team, contributing to a documentary about Martin McGuinness. The programme led to calls at Westminster for McGuinness's arrest. The RUC promised a full inquiry. Some weeks later I was asked if I would be prepared to see two RUC officers in relation to that investigation, and a few days later was paid a visit. The RUC had decided to begin a full-scale investigation into McGuinness, with a view to bringing charges against him. I said that I would help, even though I didn't believe that in the present political climate there was any chance that the government would allow charges to be brought against him. On 28 November 1993 the *Observer* newspaper broke a story long suspected by many people, including myself. The government, in spite of official denials, had been in secret contact with the IRA for some time. The chief negotiator on the IRA's side had been Martin McGuinness. In the light of this there was no way he was going to be charged with anything.

Even though I continued to meet the RUC regularly in connection with the McGuinness case, until the late spring of 1994, any prospect of a successful prosecution looked hopeless. If the government was intent on doing business with the IRA, there was no point in locking up the mouthpiece. I was also convinced that the ceasefire could not be long delayed. It was obvious from any examination of what the IRA were saying in public that they had already decided to call a ceasefire, but they would do so only when it suited them.

The IRA/Sinn Fein leadership understood that what was on offer from the British government was nowhere enough for them, but the existence or otherwise of the ceasefire had little to do with the intentions of the British government. From a position of weakness the entire IRA peace strategy, cleverly disguised though it was, had turned into a full-scale assault on constitutional nationalism, thanks to the gullibility of some nationalist leaders. The British government was unable to deliver a united Ireland even if it had wanted to, for the simple reason that the majority of people in Northern Ireland would never accept it. Adams and McGuinness were well aware of that. They also knew that if they could present Sinn Fein as interested in a peaceful solution, constitutional nationalists such as John Hume, and the Dublin government, led by Albert Reynolds, as well as a substantial section of influential Irish America, would find themselves lined up alongside Sinn Fein in a pan-nationalist alliance. Nothing was more guaranteed to both frighten and infuriate unionists, thereby making the prospects for resolution even less favourable.

Already the broadcasting ban, which had forbidden the broadcasting of republican spokespersons since 1973 in the Irish Republic, had been revoked. For the first time for twenty years the Irish state decided that it was acceptable to have known IRA personnel interviewed on state-owned television. In early 1994 I wrote in a *Sunday Times* article that the IRA would call a ceasefire, and that ultimately the object of the exercise would be to heighten nationalist expectations to ridiculous levels and to portray the British and the unionists as the intransigent party. The unionists and the British government would appear unwilling to negotiate seriously in the light of changed circumstances and this would anger and radicalize constitutional nationalism. The IRA leadership could never have forecast how easily its plan would work.

That spring speculation was rife that the ceasefire was imminent. Then, on 3 June 1994, an event occurred that was to have a dramatic effect not only on my life and the lives of many other individuals and families, but also on the entire security infrastructure of Northern Ireland. A Chinook helicopter, carrying almost all of the senior security personnel, crashed off the Mull of Kintyre. There were no survivors. Among the victims was the head of RUC Special Branch and several of his most senior staff. A number of key members of the security service also perished. It was a devastating blow to the service. Its effect was sudden and dramatic.

A couple of months after the end of my strike I had been visited by a senior prison official, whom I knew slightly. He had been charged to begin the investigation promised by the head of the prison service. We met on several occasions and though he continued to visit quite regularly for a long period nothing happened. He told me that the prison authorities were having very little success, and that this was due to the RUC, who had complete control over the matter and who were proving to be wholly uncooperative.

Two weeks after the helicopter crash he came to see me again. To the best of my recollection, he said the following to me: 'If I had come to see you two weeks ago, I would have said that we had comprehensively failed to make any progress. We went everywhere with our report – Stormont Castle, everywhere – and were told to go away. That O'Callaghan does not qualify for one minute off his sentence.' Then came the helicopter crash and the subsequent appointment of a new head of Special Branch. Within days, the prison official now told me, the new Special Branch boss contacted the head of the prison service and asked to see the report. When asked why he wanted to see it, he replied, 'Because I'm unhappy at some of the things I'm reading and hearing.' Within days of his receiving the report, a new document was sent by Special Branch to the Life Sentence Unit, fully acknowledging my work for the RUC since 1979. It was all that I had ever asked for – that the people who would make the decision regarding my release date from jail should be given all of the relevant information. Now that that had been done I was content.

By August 1994 it was clear that a ceasefire statement was close. On 31 August almost everyone knew that an announcement would be made that day. I sat in my cell and waited for the lunchtime news. When it finally came, I felt emotional, close to tears and wondered whether it could really be over. Was the IRA really serious about peace? But later, when I saw the complete statement on the television, I knew that I had been correct in my assessment. It was apparent, at least to me, that the language did not demonstrate a genuine commitment. However, there was sufficient promise for those who wanted to project an optimistic interpretation on to it. But understandably at that point, amid the euphoria, very few people wanted to listen to words of caution.

They certainly did not want to believe that the peace process also carried great dangers. Making peace can be a noble thing, but peace at any price is not. Those of us who warned that there were problems implicit in the current process were accused of being against peace, and anyone who said they were doubtful about the motives of IRA/Sinn Fein was vilified and accused of being a warmonger.

Even though rationally I knew that it was far from over, there were moments when my heart overruled my head. Like so many other people I desperately wanted to believe that the ceasefire was for real. The investigation into Martin McGuinness was over and, because there was a lack of evidence that would stand up in court, no charges were to be made. Rumours swept through both the loyalist and republican communities that the ceasefire was the result of some secret deal between the British government and the IRA. Expectations in nationalist Ireland were at an all-time high, and the initial feeling within the unionist community was one of apprehension combined with hope. Thus the stage was set for a conflict between unrealizable expectation on the one hand and, on the other, fear about the future.

On 13 October the loyalist terrorist organizations announced their ceasefire, conditional on an end being made to republican violence and on the continuation of the union between Great Britain and Northern Ireland. The loyalist ceasefire has never been other than conditional and depends essentially on the maintenance, in real terms, of the status quo. As the year progressed the stability of the IRA ceasefire became threatened by their refusal to attach the word 'permanent' to their statement. There was also controversy about the continuing 'punishment beatings' and forcible expulsions from Northern Ireland by terrorists, loyalist and republican, of people who had fallen foul of them. And the terrorist organizations' refusal to countenance even token de-commissioning of weapons did not imbue government with the confidence to move forward on the basis that the violence was over for good.

The ceasefires continued throughout 1995 amid high-profile visits to America and London by Gerry Adams, but there were signs that things were not going well. Undoubtedly, Adams and McGuinness were under pressure from the different factions in the republican movement, some of whom were unhappy at the drift from pure militarism and others of whom believed that the ceasefire would produce much quicker dividends. There were also those at grass-roots and sympathizer level who could not for internal security reasons be told the reality behind the leadership's strategy.

My own position had not changed significantly. By this stage both Andrew Neil and Charles Moore, editor of the *Daily Telegraph*, had visited, and I had written a number of articles for different newspapers. I had been introduced to Ruth Dudley Edwards, the Dublin-born and London-based historian, writer and journalist who was brought to visit me by Henry Robinson and who in turn brought others to meet me. By now telephones had been installed in the jail and it was easier for me to make and receive calls. I had more or less constant discussions with prison governors and officials about how I felt the situation was progressing, all of which was fed back to security force sources. As a result, I was usually very well informed about what was going on in the wider world.

At the end of November 1995, Northern Ireland seemed to be on the brink of a new era. President Clinton came to visit and the people of Northern Ireland responded with enthusiasm. Peace, it seemed to many ordinary people, was at long last here to stay. The emotion on the day of Clinton's visit seemed to promise a momentum for permanent peace that would prove unstoppable. Others, however, me included, were watching the rumblings within the republican movement and knew that the reality was quite different.

I believed that the IRA ceasefire would not hold beyond the end of the Christmas period, probably February, and that it would most likely end with a large bomb aimed at a prestige London target. It would later transpire that the IRA had moved many tons of home-made explosives to London days after the ceasefire had been called – hardly the actions of an organization that was serious about a commitment to non-violence. By October 1995, a month before President Clinton's visit to Belfast, the IRA had made plans to end their ceasefire. Even while the president was in Belfast the IRA was organizing the bomb that would signal the end of their ceasefire when it rocked London's Canary Wharf development on Friday, 9 February 1996.

Two people died in the blast. Many in Britain, Ireland and America who thought the ceasefire was for ever were devastated. Just as the IRA had planned, many nationalists had come to believe that the intent of the IRA leadership was peaceful and now blamed the fact that the IRA's actions were not always peaceful on the British government, the unionists, or 'hawks' within the organization itself – in fact, anybody but the people who had actually authorized the violence.

The major question that arose from the Canary Wharf bombing was whether Gerry Adams had known about it in advance. He certainly tried to give the impression that he hadn't. But while he might have chosen not to know precise details of the target, it is inconceivable that he did not know that the ceasefire was going to be broken on that day. His not knowing would have implied a serious challenge to his authority, and indeed one that would have brought about his overthrow. Yet in the following months and right up to the present day he and Martin McGuinness have been firmly in charge of the republican movement. They could not possibly have remained if the Army Council of the IRA had approved the ending of the ceasefire and sanctioned the Canary Wharf bombing without their knowledge or agreement. It simply does not make sense.

The IRA and Gerry Adams blamed John Major and the British government for the breakdown of the cease-fire. The prime minister responded by saying, 'All the time that Sinn Fein were calling for all-party talks we knew that the IRA continued to train and plan for terrorist attacks.' In the following months there were a couple of bombings and attempted bombings in London, one of which resulted in the death of a young IRA volunteer, Eddie O'Brien, from Wexford, who blew him-self up and seriously injured several other people on a bus in the Aldwych. *Republican News*, the IRA news-paper, said that his 'daring and courage . . . in the heartland of Britain's war machine did not go un-noticed'. That his heroic characteristics did not go unnoticed must have been a great source of comfort to Eddie O'Brien, his family and those people he had griev-ously injured. To the IRA leadership he was simply cannon fodder, and the people injured were of no account. For his part, McGuinness told BBC Radio Ulster that the cessation had never been permanent and that everybody connected with the peace process had always been aware of that fact.

On 30 May 1996 Northern Ireland went to the polls to elect a new forum as a means of getting political talks under way. Sinn Fein announced its intention to contest the election but said that it would boycott the forum, following John Major's announcement in the House of Commons that elections to such a forum would open the way for all-party talks in a manner that would clearly represent each party's electoral mandate. These were due to begin on 10 June. Sinn Fein would be permitted to attend the talks only if there was an IRA ceasefire in place. Sinn Fein won a record 15.5 per cent of the vote. Clearly, Northern Ireland's nationalists either did not blame republicans for the breakdown of the ceasefire or simply supported the IRA's right to wage a violent campaign if it saw fit. Sinn Fein won seventeen seats and the SDLP twenty-one. The IRA/Sinn Fein leadership was within touching distance of realizing its great ambition – to overtake the SDLP as the leading voice of Northern Ireland's nationalists – and this without an IRA ceasefire in place. If anyone had suggested that such a thing could happen as recently as six months previously they would have been dismissed as a raving lunatic. Some of us had, and were.

In spite of the absence of an IRA ceasefire, senior Irish civil servants continued to meet Sinn Fein/IRA representatives on a regular basis. Yet on the eve of the talks the IRA announced that the prospects for an IRA ceasefire were 'remote in the extreme'. Four days after the opening of the Stormont talks the IRA delivered its opinion when a one-and-a-half-ton fertilizer-based bomb exploded in the centre of Manchester. More than two hundred people were injured and scores of shops and businesses devastated.

But in spite of this spectacular opening salvo, things did not go well in many respects for the IRA as they attempted to step up their campaign in England. One IRA man was shot dead during a police raid in London and five other suspects were arrested. Police also made significant discoveries of many tons of homemade explosives, Semtex and timer units as well as vehicles. These were crippling blows to the IRA's plans. For political reasons the IRA did not want to resume its campaign in Northern Ireland, but this meant that, for the first time in its campaign, it was obliged to confine its operations to one small theatre of activity, enabling the security forces to concentrate their efforts, too, in that area. It was obvious that the IRA could not continue to operate in this way for much longer, and I wrote at the time that a return to IRA violence in Northern Ireland would not be long in coming.

It came on the eve of the 1996 Conservative Party Conference, 8 October. Without any warning a bomb exploded inside the grounds of Thiepval Barracks, the headquarters of the British Army in Northern Ireland. Fifteen minutes later, as the injured were being removed to a medical centre, a second bomb exploded. It was a miracle that only one soldier was killed.

Did the key people in the leadership of IRA/Sinn Fein know about this in advance? The simple truth is that they must have done. Resuming the campaign in Northern Ireland was a major decision for the republican leadership, and to do so on the eve of the Conservative Conference was a direct challenge to the prime minister, John Major. It also raised the spectre of a return to violence by loyalist terrorists. Gerry Adams and Martin McGuinness, and others like them, had devoted their entire adult lives to the republican cause. It was impossible to believe that they would be content for other people to make decisions that had the potential to damage that cause. Adams and McGuinness might be lots of things, but patsies for other people they certainly are not.

As 1996 was drawing to a close, I knew that a decision about when I would be released was close at hand. Many prison staff and governors seemed to believe that I would be free before the year was out but none of us could do more than guess. If I were released there would certainly be protests from republicans. It was also clear that the door to another ceasefire remained open. My biggest obstacle appeared to be political. While certain prison officials believed that after serving eight years I should be released, some took the view that political considerations might weigh very heavily with the Northern Ireland Office.

After the difficulties I had experienced in persuading the RUC to acknowledge my work with them, I would never again take anything for granted in prison. If I was to be freed shortly it was unlikely that I would be told officially until the day it was due to take place, but there were at least one or two senior officials and prison governors who would tell me a day or two in advance, if they knew. When, finally, I learned that I was being released, I had difficulty taking in the enormity of what was being said. I knew what the words meant, of course, but I had no concept of what I was going out to. I had been in prison for eight years, almost all of it in very isolated circumstances. How long would it take me to adjust? Where would I be in six months' time? Would I see my children and family again? I had no answers to any of these questions.

While I was delighted that release appeared to be near at hand, there was also a degree of sadness at leaving behind people who had become friends. These included prisoners and prison staff. I never cease to be amazed at the courage, endurance and dedication to duty displayed by most prison officers. That same sense of duty is one of the rather old-fashioned qualities that are still deeply ingrained in the best of Northern Ireland's Protestants.

I was a former IRA man who had murdered and bombed in a war against them. These people had endured a savage terrorist campaign for over twenty years and had seen members of their own families, colleagues and friends maimed or murdered. Yet the vast majority of them had continued to go to work and behave in a civilized manner.

There was one particular prison officer called Ian with whom I had a good relationship. I knew that he was a widower who had raised seven young children on his own. He sometimes came into my cell to talk about his children, how they were doing at school, their career prospects, and so on. One day another prison officer warned me never to say anything to Ian about the time he was blown up. Later I discovered that within a couple of weeks of his wife's death, he had been blown up and seriously injured when his car had been booby-trapped. A couple of days before I was released, I finally spoke to him about it. He said that the reason he never wanted prisoners to know about it was because of the possibility that one day he would have to be the prison officer in charge of the person who had tried to kill him and wanted to be able to be even-handed in his treatment of any prisoner. Almost every prison officer in Northern Ireland would have had personal experience of terrorism and yet they worked in a situation which brought them into close contact with the very people who had inflicted this suffering on their friends and neighbours. Bearing this in mind, it is obvious that only people of moral strength could cope under those circumstances.

On the day of my release, a number of the prison officers with whom I was friendly, but who were no longer attached to the unit, came over to say goodbye. Several of them gave me their addresses and phone numbers and although since I left I've been a rotten correspondent, I still hear from some of them.

What about the years in jail? It was a bizarre world

inside, and never more so than in Northern Ireland, where the political/terrorist status of prisoners had created an environment where they enjoyed privileges that would have made prisoners of war blush with embarrassment and where Open University degree courses were handed out free of charge. Convicted murderers were treated better than prisoners who were innocent until proven guilty. It was a small, often bitter and spiteful world. The unit where I had spent the last five years had been at times soul-destroying; I had to struggle to rise above the trivia and the petty jealousies. And now I was going out into the world with no idea of what it had in store for me.

On the morning of 6 December 1996, the grille at the exit to the unit opened and I stepped into the back of the prison van which was to take me to the outside world and freedom. After driving for two miles we stopped at a petrol station. I shook hands with the prison officer whom I had known from my first day in Crumlin Road prison eight years before and walked across the forecourt to where Liam Clarke was waiting.

EPILOGUE

The days immediately following my release from prison were disorienting in the extreme. I was handed over by the prison officers to Liam Clarke, who had come to collect me with a *Sunday Times* photographer, and we drove off in the direction of Belfast, my heart in my mouth the entire way. I had not sat in the front seat of a car for eight years and I was convinced that we might crash at any time. Every oncoming car appeared to be heading directly for us and we seemed to be driving at a suicidal speed, even though I know we never travelled faster than 60 m.p.h.

The only clothes I had taken from the prison were some white T-shirts and a couple of pairs of jeans, hardly sensible winter wear, so we stopped at a shopping precinct on the outskirts of Belfast for more suitable attire. Even walking the distance from the carpark to the shops was a novelty. I hadn't been able to move more than thirty yards in any one direction for more than four years and for a minute or two it felt as if I was on a movable air cushion; my feet just didn't seem to make proper contact with the ground. The crowds, the cars and the general noise were overwhelming. I don't like shopping at the best of times, and this time I was so

403

anxious to be away that I bought the first things I saw, namely a nerdy anorak, a hideous tweed jacket and an almost unwearable tie.

Then we drove into Belfast, to the nationalist New Lodge district, where I posed, feeling like a prize prat, for photographs. Eventually we drove on to Islandmagee and the home of the fine Irish poet Jimmy Simmonds. Jimmy and his wife had established a Poet's House at their home which was a recognized educational trust linked with Lancaster University and offered an MA in creative writing. It concentrated exclusively on poetry and while in jail I had signed up for the course; although I had no primary degree, Lancaster had decided that my collection of poetry was good enough to earn me a place. We stayed for a while with Jimmy's other pupils and it was a great intellectual and emotional luxury to talk with them over a glass of whiskey.

Islandmagee is a tiny peninsula near Larne on the North Antrim coast. On a clear day Scotland is visible, twelve miles away across the water. More photographs were required, so we went to the seafront. Walking on the rocks there made me very nervous and the seawall, which is supposedly safe even for old-age pensioners, was an anxiety-inducing experience. The motion of the sea and the sheer space made me feel dizzy and lose my balance, and I kept thinking I was going to fall. In spite of the place's beauty, I couldn't get away quickly enough.

I spent the next couple of days in a house outside Ballymena, where I wrote an article for the *Sunday Times* while Liam concentrated on covering the story of my release. The *Sunday Times* led with the story that weekend and it was quickly picked up by some of the local Northern Ireland papers the following day. The *Daily Telegraph* also carried a substantial interview with me by Ruth Dudley Edwards, which had been based on a conversation we had had when she visited me in prison a couple of weeks earlier.

By Monday evening people from different media organizations were getting in touch, and I did a series of interviews for the BBC, ITN and radio programmes in the Irish Republic. On Tuesday I was at the airport on my way to London. I was met at the other side by a contact of Liam Clarke's on the *Sunday Times*. He drove me to a prearranged lunch date with Ruth and two friends, one of whom had instigated my writing for the *Spectator* while I was in jail, and the other of whom, Gary Kent, had visited and kept in contact during the last two years. Gary is heavily involved in a cross-party peace group called New Dialogue, which has made a tremendous contribution to combating terrorism and promoting a peace in Ireland based on reality and not wishful thinking.

Eating was impossible. Media people knew that Ruth was probably a good contact point for me and her mobile phone rang constantly throughout lunch as various people tried to get in touch. After lunch came another round of interviews. A pattern was quickly established for the days and weeks that followed.

During this period I spoke to the Conservative and Labour back-bench committees on Northern Ireland. I also got to know many journalists, peace activists and even some people who had nothing to do with Northern Ireland. It was an incredibly hectic period, undoubtedly made more so by the fact that I was used to a far slower pace. I spent Christmas with friends in England and was glad of that time to gather my thoughts.

My release and well-publicized opinions on the IRA had provoked a certain amount of vitriol from some of the more stridently nationalist commentators in Ireland, but this did not cause me any unease. What else could I expect? When I had set out to be an informer, I had known what I was doing. I knew that folk-memory would incline most Irish people to assume that I was in some way venal. The easiest thing for many of them to latch on to was the fact that I had been released after only eight years: clearly, it was said or implied repeatedly, I had done a deal with MI5 or MI6 to get out of jail in order to wreck the peace process. It was easy to dismiss my denials. For instance, on a programme on Irish radio a few days after I was released, John Hume refused to consider the possibility that I was genuine. The man who had told the world that he would talk to anyone refused to speak to me on air on the grounds that my release had come at a critical time for the peace process and therefore was deeply suspect. It was an almost impossible allegation to answer, particularly since the peace process is so shaky that it is almost always at a critical stage.

I will always be grateful to Garret Fitzgerald, Irish prime minister during the 1980s, for an act of typical honesty and decency. Around this time, while I was being widely denounced as a fantasist and a British agent, he corroborated my story about the plot to murder the Prince and Princess of Wales in the *Irish Times* and paid tribute to my work for the Garda.

Throughout this period, I was based with various friends or temporarily in a flat close to London. After eight years in prison, including almost two years in solitary and five in the very confined and isolated supergrass unit, it would take some time to adjust. Freedom is not quite as simple as it might at first appear. There were moments when I felt as though I was on auto-pilot. I had already been told by a senior prison official that it would take nine months to a year to establish some normality.

Every prisoner before me who had come out of the special unit had gone into the RUC's protection programme and had benefited from a relocation package: new name, driving licence, passport, house or flat, and so on. RUC officers had lived with them for up to a year until satisfied that everything was in order and that they were capable of making their own way. For me that would have been unendurable – my idea of life is not sitting with two bored policemen watching Clint Eastwood movies. But the downside of independence was that as well as the frantic media and political activity, I was having to cope with readjustment virtually entirely on my own; though supportive, friends knew nothing of what it was like to be just out of prison, let alone be – as the gardai and police occasionally confirmed – a priority target for the IRA.

One incident during this period was particularly traumatic. The representative of an Australian TV channel asked me if I would be prepared to be interviewed for a programme called *60 Minutes*. The American programme of the same name had put together a profile of me after my release and I found the people involved very thorough and professional. However, the Australian operation was not so slick. After a series of mishaps, one of them asked me if I would be prepared to meet Richard Martin, the husband of Eva Martin, who had been killed in the attack at Clogher in 1974. I replied that I didn't feel that such a meeting on television was the best way to achieve anything and that it would only destroy any possible good that might emerge by cheapening and sensationalizing it. I was already hopeful of the possibility of a private meeting with Richard if approaches initiated by friends were successful. The last thing I wanted to do was destroy that possibility by indulging in some cheap performance for the benefit of a TV company.

We did some filming the first day at the Dominion Theatre and the morning seemed to pass without incident. Quite early on I knew that I didn't trust the interviewer an inch, although I recognized that he was a tough professional. In the afternoon we moved to a different location and I immediately detected a change in his attitude: the tone and content of his questioning became much more aggressive. At one point he mentioned Eva Martin's name but almost in a derogatory way, in an attempt to provoke me. I was by now growing quite angry with him, at which point he introduced Richard Martin, who had been standing behind me for perhaps thirty minutes. Richard Martin and I both broke down in tears while the interviewer continued to ask questions. Richard couldn't have been more understanding or forgiving and just kept repeating, 'It was an awful black night,' and 'We must do something for the kids.'

When we were finally allowed a moment to talk privately, I told him that a group of peace activists and I wanted to make a video featuring ex-loyalist and republican terrorists for distribution to schools in Ireland, seeking to explain to youngsters the dangers of becoming involved in terrorism. I asked him if he would be interested in helping in such a project and he said that he probably would.

The filming of the Australian documentary was due to continue the following day, but I was so incensed by the behaviour of the producers and interviewer that I refused to have anything more to do with it. I haven't seen or been in contact with Richard Martin since, but I hope that as the video project moves closer to fruition we will speak again and in more appropriate circumstances.

While in jail, I had thought periodically about going to America to try to explain the true nature of the IRA and to show how Irish America's romantic views of the situation had helped the IRA in a real and quantifiable way, whether by their supplying of guns and money or by their application of political pressure. Whichever method of support they had lent, few people there knew the realities of life in Ireland. I also wanted to develop a network of people in America who would help to counter IRA propaganda. Now I had the opportunity to turn that idea into reality. Invitations came from organizations all over America – to speak at think-tanks, seminars, foreign policy groups and editorial boards; from people like John O'Sullivan, editor of the *National Review*, for which I had written. I accepted most of these invitations, keen to speak to anyone who had a constructive interest in Northern Ireland.

While we were organizing the trip I became very ill with bronchitis, something to which I have always been prone, particularly since becoming a heavy smoker. I remember Ruth saying to me, as I almost collapsed in central London, 'Your chest is going to get you before the Provos do.' Even before we set off for America I felt exhausted physically and mentally. The media interest was relentless and it was difficult to get even a minute to myself. Everyone I met wanted to ask the same questions, go over the same ground. It was an endless process.

With hindsight, I may have been over-ambitious – even making practical arrangements was a logistical nightmare. I was on the run from the IRA, with no fixed address or telephone number, and no bank account. The Irish government wanted nothing to do with me; in fact, the Department of Foreign Affairs in Dublin instructed the Irish ambassadors in London and Washington not to see me. The word went out to Irish America that I was 'unhelpful' to the peace process and consequently none of the their organizations was prepared to help, although some individuals assisted privately, albeit a little nervously. Thankfully, peace groups in Britain and Ireland were supportive – as was the *Sunday Times,* which contributed £1,000 towards the cost of the expedition (the rest of the trip was paid for from the advance I received for writing this book) and provided practical help through their Washington office. I appreciated their decency: in January when I was ill and unable to think straight, I had signed a lucrative journalistic contract with them, but a week or so later, in a more reasoned frame of mind, asked them to cancel it because I wanted to maintain my independence. They agreed with regret but without recrimination.

Making the arrangements for America involved hours of transatlantic phone calls and innumerable faxes, all of which took place in the middle of a huge controversy over my visa application and a hate campaign organized by IRA supporters in America and Ireland. Some Irish-American newspapers were lending their support to that campaign even before I had left Britain. An impressive range of false and increasingly bizarre allegations were levelled at me.

On Friday 21 February I had a memorable encounter with an old friend. When I walked into the television studio in London to take part in CNN's *Questions and Answers* current affairs programme I knew that Danny Morrison, a former senior member of the IRA, would also be appearing, courtesy of a telephone link from Belfast. The initial exchanges were almost friendly: 'Hi, Sean.' 'Hi, Danny.' But he was a member of an organization that wants to murder me. Morrison had just completed a prison sentence after being convicted of the abduction of RUC informer Sandy Lynch, who was on the point of being murdered by the IRA when he was rescued by the security forces. Morrison's nickname was 'Lord Chief Executioner'. No one present on that day can have been unaware of the reality of the situation: the representative of the would-be executioners was talking to their potential victim.

I have a reluctant liking for Danny Morrison, mainly because of his sense of humour and because I believe that he just might break free of the republican straitjacket. We encountered each other later, on a radio programme in New York, when he spoke of how sorry he was for me because I had no family and no friends and would face a desperately lonely existence when my new friends dropped me. That, in essence, is the reason why so few republicans quit: they cannot imagine that there is life, fun, decency and honour outside the ghetto. They don't know what they're missing.

By now a three-week, coast-to-coast, media-cum-lecture tour was more or less in place and fourteen hours after leaving the London studio I was at Heathrow airport with Ruth Dudley Edwards, who had proved to be such a staunch ally since my release from prison. Like my friend Bert Ward, an ex-communist and now a pillar of New Dialogue, Ruth is ferociously anti-fascist and hence anti-IRA. Henry Robinson, another great ally, hates fascism because ideology had made a teenage terrorist of him too. I have met many other people as sceptical and committed as them since I left jail: like me, they believe the truth will out, but that it still needs help.

When we landed in Washington the following day, we had no idea of what to expect. We were met at the airport by Allison Bozniak from the Washington bureau of the *Sunday Times* and driven straight to a television studio for the first of many interviews. That night we stayed in a house lent to us by old friends of Ruth, who were holidaying in Mexico. Washington was beautiful, the weather unseasonably warm, with clear blue skies and a crisp freshness in the air.

On Sunday morning we relaxed – the next three weeks would be hectic and we had planned to take the day easy. We strolled along in the sunshine, stopped for a coffee at a little café and glanced through the newspapers. While I knew that the IRA would kill me given the opportunity, it was Ruth's rather absentminded habit of stepping out into busy roadways while reading the newspaper, or simply not looking where she was going, which really scared the life out of me.

At about 2 p.m. I decided to get a couple of hours' sleep; James Adams, the *Sunday Times*'s Washington correspondent, had organized a press dinner for the evening and I wanted to be fresh for it. But shortly after 3 p.m. Ruth woke me: 'I have something to tell you,' she said. I knew something was wrong straightaway. Then she told me my father had died. I had known he was ill, but the news still came as a shock. All I could think of to say was, 'The old bastard always had a perfect sense of timing.' I rang Liam Clarke; no answer. I rang Sam Cushnahan, the director of FAIT, Families Against Intimidation and Terror; no answer. Eventually I got through to Toby Harnden, the *Daily Telegraph* Ireland correspondent, who had phoned the *Sunday Times* in Washington to pass on his condolences on my father's death. He told me that there was to be a funeral with full republican honours and that Martin Ferris would be giving the graveside oration.

In fact my father had died on the Friday, even before I had gone to the CNN studio in London, but there was no way I could have been told. My family hadn't been able to get in touch with me. Nor did I expect they would have wanted me to run the risk of going back to the republican hotbed of Tralee. What was I to do? My father was to be buried the following morning. I wanted to go to the funeral and would have done so had it been at all possible, but time was completely against me. I was appalled to discover that I had an interview scheduled for Sky TV in the morning that would be going out in Ireland just after my father's burial. I was worried that my family would see the piece and be even more upset. It would look like I didn't care, which wasn't the case. Eventually I phoned Liam Clarke again; this time he was at home. I told him about my father and he arranged for an undertaker in Tralee to deliver a wreath.

I had missed my mother's funeral while I was in Full Sutton, and my grandmother had also died while I was in jail. Now I was about to miss my father's. Even if I could have reached Ireland in time, the threat from the IRA had to be taken very seriously. I talked it through with Ruth, friends in Ireland and some of the American people who were helping with the tour. Everyone I spoke to was of the same mind: I would be mad to go back to Ireland, and the tour should go ahead. It wasn't what I wanted to hear, but there was an irrefutable logic to what they said. I showered, changed my clothes and went to the press dinner.

One of the reasons I was in America was to begin to make the sorts of contact that would enable different peace groups in Ireland to get their message to America as quickly and efficiently as possible. Right from that first dinner in Washington, and everywhere we went, we met intelligent, informed people, who had never bought the IRA propaganda and were eager to help.

The following morning I was at the National Press Club in Washington for a press conference attended by about fifty journalists and camera crews. I knew that my father's funeral was taking place in Ireland at about the same time and it was difficult to concentrate. That day and the following one in Washington were crammed

413

with media interviews, speaking engagements and some private meetings with influential individuals. Then John O'Sullivan from *National Review* got in touch. He was eager to arrange a public debate between me and Congressman Peter King, a long-time supporter of the republican movement. I was more than eager to take up the challenge.

The debate took place on Capitol Hill and was well attended. Many in the audience from the crazy fringe of Irish America were very hostile and the questions they asked did more to demonstrate their abysmal ignorance of affairs in Ireland than anything I could have said. King had been fairly well briefed by Friends of Sinn Fein, the IRA support group based in Washington, but he is not a good debater and concentrated on personal abuse rather than any discussion of the issues. There was one ludicrous moment when he accused me of having been seen eating lightbulbs in prison. A desire to concentrate on the issues encouraged me not to point out that there are no lightbulbs in prison – unless, of course, you can extract fluorescent tubing from the ceiling after removing the wire mesh that surrounds it. For months afterwards I had to endure friends asking me how I would like my lightbulbs: fried, poached or boiled.

After Washington it was on to New York, and while there I had a meeting that I had looked forward to for a long time. John O'Sullivan had arranged a lunch with Conor Cruise O'Brien and his wife, Maire Mac an tSaoi, a distinguished Irish-language poet. I had written to Conor from jail to thank him for all that he had done to stand up to extreme nationalism and for his writings and speeches, which had influenced me profoundly over the years. Throughout a long and distinguished career he has displayed remarkable intellectual clarity combined with enormous moral and physical courage. They asked Ruth and me to dinner that evening as well; while there I fell under Maire's spell and we talked all evening of Kerry and poetry, the kind of conversation I had craved through my years in jail.

The rest of the trip disappeared into a haze of interviews, speaking engagements and meetings with editorial boards of influential newspapers in every city we visited. Everywhere we went we found people eager to help and were able to announce plans to put together a network of people we called Friends of Peace in Ireland, which I hope will go on to play a role in combating IRA propaganda in America. We travelled back to England in the middle of March. I was exhausted but there was still a lot of work to be done.

It was around this time that Ruth asked me if I would be prepared to speak to a group of people from the leadership of the Orange Order. It was to be an attempt to persuade them that they were playing right into the hands of the Provisional IRA by pushing ahead with controversial parades that then allowed republicans to portray unionists as bigoted and intransigent – which indeed some of them are. Ruth has made a lot of contacts with unionists and Orangemen over the years and has written extensively in an attempt to explain their case to a very sceptical and often hostile world.

I had come across many Orangemen while I was in prison in Northern Ireland and as a result had a reasonable understanding of their position. The rules of the Orange Order forbid them to meet with convicted terrorists and it was a very delicate situation for them. However, most of them are prepared to make an exception for us penitents, and four of them travelled to an airport hotel near Heathrow, where we spent the day discussing how best the situation could be handled. The fact that these people had travelled to London to talk to me was indication enough that they were serious about trying to resolve the situation. I could tell them little that they did not already know, but perhaps information from a former IRA member who could be expected to have a clearer understanding of long-term strategy carried some weight.

That initial meeting led to extensive further contact on the phone and several more meetings in London and in Northern Ireland as the marching season drew closer. There was an atmosphere of fear and apprehension on the ground in Northern Ireland as tension grew. In June, at my suggestion, Viscount Cranborne, Conservative leader in the House of Lords, Andrew Hunter MP and I travelled to Northern Ireland to speak with Orangemen from Portadown in an attempt to persuade them to reroute their annual church parade to Drumcree Church, the scene of serious clashes in previous years.

Though the meeting was quite friendly, the local Orangemen were determined to follow their original plans, come what may. But I was still hopeful that, if everyone remained calm and continued to work quietly, we could still avoid serious confrontation. Much of the detail of what went on during this period may not yet be revealed, but late one night as 12 July approached, with tension at its highest for years and serious street violence seemingly inevitable, the Orange Order announced that it was voluntarily rerouting or cancelling the four parades that were likeliest to end in confrontation and violence. The decision was greeted initially with disbelief and then with enormous relief. The IRA/Sinn Fein's attempt to create mayhem, for which the Orange Order would have been blamed, lay in tatters.

Within weeks the IRA declared a ceasefire, the timing of which I believe was forced on them by the hard work and courageous leadership of those within the Orange

Order who had decided that they were no longer going to be led by the nose by republican strategists. I was glad that those of us who had tried to provide what help and advice we could might have played some small part in making that decision possible. At least for one summer Northern Ireland was not plunged into chaos and murder.

Those months were incredibly busy: if I wasn't on the telephone I was rushing to meetings. Gradually, a more definable framework of democrats, human rights activists and people who understood that working for peace entailed more than lighting candles, admirable though that is, was emerging.

Through all of this there were still the problems of adjusting to life outside prison. A lot of new technology, from mobile phones to computers, caused me all sorts of difficulties. I still hadn't driven a car, I had no bank account and by now I had a book to write as well as journalism to keep me busy. Around August a proposal for a new pro-union think-tank based in London began to gather momentum. I had been interested for some time in trying to win support for a conference that would bring together the democratic strands of unionism. The idea was to reach out to people who, like me, though not unionist in the ideological sense were committed to the principle that there should be no change in the status of Northern Ireland without the freely given consent of its people.

After much work and against all the odds the conference took place in October 1997 at Hatfield House, the home of the Marquess of Salisbury, Viscount Cranborne's father. Amongst those present were the leaders of all of Northern Ireland's democratic unionist parties, including Robert McCartney, David Trimble and both Ian Paisleys, senior and junior, the Grand

Master and other members of the Orange Order, representatives from both Houses of Parliament, as well as a wide range of academics and journalists. While there were undoubtedly differences between the major unionist parties, much solid work was done and it is intended that a similar conference will take place later this year to move the discussion forward.

I have met an enormous number of people since my release from prison, some of whom have become good friends. Contrary to the rather widely held belief that an informer's life consists of looking over his shoulder or skulking in the shadows, afraid of revenge from former comrades, I enjoy as normal a life as possible under the circumstances. Though I have had to put aside work for my poetry MA, I still write when I get the opportunity. The novel I worked on in prison over the years is also nearing completion, as are a couple of television scripts.

I look forward to the future with a mixture of confidence and apprehension. I hope that I will continue to cause problems for terrorists and that the battle for ideas, so important for the future, will be won by democrats and not by the terrorists and their propagandists. It would be refreshing to see those in the Irish media who can't write about Gerry Adams without indulging in an orgy of adulation and anti-Brit polemic rein in their wilder enthusiasms. They don't seem to care about the terrorized communities, murdered petty criminals, mutilated youngsters and brainwashed inadequates – perhaps it's just not sexy enough.

My main fear for the future of Northern Ireland lies in my belief that the essential aim of the IRA peace strategy has been to radicalize nationalist sentiment, particularly in Northern Ireland but also to some degree in the Republic. The available evidence so far suggests that they have been successful in that. In recent times we have seen the IRA/Sinn Fein vote increase substantially in both Northern Ireland and the Republic. Sections of the Irish media have slavishly followed the IRA/Sinn Fein line and the IRA still murders people when that serves their purpose. The constitutional nationalists of the SDLP are looking increasingly old, anaemic and irrelevant when compared to the young, articulate coherent and disciplined organization that is Sinn Fein. Awash with funds from America, and with confidence riding high, Senn Fein are convinced that the future of Irish nationalism resides with them. If they are right, then the future is bleak and any prospects of a rational accommodation with unionists is all but impossible. That is the challenge that faces us in Ireland today: to defeat the forces of extreme nationalism. It will take the combined forces of everyone committed to democracy on both islands if we are to succeed. I look forward to helping in every way possible until real peace based on co-existence between democrats has been established.

I know that the organization led by Gerry Adams and Martin McGuinness would like to murder me. I know that that organization will go on murdering other people until they are finally defeated. It is my belief that in spite of IRA/Sinn Fein's strategic cunning, and no matter how many people they kill, the people of the Irish Republic expect, because they have been told so by John Hume, that there will be peace. There may come a time when their patience runs out. If that were to happen there would be no place for IRA/Sinn Fein to hide. We must work tirelessly to bring that day forward.

THE VOLK

Heaney's a sound man,
And your man Tim Pat
He's sound as well.

Old stock, part of who we are,
Of time and race and place
Beyond ourselves.

That's the story anyway,
A bit of hard sell
If you ask me.

I'll choose my own race and place
And won't thank you for the choice.

I can do without your mystic twist.

This poem was written on the day Seamus Heaney was awarded the Nobel Prize for Literature in 1995. Tim Pat refers to Tim Pat Coogan, Irish historian and author.

APPENDIX

Hijacking Mr Hume

Thirteen years ago this month, Gerry Adams rose to address Sinn Fein's National Executive following a series of public exchanges between himself and John Hume, leader of Northern Ireland's constitutional nationalists. I was a member of the Sinn Fein National Executive at the time and I remember clearly what Adams said: 'We may have nothing to say to John Hume but northern nationalists will not forgive us if we refuse to talk.'

As we move closer to a referendum on the future of Northern Ireland – possibly in May 1998 – one important question remains unanswered: after thirteen years of negotiations between Hume and Adams, what is the position of Northern Irish constitutional nationalism? Have the years of contact between the two leaders undermined the capacity of the Social Democratic and Labour Party (SDLP) to deliver a fair and sustainable deal for Northern Ireland's nationalists? Or has Hume's courage and skill succeeded in drawing the militant republicans into the democratic fold? One thing is clear: if John Hume is afraid to reach a sensible compromise with David Trimble and his Ulster Unionist Party (UUP) for fear of Sinn Fein, we are in deep trouble.

I watched Adams carefully at Executive meetings in 1985, in the period just before the signing of the Anglo-Irish Agreement. Adams learned two lessons at that time: John Hume was a much bigger player than the combined Sinn Fein leadership; and a British government, even one led by Margaret Thatcher, would ignore the wishes of unionists if it suited it.

The IRA/Sinn Fein was opposed to the Anglo-Irish Agreement, which it rightly saw as an attempt to bolster the SDLP and stem the electoral rise of Sinn Fein following the 1981 hunger strikes. Why, then, from late 1988, did the Army Council of the IRA, with Adams and Martin McGuinness as its dominant figures, begin to formulate a 'peace strategy'? Why, less than four years after insisting that every Sinn Fein election candidate had to sign a pledge of 'unequivocal support for the armed struggle', was the same leadership now proposing something different? The answer is to be found in part in those two lessons learned by Adams; but above all it lies in the IRA's weakness. Despite a generous supply of weapons from Libya, the IRA was unable to escalate its campaign to the point where the British government wanted to withdraw and unionist will to resist was undermined.

This weakness manifested itself in several ways. The IRA's terrorist campaign had been largely contained by the security forces: with the exception of South Armagh there was no part of Northern Ireland not patrolled by the RUC. The IRA could and did kill people, but every indicator of republican violence – with the exception of so-called punishment beatings and shootings – showed an organization in decline.

American support was on the wane, too. The core leadership of Noraid, the republican fundraising group, comprised men in their seventies and eighties who had no access to or even an understanding of how to use political influence in Washington. Respectable Irish America, Hume's power base, was embarrassed by the IRA and wanted no contact. The IRA's supply of money and guns from the US was dwindling.

Meanwhile, in the Irish Republic, attempts to make political progress had ended in farce. The goal of the Adams/McGuinness axis from 1979 to 1980 had been to make Sinn Fein a real political force there. In 1986 Sinn Fein abandoned its abstentionist policy of refusing to recognize the legitimacy of the Irish parliament; it announced that its candidates would in future, if elected, take their seats. But its candidates usually succeeded only in losing their deposits: the Southern electorate wanted nothing to do with an organization whose only policy was 'Brits out.'

In Northern Ireland itself the SDLP had halted and then reversed the electoral rise of Sinn Fein, which had reached its peak a couple of years after the 1981 hunger strikes. Thanks to the Anglo-Irish agreement – and the failure of the unionist opposition to persuade Margaret Thatcher to change her mind – the SDLP became the dominant voice of northern nationalism and John Hume its patron saint.

This was the bleak situation faced by the republican leadership in the late 1980s. At a senior IRA meeting in 1989, Kevin McKenna, then IRA Chief of Staff, said, 'If they get an assembly in place in Northern Ireland with SDLP involvement, we're finished.' The IRA's peace strategy was a rational response. The deal offered to constitutional nationalism was the possible end of IRA violence in return for a nationalist consensus that agreed there could be no internal British settlement.

One short-term effect of this 'offer' appears to have

been to undermine the Peter Brooke/Patrick Mayhew-led talks, between 1989 and 1992, which were coming close to an agreement between the constitutional parties. It is hard to say whether that agreement would have stuck, but John Hume was evidently distracted by the prospect of militant republicanism (without guns) united with constitutional nationalism in opposition to the union and unionism. Gerry Fitt, Hume's predecessor as SDLP leader, said, 'John Hume can talk to anyone in Dublin, Washington and London. The only people he can't talk to are unionists.' The failure of the Brooke/Mayhew talks certainly left the unionist leaders who believed they had a deal – especially the liberal unionists – feeling doubly distrustful.

As Adams and Hume began to meet regularly and representatives of the Irish government held meetings with the republican leadership, the British government, too, reopened a 'line of communication'. Slowly, perception of Adams and McGuinness within the nationalist family was changing. Adams was becoming respectable. If Hume thought it was worth trying, nationalist Ireland in the main held its breath and trusted him.

When Albert Reynolds became Taoiseach in 1992 the process was stepped up. Reynolds was a dealer – the kind of businessman who split the difference and shook hands. And like many southern nationalists, he was painfully naive in his dealings with the IRA. Contrary to the assumptions of some southern nationalists, the IRA bears no meaningful relationship to the historic organization founded in 1919 to fight the British, which then rejected partition in 1921. It is essentially a Northern Irish organization hardened by twenty-five years of armed struggle and sustained by sectarianism.

But the hard men who came through the politicization of the hunger strikes had learned to be pragmatic. They were not, with some exceptions, addicted to violence. Tom Hartley, one-time general secretary of Sinn Fein, summed up the new thinking: 'There is one principle riding above all other principles and that is the principle of winning.' That is what Adams and his comrades appeared to be doing as they probed the soft underbelly of Irish nationalism and found little or no resistance.

Wolfe Tone is regarded as the father of militant Irish republicanism: the annual oration delivered in his name at Bodenstown is an important ritual for republicans. The speaker is chosen by the IRA's Army Council and the speech is written and approved in committee. In 1992, Jim Gibney, a senior member of Sinn Fein close to Adams, delivered the oration. In a widely reported speech he said, 'We know and accept that the British government's departure must be preceded by a sustained period of peace, and will arise out of negotiations.' This passage was seen as highly significant – which it was. But it was careful to promise peace only once the British agreed to withdraw from Northern Ireland – something no British government could contemplate in the foreseeable future.

Meanwhile, on 24 April 1993, Adams and Hume issued a new statement: 'We accept that an internal settlement is not a solution. We accept that the Irish people as a whole have a right to self-determination. This is a view shared by a majority of the people on this island, though not by all its people.' Both men were looking at the problem and its solution in identical terms. What separated them was violence.

It was to be more than a year before the IRA delivered that first ceasefire. By that time, aspects of the Hume/Adams statement were incorporated into the Downing Street declaration – the 1993 statement in which the British government renounced all 'selfish strategic or economic interest in Northern Ireland' – but still there was no ceasefire. Then, after the IRA had maximized public attention, raised nationalist expectations, entertained Irish-American delegations in West Belfast and talked up the personal risks that republican leaders were taking for peace, it called a ceasefire in August 1994.

Nationalist West Belfast was euphoric. People believed that a secret deal had been done with the British. Adams, Hume and Reynolds posed for a public handshake in Dublin. The nationalist consensus was alive and well and there would be no internal settlement. Two nationalist parties in Northern Ireland, the Irish government and a powerful section of Irish America had come together to argue the nationalist position. It looked as if Hume and his constitutional nationalism had achieved a historic feat. They had tamed the republican tiger.

Then the IRA ceasefire became bogged down over the failure of the IRA to use the word 'permanent' and the refusal, by any terrorist group, to countenance decommissioning of its arsenal. Something unexpected began to happen: Adams, McGuinness and other republican spokesmen began to look aggrieved; and people – particularly young people in Ireland – forgot about the history of terrorism and began to blame the 'Brits' and the unionists for their refusal to engage. By now Reynolds and Fianna Fail were no longer in government. John Bruton, leader of Fine Gael (traditionally regarded as anti-republican), had replaced them. He found himself under fire from all members of the nationalist family for failing to stand up to the Brits. When he responded that he thought he had a duty to consider unionists too, he was held up to derision.

When the first IRA ceasefire was blown apart at Canary Wharf in 1996 – and even after it was proved that the IRA had moved ten tonnes of explosives to London within days of calling its ceasefire – it was the Brits, the unionists, John Bruton or the 'hawks' within the IRA who were blamed. And then, with no IRA ceasefire in place, two by-elections took place, in Donegal and in Dublin. From very small bases, Sinn Fein's vote doubled in Donegal and trebled in Dublin.

These results challenged the accepted wisdom. Until then it had been understood (even by Sinn Fein) that the Sinn Fein vote could not increase in the Republic while the IRA campaign of violence continued. But the 'peace process' had begun to stretch the definition of what was and was not acceptable. Although the evidence for this was still thin, it made me nervous. Something was happening that had not happened since the beginning of the IRA campaign in 1970. In these circumstances, it seemed likely that Sinn Fein's vote would rise fairly dramatically in Northern Ireland too. That is exactly what happened.

Sinn Fein is now the third largest party in Northern Ireland behind the SDLP and the UUP. At the last Westminster election the party's vote rose in every constituency it contested. The same thing happened in the Irish general election and, for the first time since the 1920s, a bona fide Sinn Fein candidate was elected to and took his seat in Dail Eireann.

Sinn Fein's position today is far superior to its position in 1989, thanks to its brilliant political finessing of the 'peace process'.

On the terrorist front, the situation has scarcely changed. But this is relatively unimportant. Everyone knows that a significant IRA terrorist capability remains intact. The IRA reminds us about that now and again – when it needs to. Orange parades, sectarian murders by loyalists and the continuing instability of Northern

Ireland make it easy for IRA/Sinn Fein to exploit the 'politics of tension' and present itself as defender of an embattled minority.

Sinn Fein's political influence in the US, its fundraising capacity and the stature of its leadership are in a different league today – witness the success of the Gerry Adams visa campaign in 1994. Young, educated, sophisticated Irish America adores Adams. The same is true in the Irish Republic. A respected Irish commentator recently said that Sinn Fein's influence in the South of Ireland is at its highest since the 1920s. The election of Mary McAleese as president shows that it is possible for a northern nationalist, whose emotions and instincts are closer to Sinn Fein than to the SDLP, to achieve popular support in the South.

The 'greening of the South' is belatedly beginning to cause anxiety in political circles in Dublin. When Adams comes to visit drug-savaged, inner-city Dublin, he comes not as a politician but as a rebel hero, a man of integrity back from the war – in contrast to the seedy democratic politicians of whom people have grown tired. Futhermore, with a few honourable exceptions the Irish media have been supine in their approach to Sinn Fein. When section 31 of the Broadcasting Act was relaxed to allow Sinn Fein spokesmen to appear on Irish television and radio for the first time since 1973, the assurance given was that they would be exposed by tough questioning. This has not happened. Radical chic and the whiff of cordite have seduced a significant section of the southern intelligentsia.

In Northern Ireland itself, Sinn Fein's vote has increased dramatically. It now commands 17 per cent of the electorate – 43 per cent of the nationalist electorate – and is likely to replace the SDLP as the largest nationalist party at the next general election. John Hume still commands tremendous loyalty, but he is almost a separate entity from his party.

During the last general election Hume said that a vote for Sinn Fein was a vote for murder. Forty-three per cent of the nationalist electorate heard what he said and voted for Sinn Fein regardless. Sinn Fein now occupies the same political space as the SDLP, but it is a party steeped in IRA discipline – young, vibrant and confident, with tough, centralized control and a burning desire to take on the ageing SDLP. Sinn Fein has in fact already replaced the SDLP on the ground in much of nationalist Northern Ireland. In many areas, there is no SDLP organization worth talking about. On every level, from their MPs downwards, the SDLP looks tired and dispirited.

Sinn Fein's work on the ground in forcing confrontation over Orange Order parades has also helped to radicalize nationalist sentiment in its favour. Adams has admitted privately that the Drumcree confrontation 'did not happen by accident' and praised the local Sinn Fein activists who made it happen. None of this was possible when the IRA was engaged in its low-level and ineffectual violence of recent years.

As people in Northern Ireland become better off and the working class shrinks, demographic factors should be working in favour of the more middle-class SDLP and against Sinn Fein, whose power base has always been on the council estates. But Sinn Fein has managed to buck the socio-economic trend. You can, it seems, drive a BMW and vote for Gerry Adams.

How permanent is the shift in Sinn Fein's favour? The indications are ominous. Election results are consistent. Moreover, there is a growing sense of confidence among northern nationalists – the sense that history is on their side. One of 'their own' is president of the Republic and she converses on first name terms with Brendan

McFarlane, who was convicted of a sectarian bomb-and-gun attack on a Protestant bar in which five men died.

But if it is too late to stop Sinn Fein's march towards leadership of the nationalist community, some people argue that perhaps this is no bad thing: if Sinn Fein displaces the SDLP, it will be trapped in the world of constitutional, democratic politics. The trouble is that, as those recent election results suggest, resuming violence is no longer incompatible with electoral success. And the prospect of achieving electoral dominance over the SDLP is tempting Sinn Fein to escalate its demands.

Many nationalists no longer wish to settle for power-sharing, a bill of rights and a couple of symbolic cross-border bodies. They want police and judicial matters to be dealt with by a Council of Ireland which may not deliver full 'unification' now, but holds out the prospect later. This, of course, is just what unionists – even the most pragmatic and enlightened 'new' unionists – cannot possibly accept. A cross-border body, with some shared sovereignty, is acceptable to the UUP, but its limited powers must be very clearly drawn and it must not be subject to 'sovereignty drift'.

Adams appears to believe that most northern nationalists now want more from the peace process than is available. The Sinn Fein activists on the ground – many of them graduates – report back that they can take on Hume and the SDLP in a referendum and earn the support of a majority of nationalists for their rejectionist cause. If a majority of Northern Ireland's nationalists do vote against 'Sunningdale 2', together with a substantial minority of unionists, the deal will be worthless.

Some people still believe that it is John Hume who has outmanoeuvred Adams. What happens to the IRA, asks this school of thought, when the British, Irish and US governments line up alongside the SDLP, UUP, Alliance and one or both of the fringe loyalist parties and say, 'Here is the deal – take it and work on it, or go back into the wilderness'?

We must hope that this is what will happen, but there are reasons to doubt it. Bertie Ahern, the Irish prime minister, is a pragmatist. But Ahern leads Fianna Fail – 'the republican party' – and at least a fifth of his back-benchers will be unhappy if Adams is unhappy. Given Ireland's electoral arithmetic, that is a substantial group. In any case Hume, who has a limited record of engagement with unionism, is unlikely to allow a wedge to be driven between himself and Adams. He would prefer both governments to come to a pro-nationalist deal – Anglo-Irish Agreement 2 – and then impose it. No Irish government has ever faced down John Hume on Northern Ireland. He has always done what he liked in 'taking the risk for peace'.

Since the foundation of the Irish state there has been a clear dividing line between extreme violent nationalism and constitutional nationalism. But without any debate, and denouncing his critics as 'anti-peace', John Hume has blurred that line and given life and energy to extreme nationalism. He has brought the political arsonist into the house without taking the box of matches from his pocket.

This article originally appeared in the April 1998 edition of the current affairs monthly magazine Prospect. *The magazine can be reached at 0171 255 1281, or via its website at www.prospect-magazine.co.uk*

POSTSCRIPT

In the early hours of the morning of Friday 10 April, an agreement was endorsed by both the British and Irish governments and the leaders of the political parties represented at the talks, subject to ratification by their respective parties. But will it bring real peace and lasting stability to Northern Ireland?

It is, quite simply, too early to arrive at any firm conclusion. Inevitably much of the agreement is a fudge, designed to allow all parties to claim that they won the best deal. Only days later, serious problems have already surfaced. What will the commission on the RUC decide? Will loyalist and republican terrorists really decommission their weapons? Could IRA/Sinn Fein participate in an assembly without using their position to destabilize Northern Ireland?

If David Trimble can bring a majority of unionists with him and if IRA/Sinn Fein prove to have been boxed into a corner, there is real hope. If both of the above do coincide, then we should remember what thanks are owed to the Garda Siochana and the RUC. We should also acknowledge the courage of individuals from the Irish nationalist tradition like Conor Cruise O'Brien, John A. Murphy, Ruth Dudley Edwards, Eoghan Harris,

Kevin Myers and Eilis O'Hanlon, without whom the southern Irish press would have shown precious little intellectual or moral opposition to the cancer of violent nationalism. If, in spite of the massive hurdles ahead, this agreement works, their dogged persistence in the face of constant threats and abuse should never be forgotten. Societies should treasure their sceptics.

SO'C
14 April 1998

POSTSCRIPT II

Rereading the postscript I wrote on 14 April 1998, it is now clear that much and little has changed in Northern Ireland. On 22 May, referenda in both the Irish Republic and Northern Ireland comprehensively endorsed the Good Friday Agreement. I supported and actively canvassed for a 'yes' vote and, while any influence I may have had was strictly peripheral, I was glad to be of assistance wherever possible. Shortly after the referenda, elections took place for the new Assembly and once again parties that supported the Agreement received a strong mandate, in spite of the fact that unionist support was divided almost equally for and against. Inevitably, such a result placed restrictions on the scope and pace of the possible progress.

Even days after the final words of *The Informer* were written, and before the momentous events of 22 May had taken place, my own life was changing. In 1990, while still in prison, I had agreed to give evidence on behalf of the *Sunday Times* in a libel case brought by the then IRA chief of staff, Thomas 'Slab' Murphy. Mr Murphy had instituted legal proceedings following the publication of a *Sunday Times* article in 1989 accusing him of being an active and senior member of the IRA. He had lost the action but had successfully appealed. I knew him to be involved in the IRA at the highest level and had attended meetings with him in that capacity. The appeal was due to take place in Dublin just days before the scheduled launch of *The Informer*, and that represented a number of problems for me.

It was suggested to me that I should not travel to the hearing in Dublin at all, not only on account of the significant risk to my own safety. There was also the possibility that prolonged and intensive cross-examination might damage my credibility. In my capacity as an informer I had for many years lived a shadowy life of lies and deception, and this was bound to provide Murphy's legal team with much ammunition. It wasn't the case that I couldn't defend my actions, merely that they would be exposed to the harshest light and subject to wilful misinterpretation. Thomas Murphy's hearing was to be the first time in the history of the Irish state that a known informer had given evidence in a libel case, and as a result opinion and prejudice was already formed. Such certainties would have been a luxury in my past life. And as if this wasn't enough, it was quite likely if I travelled to Dublin that I would be arrested and questioned by the Irish police in relation to the murder of Sean Corcoran and other IRA activities undertaken on the Garda's behalf. I knew that I was not guilty of Corcoran's murder but I was also aware that it had become a political issue and was unlikely to go away.

As far as I was concerned, it would be the ultimate obscenity if Murphy were financially rewarded for his activities by an Irish court and I knew in my heart that I would give evidence, irrespective of the risks involved. Having made the decision, for many reasons I had to keep it as close to my chest as possible until my departure was imminent. On Tuesday, 28 April, the day before my evidence was to commence, I phoned one of the *Sunday Times* legal team in Dublin and told him that I would be on a flight there the following morning. He sounded relieved: I was one of the few people who could place Murphy as an IRA member and cement their case.

Arriving at Heathrow the following morning, I felt extremely nervous. Because I had been in prison when the *Sunday Times* had first approached me, they had made an application for my evidence to be heard in commission in the jail, and I was then at least under protection. This time, however, I had no such protection from the British or the Irish police. Murphy knew that it was likely that I would appear and that I would be one of the first witnesses called; I couldn't guarantee that the IRA would not be on alert at either Heathrow or Dublin airports. It was a chance I had to take. Since my release I have always felt more comfortable making my own arrangements, no matter how much I trust the people concerned. It allows a degree of control over my life that I treasure.

My heart was thumping when the plane landed at Dublin. I had last been there thirteen years before, and at that moment I would gladly have stepped back on the plane and waited another thirteen, but that wasn't an option. The solicitor from the *Sunday Times* stood waiting for me in the lobby, pretending, unsuccessfully, to be a local taxi driver. He had been working on the case for some time and ironically was probably even more familiar to Murphy's team than I was.

As a result he and I were equally anxious to leave the airport as quickly as possible. Driving to the Four Courts, I could see how Dublin had changed in the intervening years. There was an air of prosperity, and the city seemed in some ways new, like it had reinvented itself with a more cosmopolitan flavour. I recalled the last time

I had been there, setting up a bogus escape attempt that involved hiding a gun in the gents' of the Four Courts. It didn't help my nervousness – I knew how ill-protected the court was and therefore how much access the general public had. Just as when I had laid the ground for the abortive break-out, I now had to be prepared for any eventuality. We drove in via a side entrance and quickly made our way to a cramped ante-room allocated to the *Sunday Times* legal team. It was now 11 a.m. and I was told that I would be called to begin my evidence immediately after lunch.

It was obvious that the first day would be relatively easy. As defendants, the *Sunday Times* would be leading off, and their questions would be designed to establish my credibility rather than weaken it. At about 1.45 p.m. we left the room and made our way to the courtroom. Passing through the central lobby, I noticed Tom Murphy in conversation with a well-groomed man in a smart suit whose face I recognized. He saw me immediately and whispered to Murphy who had to turn slightly to look. Murphy stared almost blankly for a second or two. By then I was right beside him and he had the vacant gaze of a man who wasn't aware of what he was looking at. After a moment of disorientation, Murphy focused and then gave a very slight, almost imperceptible nod of his head in recognition. He hadn't changed much in the thirteen years since we had last attended meetings together. He was balder and greyer but still the stocky wall of a man I remembered. His physical presence has always enabled him to exude menace. With over twenty years of practising terror behind him, Murphy, the warlord from South Armagh, knew how to get his way. A man I later discovered to be his older brother Patrick glared at me and hastily followed us into the court, which was not yet sitting.

The room was large, square, and wood-panelled, with a high judge's dais, a raised jury box and a tiered public gallery. Ironically, for a place dedicated to the pursuit of close scrutiny, the lighting was extremely poor. I sat in the press area near the dock, along with some of the *Sunday Times* team. Patrick Murphy sat in the public gallery and glowered at me until I became bored and blew him a kiss. This, for some reason, seemed to enrage him. Within minutes the judge entered and my name was called. I walked to the dock, took the oath and waited for the first question.

By now the court had filled up. A crowd of Murphy's heavies and other associates from South Armagh and the border area outside Dundalk had colonized the public gallery. It was an error of judgement on their part. Murphy was trying to portray himself as a humble farmer, but the menacing presence of his supporters suggested that this was anything but the case. It was as though they believed that the attitudes that gave them such power in South Armagh would transfer to the democratic atmosphere of a Dublin court. Outside the courtroom, their behaviour had already betrayed their arrogance and the existence of an obviously organised group. Flashy new cars, pagers and mobile phones proliferated. The men were even quite openly taking photographs of people entering and leaving the court. It was difficult to believe that a simple farmer would have such resources at his disposal and begged the question of how such an operation was being financed.

Once in the court, Murphy's heavies positioned themselves directly in the sight of the jury in an attempt to intimidate them. The jury could do little else but focus on them, rather than observing me and the business of the case taking place below them. It was immediately apparent from the jury's body language that they regarded Murphy's crew as thuggish rather than frightening. This was Dublin, not Belfast or South Armagh, and the jury obviously felt sufficiently secure not to be intimidated. Incongruously, in such a menacing atmosphere, a large party of perhaps thirty schoolchildren sat directly behind the heavies. I wasn't sure that their presence was advisable and, as it turned out, their teacher removed them from the proceedings when my evidence began to relate to the business of terrorism.

In addition, there was a group of people I knew to be policemen standing implacably at the back of the court. I had always expected to be arrested once my presence in Dublin was known, and when I saw a particular officer among them, whom I knew well, I was convinced beyond doubt that when proceedings adjourned at 4 p.m. I would be taken into custody by the Garda. The case was due to recommence the following Tuesday.

As expected, the first day went smoothly and I had plenty of opportunity to land some heavy blows on Murphy's credibility as the innocent farmer he portrayed himself to be. Inevitably during this cross-examination I had also to describe in some detail the inner workings of the IRA leadership and the personnel involved. It was not surprising that the press focused more on these elements of my evidence than on the case itself. As the session drew to a close I could feel the tension in the court rising by the minute. By the time the clock reached 3.45 p.m., the various factions were already jockeying for position. There were a couple of uniformed police on routine court duty, but their plainclothed counterparts, obviously summoned at short notice and underbriefed about the identity of some of the participants, were unsure about how to proceed. Murphy's people were constantly entering and leaving the room to consult with each other, presumably about how they thought I would leave the courtroom and what they would do when I did.

As soon as the judge adjourned the court all hell broke loose. The police, press and Murphy's crew milled around chaotically, frantically trying to discern who was on which side. It was utter chaos. I had no wish to get involved and remained standing by the dock, where it was relatively clear. If the situation had not been so dangerous, it would have been funny.

At my insistence, one of the *Sunday Times* people finally asked a uniformed policeman to provide an escort, but as we tried to leave through the court, the crowd swarmed around us. Somehow we eventually made our way through, jostled on every side by the throng until we found ourselves in a narrow corridor. But even there confusion still reigned; the police had not yet gained control of the situation. Murphy's smartly dressed friend had attached himself to the jacket of one of the *Sunday Times* team and seemed unwilling to let go. It wasn't until the *Sunday Times* lawyer pointed out the man's identity as one of Murphy's associates and not, as they presumably believed, a policeman, that the Garda finally persuaded him to leave.

Finally, after twenty minutes of scuffling, the garda regained control and I was formally arrested. Outside, we were hustled into a car waiting in the main yard. We drove out of the High Court and headed south until we arrived at the quiet, rural Garda Station in Naas in County Kildare.

I was held in Naas for 48 hours. It was quite obvious that the Gardai had insufficient time to prepare, having received word of my presence in Dublin only a couple of hours before. After a brief but formal interview, it became apparent that there were political implications to my arrest, which left the police involved unsure about how to proceed. I was questioned more or less continuously about Sean Corcoran's murder, which I strenuously denied. The gardai were mostly civil, although the questioning did on occasion degenerate into abuse. This wasn't a problem – I was all too familiar with the insides of police stations and knew what went on in them. I had known it since the age of fifteen. In a sense my arrest suited me, as I had waited some time for the opportunity to talk to the Garda, knowing that the inquiry into Corcoran's death had been reopened. I was keen to make it clear that I wanted to co-operate in any way I could. I answered their questions to the best of my knowledge and, once the 48-hour period expired, I was released without charge.

Having had the chance to question me, the police were now intent on getting me out of the country as quickly as possible, until the court case reconvened. The press knew that I had been brought to Naas and had been badgering the station with calls since my arrival. However it appeared that somehow their interest had been deflected and by the time I was released they had moved on. But if the press knew I was in Naas, then so too would the IRA. It was worrying for us all, although by this stage the Garda seemed even more paranoid about my safety than I was, saying things like, 'If you even catch a cold we'll be looking for a job.'

I left the police station lying flat in the back of a Garda car which drove me to a remote area several miles away. There I was greeted by the same *Sunday Times* solicitor who had met me at Dublin airport and together we drove to the Wicklow Mountains, where he had rented a holiday cottage, intending that we stay there until the court resumed on the following Tuesday. I had politely rejected the Garda's efforts to make me leave the country immediately and had told them that I would keep them informed of my movements as best I could.

Unknown to the *Sunday Times* man, I had no intention of remaining holed up in the cottage for several days. It was isolated and probably very safe, but if the IRA were to get wind of it I would be a sitting duck. Again, it was important for me to make my own arrangements, and in this instance I had every intention of taking the first flight out in the morning, by which time I hoped I would able to leave the country unobserved. For my own security, I couldn't mention the change of plan to anybody until the last possible moment however and thus waited until the early hours of the morning to do so. Unsurprisingly my announcement was not greeted with a wave of enthusiasm but the *Sunday Times* managed to book the flight anyway. At first light I phoned the police and told them we were on our way. As I suspected, the airport was fairly quiet at that time and it was easier for me to spot any potential danger. We boarded the flight and I tried to concentrate on writing an article commissioned the day before by the *Sunday Telegraph*.

Once back in London I finished the article and attempted as best I could to relax, knowing that on Tuesday I must return to court to face cross-examination from Murphy's legal team. When the time came, the police were on hand at Dublin airport to ensure our safe arrival. But whereas the week before I had been able to slip quietly into the country, this time, after the weekend's explosion of press coverage, it was less easy to remain anonymous. It was obvious that I was recognized by some of the airport staff, and when a complete stranger waved cheerily to me while our car was waiting at a set of traffic lights in the city I felt extremely exposed for the first time, and very vulnerable with it.

Happily we reached the Four Courts without encountering further problems. They were all waiting for me inside the court. It was now that the legacy of my IRA involvement would be made to count against me in the witness box. Senior Counsel for Murphy, Mr Leahy, began his cross examination on Tuesday afternoon in a relatively low-key manner, carefully attempting to lay the ground for his later assault upon my credibility.

I was in the dock from Tuesday morning until Thursday afternoon, during which time Mr Leahy made a sustained, if at times apparently unfocused, attack on my character. At no point, however, did he succeed in undermining the central core of my evidence: that I had attended senior IRA meetings in the company of Tom Murphy, who had been present in his capacity as OC of Northern Command and a member of the IRA'S Army Council. I was aware almost from the beginning of Mr Leahy's cross-examination that Murphy would not have been comfortable with the lines of questioning that would once more bring the press's attention to the IRA leadership, particularly at a time when the IRA was determined to present a more respectable political face to the world. It appeared to me that Mr Leahy seemed more concerned with avoiding any questions that might link Murphy to the republican leaders who had risen to political pre-eminence during the peace process than with pursuing the obvious lines of enquiry. Mr Leahy's job may have been made no easier by the instructions he may have received from Murphy. I later discovered that a high-level IRA meeting had taken place the previous weekend and could only imagine that the Murphy case must have been discussed. It didn't take a genius to imagine that the leadership was not happy to have their personnel and operations exposed in a Dublin court.

Even though these factors obviously restricted the cross-examination, I had been in the witness box for almost three and a half days and was relieved when my stint was over. Although I had nothing to hide, such intense scrutiny, unfocused or not, can be very wearing and can produce a peculiar disorientation. I felt confident that my evidence had helped to ensure that Murphy would fail in his grotesque attempt to gain financial reward for his terrorist activities.

Once my evidence was completed, I returned to England to await the verdict. I read about Murphy's own evidence with interest and some humour, particularly when he was asked whether he had heard of the Maze prison; his reply was that he might have, at which point the judge, by now exasperated said, 'Come on, Mr Murphy. You must have heard of the Maze.' Even from a distance it appeared to me that Murphy's impersonation of a simple farmer was hopelessly overexaggerated and would strain the credulity of any Irish person.

It took a week for all the evidence to be heard, including that of Eamon Collins, another former IRA member, at which point the jury retired to consider. After only an hour, they found in favour of the *Sunday Times*. Murphy's appeal had failed miserably and the consequences for him were considerable. On a personal level he faced crippling legal costs, but more importantly his credibility within the IRA was shattered. He had come across in court as having needlessly subjected the internal workings of the IRA to the glare of unwanted publicity. For an IRA chief of staff and a legendary hard-man who had for years managed successfully to live in the shadows, Tom Murphy had finally been exposed for what he really was.

With the case out of the way, the publication of the book could finally take place, preceded by serialization in the *Daily Telegraph*, and a series of media interviews. On 20 May a press conference was held on my behalf at the House of Commons. With the referenda in Northern

Ireland and the Irish Republic looming within days, I was able to publicize the book and to advocate a 'yes' vote.

The referenda that at last took place on 22 May resulted in a clear victory for the 'yes' campaign, which took over 71.2 per cent of the vote in Northern Ireland. In the Irish Republic 94 per cent voted in favour of changes to Articles 2 and 3 in the Constitution, which claimed jurisdiction over Northern Ireland. No one, in all honesty, could now claim that the Good Friday Agreement did not have a democratic mandate. Admittedly the Agreement was designed to be all things to all men, and was thus so carefully phrased to avoid dissent that its various complicated clauses would provide as much heartache as illumination. Not surprisingly, each side insisted that its interpretation of the more controversial sections was the correct one.

It struck me as extraordinary and perverse that those people who were loudest in their calls for everybody to be included in the process could dismiss virtually half of the unionist electorate as fascist, as did John Hume, the SDLP leader. He didn't seem to understand that a size-able section of those who would vote 'no' would do so because their lives had been shaped by tragedy over the previous twenty-five years. Their consciences would not let them vote for an agreement that promised to release prisoners, the very people responsible for deaths of friends or family. Having made their point, many such people could then go on to accept the result and embrace the hope that it represented. The nationalists, on the other hand, were to vote overwhelmingly in favour of the Agreement, even though there remained serious reservations within some sections of the republican community.

Around this period I had direct and indirect contact with Downing Street. In the weeks leading up to the referenda, both the media spin and broad strategy emanating from Downing Street, Dublin and the Northern Ireland Office had had a detrimental effect on moderate opinion. In the days preceding the referenda the Dublin government released on parole the members of the Balcombe Street gang, who had recently been transferred from prison in England to the Irish Republic. While on parole they attended a Sinn Fein meeting in Dublin and were fêted in a triumphalist manner in the full glare of the media spotlight. A few days later Michael Stone, an infamous loyalist killer, was similarly released from prison in Northern Ireland and appeared at a UDA rally to an ecstatic response. Both releases seriously undermined the 'yes' campaign. Tony Blair and his advisers realized the seriousness of the situation and moved quickly to take a firm control of the details that could so easily derail the process.

Until this point the government had been treating the process as if it were a mainland electoral campaign without comprehending the fundamental differences between the language of what passes for political discourse in Northern Ireland and that in the rest of the United Kingdom. I was able to help put Downing Street in touch with people close to the grass roots of unionism, making it possible for them to finetune the language to avoid giving unnecessary offence and to root it in the moral tones understood by moderate rural unionism.

Both sides of the British parliament had their parts to play. Viscount Cranborne, then Conservative leader in the House of Lords and much respected among unionists, had travelled to Northern Ireland to canvass for a 'yes' vote, to the surprise of many people who would not have expected him to espouse an obviously Labour government initiative. His presence gave the waverers some reassurance at a time when uncertainty was in the air and demonstrated him to be a pragmatic and very able politician with a solid understanding of the complexities of Northern Ireland.

The way was now clear for an election to the new Assembly, which would form the basis of a devolved administration. The election on Thursday, 25 June duly returned a large number of candidates across the political spectrum who were in favour of the Agreement. The largest unionist party, led by David Trimble, had supported the Agreement, but even they could not guarantee unqualified backing. There were too many areas of concern and only a small majority could be counted upon to embrace the Agreement unequivocally. In all likelihood, the unity of Trimble's party would evaporate if there was any political slippage on prisoner releases, decommissioning or the future of the RUC. In spite of the fact that Northern Ireland had voted for a new assembly and had indeed elected members to it, there was still considerable distrust on both sides of the political spectrum. In the absence of any viable alternative, unionists and republicans appeared to have no choice other than to take their leaders' advice. However, this did not guarantee that they would not withdraw that mandate if the process evolved in a way that either community believed was contrary to their expectations. It was by no means the substantial bedrock required to build a new democracy.

As the debate raged on in Belfast, Dublin and London, we were once again faced with the spectre of another major confrontation. For the fourth time in as many years, the Orange Order parade to and from Drumcree Church on the outskirts of Portadown, long regarded as the cradle of Orangeism, threatened to push Northern Ireland into the abyss. The parade, held on the first Sunday in July, commemorates the Battle of the Somme, when thousands of men of the 36th Ulster Division were killed. As always in Northern Ireland memories are long, and within the unionist community there burns a deep pride for the memory of those who lost their lives. While to the outside world their behaviour appears absurd, to a community that believes itself under siege such expressions of unity, culture and resistance are overwhelmingly important. For them and their very existence as a separate entity on an island overwhelmingly Catholic and nationalist, such issues can literally be a matter of life or death.

Within the largely Catholic community many nationalists were genuinely angry at the Orange Order's insistence on parading through areas where demographic changes had led to areas once staunchly unionist now being mixed or nationalist. The entire parade issue was manipulated and orchestrated by Sinn Fein/IRA in a deliberate attempt to force the unionist community into confrontation with the state.

The combination of Sinn Fein/IRA's determination to exploit the issue and the stupidity, indeed bigotry, of certain elements within and outside the Orange Order has always made it difficult to arrive at a solution. Compromise has long been a dirty word in Northern Ireland politics. In spite of such entrenchment, however, it is always worth one more try. Otherwise you surrender the asylum to the lunatics.

In the build-up to Drumcree I was in fairly regular contact with Downing Street and, along with other people, presented a number of proposals to them, some of which they acted upon. Much of what took place was of course on the basis that it would never be disclosed publicly, but one incident did come to the public's attention and proved to be controversial, at least in Irish terms.

Shortly before the day of the parade, I decided to travel to Northern Ireland with the hope of trying to help to avoid the forthcoming confrontation. I had a number of contacts within the Orange Order whom I thought might be willing to listen to reason. But as I prepared to board at Heathrow, I was stopped by a detective who recognized me and was plainly horrified that I was travelling on my own to Belfast without any security. In spite of my protestations that I was late for my flight, he insisted that I accompany him to an office. I told him and one of his colleagues that Downing Street knew I was going to Belfast and that my first call was at the US Consulate in Belfast. I gave them the name of an RUC officer in Belfast whom I knew from my time in prison. They delayed the flight, insisting that they would have to call the RUC. A little while later they told me that there had been a change of plan and that I would be met at the airport by RUC officers. I gave them the name of the friend whom I had asked to pick me up from the airport. They walked me to the plane and then left. When we landed at Belfast, the RUC were duly waiting for me. I pointed out my friend to them and we walked to his car. They followed close behind as we drove into Belfast city centre. I attended my meeting at the Consulate, and my friend then drove us to another friend's house in Belfast, from where I phoned Downing Street and suggested that a group of academics and other people conversant with the situation should write a speech, or at least compile a series of recommendations which the Prime Minister could incorporate into a speech aimed at settling the situation while insisting that the position of the Parades Commission, which had banned the parade from proceeding along the Garvaghy Road be upheld.

The following day I met up with Professor Paul Bew, Dr Liam Kennedy and Ruth Dudley Edwards and we set to work preparing a document of ideas and thoughts to help to reduce the tension while still maintaining that the rule of law should prevail. During the Ulster Workers'

Strike in 1974, which had brought Northern Ireland's last attempt at forming a devolved power-sharing administration crashing to the ground, the then Labour prime minister Harold Wilson had accused Northern Ireland's unionists, or at least the majority, who were opposed to the Agreement, of sponging off the British taxpayer. The 'Spongers' speech, as it became known, made a mark in Northern Ireland, to the extent that the strikers and their supporters took to wearing pieces of sponge on their lapels as a badge of honour.

It was our hope that a speech from Tony Blair extolling the virtues of the decent people of Northern Ireland, whose sense of community values and morality had prevented Northern Ireland from sliding into another Bosnia, would expunge the memory of Wilson's speech, thereby providing leadership and, by repeating publicly his pledge on the principle of consent[1], would calm the prevailing mood in the unionist community and help avert a catastrophe at Drumcree.

We worked through the day, eventually arriving at an agreed position and faxed the document to Downing Street. We were under no illusion that the prime minister would use any of our material, but we were hopeful that at least some of the language and sentiments would permeate the walls of political efficacy.

What we were not prepared for was that word of this would leak out and be presented negatively as a pro-Orange document, which it certainly was not. All the same, some of the worst elements in the nationalist media tried to use the occasion to impugn the integrity of respected academics such as Bew and Kennedy, and for a while things became worse rather than better. Needless to say, the speech was never delivered, although since

[1] That there be no change to the constitutional position of Northern Ireland unless a majority of its people freely decided.

then the tone of and certain expressions from the document have been in evidence in government parlance.

By this stage I had visited Downing Street twice to speak with senior officials. I can feel free to say this now that my visits are known to the public. Someone had seen me enter Downing Street and had tipped off the newspapers; a couple of them ran the story under the characteristically subdued headline 'IRA KILLER HELPS BLAIR AT NO. 10'.

The period leading up to Drumcree was fraught with all sorts of difficulties. It came as no surprise when the parade was banned and the scene was set for a confrontation that is continuing as I write, seven months later. I began to detect a feeling among many Orangemen and their supporters, especially those in the western counties of Fermanagh and Tyrone, that they were increasingly at odds with the entrenched attitude of some Orangemen from the Portadown district. Now that the parade was banned, there were nightly protests at Drumcree. Mobs of loyalists erected barricades, fired shots, threw grenades and generally created havoc. There were similar incidents elsewhere, but what was noticeable, at least for me, was that there was hardly a protest to be seen in Tyrone and Fermanagh. Drumcree was no longer about a parade along the Garvaghy Road; it had been turned into an all-out assault on the Agreement, hijacked in effect.

I had been in Tyrone in 1974 when a combined unionist opposition mounted a massive campaign of strikes, powercuts and general civil disobedience across Northern Ireland, which destroyed the Sunningdale Agreement and collapsed the power-sharing executive. At that time there were roads in some parts of Tyrone that were impassable. Now, however, in 1998, things were utterly different. It was obvious that many grassroots

Orangemen were disgusted by the scenes of nightly violence at Drumcree and the blatant involvement of loyalist terrorists. Support among Orangemen and unionists was melting away at the sight of so-called loyalists in balaclavas throwing blast bombs at the RUC.

During this period we continued to be in contact with Downing Street and with senior officials at the Northern Ireland Office. My effectiveness, though, was somewhat limited. It was dangerous for me to travel in Northern Ireland, particularly in Belfast. The prospect of being stopped at loyalist road blocks was extremely nerve-racking; it was entirely possible that I would be recognized by people who, fuelled by a combination of anger and alcohol, might be incapable of analysing the realities of the situation. When driving through loyalist areas such as Sandy Row, hostility and hatred towards the outside world in general was all too obvious.

Tempers flare in such a charged and violent atmosphere, and the possibility of an Orangeman being killed by security forces at Drumcree looked likely. If that were to happen, the reaction among even moderate unionists could be catastrophic. During a discussion about this with an NIO official at Stormont, he pointed out that it was just as likely that one of the ever-more-frequent petrol bomb attacks on the homes of nationalists or RUC officers could result in a major tragedy and result in the collapse of support for the Drumcree protesters.

His words turned out to be prophetic. On the early hours of Sunday, 12 July, three children were burned to death in Catholic Ballymoney after their home was petrol-bombed. The precise circumstances that led to the attack are still unclear, but the immediate reaction in the local community was one of uncontained horror. The blame in many people's minds was laid squarely at the door of the Orange Order. From that day support for the Drumcree protest declined rapidly and it was obvious that the sting had been drawn, at least for the time being. Even so, this year, because 12 July was a Sunday, the traditional parades in celebration of William of Orange's victory at the Battle of the Boyne in 1690, had been postponed to the following day and had yet to take place.

Although everybody who had been involved in trying to broker a solution or find a way through the Drumcree impasse had failed, so too had those who had attempted to use the protest as a focal point to muster support against the Agreement. One way or another the situation had run wildly out of control and served only to demonstrate how divisive the parades issue had become over the previous four years. While one function of the parade was to consolidate the unity of the Orange Order, in fact it had done the opposite and had shown the weaknesses inherent in the organization. The Orange Order has little in the way of a central structure and had found itself unable to control the local Orangemen, some of whom were complicit in allowing their protest to be hijacked by extreme loyalists. Strange as it might seem, for historical reasons the organization is controlled by the grass roots and the Grand Lodge, nominally the governing body of the Orange Order, has no jurisdiction over individual parades. Many unionists who had campaigned against the Agreement were appalled by the violence and the cynical attempts by some people to use the parade issue for political means. Whoever was responsible or whatever the motivation behind the murder of the three Quinn children, it will be regarded as a defining moment in the history of Northern Ireland. No longer would the Orange Order have the power to enforce its will on the British government. The Orange card would never carry the same weight again.

On the morning the children were murdered, Reverend William Bingham, a Presbyterian minister based in Pomeroy, County Tyrone, and pastor to the County Armagh Lodge of the Orange Order, made an impassioned plea at his Sunday church service for the Orangemen remaining dug in at Drumcree to return home. Broadcast on national television, the appeal was powerful and had a dramatic effect. Reverend Bingham had worked day and night to find a solution to the crisis. His call was met with fury from the most extreme elements in the Orange Order and by some politicians opposed to the Good Friday Agreement.

There was an interesting postscript to all of this. The day after the Quinn children were murdered, I, perhaps foolishly, decided to attend the Orange parade in Pomeroy with a well-known British journalist. I knew that Ruth Dudley Edwards and another friend would also be there and it was a chance to catch up on events. I had intended to stay near the police station in Pomeroy and simply observe events, but was inexorably drawn towards the field where the Orangemen were gathering before the parade.

We met Ruth and Mark and were standing talking and observing when Ruth saw Joel Patton, leader of the Spirit of Drumcree, an extreme pressure group within the Orange Order that refused to countenance any accommodation over the parades. The other journalist was keen to talk with Patton, and Ruth went with him to provide an introduction. I was apprehensive about this, as Ruth had been interviewed on Radio Ulster the day the Quinn children were murdered. She had been very critical, and rightly so, of extremists and the Spirit of Drumcree.

Ruth met with a very aggressive response from Patton and his pals. Patton refused to talk to her and his cohorts around him were generally abusive. Later, one of them saw me and began to shout, accusing me of being a Provo. It was obvious that Patton would attempt to use my presence to attack Reverend Bingham, who was officiating at the service following the parade. He had intended to cause trouble all along, but my presence unfortunately gave him an extra weapon. I left as quickly as I could.

Watching television that night, I saw Patton launch an attack on Reverend Bingham, accusing him of abandoning the Orangemen at Drumcree and of inviting me, a 'Provo', to the parade. The allegation was untrue. The fact that I had travelled to Pomeroy with a British journalist and had gone of my own volition, without the invitation or the knowledge of the Reverend Bingham or of any other Orangeman, completely escaped him. He might also have noticed that over the past few years I have written for almost every major British newspaper and serious political journal about the situation in Northern Ireland. Of course I would want to be in Pomeroy to witness events firsthand.

Nonetheless, Patton was seen on television screaming and shouting and in so doing effectively destroying much of his hard-won credibility. As a rule, he is one of the more articulate extremists and an impressive media performer, characteristically using a soft tone and a slightly wounded expression. This time, however, he showed himself in his true colours. Certainly consistency and clarity of thought seemed to have deserted him. Afterwards, in an interview with a Dublin newspaper, Patton tried to explain his behaviour by saying that I was variously an MI6 agent, a Provo, or working for the Irish government. In his fevered mind it was clear that my intention was to split the Orange Order.

Eventually I was forced to respond to these ludicrous

allegations by writing an article for the *Belfast Newsletter*, Northern Ireland's oldest newspaper, explaining the facts to demonstrate how indicative Patton's reaction was of the paranoia and unwillingness to face external reality that afflicts the most extreme elements in Northern Ireland. In describing me as a British agent, Patton, a unionist, succeeded only in underpinning the IRA propoganda campaign against me. It is much more important that his antics at Pomeroy, Drumcree and elsewhere did more to damage the cause they profess to espouse than the Provos could ever hope to do. For my part, in responding I wanted Orangemen to know that I had not been invited to Pomeroy by Reverend Bingham. I will leave his ludicrous claim that Ruth Dudley Edwards and I exert an undue influence over Reverend William Bingham to the judgement of those people who know Reverend Bingham for the independent, hard-headed, disciplined man that he is. As I said in my rebuttal: 'The Spirit of Drumcree is the Spirit to Nowhere. Patton is chasing the ghost of 1912 down the misty lanes and byways of history – the Pied Piper without a tune. I for one do not believe that Orangemen will dance down the road to destruction and despair.'

The level of abuse did not dissipate, but it is significant to note that Patton claimed in yet another interview with a Dublin newspaper, that he refused to meet me in 1997. What he omitted to say was that he had in fact agreed to a meeting but had subsequently backed out, not because of principle but because he was afraid that word might leak out and compromise his 'purist' stance. If the meeting had taken place, I would have told him what I have consistently told other Orangemen: the Provisional IRA strategy was designed to force the Orange Order into a confrontation with a British government enjoying a large majority. I also told them that if the government upheld the Orangemen's right to march this year and if they exercised that right, that same government would not grant them the privileges again and allow them to walk down that road in defiance of the rule of law. People can judge for themselves how much they listened to that advice! It is interesting to note that, as a result of his attack on Reverend Bingham, Joel Patton has been expelled from the Orange Order.

Back in London there was in many respects a sense of anti-climax. The referendum and election were over, the Drumcree protest dragged on, but the outside world and media had lost interest and the Orange Order was in turmoil. Moves continued behind the scenes to resolve the Drumcree stand-off, with little or no success. The formation of a new executive was stalled over Sinn Fein's refusal to countenance decommissioning, and the accelerated release of prisoners was causing relatives and friends of victims genuine hurt. There was also a slippage of support for the Agreement among some of the soft 'yes' voters, which was not confined to the unionist community.

Many republicans became unhappy or unsure about the Good Friday Agreement once it had become obvious that it did not represent a victory for the IRA as had been suggested by their leaders. The new constitutional arrangements could hardly be described as a thirty-two county democratic socialist republic, even though Adams and his cohorts would claim that the Cross Border Council was a clear move in that direction. Under the pressure of such differences of opinion, the unity of the organization began to buckle.

In December 1997 an IRA convention had resulted in a small group of ultra-militants breaking away, and soon afterwards an organization calling itself the 32 County

Sovereignty Committee had announced its existence. Fronted by Bernadette Sands, a sister of Bobby Sands, the republican icon who had died on hunger strike in the Maze prison, the Committee denied that it had a military wing, but those who understood republican history and were familiar with some of the individuals involved knew that this was unlikely.

In the New Year of 1998 another group, styling itself the Real IRA, carried out a series of bomb attacks in Northern Ireland, mainly in the County Armagh area. It was obvious that some of these attacks could not have been carried out without assistance from, at the very least, some IRA members on the ground. No one had any doubt that the Real IRA was firmly linked to the Sovereignty Committee, that it was in effect its military wing.

Sporadic violence continued throughout the year, mainly bomb attacks on town centres like Banbridge in County Down, where dozens of people were injured. No one was murdered in the attacks, but that was only a question of time.

By this stage the nationalist insurgence was beginning to stretch to breaking point. There were already four republican groups:

IRA/Sinn Fein was still the largest and most mainstream republican movement. It had implemented a ceasefire of sorts, and although the mutilations, expulsions and general intimidation continued, these were mainly confined to their sectarian group, and as result few people, in particular governments, appeared bothered by it.

INLA/IRSP, in existence since 1974, when it split from the Official IRA, was still a small quasi-Marxist group with a turbulent history of ideological and personal differences that had often resulted in outbreaks of internecine murder or attempted murder. They too were on ceasefire but it was already apparent that the rumblings of discontent might split the group again, this time with more violent consequences.

The Continuity IRA was linked to Republican Sinn Fein which had split from Sinn Fein in 1986 and was led by Rory Brady, for many years President of Sinn Fein and member of the IRA's Army Council. I had long believed that the Continuity IRA represented the greatest long-term threat to the control that Adams and McGuinness enjoyed over the broad republican constituency. The group had mounted only a couple of attacks, but it was obvious that they were capable of much more when the time was right. They have never declared a ceasefire and at the time of writing there is considerable evidence to show that their activity and influence is steadily increasing.

The fourth and most recent addition to the republican fold was the Real IRA. On 15 August 1998, the Real IRA exploded a car bomb in Omagh, County Tyrone, and this action was to have profound consequences. Twenty-nine people were murdered on a busy Saturday afternoon in a central shopping street. It was the single worse atrocity of 'the troubles'. The date of the bombing was significant: it was the Feast of the Assumption of the Blessed Virgin and was traditionally one of the busiest shopping days of the year. Families were preparing for children returning to school and the bombers would have been well aware of that. Though the Real IRA were the prime instigators, and admitted blame, there is little doubt that Provisional members on the ground locally provided assistance.

The first I knew of it was when I received a phone call from a friend who lives outside Omagh. He had heard that there had been a bomb in town, where his wife and two young children were shopping. As it turned out, they

461

were in the car when the bomb detonated close to them and were lucky to escape alive.

Although Omagh is a mixed town with substantial republican support, particularly in the outlying rural areas, that Saturday the streets were full of shoppers from both sides of the community. It goes without saying that bombs do not make distinctions in such circumstances. Afterwards there was a huge outpouring of anger and grief on a scale rarely witnessed before. Like many other people, my first thought was that we had been there before. This time, however, something was different. The relatively peaceful conditions of the recent past had led many people to believe that the worst was over, and this heightened the shock, grief and anger. The Real IRA, which until then had been gathering support, came under enormous pressure to call a ceasefire, not least from the republican community that had lost so many of its number in the cataclysm.

Following the bombing, emergency anti-terrorist legislation was rushed through the Irish and British Parliaments. I, for one, doubted its effectiveness, were it ever to be used. Another significant consequence of the tragedy of Omagh passed largely unnoticed. For some time before the bombing, there had been increasing dissension within the ranks of the Provisional IRA, demonstrated by the growing support for other dissident groups. Senior republicans such as Brian Keenan had become increasingly unhappy with the Adams/ McGuinness strategy of amelioration, but the bombing was to put a stop to any ideas these men were entertaining about a return to 'armed struggle', at least in the short term. It did not, of course, mean that they were, or are, any happier about the strategy than before, just that they could do little about it. In the aftermath of the bomb, the Provisionals forced the Real IRA to call a ceasefire, with the tacit approval of both British and Irish governments.

At the time of writing, the Continuity IRA is the only republican group not to have called a ceasefire, nor will it. The Chief Constable of the RUC has recently warned that the CIRA intends to extensify its activities from the border counties to other areas of Northern Ireland. Simultaneously there has been a serious intensification of paramilitary mutilations, expulsions and general intimidation, all of which activities Sinn Fein describes as 'a rough form of community justice', which, of course, it does not condone. No one in Northern Ireland, with the apparent exception of the Secretary of State and senior officials, believes such feeble statements. Beatings and expulsions are often organized from Sinn Fein offices, a state of affairs for which there is much documented evidence.

Against such a background, the Patten Commission into the future of the Royal Ulster Constabulary continues to cause controversy and disquiet, particularly, but not solely, amongst the unionist population. The report is not due to be submitted until August 1999, but already rumour, supposed leaks and speculation have fuelled entrenched positions on both sides. The more extreme section of the nationalist community, which tends to support Sinn Fein, will settle for nothing less than the abolition of the RUC, a course of action that is anathema to even the most moderate of unionists.

It is indisputable that when the report is finally delivered, it will not meet with universal approval. More importantly, it has the potential to poison further the body politic, making the full implementation of the Agreement even more problematic. The future arrangements for policing in Northern Ireland go right to the heart of the Agreement's precepts and in such conditions terrorism remains a powerful obstacle to a successful implementation. Whatever is decided about policing will necessarily have to take that into account.

Many people have been at a loss to understand the rationale behind the recent increase in paramilitary violence – the so-called 'community justice'. Families Against Intimidation and Terror, the Northern Ireland-based human rights group, mounted a widespread and effective campaign against such acts of violence, and Sinn Fein and the loyalist groups faced a torrent of critical publicity, all of which begs the question: why now? Is it the simple lack of discipline? A desire to keep the organizations in a state of preparedness? Or merely the need to maintain some form of diminishing control over the communities? Whatever the reason, there seems to be a sinister agenda at work. While the above explanations, of course, have some validity, it stretches belief that people like Adams and McGuinness are happy with a situation that not only puts them in a bad light but could also, in certain circumstances, trigger their suspension from the peace process. Unless, of course, there is a more pressing justification. Sinn Fein and loyalist representatives routinely say that they are opposed to punishment beatings. They suggest that such things will continue because the community has no faith in the RUC and that as a consequence there is a policing vacuum. I can draw only one conclusion from all of this: the IRA and, to a certain extent, their loyalist counterparts are escalating these activities in a deliberate attempt to influence the report of the Patten Commission and therefore the future of policing in Northern Ireland. Both sets of terrorists are deliberately using violence against their own communities as a deliberate political strategy. If they stopped the beatings, which they have done before when it suited them, much of the problem would disappear and their negotiating position with regard to policing would be seriously undermined.

Of course, there is a real need for the RUC to adapt to changing circumstances, and a police force that is 92 per cent Protestant will inevitably project a unionist ethos. There are many reasons, historical and cultural, for the composition of the RUC, but change is now both right and necessary. However, it is also necessary that changes be designed to improve the quality of policing, take full account of operational difficulties and not be designed or implemented to satisfy any particular political agenda. If he was not aware of the difficulties beforehand, then I am certain that by now Chris Patten realizes that he has stepped into a political minefield. There is no obvious solution to the problem. How he deals with it will have an enormous impact on the future of Northern Ireland and the success or otherwise of the present Agreement, not to mention Mr Patten's own political future.

Meanwhile, the argument over the decommissioning of terrorist weapons continues. Until now, in spite of large-scale prisoner releases, only one small loyalist terrorist group has decommissioned. The Loyalist Volunteer Force, a small terror group founded by the infamous Billy Wright, known as King Rat, decommissioned a small amount of weaponry in December 1998, following agreement in negotiations at Stormont about the nature and extent of cross-border bodies. I had been aware for some time that the LVF were discussing decommissioning, and I believed that they should be encouraged to do so. I contacted Kenny McClinton, a former loyalist terrorist with convictions for murder, who I knew was working hard in that direction, to congratulate him and offer encouragement. The failure to decommission by the IRA, UVF and UDA has delayed progress towards the full implementation of the

Agreement. David Trimble, leader of the Ulster Unionist Party, the largest political party in Northern Ireland, and First Minister designate in the new administration, is refusing to allow Sinn Fein to assume ministerial posts, to which they are entitled as a result of their electoral success under the terms of the Agreement, until they begin the actual physical business of decommissioning. Trimble enjoys the support of almost the entire unionist community in his stance on this issue as well as a broad swathe of public opinion across the political spectrum in these islands. Most sensible people find it difficult to accept that people who are serious about involving themselves in democratic politics find it necessary to hold on to an illegal private army with a huge arsenal of guns and explosives. None of these issues will be easy to resolve but resolved they must be if the Agreement is to move forward and take root.

At the end of 1998 I was asked to deliver the Ian Gow Memorial lecture. Ian Gow, one-time Conservative MP and Private Secretary to Margaret Thatcher, was murdered by the IRA in July 1990. I agreed to give the lecture, which took place in the Grand Committee Room at Westminister and which was attended by a wide range of journalists, politicians, peace activists and unionist supporters. Also in attendance was Ian Gow's widow, Dame Jane Gow. I thought that it was both brave and charitable of her to attend what cannot have been an easy or pleasant occasion.

I continue to work to help, in whatever ways I can, to promote a better and decent future for the people of Northern Ireland. On a recent trip, I found the mood sullen and disappointed among the people to whom I spoke, including some who had voted 'yes' in the referendum. The early release of prisoners has upset many. Victims' families are shocked and angered to see murderers released with no sign of remorse or respect for the relatives, amid scenes of jubilation outside the Maze prison. The Patten Commission is still causing deep resentment among law-abiding people in Northern Ireland who fear that the RUC will be disbanded. Even though such an outcome is unlikely in the extreme, it is impossible to tell that to people who feel that they have been betrayed at every turn. The fact that the IRA and loyalist paramilitaries still refuse to countenance any decommissioning of arms is not surprisingly also causing grave disquiet.

As we enter perhaps the most crucial part of this process, David Trimble's room for further manoeuvre appears to have evaporated. It is most unlikely that an executive including Sinn Fein can or will be formed until the improbable advent of their decommissioning. Only months from the time when Ireland appeared to be on the brink of a momentous sea-change, so much is still speculation. Even though there was much euphoria when John Hume and David Trimble were awarded the Nobel Peace Prize for their part in the Good Friday Agreement, one-off events or daily realities that were to have been eliminated from the New World Order continue as before. All carry with them the potential to delay, damage or destroy the process. Quite simply, no one can know what the future holds. It seems likely that the process will stagger on at a slower pace than previously envisaged by its architects, and may indeed develop in ways not yet defined. At the moment it is still moving ahead, but any sane observer would hazard two guesses: that republican groups will be responsible for further attacks in Northern Ireland and the British mainland; and that this process has carried in its wake a political and moral corruption that bodes ill for the future development of Northern Ireland.

Even events of the days before I wrote this postscript demonstrate how quickly observations and prognoses can become redundant. Only a few days ago, early on the morning of 27 January, Eamon Collins, a former IRA member, was murdered as he walked his dogs. In the mid-eighties, Collins had been arrested by the RUC, had admitted his role in five murders and had offered to give Queen's Evidence. He later retracted that offer and was promised an amnesty by the IRA. At his trial in Belfast he was acquitted of all charges and went on to write a book about his IRA involvement. In spite of threats from the IRA he and his family continued to live in Newry, County Down, where he was horribly tortured and killed. As yet, no group has claimed responsibility for his death.

I was having lunch at Westminster when I heard the news of his death. If I ever needed a vivid reminder of the realities of my own situation, this was it. Whilst my initial reaction was one of shock and outrage, I was not surprised. In a political climate where violence was escalating once more, Collins was an easy target. He made no attempt to conceal himself and continued to live in a border town with a strong republican history.

Saddened as I am by Collins' murder, I will not allow it to intimidate me. It is over two years since I was released from prison. During that time, and in spite of the threat that shadows me, I have experienced a freedom like never before. For the first time in my life I am very much my own man. I can say and write what I please without paying lipservice to any political doctrine, a great luxury in a world constrained by such limitations.

We must look forward to a future in Northern Ireland where politics can be conducted as part of a civic debate, without descending to the levels of violence we are still experiencing as I write. Such an outcome is by no means assured. All those concerned must work to ensure that any future is informed, but not governed, by the past. The peace process has a long way to travel, and no one can predict whether or not we will reach the end of our journey.

Sean O'Callaghan
February, 1999

GLOSSARY

Active service unit (ASU). Term used to describe self-contained active cells of the IRA.

Adams, Gerry. Sinn Fein MP for West Belfast/President of Sinn Fein and leading strategist within the republican movement. Senior figure in the leadership of the IRA since 1972.

Anglo-Irish Agreement. Signed on 15 November 1985 at Hillsborough Castle in Northern Ireland by British prime minister Margaret Thatcher and Irish taoiseach Garret Fitzgerald. Opposed by both unionists and republicans, the agreement established a joint ministerial conference of Irish and British ministers serviced by a permanent secretariat to monitor issues of concern to the nationalist minority.

Anglo-Irish Treaty. The treaty signed in London in 1921 which led to the establishment of the Irish Free State and the formal acceptance of partition between the New State (Republic of Ireland) and Northern Ireland. The IRA and Sinn Fein split over acceptance of the treaty led to a civil war between the New Free State government and the republicans, who were opposed to the treaty.

Army convention. A convention that brings together representatives of the IRA at every level, from Army Council to local leadership. Representatives are elected at regional meetings and vote in accordance with the wishes of the majority of volunteers in their area. Each representative controls a block of votes, the size of which depends on the strength of local membership. Conventions are attended by upwards of 100 members and pose a serious security risk. IRA leaderships are consequently reluctant to call one unless it is absolutely necessary. There have been only three conventions called since the Provisional IRA was formed in 1969. The first was in 1970, when the organization was formally set up. The second took place in County Meath in 1986 to enable the election of a new Executive loyal to the Adams/McGuinness leadership, which would better reflect the mood and membership of the organization sixteen years after its establishment. The third was held in County Mayo not long before the first IRA ceasefire ended in February of 1996.

Army Council. The seven-person supreme governing body of the republican movement, elected by the Army Executive and run by the Chief of Staff.

Army Executive. The primary function of the twelve-person Executive is to elect an Army Council. Its secondary purpose is to advise the Council on strategy. Once an Executive has been elected it remains unchanged until a convention is called, when a new Executive may be elected. If a member dies, resigns or is imprisoned a replacement is co-opted from a list of substitutes. No person may be a member of both the Executive and the Council.

Bloody Friday. Friday, 21 July 1972, the day the Provisional IRA exploded twenty-six bombs in Belfast, killing eleven people and injuring over a hundred.

Bloody Sunday. Used to describe the events that took place in Derry on 30 January 1972, when thirteen people taking part in a civil rights march were shot dead by soldiers of the First Parachute Regiment of the British Army. The killings were extremely controversial, and a source of great anger in the nationalist community. The British government has recently announced plans for a full independent inquiry into the events of that day.

Chief of Staff. Chosen by the Army Council, the Chief of Staff is not the 'Boss of Bosses' but rather a part of the collective leadership. He has two primary responsibilities: to ensure that the IRA has the equipment to wage war, and that the organization operates at maximum efficiency. Essentially a functional role, no Chief of Staff in recent years has carried anything like the internal influence of Gerry Adams or Martin McGuinness.

Civil War. Took place in 1922–3 in the newly established Free State between the government forces and those of the IRA opposed to the New State. It was fought savagely, but the government forces quickly established control and the IRA was routed.

Combined Loyalist Military Command. Umbrella body of loyalist paramilitary organizations which first emerged in 1991. It called the loyalist ceasefire in October 1997. Because of factional problems it is not functional at the time of writing.

Continuity Army Council *see* **Republican Sinn Fein.**

Council of Ireland. A proposed ministerial body with representatives from the Dail and a Northern Ireland assembly. First proposed in the Sunningdale Agreement of 1974.

Dail Eireann. Gaelic name for Irish parliament, first used in 1918.

Democratic Left. Formed in 1992 as a result of a split in the Worker's Party. The split arose out of allegations that certain members of the party had links with Official IRA, which was believed by some security sources to be still active.

Democratic Unionist Party. Founded in September 1971 by the Reverend Ian Paisley, the Democratic Unionist Party has long been identified as the most extreme of the mainstream unionist parties. Very much under the control of Revd Paisley, it has begun to lose support in recent years. It is opposed to the present peace process.

Easter Rising. Took place Easter 1916, when a small group of Irish Republicans took over buildings in Dublin and proclaimed an Irish Republic. After a week of fierce fighting the rebels surrendered. The leaders were subsequently executed by the British government, which led to an outpouring of sympathy and support among many Irish people. Easter 1916 was a key moment in Irish history and its effects are still felt today.

Fenian Brotherhood (also **Irish Republican Brotherhood (IRB)**). Secret revolutionary organization active in both Ireland and America, particularly in the 1860s.

Fianna Fail. Political party formed from the section of

Sinn Fein/IRA opposed to the Anglo-Irish Treaty of 1921. It has always been the most republican of Southern Ireland's constitutional parties and has been the governing party for much of its history.

Fine Gael. Formed from the wing of Sinn Fein/IRA that supported the Anglo-Irish Treaty of 1921. It constituted the first government of the Irish Free State.

Fitzgerald, Garret. Leader of Fine Gael, 1977–87, and taoiseach (prime minister) in the Republic, 1981–March 1982; December 1982–February 1987.

Garda Siochana. Gaelic name for the police force of the Irish Republic, created after the formation of the Irish Free State.

General Headquarters (GHQ). A group of individuals appointed by the IRA Chief of Staff to run the various departments reponsible for the day-to-day operational functions of the organization. It varies in numbers, depending on the IRA's requirements at any particular time and meets secretly and regularly at different venues in the Irish Republic.

H-blocks. The Maze prison cell blocks, so called because of their shape. Home to terrorist prisoners since 1976, the H-blocks became world famous in 1981 after the deaths of ten republican prisoners following protracted hunger strikes.

Hume, John. First came to prominence in the Civil Rights movement in Derry in 1968. Founder member of the Social Democratic and Labour Party (SDLP) in 1970, leader since 1979. MP for Foyle from 1983. In recent years he has been engaged in controversial talks with Sinn Fein/IRA.

Internment. Emergency legislation used both in Northern Ireland and the Irish Republic at times of civil disorder or terrorist threat, when the normal processes of law were found incapable of dealing with the situation. Suspects were detained without trial for an indefinite period of time.

Irish National Liberation Army (INLA). Formed in 1975 by members of the Official IRA angry at the ceasefire declared in 1972. A small, extremely violent quasi-Marxist group, its effectiveness has been regularly damaged by its propensity for violent internal feuds that have claimed the lives of many of its members. At the time of writing it has declared a ceasefire. Its political wing, the Irish Republican Socialist Party (IRSP), has failed to make any serious impact.

McGuinness, Martin. An active republican since 1970. Chief of Staff of the IRA 1977–82. Leading member of the IRA Army Council from 1976. MP for Mid Ulster from May 1984. Sinn Fein's chief negotiator in present talks.

National Executive (Ard Comhairle). The governing body of Sinn Fein.

New Ireland Forum. Conference of four mainstream nationalist parties: Fianna Fail, Fine Gael, Irish Labour Party and Social Democratic and Labour Party, which first met in Dublin in 1983 with the goal of reaching an agreed approach to a Northern Ireland political settlement. Even though British prime minister Margaret

Thatcher comprehensively rejected its proposals, it played a pivotal role in the establishment of the Anglo-Irish Agreement in November 1985.

Noraid. American-based committee established in 1969 ostensibly to provide aid for the families of Republican prisoners. There have been frequent accusations that much of the money has been redirected to buy weapons for IRA.

Official Irish Republican Army (Official IRA). The term first used when the republican movement split in 1970 into two movements, the Officials and the Provisionals, each with a political and military wing. The Officials have been largely inactive since they called a ceasefire in 1972.

Partition. The Government of Ireland Act of 1920 effectively partitioned the country into two separate entities: Northern Ireland and Southern Ireland. The Act allowed for the establishment of a Northern Ireland parliament, at Stormont Castle outside Belfast. Following the Anglo-Irish Treaty in 1921, the Irish Free State was established with jurisdiction over twenty-six of the thirty-two counties. The remaining six – Northern Ireland – remained part of the United Kingdom.

Progressive Unionist Party. Formed in 1979 in the Shankill Road area of West Belfast. Has close links with the paramilitary loyalist group the Ulster Volunteer Force (UVF).

Provisional Irish Republican Army (PIRA). The dominant paramilitary group in Northern Ireland. Formed out of the split in the republican movement in

1970. Its aims are: to end the union between Northern Ireland and Great Britain; and to establish a thirty-two-county democratic socialist republic. PIRA is inextricably linked with Provisional Sinn Fein, its political wing.

Republican Sinn Fein. Split from the republican movement in 1986 when the IRA and Sinn Fein decided that any future parliamentary candidates in elections in the Irish Republic would, if elected, take their seats in the Dail. A small ultra-traditionalist group, it has a military wing called the Continuity Army Council, which has carried out several bomb attacks in Northern Ireland since the IRA ceasefire.

Revolutionary Council. Republican think-tank established by the IRA leadership in the early 1980s. Ceased to operate effectively, at least under that name, from the mid 1980s.

Royal Ulster Constabulary (RUC). Northern Ireland police force established in 1922. Has often been controversial because of its dominant Protestant/unionist ethos and is unacceptable at present to many nationalists. It has borne the brunt of the Provisional IRA campaign, having had over 300 of its officers murdered and thousands more injured.

Sinn Fein. Founded in 1905 by Arthur Griffith, Sinn Fein is nowadays effectively the political wing of the IRA and comes under the control of the Army Council.

Social Democratic and Labour Party (SDLP). The largest nationalist party in Northern Ireland, in recent years its dominance has been under serious threat from Sinn Fein.

Founded in August 1970, it presented itself as a left-of-centre party but has increasingly been seen to be little more than the old Nationalist Party under a new name.

Southern Command. Established in 1977, Southern Command's area of operation covers nineteen counties, excluding Northern Ireland and the border counties as well as County Meath, which is an Army Council 'back-up' area, home to most of the IRA's large 'reserve dumps'. Essentially Southern Command provides practical support for the 'war effort', which is spear-headed by Northern Command. Its remit is to raise finance, usually by means of armed robbery or by assisting in GHQ operations such as kidnapping, and to help provide assistance for the training, engineering, finance and England departments. Its secondary function is to strengthen the 'republican base' by means of working with Sinn Fein prisoner support groups and with general propaganda. The OC (Officer Commanding) Southern Command is always a member of GHQ staff.

UK Unionist Party. Small unionist party led by Robert McCartney, MP. Its main policy is one of integration between Northern Ireland and Great Britain. It is opposed to the present talks.

Ulster Defence Association (UDA). The largest Protestant paramilitary organization, outlawed on 10 August 1992 by Northern Ireland Secretary of State Sir Patrick Mayhew. The UDA has been responsible for hundreds of sectarian murders, often under the cover name of the Ulster Freedom Fighters (UFF). It has close links with the Ulster Democratic Party (UDP).

Ulster Defence Regiment (UDR). Intended as an

acceptable replacement for the B Specials, a locally recruited and almost exclusively Protestant militia. It became operational on 1 April 1970 but proved unacceptable to most Catholics, who saw it as the B Specials under another name. There have been a large number of cases in which serving or former UDR members have been convicted of involvement with loyalist terrorist organizations. In July 1992, it was merged with the Royal Irish Rangers to become the Royal Irish Regiment.

Ulster Unionist Party. Popularly styled the Official Unionist Party, this is the largest political party in Northern Ireland and is usually regarded as the most moderate of the unionist parties. Its present leader is David Trimble.

Ulster Volunteer Force (UVF). Illegal Protestant paramilitary force. Formed in 1966, it revived the name used to describe the Protestant-Unionist force established in 1912 to fight against Irish Home Rule. When war broke out in 1914 its members became the 36th Ulster Division which suffered heavily at the Battle of the Somme in 1916. The present-day UVF has been responsible for many horrific sectarian murders. The 'Shankill Butchers' who tortured their victims before killing them were members of the UVF. It is closely linked to the Progressive Unionist Party (PUP).

INDEX